Acts of Compassion in Greek Tragic Drama

Oklahoma Series in Classical Culture
Ellen Greene, Series Editor

Acts of Compassion in Greek Tragic Drama

James Franklin Johnson

University of Oklahoma Press : Norman

Library of Congress Cataloging-in-Publication Data

Johnson, James F. (James Franklin), 1946– author.
Compassion in Greek tragic drama / James F. Johnson.
pages cm — (Oklahoma series in classical culture ; volume 53)
ISBN 978-0-8061-5166-3 (hardcover : alk. paper)
1. Greek drama (Tragedy)—History and criticism. 2. Compassion in literature.
I. Title. II. Series: Oklahoma series in classical culture ; v. 53
PA3136.J64 2016
882'.0109—dc23

2015033021

Acts of Compassion in Greek Tragic Drama is Volume 53 in the Oklahoma Series in Classical Culture.

The paper in this book meets the guidelines for permanence and durability of the Committee on Production Guidelines for Book Longevity of the Council on Library Resources, Inc. ∞

1 2 3 4 5 6 7 8 9 10

Contents

Acts of Compassion in Greek Tragic Drama

Introduction

χάρις χάριν γάρ ἐστιν ἡ τίκτουσ' ἀεί.

For one kindness always engenders another.

Sophokles, *Aias* 522

Like the ancient Greeks, we live in a world that continues to be rife with devastating and disastrous wars, violent struggles for power, and refugees in desperate flight. Unlike the ancients, in contemporary Western culture most of us witness these overwhelmingly cruel events from a distance on our televisions and through print and other nonprint media, though some Western citizens, such as soldiers and international aid workers, do become involved more directly. Along with great natural disasters, horrific accidents, plagues, and fatal diseases, these events have brought home to the world at large the realization that human life is fragile and subject to devastating loss and misfortune. Many people around the world have responded to large-scale disastrous occurrences with an outpouring of aid, both physical and monetary. Some have provided compassionate responses by personally helping in the wake of catastrophic events. Such responses remind us all how widespread and nearly universal is the potential for compassionate response in the human psyche. At the same time, we see that such compassionate responses have limits and are hard to sustain over a long period of time. Also, we recognize that the world we inhabit is not always a place of peace and harmony: distrust and conflicts continue to develop and persist between individuals, groups, ethnicities, and nations. Sometimes, perhaps even often, we fail to display an appropriate compassionate understanding and response to the suffering we witness in our human relationships—both between and even within our social groups: families, communities, and nations. Still, it is likely that many—if not most—human beings on our planet today do feel and show compassion in their daily lives. Furthermore, the existence of peacemaking and disaster-assistance institutions, and the stories we hear of compassionate individuals coming to the rescue of fellow humans in extreme circumstances, are reassuring and suggest that human beings are at least capable of responding compassionately when confronted with misfortune and suffering.

Many of us attribute our compassionate responses to great natural disasters and other catastrophic misfortunes to values that stem from our religious faith or from philosophical assumptions about life and humanity—about the human condition, if you will. The traditional stories or myths of many cultures include tales of compassionate treatment and assistance. The story of the Good Samaritan is one such story from the Christian tradition, but virtually all other cultures and religious traditions have comparable myths or archetypal narratives portraying compassionate responses to misfortune and suffering. Scholars who study ancient religions and ancient cultures from the perspectives of anthropology or other comparative disciplines have concluded that the compassionate response to the helpless person in dire need, especially to infants or other children in such situations, is practically a human given—or, at least, is something basic to the survival of human culture and human society.[1]

For an ancient Athenian citizen of the fifth century BCE, lessons concerning the need for compassion and the proper application of compassionate assistance could be learned not only from teachers and from philosophers one might encounter in the agora or elsewhere, but also from the tragic dramas performed each spring in the Theater of Dionysos. Those dramas presented great tragic conflicts and serious tales about human vulnerability and fate. The saga of a great hero such as Oidipous or Philoktetes was a drama to which the Athenian spectator (most often an Athenian male) could relate and that he would take to heart in considering the path of his own life and that of his loved ones. Douglas Clapp and I recently collaborated on a chapter in which we argued that Athenian tragedy provided lessons about and models of proper compassionate behavior for Athenian citizen-spectators despite the demands of life in an ancient polis that was often at war.[2] In that chapter (141–52) we also challenged Plato's negative view of the "tragic emotions."

The goal of this study is to extend that smaller study through a more comprehensive analysis and interpretation of the representation of compassion and compassionate action in ancient Greek tragic drama. In the pages that follow, I examine appeals for compassion and the display or lack of compassion as they are depicted in Greek tragedy. This approach differs from the more common interpretive approach to pity in tragic drama. That approach derives in large part from Aristotle's linking of pity and fear (*eleos kai phobos*) as the primary emotional effects produced in the spectator by the enactment of tragic drama. Furthermore, it focuses on the emotional response of the spectator/reader to the fictional representation of suffering in tragic drama, a primarily aesthetic or educational response.[3] This kind of response differs greatly from the one we have in life when directly confronted with the suffering of another human being. If that human being appeals to us for assistance or relief of that suffering, our experience differs even more from that of Aristotle's theatrical spectator. This type of interaction—that of one human being responding to another human being's perceived or expressed need, rather than that of a spectator responding to the poet's fictional representation of human misfortune—is what I seek to analyze in Greek tragic drama.

I will, therefore—somewhat like Aristotle's spectator, perhaps—examine representations of suffering or misfortune in tragedy, but I will also look closely at the representation of the champion or other person on stage who responds or fails to respond to that suffering, as though he or she and the sufferer represented real people. The sort of compassion that I find in tragic characters who show compassion or are asked to show compassion should be more like that of real-life situations than like the pity that Aristotle and others describe as the spectator's experience of the tragic.[4] It should not, however, be exactly like the pity or compassion that we experience or expect to experience in real life today. One difference that will become obvious is the cultural difference: the characters of tragedy are products of Athenian culture in the fifth century BCE; therefore, the experiences they are represented as having to some extent reflect features of compassion as experienced in that time and place.

A second difference relates to the tragic genre and its medium: we must not forget that the persons we are examining are dramatic characters in a tragedy rather than real people; we therefore can expect them to display some emotions and actions that the average Athenian spectator would be unlikely to exhibit in real-life situations. This is especially likely to be true, since they represent ideal or heroic types rather than "normal, everyday" types of people. Traditional criticism of classical Greek drama has made this kind of distinction by contrasting tragedy with the other major dramatic genre, comedy. Aristophanes' characters are said to typically represent average Athenian men and women in contrast to the heroes whom Aischylos and Sophokles, in particular, depicted in their tragic plays. We therefore would expect a heroic character in a play by Aischylos or Sophokles to express emotions of compassion or its contrary in accordance with the Greek audience's expectations of heroic characters.

But this raises a problem: how do we know what emotions tragic heroes were expected to feel and show? Ancient critics of drama, such as Aristotle, can be of assistance here, but the best approach seems to be to examine and analyze the representation of such characters and their emotions in the tragic dramas that we possess. Also, since tragic heroes are commonly said to derive from and to reflect, at least to some extent, the heroes of Homer's epics, it will be beneficial to examine the representation of compassion and its lack in the Homeric epics as well. The latter, at least, can help us establish traditional features of Greek compassion and traditional standards or precedents for the display or denial of compassion by heroes. The heroic characters of Greek drama, whether by Aischylos, Sophokles, or Euripides, can then be compared to Homer's heroes in light of their expression or denial of compassionate emotion and compassionate action in the face of misfortune or suffering.

This work seeks to treat the topic in all three tragedians in some depth. My publications in this field have included an article on compassion and friendship in Euripides' *Herakles* (J. F. Johnson 2002) and a collaborative study on the educational benefits of the representation of compassion in Greek tragedy (Johnson/Clapp 2005). I mention here some recent general studies of ancient compassion or pity and how they differ from mine in scope; more specialized studies are cited in the relevant chapters ahead. Stanford's *Greek Tragedy and the Emotions* (1983) deals more broadly with emotion in tragedy but includes pity and fear among these. Vickers's *Toward Greek Tragedy* (1973) is a general study of Greek tragedy that deals with many interpretive issues and themes, including the sympathy and suppliant themes. Nussbaum's *The Fragility of Goodness* (1986) employs a philosophical approach to examine issues of luck and morality as they apply to Greek tragedy and philosophy; pity comes up in her discussion of Aristotle and the tragic emotions. Konstan's *Pity Transformed* (2001) deals specifically with the topic of pity as an emotion, but his study has a much broader scope, encompassing both Greek and Roman literary and nonliterary culture over the entire classical period. While his analyses are basically sound, my study will focus more on the integral role that reciprocity plays in the working of compassion in Greek epic and tragedy. The collection edited by Rachel Sternberg (2005) contains several articles dealing with pity in Athenian tragedy, including Johnson/Clapp (2005), mentioned above. Munteanu (2012), adopting a predominantly Aristotelian approach, interprets pity and fear in several tragedies as they may affect the spectator/reader and as they relate to the historical context of the plays. Tzanetou (2012) focuses on Athenian political ideology as represented in Greek suppliant tragedies. The present study takes into account the work of these and other scholars who treat the representation of pity or compassion as a prominent theme in Greek tragic drama. One difference in my approach from that of most other scholars is that I approach the theme in tragedy from its specifically Homeric foundation rather than reading back from Aristotle's fourth-century philosophical perspective.[5]

A word about my theoretical underpinnings is in order here. My training has been in New Criticism and classical philology, both of which promote close reading of texts to discern their meaning, but I have also been influenced by approaches, such as those of M. I. Finley, Alvin Gouldner, and E. R. Dodds, that employ the perspectives of cultural anthropology and sociology to view the ancient Greeks as a culture markedly distinct from our own. A. R. Hands's book, *Charities and Social Aid in Greece and Rome,* has provided a foundation of this study in terms of real-world phenomena, while the work of Christopher Gill and others on reciprocity in ancient Greece has provided a touchstone in regard to one of my primary subthemes.

My approach to this study is literary. I emphasize the representation, in Greek epic and tragedy, of the emotion of compassion and of the behavior that flows from that emotion. The Greek texts of epic and tragedy furnish the primary contexts, the dramatic situations, in which the working of compassion is examined. Words denoting pity or compassion will help locate where pity is in operation in a text; the *Thesaurus Linguae Graecae* (*TLG*) has been most helpful in locating these occurrences. Still, the depiction of appeals for pity and of expressions of compassion in action must be examined within the larger context of the epic or play containing them. No act of compassion exists in a vacuum. Indeed, the compassionate response or lack thereof is often integral to the plot and larger meaning of the work that contains it.

I also hope to situate the representation of compassion in these works within the larger contexts of Homeric epic performance and Athenian dramatic performance. Although my emphasis will not be on the spectator's own responses of pity, fear, and catharsis—Aristotle's concern—nevertheless, I seek to remain sensitive to likely audience responses to what is being represented onstage or in epic narrative, since epic and tragedy are forms of communication that require and are shaped by author, performers, and audience members all working together in their respective modes of action and response.

I will also employ close study of the texts, especially those passages where a character spontaneously expresses compassion or a character appeals for pity and is consequently either granted or denied it by another character. Compassion is not a purely rational process; rather, it normally relies on a combination of emotion, reasoning, persuasive speech, and action. The language used to describe these transactions must be carefully noted, along with the situational and behavioral features that tend to recur in such encounters.

Since my study encompasses both Homer and a representative number of Greek tragedies by Aischylos, Sophokles, and Euripides, a comparative approach is naturally required. The benefit of comparative study is that it can reveal both significant similarities and significant differences. In the representation of compassion by all four ancient Greek authors, I expect to find some common features but also some differences, especially in the transition from the epic to the tragic genre and from the archaic era of Homer to the world of fifth-century Athenian democracy in which tragedy flourished. We can also expect there to be significant differences among the three tragedians in their representation of pity, just as scholars have shown that there are important differences in their worldviews, depiction of character, use of language, and dramaturgical styles.[6] In general, Aischylos tends to show compassion from a distance; Euripides tends to depict compassion as problematic and on trial; and Sophokles tends to explore the depths of human vulnerability is his portrayal of compassion. This book, therefore, will examine these varied treatments so as to provide a comprehensive narrative and thematic commentary on the portrayal of compassion in Greek tragedy.

Compassion in the Greek Language

We begin with a brief survey of the principal Greek words denoting pity or compassion and a general account of how pity or compassion commonly functioned in early Greek culture. The language by which compassion is commonly represented or through which it is expressed reflects cultural values and assumptions. Even the individual words used to denote the feeling develop different connotations, and synonyms may differ as a result. For example, the most common English words used to denote a sympathetic feeling for the suffering or distress of another person differ considerably, as the following quotations from *Webster's New Dictionary of Synonyms* reveal:

> *Sympathy* is the most general term, ranging in meaning from friendly interest or agreement in taste or opinion to emotional identification, often accompanied by deep tenderness. . . . *Pity* has the strongest emotional connotation; the emotion may be one of tenderness, love, or respect induced by the magnitude of another's suffering or of fellowship with the sufferer. . . . *Pity* sometimes may suggest a tinge of contempt for one who is inferior whether because of suffering or from inherent weakness; there is also a frequent suggestion that the effect if not the purpose is to keep the object in a weak or inferior state. . . . *Compassion,* which originally meant fellowship in suffering between equals, has come to denote imaginative or emotional sharing of the distress or misfortune of another or others who are considered or treated as equals; it implies tenderness and understanding as well as an urgent desire to aid and spare. . . . But while *compassion* suggests a greater dignity in the object than *pity* often does, it also implies a greater detachment in the subject. . . . *Empathy,* of all the terms here discussed, has the least emotional content; it describes a gift, often a cultivated gift, for vicarious feeling, but the feeling need not be one of sorrow. . . . *Mercy* implies compassion so great as to enable one to forbear, even when justice demands punishment, or to give help or comfort even to the lowliest or most undeserving. (Gove 1973: 809–10, 536)

We see here that "pity" and "compassion" are synonyms, but that "pity," although it has long been used as the standard English equivalent of *eleos* in Aristotle's famous phrase *eleos kai phobos* (pity and fear), often carries with it an assumption of superiority, so that it can be used to express contempt or even hostility toward the sufferer; consequently, it carries something of a taint even when not employed in a negative way. "Compassion," on the other hand, is more positive in tone and implies equality in status or dignity between the subject and object. An element of detachment is also implied in "compassion" in contrast to the closer personal engagement of "pity." "Mercy" applies specifically to compassion for one who perhaps should be punished and so refers to situations where justice is a primary issue.

But what about the Greek words used to express such concepts? We can forgo a full word history of the various Greek terms, since work has been done in this area and the results may be summarized briefly.[7] The two most common words for "pity" in ancient Greek are *eleos* and *oiktos,* together with their cognates. The etymology of *eleos* is uncertain, although some have sought to connect it to lamentation; *oiktos,* however, has been traced etymologically to lamentation in the form of the interjection *oi.*[8]

In usage, *eleos,* beginning with Homer's *Iliad,* normally denotes an emotion that entails action of some sort, whereas *oiktos* is more likely to be used of the emotion itself or of its expression by means of words.[9] The connection of *oiktos* with words, specifically with words of lamentation, is a strong one. In fact, the noun and its cognates are often used to denote the act of lamenting, sometimes without any reference to a specific object of the lament.[10] On the other hand, Pohlenz (1956: 51–53), relying in part on Burkert's evidence, discusses the tendency of *eleos* to involve action and describes Homeric *eleos* as an emotion that also contains an impulse to act.[11] Because it is regularly used transitively, it refers not merely to a feeling isolated in the soul, but is used in connection with an object—typically another person who is suffering or is imminently threatened by grievous harm. When a suppliant in battle begs his conqueror to have *eleos,* he hopes to elicit not only the feeling but also, more importantly, the action that feeling may motivate. Thus, according to Pohlenz, *eleos* essentially involves the contact between persons: it is always aroused by someone else's distress, and it often results in action. More specifically regarding comrades in battle, as Kim (2000: 67) has now analyzed it in the *Iliad*, *eleos* prompts one to avenge one's fallen comrade, to rescue friends in danger on the battlefield, to seek to heal a friend who is wounded, or to give proper burial to a dead friend.[12]

Although these two word groups may have had different origins and did have distinct early uses, they later seem to have become roughly synonymous. Burkert (1955: 35–42) gives examples of many expressions in which parallel forms from the two groups are used almost interchangeably, although they probably continued to preserve at least some of their distinct connotations, just as the English equivalents do.[13]

Of the English synonyms mentioned above, none would seem precisely equivalent to either *oiktos* or *eleos*, although "compassion" comes closest to both. *Oiktos* would have a range extending roughly from "lamentation" to "compassion," whereas *eleos* would extend from "compassion" to what we would call "mercy." I will, therefore, favor the use of "compassion" or "have compassion" as equivalents where possible, but for the sake of readability I sometimes employ the other equivalents where they fit better syntactically, with the understanding that these equivalents are being used to represent Greek *eleos* or *oiktos* rather than carrying their full weight as concepts in English.[14]

Greek compassion (*eleos* and *oiktos*), like English "compassion," suggests fundamental equality between the pitier and the pitied. Of course, the situations of the two individuals are radically different: the suppliant has experienced a downward change of fortune and is in a state of misery, whereas the champion is in a position of power and prestige. The suppliant may also suffer shame when he or she recalls their former state of prosperity, power, and prestige. But Greek epic and tragedy do not stress social inequity between the two parties: both tend to be nobles, one of whom has fallen into misfortune. What makes them inherently equal is the idea that the champion could also experience such a fall, the notion that vulnerability is inherent in the human condition. If I assume that I can suffer the same fate as my suppliant, my compassion for him or her does not imply disdain or express derision. Any such assumptions of superiority or expressions of disdain for the sufferer are the mark of a hubristic or self-righteous person who assumes that he or she is exempt from such a fate.[15] Compassion among the Greeks in epic and tragedy therefore tends to preserve the dignity of the suppliant as a fellow human being.

Where other Greek words that specifically denote emotions of sympathy (such as *sunalgein, sugkamnein, sullupeisthai, sumpathein*) are used, I will mark their usage and give them meanings appropriate to their context. I accept these words as synonyms of *eleos* and *oiktos* that also express "compassion" broadly understood, but recognize that they focus specifically on the other person's pain and suffering rather than on the person's misfortunate circumstance. Although they are capable of denoting deep sympathetic distress, they often lack the intensity or impulse to respond that we find in the primary words. At times, they may suggest an early stage in the development of a sympathetic relationship that will later entail a saving response. Often they function as expressions of sympathy for an acquaintance, friend, or loved one, as when we say, "I feel your pain" or "I know what you are going through" to a friend who has expressed his or her suffering; at such times, we may be unable to provide behavioral assistance due to circumstances or the nature of the suffering or our own personal inadequacy. At still other times, we might even be unwilling for one reason or another to provide the helpful assistance or salvation needed; in fact, such expressions of sympathy can be false and can be used to conceal one's true feelings.[16] These synonyms therefore more likely occur as expressions of sympathy in circumstances where saving action is impossible or is being considered or is about to be denied.[17]

Narrative and Dramatic Representations

Beyond the insight and clarity provided through the traditional philological approach of word study, we must also take into account the representation of narrative and dramatic situations and interactions in which compassion is appealed for and either granted or denied and those in which compassion is shown spontaneously without being explicitly requested.[18] Indeed, we occasionally find interactions in which compassion is explicitly requested and appealed for, but in which the champion does not openly express his personal feeling of compassion. In such cases, it will be important to note whether the champion provides the compassionate action that has been requested. Such interactions require especially close examination.

In this study, I also emphasize two important features of ancient Greek compassion that have not received emphasis in the past: (1) the contrast between "active" and "passive" forms of Greek compassion and (2) the tendency of Greek compassion, unlike our modern concept of "altruism," to operate reciprocally both in its expectations and in appeals used to elicit it. Let's now look at these two features in turn, beginning with the two forms of Greek compassion.

Active versus Passive Compassion

In *On the Basis of Morality,* Arthur Schopenhauer argues that compassion is the basis or foundation of all moral action. Despite his modern concept of morality, which differs from ancient Greek concepts, Schopenhauer, nevertheless, is helpful in the way he defines compassion and the way he connects it to behavior that he considers moral. Specifically, he distinguishes between two degrees or forms of compassion. One degree of compassion, he argues, inhibits one from doing harm: "By counteracting egoistic and malicious motives," he argues, "compassion prevents me from causing suffering to another and hence from becoming myself the cause of another's pain" (1995: 148–62). He connects this form or degree of compassion to the maxim, *neminem laede,* "harm no one," which he sees as the fundamental principle of justice. This principle, he argues, is the foundation of society's laws, which, by and large, serve to keep us from doing harm to one another. Here, "wrongdoing" is defined as active, positive injury to another person; "right," on the other hand, which restrains wrongdoing, is "negative" or passive and denotes merely those actions that are done without injury to others. Right, therefore, consists of not doing harm

(1995: 152–54).[19] According to Schopenhauer, compassion is that natural feeling brought about by our imaginative anticipation of or participation in the pain of others that checks any impulse we might have to harm that other person.

Schopenhauer also defines a second degree of compassion as "the higher degree where compassion works positively and incites me to active help of others" (1995: 162–67). This active degree of compassion also has its own maxim: *omnes, quantum potes, juva,* "Help everyone as much as you are able."[20] Schopenhauer sees this type of compassion as the basis for what he considers loving-kindness, philanthropy, *caritas,* or *agapê.* He says that this was first formulated as a virtue by Christians rather than by ancient philosophers, although he notes that it occurred much earlier in Asian texts of Buddhism and Hinduism, with "traces" as well in classical authors, such as Pythagoras and Cicero (1995: 162–63).[21] This second degree is distinguished from the first in that it is positive or active in nature: compassion not only restrains me from harming another person but also impels me to help him or her (1995: 163). To quickly summarize, Schopenhauer posits two degrees of compassion: one, a negative or passive compassion, which keeps me from harming another person; and two, a positive or active compassion, which not only keeps me from harming the other person but also impels me to offer aid or assistance to him or her in order to remove or at least relieve that person's suffering or misfortune.

Schopenhauer therefore observed some fundamental manifestations of compassion that seem recognizable in most cultures, including that of the ancient Greeks. The Greeks did not analyze these in the neat philosophical terms that Schopenhauer developed, but these contrasting forms are observable in Greek literary texts. A few examples will serve to illustrate this distinction. Let's begin with the passive form, which I call the inhibiting or restraining force of compassion.[22] Often it is depicted as an emotion that arises in conflict with a person's duty or job to harm an innocent individual. A classic example of it is in Herodotos's story about Labda's child Kypselos (Hdt. 5.92).[23] Ten men are sent by the rulers of Corinth to kill this infant child, because the child's survival represents a threat to the rulers. The text says that when the first man held the child, the smile of the infant aroused in him compassion (*oiktos*), which restrained him from killing it. As a result, he passed the child to the next man in line, who experienced the same feeling, with the same result, and this continued, until eventually the child was passed through the whole line and was handed back unharmed to his mother. Later, after they had gone outside and reproached each other for their common failure to do the job, the men came back determined to finish it. By this time, however, the mother had overheard what they were up to and had hidden the baby in safety. Here, compassion is depicted as a powerful emotion that affects each of the ten men when he takes the helpless infant into his arms and that furthermore restrains or inhibits him from carrying out the heinous job of slaughtering the infant.

Similarly, in Euripides' *Ion,* when Apollo's priestess finds the infant Ion on the steps of the temple, where Hermes had placed it, she assumes that some Delphian girl had abandoned it as unwanted. She is about to take it outside Apollo's precinct to expose it, when, according to the text, out of compassion (*oiktos*) she sheds her cruelty (*ômotês*) and decides to rear the infant instead (Eur. *Ion* 47). The narrator, Hermes, adds that the god Apollo also played a role in the child not being removed from his temple. Here, compassion again is of the passive, inhibiting kind and is characterized as a powerful emotion (D1b; for an explanation of this annotation system, see "General Features of Greek Compassion," below). Note also that, although she takes the child and rears it, an act of positive benefit, compassion is described specifically as restraining her from the cruel action of exposing the child. This form of compassion does not always succeed in Greek tragedy. Since it often arises in conflict with a duty or requirement to do harm, this impulse to spare will sometimes be overpowered or suppressed by that contrary compulsion, often to the regret of the agent or agents involved. Indeed, we can hardly be surprised that such failures of compassion occur in drama that is inherently tragic. Such failures also frequently occurred in real life, as the records from history, oratory, and other areas of ancient Greek life reveal.[24] Also, note that in the two examples we have seen, this form of compassion has arisen in connection with doing harm to an infant—the archetypal innocent.[25] We will see, as has often been observed, that innocence or worthiness is an important factor in the working of compassion.

The other degree of compassion analyzed by Schopenhauer, the positive degree of loving-kindness or *caritas,* does not conform so neatly to the active compassion that we commonly find depicted in classical Greek literature. Nevertheless, a positive type of Greek compassion does exist and is traditionally denoted by the word *eleos* beginning with the Homeric texts, although *oiktos* may also be used to denote it in the classical period. This type normally consists of an act of salvation or rescue, both in Homer and in tragedy; it may be associated with *aretê* and *kleos.* In the latter genre, this form of compassion is typically sought and sometimes granted in suppliant dramas, such as Aischylos's *Suppliants,* Euripides' *Suppliants,* and the latter's *Children of Herakles.* We will examine this form in depth as we encounter examples in Homer and tragedy.

The Reciprocal Functioning of Greek Compassion

We can now turn to the second feature mentioned above, compassion's reciprocal functioning. In the modern era, especially since Kant, we in the West have by and large adopted the assumption that morality should be independent of an expectation of reward. Moral action in its purest form, we say, does not expect a reward or recompense; we act morally simply because it is "the right thing to do." We speak of "the moral choice," by which we mean that which we ought to do regardless of consequences.[26] We, in fact, pride ourselves on the absence of "self-interest" in our motives and see any consideration of "benefit" or "reward" or "harm" in determining that choice as a corruption of moral purity. In regard to compassion, we reserve a special category of moral choice that we call altruism. By this we mean that we show compassion for another suffering human being based on a pure moral choice or based solely on the other person's interest rather than out of consideration of any reciprocal benefit that we might receive as a result.[27]

Ancient Greeks, at least as depicted in Homeric epic and Greek tragedy, did not commonly appear to make such assumptions or to employ such reasoning. Instead, they considered compassion along with other forms of social behavior as operating within a framework of reciprocity or mutual benefit.[28] In part this connection is illustrated by the basic Greek concept of morality as helping one's friends and harming one's enemies. As far as compassion is concerned, the predominant ethical rule was: "I should show compassion to someone who has shown compassion to me." Also, the converse assumption was: "I should not show compassion to someone who has refused to show it to me." In regard to the recipient of compassion (as suppliant, for example), the proper reciprocal response to such an act is first of all an expression of gratitude or commendation, such as calling the person "noble." Also, later on, the recipient of compassion, now secure and prosperous, may in turn become the provider of compassion to the person who earlier showed him or her pity (reciprocity at its clearest) or, more likely, to someone else who is in dire misfortune, just as the former recipient had been.

Compassion versus *Philia* and *Xenia*

This would seem to make it appropriate, then, for my *xenos* ("guest-friend," "stranger with whom I have established a relationship based on reciprocal benefit") and at times even my *philos* ("friend" or "loved one" or "kinsman") to request compassion based on their relationship to me. Of course, *xenoi* and *philoi* typically benefit one another positively through the simple reciprocity expected of *xenia* and *philia*. Do they also appeal for compassion from their *xenos* or *philos?* One important difference is that compassion arises only when one party is in dire circumstances or in desperate need of assistance. This would exclude simple, customary acts of *philia* or *xenia* that apply to "normal," everyday situations. This, however, does not mean that *philia* or *xenia* is not thought to be operating at all in situations involving compassion between such parties, but that extreme sufferings or personal crises make compassion the primary concern of the parties involved. Indeed, compassion for a loved one may come into play when, in extreme or desperate circumstances, that loved one becomes in a sense an "other" who requests or needs compassion. Such extreme situations are, of course, to be expected in Greek tragedy. Indeed, the refusal or denial of pity or compassion to a loved one is inherently tragic by nature. We will see specific examples in the chapters ahead.

Also, anthropologists have found in their study of "primitive" cultures that compassion tends to be felt most strongly toward those closest to us and to diminish in emotional intensity and action as the pitied one is more distant from us.[29] This pattern is usually represented in the form of concentric circles of affiliation, with the household (close family) being the inner circle and intertribal groups or cultural outsiders being the outer circle, farthest from the perspective of the person supplicated or the one who pities.[30] In regard to the texts I examine, the continuum would likely resemble the following:

self > close family > extended family / kin > *philoi/xenoi* >
fellow Greeks > non-Greeks > enemies

We will see how this model works out in our study.

Claims Based on Reciprocity and Generalized Reciprocity

The suffering individual may therefore buttress his or her appeal for compassion by claiming that he or she has provided the champion with a past benefit or kindness. The most powerful of these claims is, "I showed compassion to you when you were suffering." Conversely, the most powerful justification for refusing to show compassion to an individual is that he or she showed no compassion to you when you desperately needed it! Also, active harm unjustly inflicted by another person typically arouses a strong impulse to enact retribution rather than an impulse to show compassion. In fact, retribution itself may be seen as a form of compassion desired by the victim.

The appeal may also raise the prospect that, someday, somebody may show you similar compassion. Even if not explicitly mentioned by the suppliant, the likely prospect of future compassion for the compassionate person or a thought like the Golden Rule ("I will show compassion to you just as I would want to be shown compassion in your situation") may prompt an individual to show compassion to another suffering human being. This latter type of reasoning connects with the notion of universal human vulnerability to misfortune (see D2 below, pp. 21–22). In some cases a champion may show compassion unprompted by the recipient and based on the champion's sense of his own long-term self-interest. This accords with the concept of "generalized reciprocity" discussed by Walter Donlan and others.[31] Does this verge on altruism? Some might so conclude, but I find a persistent element of self-regard in the cases I analyze in this volume; this keeps it as a "reciprocal behavior" category rather than a category of "purely other-interested behavior" that we normally associate with altruism.[32]

Compassion and Reverence

There is also a connection between compassion and "reverence." The inhibition aroused by a suppliant is typically denoted by the word *aidôs* (reverence, respect).[33] *Aidôs* is a sense of respect, fear, or awe that inhibits the champion from harming the suppliant; in some texts, this is associated with the notion that Zeus protects suppliants from harm. In contrast to compassion, which refers to the human-to-human relationship, *aidôs* tends to bring in a notion of divine protection of the weak party.[34] As John Gould (1973) shows, the suppliant's ritual in large part inspires *aidôs.* Compassion (*oiktos* or *eleos*) typically functions in supplications in one of the two forms analyzed above, as either (1) a second inhibiting emotion that the suppliant may arouse or seek which strongly reinforces the inhibitory effect of *aidôs* or (2) as an emotion that entails helping or saving action in response to the suppliant's situation or appeal. The frequent association and occasional overlap of *aidôs* with compassion will be a persistent theme of this study. In general, I show that both reverence and reciprocity reinforce and are reinforced by compassion. Compassion, properly applied, is a gift that keeps on giving.

General Features of Greek Compassion

Here follows a summary of prominent features of Greek compassion in epic and tragedy that I shall exemplify and develop in the chapters ahead. This summary includes basic definitions, conditions, and assumptions of compassion, marked by the letter D. In the chapters that follow, I refer to the following sections of the introduction by simple references, such as D2. The general features are as follows:

D1. Basic Definitions. Greek compassion (*eleos, oiktos*) in Homeric epic and Athenian tragedy is a strong, painful feeling of concern for another person's extreme distress or misfortune that (a) impels one to provide help or saving action to the person (D1a) or (b) restrains one from inflicting harm on the person (D1b), or (c) both. The Greeks also considered the action or restraint that results from this feeling as compassion. At times the compassionate impulse may be muted or suppressed by circumstances so that saving action or restraint is not possible. At such times, a sympathetic emotional response based on an awareness of the other person's distress or pain may be signaled by *oiktirein* or a compound synonym such as *sunalgein.*

D2. Recognition of Common Humanity: likeness and vulnerability. (a) The impulse or restraint of compassion, at the most basic level, stems from the understanding that the other person is a human being just like oneself, and that also, like oneself, that person does not want to be harmed or to continue to suffer. (b) That impulse or restraint may be aided by the further consideration that such a misfortune could also happen to you or to someone you love (family or close friend).[35] Macleod (1983a: 14) insightfully comments, "Such understanding is, in fact, the cognitive and rational element in compassion."[36] Greek epic and tragedy typically express a worldview that conveys a strong sense of the fragility of good fortune or happiness. A common type of statement in tragedy is the gnomic utterance that expresses the common frailty of humanity, the brevity of life, and mankind's relative lack of power and knowledge, usually in contrast to the gods' superiority.[37] Such a worldview greatly strengthens the impulse to feel and show compassion.[38] (c) Beyond the fundamental recognition of the other person as a fellow human being, there may also be further points of situational closeness or likeness that promote a compassionate response. In *Rhetoric,* Aristotle says that we pity those who are "like us in age, character, disposition, social standing, or birth" (1386a, Roberts tr.). These "accidental" likenesses allow us more readily to comprehend the other person's situation as like our own and thus deserving of our concern and compassion. In fact, in epic and tragedy suppliants often use likenesses as major components of their appeals for compassion: assertions such as "like me you have a father" or "like me you have children" serve to establish a further basis of similarity that should increase compassion.

D3. Intensity of Suffering. The intensity or severity of the person's suffering or the direness of the person's misfortune may prompt or increase compassion for that person. The common tragic motif of "the fall from high to low" emphasizes the extremity of the sufferer's calamity. Also, intense, long-term isolation with consequent hardship and loneliness is often seen as both extreme and as especially pitiable. Furthermore, the senses—particularly sight and hearing—may intensify the effect of the pitiable. Sternberg (2005: 31–36) finds in oratory and history that tears also tend to prompt pity in the form of another's tears. In this regard, Aristotle remarks that we pity sufferings that are close to us (*Rhetoric* 1386a–b), although we should note that this assertion in the context of *Rhetoric* refers specifically to strategies that orators can employ to make suffering seem more immediate and compelling to their audience. In epic and tragedy, perhaps the closest parallel are those intense visualizations of prospective calamity made by characters in their appeals to their loved one (such as Andromache in *Iliad* 6, Priam and Hekabe in *Iliad* 22, and Tekmessa in Sophokles' *Aias*). In these cases the vivid visualization intensifies the appeal in a way not unlike that which Aristotle recommended for orators.[39] In epic and tragedy, however, a character is often confronted directly with the calamity of the suffering individual or group.

D4. Compassion and Worthiness. The compassionate impulse may be promoted or, conversely, repressed by a judgment as to the worthiness of the person to receive compassion. Is the person, for example, innocent, not an enemy, and not likely to be treacherous?[40] In *Poetics,* Aristotle touches on this topic when he discusses the type of character appropriate for tragedy, namely, the type that can arouse tragic pity and fear. He concludes that this is a "good" (*chrêstos*) person with whom we can readily sympathize—not, however, a "saint" (1454a, cf. 1452b–53a).[41] But the requirements of a dramatic character for satisfying a theatrical audience need not necessarily be the same as what a sufferer needs to arouse compassion in a fellow human being. Whenever a suppliant exhibits unworthiness due to wrongdoing, cruelty, treachery, or enmity, compassion will be suppressed in favor of a contrary emotion such as indignation or hostility.[42] On the other hand, when the person is not obviously unworthy, he or she is normally considered worthy simply by virtue of being a human being. We might recall here the infants that were spared in the examples given above: they had nothing to recommend them other than their obvious innocence, their helplessness, and their humanity. If, however, the person has positive points of worthiness that make him or her admirable, we would expect those qualities of goodness to make him or her especially worthy of compassion.[43] Not so clear-cut, however, are the cases of suppliants who may have exercised bad judgment or have otherwise shown undesirable attitudes, but who are not dangerous or deceitful. Such people are not clearly unworthy of compassion, but their actions or attitudes may inhibit a sympathetic hearing (e.g., Adrastos in Euripides' *Suppliants*). In such cases, suppliants normally need to present arguments for or inducements to compassion other than simply their worthiness of character. In such cases, those other considerations likely determine whether or not the appeal for compassion succeeds.

D5. The Pitier's Situation or Character. According to Aristotle, the person who feels compassion and shows compassion is normally not in a state of severe suffering or grief himself or herself, although if that person has experienced such suffering in the past, his or her compassion should be facilitated (*Rhetoric* 1385b–86a). Also, some people by nature are more prone to feeling and showing compassion than others; some, at the other extreme, are characterized as cruel or pitiless.

D6. Compassion and Gender. Both male and female characters in Greek tragedy may appeal for compassion and may show or refuse to show compassion to another person. In general, females appear to be more prone to express compassion or sympathy for others, especially in subordinate roles such as that of the typical chorus.[44] But whereas female characters are more likely to express feelings of sympathy and compassion than male characters, it is more often the male characters that are in positions of power and are asked to show saving compassion. As we shall see, these male characters typically do so, although they may be chary in expressing openly their personal feeling of compassion. At other times gender differences are accentuated explicitly, especially when a male hero, such as Herakles or Aias, suffers extreme misfortune and expresses self-pity or grief or contemplates asking for compassion. Also, since lamentation in Greek culture was specifically associated with women, male heroes in these situations may express shame because they are acting "like a woman." Still another aspect of gender has to do with the suffering of women and girls, especially in situations of war, an issue recently explored by Kathy Gaca (2014).

Now we are ready to begin our analysis, first, by surveying traditional modes of compassion in Homer's epics and other early Greek literature. The second chapter briefly surveys compassion in fifth-century texts mostly outside tragedy in order to provide a historical and cultural context for the plays to be examined. We can then turn to the three great tragedians, Aischylos, Euripides, and Sophokles, whose works we examine in depth.[45] We conclude with a comparison of the three tragedians' employment of the compassion theme and with further reflections on the nature of Greek compassion, particularly as depicted in Greek tragic drama. In particular, I reflect on the relationship of reverence and reciprocity in the working of compassion in Greek tragedy.

CHAPTER 1

Homer and Archaic Greece

The Traditional Elements

Perhaps the most conspicuous occurrence of compassion in ancient Greece is in response to the phenomenon of supplication: the suppliant falls to his or her knees or crouches, clasps the knees and sometimes touches the chin of the person being supplicated while reciting, either briefly or at length, his request. He or she usually tries to encourage a positive response by citing reasons why he should receive compassion or mercy, such as recalling previous service to the *supplicandus*, promising future ransom, or invoking family ties.[1] Supplication can (1) be made directly to the person to be supplicated or (2) take the form of first seeking asylum at the altar of a god or on other sacred ground and then asking for aid or protection from an individual or a group. Although the latter method does not occur and is very rarely alluded to in Homer, the former technique or ritual is common even in our earliest Greek epics.[2]

The Religious Nature of Supplication

Apart from previous ties that the suppliant may invoke as an owed debt, the sanction that allows a suppliant to expect that his request for compassion or mercy will at least be heard and possibly be granted is primarily religious in nature. Zeus is not only the protector of oaths (Zeus *Horkios*) but also the protector of strangers, hosts, and guests (Zeus *Xeinios*) and the protector of suppliants (Zeus *Hiketesios* or, later, *Hikesios*).[3] The aspects of Zeus *Xeinios* and Zeus *Hiketesios* are occasionally linked.[4] Zeus's protection is so formidable that even other gods are said to be obliged to respect the sanctity of suppliants (*Odyssey* 5.447–48), for aggression against Zeus's ward is aggression against Zeus himself. Pedrick (1982) denies that divine sanctions enforce acts of supplication in the *Iliad,* but finds such protection in the *Odyssey.* Indeed, the latter epic makes Zeus's protection of suppliants much more explicit, but Zeus's assurance to Priam (*Iliad* 24.184–87, discussed below) that Akhilleus "is neither senseless nor rash nor sinful, but will very thoughtfully spare a suppliant" suggests that suppliants in the *Iliad,* apart from the crisis situation on the battlefield, also have some protection from the gods against being harmed by the champion they supplicate. Furthermore, Apollo's reinforcement of Chryses' supplication in *Iliad* 1 is a dramatic example of divine protection.[5] Pedrick, nevertheless, correctly asserts that whether the suppliant succeeds in getting his or her request granted generally depends on the suppliant's ability to arouse compassion in the champion and/or persuade him or her with claims of past benefits or with promises of rewards to come. My argument will seek to show that claims of reciprocity in suppliant appeals, including offers of ransom, need not inhibit the suppliant from seeking to arouse the champion's reverence and compassion as well.[6] Priam, indeed, does both in *Iliad* 24 (501–6). Indeed, Naiden (2006: 82) correctly argues that the reciprocity of ransoming found in Homer should not be confused with a notion of "compensation," which implies guilt on the part of the suppliant.

The language used of suppliants and those who honor them emphasizes the religious nature of Zeus's protection of suppliants. For example, Pausanias, in discussing Zeus's anger at those who violate suppliants, cites an ancient oracle of Zeus himself at Dodona: "Do not kill these, nor do injustice to suppliants, for suppliants are holy and sacred."[7] This religious connection is continued into the fifth century, in which those who succor suppliants are called *eusebês* (pious) and *hosios* (holy), as noted by Adkins (1960a: 132–33). In Herodotos's story of Paktyes' supplication at Kyme (1.157–60), the oracle of Apollo described the people of Kyme as "having committed sacrilege" (*asebêsantes*) for even consulting the god about whether they could give up the suppliant to his pursuers. Euripides describes the religious sanction that protects the suppliant as a pollution of "blood which cries out for vengeance"[8] upon those who kill a suppliant. The connection between supplication and religion is also reflected in the use of the concept of *aidôs* (reverence, awe, shame) in the Homeric poems.[9] Both Schadewaldt (1955: 138) and Pohlenz (1956: 56) define *aidôs* as quasireligious, quasimoral restraint or reverence that is shown both toward superiors, such as kings and parents, and toward inferiors, such as the weak and suppliants. The religious quality is brought out explicitly by the use of *aidôs* and its cognate forms to refer to the gods' protection of suppliants: one's reverence toward the gods should lead one to revere and show restraint toward suppliants.[10] The same authors also discuss Homer's yoking of *aidôs* with *eleos,* and they agree that whereas *aidôs* represents a feeling of divine-moral obligation (imposed by the gods and society), *eleos* is the complementary feeling of "pure" or internally aroused compassion that one feels at the sight of human misfortune.[11] Pohlenz, who describes *eleos* as an emotion that stimulates action (see above, intro. p. 10), argues that it is *eleos* which turns the inhibition or awe caused by *aidôs* into an act of deliverance.[12] In any case, this aggregate of religious, social, and personal feeling not only strongly inhibits the supplicated from harming the suppliant but also provides an impulse to assist him or her. *Aidôs* is the specifically religious element of the mix and, as Gould shows (1973: 87–89), continues to denote a feeling of inhibition with religious overtones in fifth-century tragedy. According to Gould, this *aidôs* "represents, more than any other quality, the characteristic feeling-tone of the supplication situation."[13]

Not only language but also action reveals the religious nature of supplication. The suppliant can either seek asylum at an altar or some other holy ground before supplicating an individual, or as happens often on the battlefield in the *Iliad,* he can or must approach the *supplicandus* directly and assume the suppliant posture. Whereas the religious nature of asylum at an altar is obvious, that of supplication of an individual is less patent. Gould (75–78) argues that the link between the two forms is the "ritual significance of physical contact," which is made with either the altar of a god or the body of the supplicated.[14] With this assumption, he develops a distinction between "complete" supplication, in which the ritual contact is made and maintained, and "figurative" supplication, in which it is not made, avoided, or broken. His argument is that "figurative" supplication lacks the "full ritual significance" and the "full binding force" of the "completed" supplication. In spite of some uncertainty about the validity of this distinction,[15] I do agree that supplication of an individual by assuming the suppliant stance and touching the supplicated is a ritual or ceremonial act involving assumed religious sanctions, specifically the protection of Zeus, just as asylum at the altar of a god would be.[16] So far we have seen the religious quality of the language and behavior of supplication, but let us now examine how the connection between compassion and reciprocity is developed in Homer (cf. n.6, above).

Compassion and Reciprocity: Early Connections

That the ancient Greeks in general had a strong sense of reciprocity is evident in their literature from Homer on.[17] M. I. Finley describes the reciprocity of gift-giving in the Homeric world, which he likens to other "primitive" or traditional societies in this respect:

> The word "gift" is not to be misconstrued. It may be stated as a flat rule of both primitive and archaic society that no one ever gave anything, whether goods or services or honors, without proper recompense, real or wishful, immediate or years away, to himself or to his kin. The act of giving was, therefore, in an essential sense always the first half of a reciprocal action, the other half of which was a counter-gift. (1965: 62)

This reciprocity is part of the distinction that Bolkestein (1939) draws between "charity" in the pre-Christian West (Greece and Rome) and East (Egypt and Israel). Whereas the autocratic cultures of the East developed a rigid class distinction between rich and poor, with relief to the poor serving to highlight the contrast between classes, the more egalitarian Greeks did not direct their charity so much toward social inferiors as toward equals who had suffered misfortune. The understanding, expressed or not, was that such peers would return the favor when their misfortune had passed. Indeed, such reciprocal service played a large role in the development of "friendship" or *philia:* the beneficent deed not only obligated the recipient to make a return but also tended to form the basis for a friendship through which both parties usually acquired status and security.[18] Such alliances would be especially important in societies, such as that which Homer describes, in which the *oikos* or household was so independent. Gill (1998a: 309–13) shows how reciprocity in Homeric society provided a basis for social solidarity and mutual benefit. He uses the famous speech of Glaukos to Sarpedon (*Iliad* 12: 310–38) to illustrate the working of this society based on ideals of reciprocity.

Here is where *xenia* (guest-friendship) and the related phenomenon of *hiketeia* (supplication) enter the picture. The reciprocal nature of *xenia* is well known: the hospitality shown to a stranger is to be returned by him when the occasion arises. This institution serves to form alliances and friendships between strangers as well as to lessen the danger and fear of travel in the ancient world.[19] *Xenia,* therefore, not only reduces the anxiety and hostility that might be felt in encountering a stranger; it also seeks to bring the outsider within the group as, for example, a potential ally against enemies. Gould (1973: 92–94) argues that *hiketeia* is closely related and that it too brings an outsider (the *hiketês*) within the group. He describes both *xenia* and *hiketeia* as forming a "spiritual kinship" between the parties involved, and he cites two passages from early Greek literature in which the *xenos* and the suppliant are described in the language of kinship or in the context of remarks about kin (*Odyssey* 8.546–47; *Works and Days* 327–32). He also mentions the encounter of Diomedes and Glaukos (*Iliad* 6.215–36), which suggests that the bonds developed through these means are passed on through generations, much like the obligations of blood kinship.

As with gift-giving between *xenoi* in Homer or the mutual service by members of the upper classes in later times, compassion tends to be shown to those who can be expected to make a return of compassion or of some equivalent service or to those with whom a relationship of *philia* (friendship, love, affection) or *xenia* has already been established by previous experience of favors or mutual service. Adkins (1963: 34–35) notes that a suppliant becomes a *philos* (friend, loved one) only if he is an equal and has the possibility of returning the favor and, furthermore, that *philotês* (friendship, love, affection) in Homer is shown by action rather than by mere intention or expression of sympathy. He says of the suppliant, "What he needs is not primarily sympathy or affection, which are luxuries for a man in his position, but actions: the provision of food, shelter, and protection if he needs it—in short *timê* [honor]" (35). Adkins rightly emphasizes the behavioral nature of *philia* to the extent that he says that "*philein* [to love] is an act, which creates or maintains a cooperative relationship; and *it need not be accompanied by any friendly feeling at all:* it is the action that is all-important." Compare with this Pohlenz's emphasis on the behavioral nature of *eleos* in Homer (see above, intro. p. 11). Here, as in our discussion of the reciprocal nature of compassion in the introduction (pp. 17–20), we need to carefully observe that compassion is not the operation of simple, normal *xenia* (*xeiniê*) or *philia* (*philotês*) but is called for in instances where the *philos* or *xenos* is in a state of serious or extreme misfortune, distress, or need that requires the action of the person supplicated.

Some examples of reciprocity functioning in supplications or other appeals for compassion are the following: in *Iliad* 1, as Akhilleus is requesting Thetis to make an appeal to Zeus to restore his honor, the hero prompts her to "supplicate (*lisai*) Zeus, if you have ever gratified (or, benefited) his heart by word or by deed" (1.394–95). Akhilleus then proceeds to provide his goddess mother with one such example: the time when she rescued Zeus from the other Olympians who sought to bind him (1.396–406). Indeed, in her appeal to Zeus, in which she performs the full suppliant ritual, Thetis begins with, "Father Zeus, if I ever benefited you among the immortals by word or deed . . ." (1.503–4). Of course, this example features a goddess appealing to a god, but there is nothing in the mode of supplication or in the rhetoric of the appeal that appears to mark it as different from a supplication and an appeal that human beings might perform among themselves. The Chryses supplication that begins the *Iliad* is clearly framed in terms of reciprocity: the father not only offers ransom for his daughter (i.e., terms of an actual exchange) but also prefaces his supplication by expressing a good wish for the Achaians' success at Troy and safety on their return home (1.17–21).[20] How do these two examples relate to compassion? If we define compassion as action that relieves suffering or misfortune (including the restoration of honor), we can see how Thetis's appeal to restore Akhilleus's injured honor and Chryses' appeal for the restoration of the daughter who has been taken from him are effectively appeals for compassion (cf. D1).[21] Further examples of reciprocity in appeals for compassion between friends are discussed below in connection to Akhilleus's relationship with his comrades.

Shared Humanity and Common Vulnerability

Another aspect of the reciprocal nature of compassion is that not only does one show compassion to someone of the same class because he or she can make a like return, but also one tends to benefit peers out of a recognition of shared humanity (a sense of one's own similar nature and vulnerability) that is expressed in terms more general than strict this-for-that reciprocity (D2, D5).[22] Thus the man who is asked for compassion by a suppliant who was once prosperous like himself tends to feel compassion and to aid the person because there is always the chance that he himself will be in the same lowly condition some day. This traditional feature of Greek compassion is given explicit expression by later writers, especially tragedians. Anaximenes, the philosopher, is reported to have said, "The rich are not accustomed to pity (*oiktirein*) the unfortunate in the same way that the poor do. For, out of fear for themselves they [the wealthy] pity (*eleein*) the misfortunes of others."[23] Herodotos (1.86) describes how Kyros came to spare Kroisos, whom he had placed alive on a burning pyre, "when he considered that he himself, a human being, was burning to death another human being who had once been no less prosperous than he was. Furthermore, because he feared retribution and discerned that nothing in human affairs was secure, he ordered the blazing fire to be extinguished."[24] And there is Odysseus's response to the humiliation of Aias in Sophokles' *Aias* (121–26); Odysseus says he pities (*epoiktirein*) Aias, even though he is an enemy: "I'm considering what concerns me no less than him. For I see that all of us who live are nothing but phantoms and empty shadow."[25] Thus compassion for others was aroused by the sight of a misfortunate human being along with the fear that one's similarity to such a person entails.[26]

Doubtless this kind of fear was increased by the evident lack of security in the ancient world (cf. *Odyssey* 18.130–42) and perhaps also, especially among the upper classes, by the notion expounded by poets and dramatists that the prosperous are especially liable to downfall because of the gods' envy.[27] From this commonplace of situation and reasoning eventually comes Aristotle's famous yoking of "pity and fear" (*eleos kai phobos*), which he puts at the heart of his description of the spectator's experience of tragedy (*Poetics* 1449b) and on which he discourses at length in the *Rhetoric* (1385b–86b).[28]

The realization that fortune was so unstable and that a sudden transition from rich man to beggar could easily happen went hand in hand with the special protection said to be afforded to beggars by Zeus (*Odyssey* 14.56–58). Unlike the poor man, who worked hard for a modest living and so had little in common with the rich, the beggar was more likely to have been well off once and to be in his present condition through some catastrophe.[29] This is the case of Odysseus who poses as a beggar in the *Odyssey* and tells his host, Eumaios, a story of previous fortune followed by disaster and treachery that reduced him to his present state of being a wandering beggar (14.191–359). In the case of such a beggar, a sense of one's own vulnerability reflected in the beggar's lot (occasioning fear and compassion) would perhaps play a more important role than the prospect of rewards; still, the latter might to some extent be present, since fallen *nobiles* can sometimes recoup their losses.[30] Eumaios, of course, has also fallen from high to low (15.403–84)—as Odysseus well knows—and so can readily sympathize with Odysseus's tale, although he perhaps no longer has fear of such a fate, since he has already encountered it. In any case, Eumaios asserts that both fear of Zeus and his own compassion (*eleairôn*) lead him to treat the needy stranger well (14.388–89). Odysseus's later words acknowledging that Eumaios is now *philos* to him (15.341–43) suggest that even benefiting a wandering beggar can induce a relationship of friendship with reciprocity understood.

Compassion toward Enemies

So far we have looked at the positive side of compassion in Homeric and early classical Greece: how religious sanctions protect the suppliant and encourage inclinations to benefit him or her, and also how the strong personal motivations of reciprocity and a tendency to see one's own vulnerability reflected in the destitute person's situation reinforce the feeling of compassion and the impulse to assist. But a negative side also comes into play when the religious obligation and the rule of reciprocity come into conflict: when an enemy becomes a suppliant. Here, the feelings of religious obligation may draw one toward showing mercy, but the feelings of hostility and the law of reciprocity demand that an enemy be returned evil for evil and not be spared. This conflict presents problems to the interpreter of Greek literature because it is not always possible to determine the poet's tone or the response that he expected from his audience when presenting an account of a person who kills a suppliant who is also an enemy. Whether the religious sanctions that protect the suppliant are meant to be perceived as being in force in instances of war, as in the *Iliad*, or in the case of revenge for, say, the abuse of one's household, as in the suitor plot of the *Odyssey*, is often problematical for the reader, as it must have also been for at least some of the ancient Greeks who found themselves in such situations.

The assumption of reciprocity is that you show compassion to friends and deny mercy to enemies. A corollary assumption, from the viewpoint of the suppliant in need, would be that you would expect compassion from your friends (and from neutral strangers under the benefit of Zeus's protection), but you would not expect it from personal enemies.[31] As a result of these assumptions, one would expect the person who refuses to show compassion to a friend or a suppliant stranger to be especially liable to retaliation from Zeus, and for someone who is so mistreated to perceive himself or herself (and perhaps be perceived by others) as entitled to carry out revenge as the agent of Zeus. This can be seen in the case of Odysseus and the Kyklops: Polyphemos refuses to honor the supplication of Odysseus and his men, and so they act as Zeus's agents in punishing him for his savagery and lack of compassion (*Odyssey* 9.478–79, 23.312–13).

This is also what is involved in the treatment of the beggar Odysseus. After having entered his house with Eumaios, Odysseus is approached by Athene who bids him to beg from the suitors, who are at dinner, as a test to see which are *enaisimoi* (righteous) and which are *athemistoi* (lawless), even though all are destined to die (17.360–64). Odysseus does this, and the suitors respond at first with proper compassion: "feeling compassion they gave" to the beggar.[32]

Then Melanthios, the disloyal goatherd who had already abused the beggar as he entered (215–34), remarks that the beggar was brought in by Eumaios the swineherd (369–73). This provokes Antinoos, who chides Eumaios for bringing the beggar in and then is rebuked in turn by Eumaios and Telemachos (374–79). Eventually Odysseus comes around to beg from Antinoos himself (414–44). In his request for food, Odysseus flatters Antinoos as having the appearance of noble breeding and then begins to tell a false story: how he himself was once prosperous and gave to wanderers in need, like himself, but then was brought down by an evil fate. Like the tale told to Eumaios, this story is tailored to fit its audience: it shows Odysseus to be Antinoos's peer by birth and, as we have seen, it is just the sort of story that ought to arouse in the latter a sense of shared vulnerability and lead to his feeling compassion for the beggar (D2). Furthermore, Odysseus adds an explicit promise of reciprocal benefit by saying that he will spread Antinoos's good reputation around if Antinoos is charitable (418). The suitor, however, responds not with the *eleos* that is expected of him but with abuse and, after a hostile exchange of words with Odysseus, hits him on the shoulder with a flying footstool. Odysseus ponders revenge in his heart and curses Antinoos for his abuse of a beggar and especially for his insensitivity to the lot of a man who is under the hard necessity of hunger (468–76). The other suitors rebuke Antinoos for his mistreatment of the beggar and warn that he might be a god (483–87). (Antinoos will be the first to die when Odysseus's revenge eventually comes.) Later, Eurymachos and the other suitors, at Athene's instigation, taunt the beggar further (18.346–48), and Penelope complains that the suitors' behavior has interfered with her ability to give proper heed to guests, suppliants, or heralds (19.134–35).

Penelope's complaint and the other suitors' earlier expressions of dismay at Antinoos's abuse of the beggar suggest norms of behavior presumably recognized and acknowledged as valid by Homer's audience. Both the Kyklops episode and the episode of the beggar in the palace are designed to show the wrong response to the appeal of suppliants and beggars, respectively. They can be contrasted with the response of Eumaios, who respectfully welcomes the beggar and enters into a relationship of *philia* with him. In both the Kyklops and beggar episodes we see that abuse of the suppliant or beggar (who does not approach as an enemy) motivates retaliation on the part of the suppliant. Furthermore, the stories are told in such a way that this revenge seems fully justified as punishment for the violation of Zeus's sacred protection (cf. *Odyssey* 22.413–16, 23.63–67, and 24. 351–52). This is reciprocity pure and simple: no mercy for him who has shown no mercy.[33]

A similar type of violation that seems to provoke this simple type of reciprocal justice is the abuse of *xenia.* The person whose *xenia* (either as guest or host) has been abused, like the violated suppliant, often takes it upon himself to carry out revenge with no quarter given. Again, the Kyklops episode may serve as an example.[34] A closely related example is the suitor plot of the *Odyssey,* although the suitors are perhaps not technically *xenoi* since they have not been invited into the house as guests. Still, Telemachos charges the suitors with consuming and wasting another man's property when they have goods of their own, a clear violation of reciprocity and of the sanctity of the household, and he prays to Zeus for retaliation (1.374–80, 2.139–45). He also remarks that, with

Odysseus absent, he himself is not strong enough to defend his house against this plunder by fellow Ithakans (2.55–62; contrast with this the procedure that the suitors should have followed, 51–54).[35] Zeus's omen (2.146–76) shows that Zeus is indeed aligned with Telemachos against the violations by the suitors. The suitors' wastefulness is further detailed by Eumaios in his description to Odysseus of the situation at home (14.80–95). He specifically mentions the suitors' lack of concern about the gods as shown by their behavior: "having in mind neither the wrath of the gods nor mercy."[36] Eumaios goes on to say that the gods dislike "cruel deeds" (*schetlia erga,* 83), with the clear implication that the suitors are liable to the gods' vengeance for their abuse of Odysseus's household. Even Antinoos suggests that there is something wrong with the suitors' squandering another man's fortune when he hypocritically argues that the beggar shouldn't be given any bread (17.450–52).

The suitors have ignored the civilized conventions of hospitality, violated the ethic of reciprocity, and shown contempt for the gods (22.39–40) by forcing their way into Odysseus' house, terrorizing his son (including a foiled ambush), courting his wife, subverting some of his male slaves, subverting and sleeping with some of his female slaves, and wasting his wealth. Odysseus's revenge for this "transgression" (*hyperbasiê,* 22.64) is severe and without mercy. Even Leodes, who adopts the suppliant posture, is not spared (22.310–29). Leodes claims to have behaved well toward the women of the household and to have tried to restrain the other suitors, but the fact that he willingly participated in the suit for Penelope's hand with the others brings down retribution upon him as well.[37] Halitherses the seer later says that the suitors deserved their punishment for consuming Odysseus's wealth and dishonoring his wife (24.454–62). We might also note that Odysseus is even more vindictive in punishing the disloyal members of his own household (22.419–77).

Likewise, in the *Iliad* a violation of *xenia* is explicitly cited as the cause of the war with Troy: Paris's abduction of Helen and the continued refusal to give her back. When Menelaos is about to spare the enemy suppliant Adrestos, Agamemnon intercedes and reminds Menelaos of the injury to his home by the Trojans; Adrestos is then killed (6.37–65). Later, after killing Peisandros, Menelaos claims revenge and describes himself as the agent of Zeus *Xeinios,* who will destroy the Trojans' city for their violation of Menelaos's hospitality (13.620–27).

War in general is a situation in which the sanctity of the suppliant's person and the demands of reciprocity are likely to come into conflict. Gould (1973) may be correct in his speculation that the original form of supplication was done at the hearth of a powerful individual, the "domestic" form, as the word *hiketês* (comer, suppliant) suggests, thus making it close to *xenia* in origin as well as in nature. He further speculates that the supplication of a king or populace from the public altar of a god was a later development as communities came to have a being apart from the king's *oikos* (household). If this was so, then the supplication of an enemy on the battlefield, which is the form that predominates in the narrative of the *Iliad,* may well be what Gould (93, n.100a) calls "merely a crisis extension, a metaphorical adaptation" of the "domestic" form. Also, we might expect this "crisis extension" to be more liable to failure, since the suppliant is now an enemy, rather than the neutral stranger or friend that he would be in time of peace; enmity places a stress on the sanction that protects suppliants, however binding that sanction might be assumed to be in time of peace.

There is a story of a king who spares an enemy, a story that is part of Odysseus's fabrication to Eumaios (*Odyssey* 14.259–84). Odysseus tells how he and his men put in at Egypt and how he sent out some men who got carried away by their greed and began plundering the territory. When retaliation came and his men were defeated, he threw down his battle gear and became a suppliant at the knees of the enemy king, who took pity on him and spared him (278–79), although the rest of the Egyptians were so angry that they tried to kill the suppliant. The king protected him, according to Odysseus, out of fear of Zeus *Xeinios,* who "above all is angered by evil deeds."[38] The reliability of this story as a model of standard behavior is perhaps less than that of narratives by the poet himself. Since the audience knows this story to be a lie, the teller is assumed to have an especially free hand in shaping "reality" to his own ends. For example, there seems to be a moral undertone that connects Odysseus's "innocence" in the plundering with the fact that he is later spared, even though the king could not know of his innocence.[39]

There is, however, other evidence in Homer that suppliant enemies in war were sometimes spared and taken prisoner, although the dominant motive seems to be a desire for ransom rather than a feeling of compassion. Menelaos is on the verge of sparing and ransoming the suppliant Adrestos when Agamemnon, eager for him to get on with the business of fighting, intervenes and demands blood (*Iliad* 6.51–53). Likewise, Akhilleus, responding to Lykaon's supplication, remarks that his practice before the death of Patroklos had been to spare Trojans and sell them into slavery (21.100–102). Still, in the context of battle, Menelaos is easily persuaded not to spare Adrestos by Agamemnon's brief appeal for vengeance, and Akhilleus decides not to spare Lykaon out of revenge for Patroklos's death.

In both cases the strong personal motivation for revenge is shown to overpower the restraint induced by a desire for ransom. Indeed, in neither of these cases does the killer acknowledge any religious obligation to spare the enemy suppliant, which suggests that *aidôs* is assumed not to be in force on the battlefield.[40] Such revenge is the stuff of which wars and warriors are made; to come by mercy from an enemy with whom and with whose friends you have been fighting to the death is an erratic possibility at best. In Odysseus's tale about the king who spared him, we may note that many of the Egyptians furiously desired to take revenge on the suppliant and were restrained from doing so only by the king, who stands out as something of a rarity. The more realistic unlikelihood of receiving mercy from an enemy on the battlefield is shown by Hektor's dismissal of supplication as a possible means of surviving Akhilleus's furious onslaught after the death of Patroklos (22.111–30). Mercy seems strictly optional; where it does occur, it seems to be primarily for the purpose of gaining wealth in the form of ransom.

The Case of Akhilleus

Akhilleus, of course, is something of a special case, and in discussing him we must be especially careful not to forget the poet and the poet's muse. Regardless of the fact that we must rely on Homer with the expectation that he is reflecting behavior and values typical of or at least understandable to his society (and helping shape the values of later Greek civilization and its poets), he is nevertheless creating characters and telling a story in a certain way to achieve his desired artistic ends. These must be taken into account.

The *Iliad*, as the story of Akhilleus's anger, is also the story of his compassion or lack of it.[41] This story falls into roughly two parts: (1) Akhilleus's anger at Agamemnon and his refusal to pity his comrades by helping them fight the Trojans, and (2) Akhilleus's lack of mercy toward the Trojans that results from his drive to avenge Patroklos's death.[42]

To continue our discussion of *eleos* vis-à-vis enemies, it will be convenient to consider the second phase first. After Patroklos's death, Akhilleus reenters the battle, and, as I have noted, contrary to his previous practice, he no longer spares and ransoms the suppliant Trojans that he encounters in fighting. Two examples are Tros (20.463–72) and Lykaon (21.74–135). This vengefulness continues to drive Akhilleus as he seeks Hektor, the killer of Patroklos, and eventually kills him.[43] The intensity of Akhilleus's vindictiveness is emphasized by his subsequent treatment of Hektor's corpse, which he seeks to mutilate and to which he refuses burial. This brings on the accusation of Hektor's divine partisan, Apollo, that Akhilleus has lost all *eleos* and *aidôs* (24.44–45). We may note here that it is not so much Akhilleus's merciless killing of Hektor and the other suppliant Trojans as it is the mistreatment of Hektor's corpse and the refusal of burial that instigate Apollo's complaint and cause Zeus to send Priam to ransom the body (65–76).[44]

Priam's supplication of Akhilleus follows, in which Akhilleus's compassion is aroused by Priam's appeal to him to think of his own father, Peleus (486–506).[45] Both men weep as Priam remembers

Hektor, and Akhilleus, in turn, remembers his father and Patroklos. Akhilleus feels compassion (*oiktirôn,* 516) for Priam's past loss of his beloved son Hektor as he also envisions his own father's future loss of him and recalls his own past loss of his dear *philos* Patroklos (507–12).[46] He thus sees himself and Priam as participants in the common world of suffering humanity, as he articulates eloquently in his speech describing the two jars of Zeus. Again, we have the process of likeness in which one man's *eleos* is aroused for a peer because of the universal human condition. Here, the likeness is not precise, because one person is depicted as a father and the other as a son, so that the connection is made through Akhilleus's thinking of the similarity of his father to Priam.[47] Indeed, the introduction of his beloved father, Peleus, makes Akhilleus's development of compassion even more poignant than the more typical "direct" recognition of likeness (D2). Of course, the fact that the two men are enemies adds greatly to the dramatic tension of the scene and to the sublimity of its resolution.[48] As we have seen, Akhilleus's treatment of Priam is the exception rather than the rule in war, but the fact that Priam comes to Akhilleus's hut rather than meeting him in hostile gear on the battlefield is important in motivating Akhilleus to revere the suppliant's sanctity here, as is suggested in Zeus's assurance (via Iris) to Priam: "But when [Hermes] leads you inside Akhilleus' hut, he himself will not kill you, and he will restrain all others from doing so. For he is neither senseless nor rash nor sinful, but will very thoughtfully spare a suppliant."[49] The mention of the hut (*klisiê*) suggests the "domestic" form of supplication, with its overtones of *xenia,* as in the case of the Kyklops. Unlike on the battlefield, here the religious sanctions protecting the suppliant are assumed to be in force, as Akhilleus implicitly acknowledges (568–70). Still, it is Priam's personal appeal and Akhilleus's very personal response to it, depicted as they are in precisely reciprocal terms, that make the scene such a powerful one.

The other part of the Akhilleus narrative that involves compassion is Akhilleus's relationship with his comrades after the argument with Agamemnon and before the death of Patroklos. This, of course, is the period in which Akhilleus withdraws from battle and watches his fellow Greeks sustain heavy losses and impending defeat from the Trojans. The notion that Akhilleus lacks compassion for his allies comes up in the story of the embassy sent to him (book 9).[50] Odysseus begs Akhilleus at least to have compassion for (ἐλέαιρε) the other Achaians (i.e., to save them with his *aretê*), if he cannot come to terms with Agamemnon. The soldiers, he argues, will honor Akhilleus as a result of his *eleos* (300–303). Phoinix warns Akhilleus not to have a "pitiless spirit" (*nêlees êtor*) and tells how even the gods themselves can be placated by compensation (496–98). As McCoy (2013: 20) notes, Phoinix reminds Akhilleus that in his youth he was once dependent on the care of Phoinix and others. He also mentions the Litai, the daughters of Zeus who see to it that prayers and entreaties are honored (502–12),[51] and he draws a parallel in Meleagros, who lost honor through his persistent refusal to relent and fight (529–99). Aias calls Akhilleus "savage" (*agrios*, 629) and "pitiless" (*nêlês*, 632), a man who refuses to be moved by the "friendship" (*philotês*) of his comrades, the friendship through which Akhilleus has acquired great honor (629–32). Later, Nestor describes to Patroklos how Akhilleus lacks care and compassion for his friends (οὐ κήδεται οὐδ' ἐλεαίρει, 11.664–65) and asks Patroklos to intercede with Akhilleus for the Greeks. Patroklos, in turn, calls Akhilleus "pitiless" (*nêlees*) for not helping his allies and says that the sea and the rocks bore him instead of his reputed parents, Peleus and Thetis (16.33–35). Thus Patroklos has compassion for his fellow soldiers and suggests that Akhilleus should as well, but Akhilleus's prayer that all the Achaians, as well as the Trojans, perish and that only he and Patroklos win glory suggests that Akhilleus still lacks complete compassion for his fellow Greeks (16.97–100). Pohlenz (1956: 56) describes Akhilleus's lack of compassion as a sign of his loss of connection with human society, and, indeed, Aias's and Patroklos's particular reproaches imply that Akhilleus's lack of compassion is a lack of humanity.[52]

There is, however, a moment just before Patroklos accuses Akhilleus when the latter sees Patroklos weep and feels compassion for him (ᾤκτιρε, 16.5). He even chides Patroklos for weeping "like a little girl." Here, we have an example of the sight of tears leading to compassion (cf. D3, D6). There is also, along with intimacy and warmth, the touch of condescension that Burkert (1955: 38) associates with *eleos/oiktos*. But it is gentle, not harsh condescension, and it does not detract from the equality and essential human dignity of the pitied one.[53] Akhilleus's compassion here does eventually prompt him to allow Patroklos to intervene to assist his fellow Achaians (D1a). And later, after Patroklos's death, Akhilleus expresses deep regret for not having helped his companions who have died fighting the Trojans (18.98–106). By the time of the funeral games, his hostility toward the Achaians seems to have vanished completely.

Again, we see reciprocity in force in the Akhilleus narrative: whereas a soldier may not be expected to help his enemies in war, he is expected to help (and to have compassion for) his friends and allies and to accept recompense if one of them has offended him, as Agamemnon did Akhilleus. Adkins (1963: 39) has said that the relationship of *philotês* in Homer "is not really co-operative, but reciprocal." Indeed, as we have seen, Akhilleus's lack of compassion and refusal to relent is usually described in terms of his unwillingness to accept compensation or his willingness to forgo the *timê* that his exhibition of *eleos* would bring him (9.300–303), but I sense an element of what I would call "co-operation" in the tone that is used to describe Akhilleus's feelings about his fellow Greeks, Agamemnon excepted. When Patroklos reproaches Akhilleus with being pitiless and the harsh and hard offspring of sea and rock for not helping the Argives who face impending destruction, and later when Akhilleus expresses recrimination for not having provided assistance to those who died rather than sitting as a "useless burden on the earth," there is an implication that the Greeks do have common interests in the defeat of the Trojans and that they should assist one another above and beyond the strict consideration of reciprocal rewards (cf. *Iliad* 5.529–32, 15.561–64). "Reciprocity" and "co-operation" need not be mutually exclusive terms.[54]

Limitations of Compassion toward Friends

The unrestricted display of compassion and consolation to *philoi*, however, tends to be limited by the competitive nature of war, especially when such compassion would or could interfere with success in war. Pohlenz (1956: 56) notes that the spontaneously rising emotion of *eleos* can be seen, in certain circumstances, as a hindrance to the performance of masculine duties (*Mannesaufgabe*), as in the case of Hektor, who must strongly resist his wife's appeal for compassion, since such compassion would involve behavior (remaining behind the walls and defending from within) that he sees as contrary to the requirements of martial valor (6.405–93).[55] A similar episode occurs in book 22 (25–91) when Priam and Hekabe also try to call Hektor inside—away from his certain death at the hand of Akhilleus.[56] The requirements of battle also place restrictions on the indulgence in lamentation for fallen comrades; see, for example, *Iliad* 19.228–29, where Odysseus says to Akhilleus about the dead Patroklos: "It is necessary to have a pitiless heart (*nêlea thumon*) and, after weeping for a day, to bury him who has died." This example and the examples concerning Hektor show that in war, success and consequent survival are necessarily the paramount values (or demands) and that occasionally compassion or lamentation, which might be expected in other circumstances, must be repressed or curtailed.[57]

The Poet's Perspective

But what are we to make of the Akhilleus narrative and of *eleos* in Homer in general? Again, we have the problem of the artist's values versus the values of the world that he is depicting. These values can be the same, but they do not have to be. Homer himself need not have been a warrior who was driven by the demands of valor in order to depict a character or set of characters who were so driven or to see the tragic implications of such a life or of such a society. The pathos of the Hektor-Andromache scene and the way in which the Akhilleus story is designed (with Akhilleus beginning in anger, then coming to pity his fellow Greeks, and, finally, coming to feel compassion for even his enemy, Priam, in the resolution of the epic) suggest to me, at any rate, that, for the Homer of the *Iliad*, *eleos* was a highly valued emotion indeed.[58]

Such an artist may draw characters who also value compassion or who see it as essential to good character or full humanity, as Patroklos obviously does when he uses lack of compassion as a reproach for Akhilleus.[59] But the tragic art (and I include epic in this concept) demands that, even though the artist may have a broad sympathy for his characters and depict them all as human, the characters themselves, or at least some of them, must possess values or drives (at least temporarily) that bring them into conflict rather than always exhibiting common respect, understanding, and sympathy for one another. Otherwise, there would be little matter for tragedy.[60]

Thus there is normally a gap between the poet and his characters as well as between the behavior of his characters and that of those who people the "real world" of the author's time. For example, whatever the behavior of the real people of Homer's age in war, the tragic consequences of war, as shown by the touching scene between Hektor and Andromache and by Akhilleus's temporary loss of humanity, may be emphasized by an artist who places a high value on *eleos,* whereas another artist who values the prizes and rewards of valor almost exclusively might have little interest in conveying pathos and prefer to tell a story in which the evil or unrighteous or disloyal are vanquished by a morally superior hero (or heroes)—in other words, to emphasize the distinctions between human beings rather than their common ground. The *Odyssey* is often seen as belonging to this second type, as Aristotle suggests with his description of the double plot (*Poetics* 1453a). Still, we might remember that one basis that is used to distinguish the good from the bad in that epic is the exhibition of *eleos* or the lack thereof: the suitors are punished, at least in part, for their mistreatment of the beggar Odysseus. Again, this shows that *eleos* is highly valued by the storyteller, even though the broad sympathy of the *Iliad* may be missing. One difference between the two epics is situational: as ironic as it seems, it is probably more difficult to make villains out of those who fail to show compassion in the generally cruel and merciless situation of war than out of those who fail to do so in peaceful situations such as those of the *Odyssey.*

Such considerations of the poet's viewpoint are, of course, highly speculative and subjective (and this matter is complicated still further if we broach the issue of multiple authorship of the epics).

These considerations do, however, serve to remind us that the Homeric poems are themselves subjective works of art rather than "documentaries" or "histories" of early Greek society; furthermore, that the degree or quality of compassion depicted in characters or conveyed by the tone of the poem may well be more reflective of the artist's particular vision than of the society in general. For one thing, Homer invests his major characters (Thersites and the suitors excepted) with a heroic stature typical of legendary figures. Their attitudes and behavior are thus made expressive of specifically heroic standards (i.e., how a hero ought to behave), whether or not various individuals in the stories succeed in meeting the requirements of these standards. Nevertheless, where the characters express standards of expected behavior, we may expect these to be comprehensible to Homer's audience and thus to some extent reflective of the real world.[61] Certainly this is true of the suppliant model, with its religious overtones and prohibitions, as well as of the reciprocal nature of compassion, which is perhaps the single most important factor defining *eleos* in Homer and which, as we shall see, continues to be in force in later Greek culture.

Compassion in the Archaic Period

Before we consider the transition from epic to Athenian tragedy in the fifth century, brief notice may be given to other writers or works of the Archaic period. I have already quoted the general statement about *eleos* attributed to Anaximenes (see above, p. 33). In general, however, the philosophers, lyric poets, and didactic poets of this period are not much interested in compassion, or perhaps it is not so central or appropriate to their genres as it is to that of epic, especially "tragic" epic. Where it is mentioned, it is usually along lines similar to those we have already seen in Homer. Some examples should be sufficient: in the *Hymn to Demeter* (137–211), the wandering Demeter is pitied by the daughters of Keleos and received into their father's house in accordance with the proper treatment of suppliants (D1a). Such all-female scenes are rare in the literature of this period. In the *Hymn to Dionysos*, mercy is awarded on the basis of reciprocity or "justice" in a way similar to that of the *Odyssey:* in his revenge Dionysos feels compassion for and spares the helmsman who had recognized the god's divinity and vainly urged his fellow pirates to free him (53–54; D1b).

Xenophanes is said to have once pitied (*epoiktirai*) a puppy that was being beaten because he recognized in its cry the voice of a dear friend (West 1972: 2.167). In Lucian's portrait of him, Heraklitos said that he pitied and lamented humanity because human affairs were always in flux (Diels-Kranz 1966: 1.471). Pindar mentions Phalaris, a tyrant of Akragas, who used to roast men in a bronze bull and acquired an evil reputation for his lack of compassion (*Pythia* 1.95–96). As in the case of the Kyklops, the complete lack of compassion is regarded as a serious fault of character. But whereas the Archaic period has left us not very many extant statements about compassion, the period does seem to have contributed an emphasis on man's general helplessness (*amêchania*) in the face of an overwhelming universe. This worldview no doubt promoted compassion as an appropriate response to one's fellow human sufferer in the face of humankind's common fragility (D2).[62]

Conclusion: Compassion in Homer and Archaic Greece

We have seen how compassion is a very important emotion in the poems that Homer handed down to later Greeks. It is a strong emotion, but in the heroic world of the Homeric poems, it usually involves action as well. It is strongly colored, stimulated, or repressed by the nature and behavior of the recipient: the total stranger who is in need, along with others who are in a natural position of weakness, such as the very old, arouse a sense of religious awe and restraint as well as compassion in those whom they encounter. When they employ the rite of supplication in their appeals for compassion, they are assumed to be protected by Zeus. Friends arouse sympathy and elicit compassionate treatment in part through the reciprocal obligations of friendship and because of natural emotional bonds, whereas enemies or those who have failed to show compassion are not considered proper objects of compassion and are subject to retaliation.[63] Greek *eleos* is primarily egalitarian, as well as reciprocal, and is built on an assumption of the universal fragility of human fortune (D2). The possession of compassion (*eleos*), within proper limits, is seen as an essential of good character and full humanity; its lack, as a deficiency.

From Epic to Tragedy

How, then, do we account for the development of pity as a prominent theme in Athenian tragedy, especially in terms of the development of Athenian democracy out of the Archaic age of Homer and choral lyric? Although we do not have ancient testimonies or other evidence that might provide an uncontestable answer, we can posit a plausible, even probable, linkage from Homer's epic poetry to the drama of the Greek tragedians.

If, as we have argued, Homer, especially the author of the *Iliad,* emphasized the pity theme beyond the emphasis by other authors or in other texts of the Archaic period, how did this theme come to resurface in Attic tragedies? The simplest answer is through Homer's prestige and his tremendous impact on Greek culture generally. More specifically, the mechanism may have been the powerful performances of the rhapsodes and the canonization of Homeric epic performance at the Great Panathenaia festivals as organized by Peisistratos.[64] The earliest tragedians, inspired by the epic performances of the Homeric rhapsodes, may have taken the step to dramatize such stories in a form (with chorus and actor) that seemed to fit the ethos of the new Athenian democratic culture even better than epic narrative.[65] In turn, the City Dionysia was changed (ca. 534 BCE) to accommodate this new mostly Athenian form of dramatic art.[66] I don't need to rehearse here the complex but extensively discussed issues concerning the origin of Athenian tragic drama. Instead, following the work of John Herington (1985), I simply want to argue that if, as Herington argues, the tragedians took much of their art from Homer, even though they took their plots from the epic cycle, it seems likely that one of the things they adopted from Homer was the "tragic" mode and, correspondingly, the emphasis on pity and compassion that are keystones of Homer's tragic mode.[67]

One piece of evidence that points in this direction is, ironically, from that great critic of tragic pity, Plato, in his work *Ion.* This well-known Platonic dialogue features a Homeric rhapsode in the person of Ion himself. Plato mentions that Ion conveys both lessons of valor and also arouses great emotions in his performance of those passages of Homer that he characterizes as conveying pathos, namely through the characters of Andromache, Hekabe, and Priam.[68] The passages of the *Iliad* that he has in mind here suggest themselves: books 6, 22 and 24. Plato as the critic of what he sees as unreflective emotion may be exaggerating the emotional impact that the rhapsodes created here, but it so happens that he selects characters who, as we have seen, made exceptionally intense appeals for compassion in Homer's *Iliad.* I take Plato at his word here and accept that the rhapsodes' portrayals of Andromache, Hekabe, and Priam in the books I have cited were often, if not always, moving and that they typically aroused pity in the rhapsodes' audiences. So much so, in fact, that this phenomenon moved Plato to cite this arousal as a pernicious, even dangerous effect of the rhapsodes' art.

Other scholars have not mentioned "pity" specifically in this story of tragedy's development out of epic, but "pity" has generally been "under the radar" in the scholarship of Greek literary history. Instead, the emphasis there has quite understandably been on the genre of tragedy itself and its more salient manifestations of form, production, and performance.[69] My argument is that the tragic poets, in adapting Homer's art to their own genre, also adopted his tragic worldview together with his interest in and high valuation of compassion. This is not to say that the tragedians all adopted these Homeric perspectives uniformly or consistently.[70] In fact, the chapters ahead examine each major tragedian's use of the Homeric inheritance in regard to the theme of compassion. Needless to say, their use of it will vary just as other aspects of their dramatic art have varied. But before we examine the three tragedians, we will look at the compassion theme as it was practiced in the social, political, and intellectual context of fifth-century Athens, the historical context in which Aischylos, Euripides, and Sophokles practiced their tragic art.

CHAPTER 2

Fifth-Century Athens

The Social, Political, and Intellectual Contexts of Athenian Tragedy

In *Sir Gawain and the Green Knight*, "pity that surpasses everything" is said to be one of the five virtues in which the noble and pious Sir Gawain excels.[1] A fable attributed to Aesop, however, depicts pity differently:

> Γεωργός τις χειμῶνος ὥρᾳ ὄφιν εὑρὼν ὑπὸ κρύους πεπηγότα, τοῦτον ἐλεήσας καὶ λαβὼν ὑπὸ κόλπον ἔθετο. Θερμανθεὶς δὲ ἐκεῖνος καὶ ἀναλαβὼν τὴν ἰδίαν φὺσιν ἔπληξε τὸν εὐεργέτην καὶ ἀνεῖλε· θνῄσκων δὲ ἔλεγε· "Δίκαια πάσχω, τὸν πονηρὸν οἰκτείρας." (fable 82, Budé edition)

> A certain farmer in the winter season found a serpent frozen by the cold. He took pity on it, picked it up and placed it next to his chest. But when the serpent had been warmed and had resumed its own nature, it struck and killed its benefactor, who, as he was dying, said, "I suffer justly, because I pitied the wicked one."

These two passages, from cultures separated by some twenty centuries, give some idea of the range of attitudes toward pity or compassion to be found in Athens in the fifth century BCE, especially as that century was drawing to a close. In this chapter, I shall examine this ambivalence and how it was reflected in three of Athens' major institutions (the theater, the courts, and the assembly) within the general context of Athenian democratic society and in contemporary speculations about society. I concentrate on the later fifth century BCE (roughly 425–400) when, as we shall see, compassion was an especially prominent topic for comment and discussion. From a different perspective, we might ask how an Athenian citizen watching tragedies during this period might relate to the language and acts of compassion presented in them.

I begin by citing some of the many testimonies that have survived to the effect that Athens was generally known in antiquity for having an exceptional inclination toward compassion.[2] Isokrates (15.20) calls the Athenians "most compassionate and gentle" (ἐλεημονέστατοι καὶ πραιότατοι) of all the Greeks. Demosthenes (24.171) says that it is characteristic of Athens "to show compassion to the weak" (τοὺς ἀσθενεῖς ἐλεεῖν). Athens is also called "compassionate and receptive of suppliants" (φιλοικτίρμων καὶ ἱκεταδόκος, *Scholium Oidipous at Kolonos* 258). Herodotos (9.27) provides early evidence for this reputation with his mention of the children of Herakles and the suppliant mothers of the Seven against Thebes who, according to tradition, were received at Athens (cf. also Isokrates 14.52). Historically, Athens' tradition as a haven for suppliants was said to reach back to the close of the Mycenean Age, when she provided refuge to those who were fleeing the Dorian invaders. Diodorus Siculus (13.22) tells of Nikolaos the Syracusan, who said that if the Syracusans showed mercy to the Athenians after the Sicilian expedition, they would surpass the Athenians in *philanthropia*—the Athenians who vaunt their superiority in civilization and who were the first to raise an Altar of Compassion. Kallimachos (fr. 51) says of Athens, "It is the only city that knows how to feel compassion" (οἰκτίρειν οἶδε μόνη πολίων). According to Plutarch (*Praecepta gerendae reipublicae* 799c), the Athenian populace was "easily persuaded to compassion" (εὐμετάθετος πρὸς ἔλεον) and "humane" (φιλάνθρωπος), even to enemies. Plato's Sokrates (*Menexenos* 244) concurs when he says that the only charge which can be made against Athens' conduct in war is that she has been "too compassionate and too favorable to the weaker side" (λίαν φιλοικτίρμων . . . καὶ τοῦ ἥττονος θεραπίς). Of course, many of these sources are late as far as evidence for the fifth century is concerned, but they are consistent enough to suggest that Athens had a long and firmly established reputation as a city disposed to compassion, a reputation reaching back before the fifth century.[3]

A particular phenomenon found in this tradition is the *Eleou Bômos* (the Altar of Mercy or Compassion or "Pity," as it is most often translated), mentioned above by Diodorus, which is said to have been in the Athenian Agora (Pausanias 1.17). The *Bibliotheke* (traditionally attributed to Apollodoros, but now thought to be from the first or second century CE) appears to be the first extant work to mention the tradition of the altar when it says that both Adrastos, after the war of the Seven against Thebes, and the children of Herakles took refuge there (*Library* 2.8.1, 3.7.1, cf. Herodotos 9.27, cited above). According to this tradition, the altar was of ancient origin, indeed. Pausanias says that only the Athenians had such an altar, but J. G. Frazer, who mentions a small Altar of Mercy at Epidauros, disputed this claim. In any case, such an altar is consistent with Athens' image as an unusually compassionate city receptive of suppliants.[4]

Of course, recent interpreters have shown that the image of Athens as the compassionate polis that readily takes all comers (*hiketai*) into its bosom is partially a construct of pro-Athenian ideology.[5] This has the ring of truth today, as we have seen the ideological constructs of many powerful modern nations, including the United States and Great Britain, cracked like America's Liberty Bell, if not shattered, by the revelations of postcolonial criticism. Indeed, it is evident that ancient Athens—much like powerful modern nation-states—had an ideology that it sometimes, if not often, violated in the interest of asserting and advancing its power and prestige in the world of its day.

For some readers/interpreters, these inconsistencies are enough to invalidate any positive meaning or interpretation that might be given to ancient Athens. But isn't this, as we say, to throw out the baby with the bathwater? In other words, if Athenians were generally a people capable of and often prone to impulses of compassion, but who, in times of extreme stress or war, may have resorted to violent, even cruel behavior, should we allow the examples of violence to completely negate the positive patterns of behavior? We may if our critical propensities or the current vogues of criticism incline us to do so, but what about the bigger picture? Shouldn't our goal be to reflect ancient realities accurately and proportionately? Isn't it as inaccurate to say that the ancient Athenians were "all bad" as to say that they were "always good and perfect"? I prefer a balanced view that says, yes, Athenian history had its share of cruelty and violence, but the Athenians nevertheless—and broadly speaking—were a people who, because of their cultural *paideia,* could appreciate the subtlety and complexity of Greek tragic drama and be moved to pity and fear and who, furthermore, could sometimes, perhaps often, be moved to pity or compassion in real life.[6]

Athenian Tragic Theater

One cultural institution that no doubt reinforced this special disposition toward compassion was the tragic theater. That Greek tragedy in general tends to elicit feelings of sympathy and compassion is an assumption inherent in the free use of the word *tragedy* by many of our contemporaries. The Greeks themselves testify to the "pathetic" effects of poetry in general and of tragedy in particular. I have already mentioned Odysseus's weeping in response to the story about him sung by the bard Demodokos in the *Odyssey* (see chap. 1, n.58). In the fifth century Gorgias, the sophist, speaking of poetry, says that it has the power to arouse "fearful shivering, tearful compassion, and sorrowful yearning" (φρίκη περίφοβος καὶ ἔλεος πολύδακρυς καὶ πόθος φιλοπενθής) in the hearer, and that the soul of the hearer "feels its own emotion" at hearing of the misfortunes (or good fortunes) of others (Diels-Kranz 1966: 2.290).[7] Xenophon (*Education of Cyrus* 2.2.13) mentions the efforts of some who compose *logoi* to lead the audience into tears. Plato (*Philebos* 48a) discusses the "mixed pleasures" of people who enjoy weeping at tragic spectacles (cf. *Republic* 605d, *Ion* 535e, *Laws* 800d).[8] And, of course, there is Aristotle's famous dictum about *eleos* and *phobos* (1449b; cf. chap. 1, pp. 32–33). These passages suggest that Greek poetry, in general, and tragedy, in particular, were especially equipped to arouse a sense of shared vulnerability and empathy with the plight of others, which I have already discussed in connection with Homeric *eleos* (see above, chap. 1, pp. 31–33). They further indicate that the audience enjoyed such emotional stimulation, except perhaps in such rare instances as the presentation of the *Sack of Miletos* (cf. n.8, just cited).

That the Athenian audiences expected to be stimulated in this way is shown, most obviously, by the fact that the Greek tragedians themselves used so many techniques for arousing strong feelings of sympathy in their audiences. Aristotle, of course, has analyzed the ways in which the manipulation of the plot can arouse and intensify such feelings. There are also the abundant laments and expressions of compassion made by various characters as well as frequent cries of pain or sorrow by the sufferers themselves, which suggest to the audience that sympathy is the appropriate emotion to feel. A common type of statement in tragedy that encouraged identification and sympathy in a member of the audience were those gnomic utterances which expressed so eloquently the common frailty of humanity, the brevity of life, and mankind's relative lack of power and knowledge (usually in contrast with the gods).[9]

One tragedy that exploits most of these elements is Euripides' *Trojan Women.* This play is laden with laments and frequent expressions of self-pity by the characters (141–43, 205–6, 585–86).[10] At one point in the play, Hekabe is asked to relate her tragic story. Before beginning, she says:

> πρῶτον μὲν οὖν μοι τἀγάθ' ἐξᾆσαι φίλον·
> τοῖς γὰρ κακοῖσι πλείον' οἶκτον ἐμβαλῶ. (472–73)

> First I wish to tell about my previous good fortune so as to inject greater pity (*oiktos*) into my present sufferings.

Such a fall from prosperity to misfortune is, as we have seen, the most pitiful of ends for the Greeks. Here we have a reflection of the poet's awareness of his own techniques and goals: to intensify the audience's sympathy by artistic means. Another example in this play of Euripides' ability to build pathos is Andromache's speech to the soon-to-be-executed Astyanax (755 ff.).[11]

That the audience could be so affected by the compassion frequently aroused by Athenian tragedy is not to say that they were incapable of detachment from it. Aristophanes' parodies of tragedy in *Thesmophoriazousai* (its diction and laments, 1022 ff.) and *Ekklesiazousai* (the kings in rags, 1063–64, and elsewhere) suggest otherwise.[12] Nevertheless, to laugh at oneself—at one's proclivity to indulge in an emotion like compassion—or, perhaps more to the point here, to laugh at a comic exaggeration of the means used by some poets to exploit that proclivity (such as Euripides, cf. above) is not to deny the validity of that emotion itself but rather to recognize its potential for excess and its absurdity when aroused inappropriately.

Two other Athenian institutions in which compassion played a role were the court and the assembly. Here, compassion was a real-life matter, and the audience's compassionate behavior was shown or denied by their votes. In both of these contexts compassion and appeals for compassion were by nature controversial, whereas they were not always so in tragedy. In the court, if one party appeals for compassion, the other party will normally oppose that appeal. Likewise, as we shall see, there can be debates in the assembly about whether or not the compassion of the *polis* is appropriate in a certain situation. Let us look at the courts first.

Athenian Courts

In his defense of Helen, Gorgias discusses the power of language (*logos*) to manipulate powerful emotions such as fear, grief, joy, and compassion (*eleos*, Diels-Kranz 1966: 2.290), whereas in the *Defense of Palamedes*, Gorgias claims that he will base his case on justice and the truth instead of making the customary appeals to emotions such as *oiktos* (2.302). The implications here are that speech can be made powerfully persuasive by arousing emotions such as pity and that such appeals to the irrational part of the psyche are qualitatively different from and may on occasion be in opposition to claims based on truth, logical argument, and even justice; consequently, they may be harmful.[13]

Thrasymachos of Chalkedon organized the various appeals to *eleos* into a system of categories for use in the courts.[14] Thrasymachos apparently taught how to arouse compassion in the juror by bewailing such things as old age, poverty (i.e., the loss of wealth), and children (Diels-Kranz 1966: 2.325). "Old age" and "poverty" or, perhaps more precisely, "poverty in old age," refer to hardship that the defendant would have to endure if convicted, while "children" of course refers to the suffering that befalls children whose parents are punished (D3). Apparently such appeals were effective in moving jurors, as was the frequent practice of parading wife and children before the jury to make an impression still more graphic than even rhetoric was able to do (Plato, *Apology*, 34–35; Aristophanes, *Wasps*, 568–74). Such appeals to compassion were based on the same principle of shared vulnerability, creating fear and then compassion, that we have seen at work in Homer and Greek tragedy: "this could happen to me" or (even more effective) "this could happen to my loved ones; I could be before a jury like this" (D2).

Such appeals were bolstered, whenever possible, by recounting services or benefits that the defendant had provided the state in his lifetime (e.g., Lysias 21.25), an appeal that used a direct claim of reciprocity and attempted to divert the issue from the narrow question of guilt or innocence on the specific charge to an evaluation of the defendant's life and value to the state in toto (cf. intro. pp. 17–19; D4). In Lysias (20.34–36) we find a novel combination of these two types of appeal: grown-up children appear in court for their father, the defendant. The son who speaks in his father's defense argues that unlike the infants who are brought into court, these children have proved their value to the state by service and deserve the opportunity to serve the state further by not being deprived of their civil rights by their father's condemnation. Prosecutors understandably criticized such techniques, particularly the exhibition of children and wives before the court, as perversions of justice. The speaker in Lysias 27.12 remarks upon the absurdity of the fact that, whereas in private suits it is the injured party who arouses pity, in public trials it is the wrongdoers who are pitied and the wronged jurors—as citizens of the state whose laws have been violated—who are asked to show compassion.[15]

In the *Wasps,* Aristophanes satirizes the interaction of the defendant, who appeals for compassion, with the waspish juror, who is inclined not to show compassion. Philokleon recounts in a long speech (548–75) the extreme self-debasement to which defendants will go to win a juror's vote, including flattery, claims of poverty, and, of course, the obligatory show of children, but the primary topic of Philokleon's speech is the feeling of power and gratification that the jurors receive from the humiliation of defendants, especially important ones.[16] Later, Philokleon's waspish nature is further exposed in the home trial of the cheese-stealing dog, Labes (836ff.). Philokleon is ready to vote guilty before the trial even gets underway (845–50) and later insists on a harsher penalty for the dog, "a dog's death" (898); his prejudice against the defendant is obvious throughout the scene. At one point his son, Bdelykleon, prays that his father's temper be mellowed and that he become more disposed toward compassion (875–84). Bdelykleon appeals to his father to have pity for Labes because the dog doesn't eat as well as his accuser, a housedog; then the puppies are called (967–78). Philokleon cries out as he feels a strong emotion of pity, which he describes as an evil (*kakon*), coming over him (973–74). His son pleads with him to have pity and show his better side (975–76, 986–88), but Philokleon resists and finally has to be tricked into voting for acquittal. When he realizes that he has acquitted a defendant, he feels tremendously ashamed (999–1002).

In this way Aristophanes lampoons the extremes to which defendants go in arousing pity in jurors, but his primary target here seems to be the vindictive old juror who is too insensitive to appeals for compassion. MacDowell (1971: 3–4) discusses how Kleon's influence over the jurors caused them to condemn men he said were guilty. Kleon thus seems to have swung the judicial pendulum toward harshness and vindictiveness and away from empathy and humane understanding, as advocated by Bdelykleon, who, according to Douglass Parker (1962: 3), speaks for Aristophanes himself. But even on Philokleon the appeal for compassion is *almost* persuasive.

In sum, an appeal for compassion was, despite prosecutors' complaints, an accepted and powerful appeal in Athenian courts and appears to have often been effective in gaining acquittals. The defendants appealed for compassion from the jury on the basis of reciprocity (service to the state) and often used what may appear to us to be extravagant techniques for arousing a sense of common humanity and like vulnerability of the sort that we have seen both in Homer and in tragedy (D2). Far from being admissions of guilt, such appeals were commonly used to buttress claims of innocence; this is consistent with the close tie between compassion and innocence (D4; cf. Adkins 1960a: 203, Konstan 2001: 27–28). Furthermore, compassion on the part of the jury meant action, namely acquittal (cf. D1a).[17] This is in line with the concept of Greek compassion (i.e., as involving behavior) that we have seen both in Homer and in appeals by suppliants in tragedy, although the court obviously lacks the "heroic" dimension of individual action so often portrayed in tragedy.

The Athenian Assembly

Likewise, as in appeals for compassion before the Athenian court, the compassion sought and awarded by assemblies or by state representatives was inherently behavioral: a positive response to an appeal for compassion meant, for example, sparing a city or assisting a city in war. The types of appeals used to arouse such compassion were similar to those that we have already seen in other contexts. Three of the principal types are exhibited in the speech of the Plataians to the Spartans after having surrendered to them (Thukydides 3.59).[18] Earlier in the speech the Plataians had recited their previous alliance with and service to the Spartans (3.54, 58), and here, in their concluding remarks, they again recall obligations of reciprocal service and alliance that bind the Spartans to them: they ask the Spartans to spare them with a sensible compassion (*oiktos sôphrôn*) and to reflect on what sort of men the Plataians are (cf. D1b). A second type of appeal is their reminder to the Spartans of the instability of fortune—how unexpectedly disaster can befall those least deserving of it (59.1). The third type of appeal is religious in nature. Calling on the common gods of

Hellas and recalling the solemn oaths made by the Spartans' ancestors to the Plataians, the speaker says that the Plataians stand as suppliants at the tombs (in Plataia) of the Spartans' fathers (59.2).[19]

The appeal to reciprocity—previous service and alliance—is the most obvious type of appeal for one state to make to another one, explicitly arousing, as it does, both good feelings about the past relationship and the expectation of more mutual benefits from the alliance in the future. Indeed, this seems to be a cardinal principle of diplomacy throughout history (cf. intro. pp. 17–19). The Plataians' use of the second type of appeal—the reminder of the instability of fortune—is, of course, aimed at inducing the same process of compassion through a sense of common human vulnerability that we note so often elsewhere (D2). Here, we find it extended by analogy to the common fragility of whole nations. Similarly, the Melians warn the Athenians that the Athenians themselves may one day stand in need of fair and reasonable restraint (5.90), and Thukydides himself speaks at one point of the general human laws that protect men in distress, which men driven by vengeance and profit violate, forgetting that they may someday be in need of them (3.84.3).[20]

Among the general human laws implied in this statement of Thukydides after his narration of the Korkyra episode is the law enforcing the sanctity of suppliants. As Gould (1973: 83) says in discussing the slaughter of suppliants who had taken refuge in temples, "The sense of shock which spreads in waves through Thucydides' comments on the Corcyra episode in iii 82–3 conveys the traumatic effect, even in the late fifth century, of happenings such as these." Gould also notes Xenophon's sense of shock at the killing of Theramenes, who was dragged away from the altar of Hestia Boulaia (*Hellenica* 2.3.52–56, cf. also Thukydides 1.128). As we have seen, Athens considered itself to have a long and distinct reputation as the recipient of suppliants, and the narratives of Thukydides and Xenophon also suggest that the notion of the divine protection of suppliants was not passé in the late fifth century.

The Spartans did not spare the Plataians, but the Athenians did send a second ship to save the *demos* of Mytilene (D1b). Kitto (1957: 151–52) remarks upon this contrast by saying that in Athens "the voice of humanity had at least the opportunity of being heard," although he also notes that ten years later the Athenians would commit a "worse crime" in their treatment of Melos. The inclination of the Athenians toward compassion can be discerned not only in their theater and courts but also in their assembly. The sheer size of the Athenian deliberative body no doubt contributed to its susceptibility to the manipulations of speakers who made eloquent appeals to powerful basic emotions such as pity (as well as the opposite emotions, such as in the trial about the battle at Arginusai). In Euripides' *Orestes,* Menelaos describes how a *demos*—here meaning the Argive assembly, but also applicable to the Athenian assembly—will eventually change from a mood of anger to one of pity, if only one is patient and waits for the right mood (696–703).

The Athenian assembly's susceptibility to appeals for compassion is shown in the debate concerning Mytilene by Kleon's attempt to dissuade the assembly from giving in to their typical compassion and leniency (*epieikeia*), which he sees as inimical to imperial rule (Thukydides 3.37.2, 40).[21] The opposing Athenian speaker, Diodotos, shrewdly avoids the direct appeal to the citizens' pity and leniency that Kleon anticipated and instead seeks to argue for reasonableness in punishing the people of Mytilene on the basis of self-interest. At one point he even ostensibly echoes Kleon's request that the assembly not be overly influenced by the emotions of *oiktos* and *epieikeia* (3.48).[22] As in the *Wasps,* Kleon is depicted again as a vigorous opponent to the Athenian disposition to compassion. In the case of Mytilene, he loses, and the Athenian assembly votes, by a narrow margin, to revoke their previous wholesale condemnation of Mytilene. In spite of Diodotos's disclaimer, compassion likely played at least some part in the assembly's reversal (D1b). Thukydides explicitly contrasts the reluctant slowness of the first ship sent to convey the "unwelcome" (*allokotos*) order for massacre with the eager haste of the second ship sent to convey the subsequent decision for reprieve (3.49; cf. Lateiner 2005: 83), yet another indication that compassion was operating at some level among the Athenians involved. Note that the reluctance of the first ship and the eagerness of the reprieving ship conform respectively to the dual action of compassion that I have described as both restraining us from doing harm to and impelling us to help those who suffer innocently (cf. D1c). Some contemporary critics understandably tend to downplay any indication of pity as they quite reasonably emphasize the cold, severe working of realpolitik in episodes like that at Mytilene.[23] Macleod and others have established that in times of conflict, ancient states tended to respond primarily to the pressures of domination and subjugation that went with empire; claims based on pity, which relied on considerations of past and future, therefore tended to fall on deaf ears, given that states were concerned only with the present and near-future. Yet it is still possible to discern the positive presence of compassion even in grim episodes of war such as these. And we may ask, in the case of Mytilene, would not the *demos* of Mytilene have suffered a worse fate, if Kleon had had his way and had not been outvoted by the *demos* of Athens? Given Kleon's irrational ferocity, it seems safe to assume they would have suffered far worse.

As we examine the role of compassion in the tragedies of Euripides and Sophokles written during the Peloponnesian Wars, we should be aware that the poets were working in response to and often in conflict with the prevailing political forces that promoted cruelty or simply allowed pity to be shunted aside when dealing with one's fellow men, women, and children, or groups of men (in the form of states) on the larger world stage. Of the plays performed during that period, the *Trojan Women,* by Euripides, seems to connect very plausibly to the events at Melos that occurred shortly before its production.[24] In general, however, we can say with confidence that Euripides and Sophokles, as well as Aischylos before them, were broadly responsive to the historical ethos around them and their audiences in the Theater of Dionysos. Our best playwrights, screenwriters, and novelists today function in a similar way in response to the world in which they find themselves.

Macleod (1983b: 157–58) found a common source in Homer for both the tragic history of Thukydides and the tragic drama of the playwrights, an observation consistent with my argument in this book. Indeed the Greeks, from Homer on, depicted the cruelty and pitilessness inherent in war. As Homer shows these qualities of war, so do the tragedians when they portray war and its human costs. And like Homer, they show the occasional moments of compassion and human understanding that thankfully can occur in war because of the humaneness of some extraordinary individuals. We saw this in the *Iliad*, and we will see further examples in the war dramas ahead. Of course, for those living in Athens in the fifth century BCE, being at war was a more immediate and palpable everyday experience than it has been for most Americans during the recent wars that have been fought mostly "at a distance."[25] It is clear, however, that troops fighting in recent wars, such as Afghanistan and Iraq, have experienced the same kinds of intense agony and deep psychological trauma as those who fought in larger wars, such as World War II and Vietnam.[26]

Following this brief survey of compassion in regard to the Athenian institutions of tragedy, the courts, and the assembly, I wish now to turn to a consideration of the relationship between compassion and the social structure: how, if at all, compassion functioned between the different classes. Of course, much of our evidence must come from drama and the courts.

Athenian Social Structure

In chapter 1, I discuss the reciprocal nature of compassion in the Homeric poems: how compassion tended to be shown by nobles to peers who had suffered misfortune rather than to members of a lower social class by members of a higher class; also, how supplication, as well as *xenia,* fit into this pattern; and, finally, how such compassion was granted on the understanding that the recipient would return the favor, or on the basis of a sense of shared humanity that understood the instability of fortune and the common predicament of humankind and that consequently impelled an epic hero to show compassion because he might himself someday be in a similar situation and would want assistance as the suppliant before him did now (D2).

These assumptions about compassion continue into the later fifth century at Athens. In this chapter, I have already mentioned fifth-century reflections on the insecurity of human fortune and appeals based on explicit reciprocity, and I have discussed the continuing efficacy of the suppliant's appeal as involving both a religious obligation and a test of the "nobility" of the person supplicated. It remains to note here that the tendency to feel compassion for the unfortunate who had known previous good fortune rather than for the perpetually poor, who spent their energies working for a meager living and were despised by men of leisure for their need to do so, also continues into the later fifth century.[27] Of the still greater contempt for common beggars who did not work and of the apparent absence of almsgiving and private charity, Ehrenberg (245) says, "We can assume that one reason for the lack of charity was the small number of beggars. It was only because they represented no real social problem that they could earn contempt as idlers instead of pity and help. 'Pity' to whom an altar was erected in the agora was not an expression of social conscience, but of personal feelings, not towards the poor, but towards every unhappy human being." In Euripides' *Helen,* Menelaus, speaking of his own circumstance, declares that the man who suffers misfortune to which he is unaccustomed is worse off than the man who has long had misfortune (417–19).[28] The contrast between good fortune and bad is especially sharp in Talthybios's description of Hekabe, once queen of Troy and wife of Priam but now an old slave deprived of her children and city (*Hekabe* 488 ff.). As we have seen, in the *Trojan Women* Hekabe seeks to increase the pitiableness of her own tale about herself by recounting her previous good fortune (472–73). One of the more common circumstances for such a sudden reversal of fortune would be the exile of the powerful or noble person. As in Homer, the pitiableness of exile and of the poverty that it often inflicts is an especially common theme in the plays of Euripides (*Herakles* 303–4; *Phoenician Women* 627–28, 1761; *Elektra* 1311–18). As traditional recipients of such suppliant exiles, the Athenians were no doubt especially sensitive to this theme.

The tendency to pity the nobles who suffer or who are about to suffer is even shown by the non-nobles (strangers and slaves) on the tragic stage, although they occasionally acknowledge their distance in station and the consequent limitation of their ability to empathize fully, as well as their usual inability to help (Euripides, *Andromache* 61–62, 141–46; *Iphigeneia at Aulis* 469–70; *Rhesos* 904–5). Apparently even the poorer members of the Athenian democracy who attended tragic performances were accustomed to being moved by the plight of fallen kings and heroes rather than by stories arousing pity for and resentment among the poor who must labor for their living and struggle against the powerful rich. In thus making previous prosperity a primary basis for sympathy, Greek tragedy did not challenge the social hierarchy, although as a democratic institution promoting sympathy and understanding, it served as a leveler or, perhaps, as an ennobler of the *demos:* the contrast between the good and bad fortune of tragic heroes showed in the most graphic terms the fragility of human fortune and happiness—a human circumstance that was applicable to every Greek citizen, however modest his fortune or limited his happiness.[29]

Although the mythical world presented in tragedy preserved a tradition of reciprocal compassion between heroic individuals (or the lack of such), compassion did play a role in the relation between the rich and poor classes of Athenian democracy. Hands (1968: 79–80) notes that "in an actual democracy, 'pity' must be shown not merely to other individual men of wealth, but to the *demos* collectively." The rich claimed to show such "pity" by their leadership of the state, their military service, and their assumption of liturgies that benefited the *demos*—indeed, the *polis* as a whole (D5). In return, they expected compassion from the *demos,* specifically in the Athenian courts where they might be the targets of vexatious prosecutions designed to arouse the people's envy of them (e.g., Lysias 21.15–25).[30]

Occasionally, moreover, the poor, as opposed to the unfortunate, are explicitly mentioned as the proper objects of sympathy. In his *Defense of Palamedes,* Gorgias claims that he has been compassionate toward the unfortunate and not contemptuous of the poor, although the denial of such contempt suggests that the poor were often so regarded (Diels-Kranz 1966: 2.302). In Euripides' *Suppliant Women,* advice is given to the wealthy to consider poverty and to fear a similar fate (176, 179), a variation on the "fear and pity" theme that, unlike most, calls attention to class distinctions, especially with 177–78 (possibly an interpolation, cf. Ehrenberg, p. 245). Euripides (fragment 407, *Tragicorum Graecorum Fragmenta*) also gives voice to an obligation of those with an abundance of wealth to benefit those less well off, although the fragment does not explicitly mention the perpetually impoverished.[31]

But the idea that compassion between the classes could result from the generosity of the upper to the lower class is most fully expressed in a remarkable fragment by Demokritos:

> ὅταν οἱ δυνάμενοι τοῖς μὴ ἔχουσι καὶ προτελεῖν τολμέωσι καὶ ὑπουργεῖν καὶ χαρίζεσθαι, ἐν τούτωι ἤδη καὶ τὸ οἰκτίρειν ἔνεστι καὶ μὴ ἐρήμους εἶναι καὶ τὸ ἑταίρους γίγνεσθαι, καὶ τὸ ἀμύνειν ἀλλήλοισι καὶ τοὺς πολιήτας ὁμονόους εἶναι καὶ ἄλλα ἀγαθά, ἅσσα οὐδεὶς ἄν δύναιτο καταλέξαι.
>
> Whenever men of wealth and power take it upon themselves to make loans to the poor and powerless and help them out and do them favors, in this process there develops compassion and the end of alienation and the development of companionship and mutual assistance and harmony among citizens plus other benefits too numerous to count. (Diels-Kranz 1966: 2.196–97, B255)

Here, compassion is, as we have so often seen, a concomitant of reciprocal service, but it is also characterized as a definitely beneficial quality that helps society (specifically the different classes within it) cohere and cooperate for the common good. Demokritos is speaking also of some of the intangible benefits of social cooperation: not only compassion but also goodwill, comradeship, regard for one another's interests and the end of isolation, harmony and consensus rather than confrontation—in short, a sense of participation and cooperation that turns the energies of the members of the *polis* toward the survival of the group and away from the conflicts that inevitably arise between members or groups within a society who are isolated from one another and feel they must compete with one another to satisfy their own individual needs or desires. In Demokritos's ideal state, the interest of the group takes precedence over competing individual interests (cf. fragment B252a).[32]

A similar connection of compassion with cooperative, mutually beneficial behavior is found in Xenophon's *Memorabilia* (2.6.21), where Sokrates, in speaking of people's tendency toward friendship, is represented as having said,

> δέονταί τε γὰρ ἀλλήλων καὶ ἐλεοῦσι καὶ συνεργοῦντες ὠφελοῦσι καὶ τοῦτο συνιέντες χάριν ἔχουσιν ἀλλήλοις.
>
> [People] need one another and so they feel compassion and help each other, working together, and since they are aware of this, they are grateful to one another.[33]

Sokrates then contrasts the competitive impulses that drive men to conflict and hostility. Still later we find fragments of Menander in which it is claimed that if all men would help one another, then no man would be in need of luck (*tuchê,* fragment 467, Körte) and that to live is not to live for oneself only (fragment 646, Körte).

In such statements we can see the continuation of the reciprocal aspect of Greek compassion—how it is based on mutual benefits and how its primary expression is action rather than mere expressions of sympathy. But whereas in the heroic world of Homer and in tragedy such compassion is usually shown between heroic individuals involved in their own individual crises, Demokritos and Xenophon's Sokrates see such compassion as part of the cooperative web that holds society together and, in the case of Demokritos at least, allows the *polis* (and the classes within it) to function harmoniously in the common interest of all its citizens.[34]

Limitations and Denials of Compassion

I wish to conclude my general survey of compassion in later fifth-century Athens by briefly discussing (in contrast to such positive notions by Demokritos and others) some general limitations on compassion in regard to considerations of vengeance and innocence as they persisted or were developed in this period. As we saw in Homer, reciprocity also has its negative side: instances in which enmity or a claim of justice require that compassion be withheld. In his article on Aristotle and tragedy (1966a: 93–95), Adkins argues that a character on the stage can expect pity only from his *philoi* (family, dependents, and friends) who value and depend on his *aretê,* and not from his enemies, who do not value it. Although this does not account for the broader human sympathy for calamity that tragedy arouses in its audience, who are neither *philoi* nor *echthroi* (enemies) of the tragic characters in the sense that Adkins means, nevertheless, his statement is generally true: characters in tragedy, as in Homer, expect compassion from *philoi* but not from enemies. We have already seen and will continue to see many instances of appeals for and expectations of compassion based on *philia* (i.e., both on the obligation of previous benefits and that of blood ties). In Euripides' *Phoinissai,* for example, the dying Polyneikes expresses pity for his dead brother, who is *philos* on the basis of their blood relation, although he had become an *echthros* in his actions (1444–46; cf. Antigone's love for the dead Polyneikes in Sophokles' play).

The traditional Greek drive to avenge oneself on one's enemies is discussed by Kitto in *The Greeks* (1957: 243–45). The demand of revenge requires that the compassion which might inhibit it be suppressed (Euripides, *Elektra* 968–70, *Orestes* 566–72). Ion denies having pity for Kreousa who has become a suppliant at Apollo's altar, and here revenge almost overrides the suppliant's claim to divine protection (1275–81); later Ion complains about the divine laws that give protection to unjust suppliants as well as to deserving ones (1312–19).[35]

The recompensatory denial of compassion is most obviously justified in the denial of compassion to those who have cruelly failed to show compassion themselves (cf. intro. pp. 17–19). In Antiphon (1.25–27), the prosecutor argues that his stepmother, who so ruthlessly murdered her husband (his father), is herself deserving of no compassion from the jury. In the next century, Demosthenes argues explicitly that no one is entitled to pity who does not display it nor to sympathetic consideration who does not exhibit such consideration (21.100, cf. 25.84). In his speech against Mytilene, Kleon uses the reciprocal denial of compassion with a view to the future: it is appropriate to show compassion to like-minded people who will pity us in turn, not to those who do not reciprocate our pity and will necessarily always be enemies (Thukydides 3.40.3). Such an assessment is based on the implication that past behavior is predictive of future behavior.[36] It is in accordance with this principle that the defeated Athenians expect to be treated as they themselves had mercilessly treated the men of Melos and other Greek cities (Xenophon, *Hellenika* 2.2.3).

No pity in return for no pity is justice at its most elemental. Several related assumptions also arise concerning the proper relationship between compassion and justice. The prosecutor's basic claim, of course, is that those who have suffered unjustly (i.e., the victims of crime) deserve compassion rather than those who have done injustice (the perpetrators of crime) and who are punished justly (cf. Lysias 2.14, 6.55, 12.79, 13.33, 22.21, 28.14, 29.8, 32.19). Compassion is thus to be directed toward the passive sufferer and hatred/anger toward the active doer (e.g., Gorgias, *Helen* B11.7 in Diels-Kranz 1966: 2.290; cf. D1a). Based on the same assumption is the appeal for compassion by the defendant who claims that he is innocent (i.e., that he has done no injustice) and therefore is being prosecuted—and would be punished—unjustly (e.g., Antiphon 5.73; Lysias 3.48). The innocent defendant thus may claim that he is suffering an injustice worthy of compassion by being put on trial.

A subtler distinction that develops is the one between the man who has done harm unwillingly and one who has purposely done harm. Both prosecutors and defendants (who claim to have acted unwillingly) in later fifth-century Athens claim that those who have done harm unwillingly deserve mercy, whereas willful perpetrators of harm do not (Thukydides 3.40.1; Antiphon 1.27, 5.92; cf. also Herodotos 1.45.2, where Kroisos pities Adrastos because he unwillingly killed his son). In this manner intention is taken into account and reciprocity is apportioned accordingly. Reciprocity thus tends to function in both the court and the assembly, as well as in tragedy, in accordance with the dichotomies of friend-enemy, guilt-innocence, intentional harm–unintentional harm.

Conclusion

The Athenian image had compassion as a major constituent; Athens had a tradition of being receptive and protective of suppliants. This was characterized as being noble, and in tragedy the defenders of suppliants (often Athenian kings) were praised as being noble and valiant: the exhibition of compassion to the unfortunate was often associated with heroic behavior and martial *aretê.* Like Homer, the Athenian tragedians regarded the exhibition of compassion as a sign of higher civilization and a mark of the educated person. The idea of the fragility of human life and fortune and the notion of the person who experiences misfortune arousing compassion in others by means of the latter's sense of like vulnerability and fear are common in tragedy and occur as well in appeals in the courts and in the assembly. This is a higher form of reciprocal compassion that has universal applications in that all humans are subject to the whims of fortune, and thus we all are capable of needing compassion someday. The Athenians seem to have been especially disposed to the feeling of compassion and also seem to have liked being told of their tendency toward compassion, although this disposal was sometimes criticized as misdirected or as a sign of weakness by prosecutors in the court and speakers, such as Kleon, in the assembly. This was especially so, of course, when a feeling of compassion seemed to interfere with the demands of revenge or justice or, in some cases, Athenian hegemony. With regard to self-interest, we can say that sometimes compassion demands the sacrifice of profit, advantage, and other types of immediate or short-term self-interest, and that sometimes it may even result in injury or a loss of life on the part of the compassionate individual or group. Still, many Athenians then and many people in our own time realize that long-term interest and the general betterment of life and society usually result from such noble sacrifices when they are appropriately made.

Therefore, in fifth-century Athens compassion continued to be discriminating and, as in Homer, still tended to be reserved for peers or for superiors who were in a position of *philia* or who claimed services performed as a basis for receiving compassion. Furthermore, in tragedy, especially, the exhibition of compassion was often associated with the heroism of individual king-protectors. Nevertheless, some political thinkers of the fifth century, such as Demokritos, saw reciprocal compassion as one of the components of the cooperation that brings the conflicting parties of society together into a strong, united state capable of defending itself and meeting the basic needs of its constituents so as to provide a harmonious and secure way of life.

An individual Athenian spectator of tragedies during this period would presumably have been aware of many, if not all, of these social, political, and intellectual connections to the acts of compassion presented on the Athenian tragic stage. Also, he (and perhaps she, if females ever attended) would have related to the chorus as well as to the heroes and heroines of the dramas. Indeed, fifth-century Athens provided an excellent cultural environment for the development, enjoyment, and appreciation of the Greek tragic drama written and put on stage by Aischylos, Sophokles, Euripides, and other dramatists of the time. We begin with Aischylos.

CHAPTER 3

Aischylos

Compassion from a Distance

In Aristophanes' *Frogs,* Aischylos and Euripides engage in a contest to decide who should win the Chair of Tragedy in the Underworld. Among the subjects they debate is the representation of character in their respective tragedies and the types of virtues and emotions inspired by those portrayals. In the following selection, we learn of Aischylos's particular strategies in his portrayals. He is speaking of the legacy he left his younger competitor, Euripides:

AESCHYLUS: Then think of the people *I* gave him, and think of the people when he got through with 'em.
I left him a lot of heroic six-footers, a grand generation of heroes,
unlike our new crop of street-corner loafers and gangsters and decadent queer-os.
Mine snorted the spirit of spears and splendor, of white-plumed helmets and stricken fields,
of warrior heroes in shining armor and greaves and sevenfold-oxhide shields. . . . [1]
I made them a martial drama.

DIONYSOS: Which?

AESCHYLUS: *Seven Against Thebes,* if you want to know.
Any man in an audience sitting through that would aspire to heroic endeavor. . . .

Then I put on my *Persians*, and anyone witnessing
  that would promptly be smitten
with longing for victory over the enemy. Best play I
  ever have written. . . .
There, there is work for poets who also are MEN. From
  the earliest times
incitement to virtue and useful knowledge have come
  from the makers of rhymes . . .
Then Homer, divinely inspired, is a source of indoc-
  trination to virtue. Why else is he justly admired
than for teaching how heroes armed them for battle? . . .
Ah, many have been my heroic disciples . . .
The man in the street simply has to catch something
  from all my heroics and braveries.
My Teucers and lion-hearted Patrokloses lift him right
  out of his knaveries
and make him thrill to the glory of war and spring
  to the sound of the trumpet. . . .

EURIPIDES: But tell me, o man without pity (*ô schetli' andrôn*) . . .
But why should it be so wrong to awaken their
  pity (*eleos*)?[2]

The debate that Aristophanes renders in this way is obviously exaggerated for comic effect, but it tells us something about these two poets in regard to the way they value an emotion like compassion. For Aischylos, compassion seems to arise only in unexpected circumstances; also, it is an emotion that he never seems to become fully comfortable with. It is largely absent in the two "martial" dramas that Aristophanes mentions in this passage, the two earliest extant tragedies of Aischylos.[3] It's only in the tragic trilogies from his later period that compassion seems to come into its own as a theme.[4] Even then, it is rarely presented as the deeply personal, strong, and dramatic emotion that Homer, and later Euripides and Sophokles, more often depict it as being.[5] Instead, we might say that Aischylos shows compassion from a distance. His life experiences as a citizen-warrior may have something to do with it, as

Aristophanes seems to suggest. He will, however, provide us with an ethical standard of sorts against which we can measure the two younger poets, Euripides and Sophokles.

Seven Against Thebes

In *Seven Against Thebes,* Aischylos uses the word *oiktos* (compassion, lament) only twice in the play. At line 51 it denotes vocal lamentation or rather the lack of it: a Theban scout reports that although the Argive warriors, preparing for battle, shed tears by the keepsakes they have hung on their leader Adrastos's chariot, no lamentation (*oiktos*) came through their lips. He goes on to describe their iron resolve and manliness (*andreia*), like lions with Ares in their eyes (50–53). In other words, they suppressed any verbal expression of impending grief or sorrow—other than silent weeping—in keeping with the military discipline that was expected of them.

Also, in *Seven Against Thebes* the chorus of Theban maidens express distress at the imminent invasion of their city, supplicate the gods to protect Thebes, and engage in interchanges with Eteokles, the king, who seeks to contain their expressions of alarm for fear they will dishearten the citizens (78–286).[6] At 263, the chorus accede to Eteokles' request that they silence their dire lamentations and pleas at the gods' statues, and, after he leaves, their prayers to the gods become somewhat more hopeful pleas for protection (301–320), but they still continue to express their anxious fears in song (288–300, 321–68). In fact, they even more vividly envision the horror of the city's destruction (D3). It would be piteous (*oiktron*) for an ancient city to be destroyed, enslaved, and ravaged dishonorably by Achaian men with the gods' approval (321–25).[7] Also "piteous" (ἐέ)[8] would be the capture of the city's women, young and old, "man-handled and dragged by the hair like horses, with their mantles torn off" (326–29).[9] They continue to imagine the city's lamentations as captives are carried off: "Lamentable (*klauton*) it is for young maidens prematurely before the customary time to finish a hateful journey from their homes."[10] Even the dead have a happier fate, they sing. "For when a city is conquered, alas (ἐέ), many miserable things are done. People carry off other people or kill them or set fires. The whole city is begrimed by smoke. Man-slaughtering Ares raving inspires them, defiling the holy" (333–44). The grim prospects of invasion, especially for mothers with babies and young women, continue to be expressed in the rest of the choral song (345–68).[11]

In this play, we have a prime example of the incompatibility between military discipline and expressions of grief or appeals for pity. We might call it "the warrior's suppression of pity." From the warrior's perspective, expressions of grief and anxious supplications for pity cannot be tolerated: they are contrary to military discipline and decorum; they undermine the fighting spirit by distracting the warrior from his primary task (killing the enemy); and they risk making the citizens cowards (see 191–92, 237–38). If warfare and the brutality it entails are to be continued, there must be some blindness to the suffering and sorrow they cause. We have seen this phenomenon in the *Iliad* in Hektor's unwillingness to stay inside the walls with Andromache (book 6). In *Seven Against Thebes,* we see it in Eteokles' response to the laments of women of the city represented by the chorus. Of course, in times of war, especially in a defensive war against outside invaders, as we have in *Septem,* survival may well depend on military success. In such circumstances, particularly in battle or in the preparation for battle, the warrior's ethic, including the suppression of lamentation, may be necessary. At the same time, this play and other tragedies tend to portray war as an inherently tragic enterprise. In such works, the typical pattern is that war occurs, and the losers (and sometimes the winners as well) have great losses to lament. Also, the execution of war may entail considerable suffering and "lack of compassion" among allies as well as between enemies on the battlefield. Homer's *Iliad* serves as a prototype of this tragic dynamic, and Aischylos's play follows that model. Of course, Thebes is ultimately victorious in this war, even though the sons of Oidipous come to a tragic end.[12] Still, the play makes us aware of the suffering on both sides of any martial conflict.[13]

Persians

This tragedy—in many ways one of the strangest—presents a drama about Persians composed by a Greek poet for an Athenian audience. Members of that audience had been at war with those Persians only eight years before, when they defeated the Persians soundly at the Battle of Salamis. To present a former enemy on stage in a tragic drama must have immediately raised questions in the Athenian audience about what they were about to witness and how the Persians and they themselves would be represented.

Before commenting on these larger issues of the play's representation, let's look first at how compassion is represented within the play. Words denoting compassion occur only a few times in the play. Early in the play, the Persian queen Atossa reports a dream in which her son Xerxes had attempted to yoke a Greek and a Persian woman, like horses, to a chariot. Atossa reports that Xerxes was unable to control the chariot and consequently was hurled to the ground. At that moment, his father Dareios stood by "pitying (*oiktirôn*) him" (198). Dareios's compassion here seems unexceptional, except that in the context of such a dream, every action, paradoxically perhaps, has a heightened "reality." Dareios's compassion is that of a father who witnesses his son's humiliation and feels compassion or "compassionate grief" for that son's intense suffering.[14] Indeed, the meaning of "compassion" appears to be uppermost here in that it is a scene of suffering witnessed by a character who responds with a strong emotion of *oiktos* directed toward the sufferer. Xerxes then expresses his grief and presumably his shame at his humiliation in the symbolic action of tearing his clothes.[15] This prefigures his later grief that the audience will see when he returns from his defeat at Salamis.

The adverbial form *oiktrôs* occurs at line 688 in the first speech of the ghost of Dareios. Atossa and the chorus of Persian elders have summoned Dareios after they have received news of Xerxes' defeat. Dareios, addressing the chorus, remarks that they have invoked him "piteously" (*oiktrôs*) with laments and shrill cries. His use of *oiktrôs* suggests that their invocation of him is a supplicatory call for help.[16] This, in fact, reflects the prayers to him in the previous choral song: what they seek is Dareios's blessing and counsel in this time of distress. The only other occurrence of this stem in the play is in line 1062, where Xerxes, having returned in defeat, calls on the chorus to "pluck out your hair and lament (*katoiktisai*) our army." Obviously, the word here emphasizes verbal expression of lamentation rather than compassion.

Consequently, we can observe that in this play the appeals for compassion and expressions of compassion appear to be "normal" and of the sort that we might expect from Greek actors no less than from Persian ones. Is their lamentation, however, somewhat over-the-top? The Persian men here seem to lament as readily as the women, not something we would expect Greek men to do (D6).[17]

I will close my treatment of this play with a few brief observations about sympathy in the play as a whole. Commentators on this play have expressed surprise at and approval of the Athenian audience's remarkable ability to give a sympathetic eye and ear to their former enemies presented in tragic guise (D4).[18] This is indeed remarkable. We don't expect such openness to the other—indeed, to the hostile other—in a society that lived in almost perpetual expectation of war over two thousand years ago. In our own time, those of us who are Americans, for example, have more often seen highly negative, unsympathetic, and even disparaging and ridiculous depictions of our former enemies, such as the Nazis of World War II, than we have seen portrayals of them that arouse our sympathy and understanding. There are exceptions, of course, but I am referring to popular works of fiction and drama, including those produced by movie and television studios—works of art roughly comparable in societal impact to the plays of the Athenian theater.

On the other hand, however, the Persians are not depicted with complete sympathy.[19] There is a distinct Greek bias within the work in two respects. First, Xerxes is depicted as a hubristic individual whose actions contribute to Persia's defeat. Also, that wrongdoing consists largely of his overweening aggression against the Greeks.[20] The Athenian audience members will naturally have taken some comfort in seeing Xerxes' and his nation's downfall presented, although they should also have seen that Xerxes' downfall conformed to the tragic potential of all human beings, including themselves.[21] Second, the Greeks come across very well in the play. Greek freedom is contrasted with Persian enslavement to a king (242, cf. 213). The battle narratives show the Greeks clearly superior and admirable, and Athenian democracy in particular is idealized; see, for example, 353–432 (especially 399–405), 447–71, 709–92, and 1025. In sum, this play is remarkable for its willingness to treat the former enemy with considerable sympathy as tragic sufferers while, subconsciously at least, it also serves to confirm in its audience their own superiority as Athenian victors.[22]

Suppliants

A common plot in Athenian tragedy that involves the exhibition of compassion by one character toward another is built around the suppliant theme.[23] In suppliant plays, the focus of interest and sympathy is placed in large part on a character who might be called the "saving hero," in contrast to the "suffering hero" of many better-known, prototypical tragedies of fate, such as *Oidipous the King*.[24] A prototype of the suppliant play from the early part of the fifth century is Aischylos's *Suppliants*.[25] In this play, the Daughters of Danaos (Danaids), who claim to be descended from Io, a Greek woman from Argos, arrive at Argos from Egypt seeking compassionate protection. They have come to Argos in flight from their cousins, the sons of Aigyptos, who have sought to marry the girls against their will. The girls' father, Danaos, supports his daughters' wishes but lacks the power to resist Aigyptos and his sons. We begin by examining in detail two supplications that occur in the first half of the play: first, a supplication to the gods, and then one to a human king.

The Daughters of Danaos begin the play in the *parodos* with a song of supplication to Zeus and the other gods whose statues adorn the stage or acting area. In the song, they appeal for Zeus's divine protection from the aggression of their cousins. The basis they use to supplicate Zeus is the threat of impious marriage (*gamon . . . asebê*, 9).[26] To support their appeal for the protection of Zeus and the other Greek gods, they cite their hereditary connection to

Greek Io and to Olympian Zeus himself through their descent from Io's Egyptian-born son, Epaphos, whom they connect etymologically to Zeus's loving "caress" of the girl Io (15–18).[27] In their appeal for sanctuary in Argos and protection from Zeus, their divine ancestor, they refer to the "compassionate spirit" (*aidoion pneuma*) of the land (28–29). At the same time, they pray that the gods will drive the sons of Aigyptos seaward to perish cruelly in a storm at sea (29–39). They then invoke their ancestor, "Egyptian" Epaphos himself, to come to their aid (40–56). They also express the hope that their lament (*oiktos*) will remind local inhabitants of the voice of Tereus's piteous (*oiktras*) wife, here identified with the nightingale who ever laments the fate of the son she herself killed (58–67). In the same way, the chorus say, they themselves being "fond of lamentation (*philodurtos*) in Ionian song," rend their cheek and their heart, which is "unaccustomed to tears, anxiously pick grief-flowers," and wonder whether there is some "friendly kinsman-protector" (*philos . . . kêdemôn*) in this land to protect them, who are exiles (68–76).[28]

Their song also contains an appeal for divine justice to punish the *hybris* (aggression) of the Egyptian suitors (77–85, 104–11).[29] They appeal to Artemis to deliver them on the basis of their common status as virgins (144–53). While they honor the power and majesty of Zeus in their appeal to him, they also recognize the prospect of neglect by the Olympian deities and show that they are determined to die by suicide rather than submitting to the will of Aigyptos's sons (154–61). They, in fact, end their song on this ominous note by tracing the cause of their suffering back to Hera's persecution of Io, a divine hatred that still pursues them, the descendants of Io. They even suggest that Zeus may be subject to a charge of injustice should he fail to protect his descendants (162–75).

This *parodos* by the chorus representing the fifty daughters serves to demonstrate their identity and clarify their situation. In particular, it shows their desperate situation (hardly unusual for suppliants!) and their strategy: having been threatened by aggression in Egypt they have sought Argos, their other "home," because of a hereditary connection. The appeal to the gods is pious and necessary since one needs local gods to be favorable and merciful.[30] But their mention of the "kinsman-protector" (*kêdemôn*) shows that they recognize their need for human compassion as well. Their claims of justice serve to ensure that they are worthy recipients of compassion both from the gods and from human protectors.

Danaos, who also recognizes the need for human protection, especially with the approach of a company of armed men, advises his daughters to adopt a suppliant pose at the altar of the gods nearby. He cautions them to be submissive and not forward in their speech, but mindful of their vulnerability as aliens and suppliants.[31] In particular, he instructs them, saying that, as they hold suppliant branches, the emblems of *aidoios* (compassionate) Zeus, they should answer the strangers in "compassion-arousing, plaintive words expressing sore need" (αἰδοῖα καὶ γοεδνὰ καὶ ζαχρεῖ' ἔπη, 192–94). Obviously this is the sort of language that will elicit compassion in the strangers.[32] Also, they should make clear that their flight has been "free from bloodshed" (*anaimaktous*) so that the strangers' compassion will not be impeded by concerns about the suppliants' innocence. The women accept their father's prudent advice, and, as they take their seats at the altar, they call on Zeus to pity them (*oiktire,* 211) and on Apollo, who like them also once was exiled, to be understanding (*suggnoiê,* 215) of them as mortals. They further invoke other deities, including Poseidon and Hermes, as their father instructs them.

When Pelasgos, the king, enters, he immediately calls attention to the foreign (non-Hellenic) dress of the maidens; their foreignness, he says, makes their unheralded appearance on Argive soil without the company of a friend or guide an act of courageous daring that causes him wonder. Only their suppliant branch makes their situation the least bit comprehensible.

In the interchange that follows, the maidens immediately lay claim to their Argive heritage based on their descent from Io (274–76). After providing the details of this claim of lineage, they make their explicit appeal: "And since you know my ancient descent, / may you act so as to raise up an Argive crowd" (εἰδὼς δ' ἁμὸν ἀρχαῖον γένος / πράσσοις ἂν ὡς Ἀργεῖον ἀνστήσῃς στόλον, 323–24). The word ἀνστήσῃς ("raise up" or, as commonly translated, "succor") means to "raise someone from misery or misfortune."[33] Here, the chorus mean that he should act as though protecting a group of citizens, possibly kin. Their strategy of appeal—both to the gods and to the human king Pelasgos—is to break down distance and alienation by asserting their consanguinity and propinquity (cf. intro. pp. 18–19).

Compassion comes out in the king's dilemma and in what the king says. As the king listens further to the maidens' explanation of the cause of their flight and supplication—that the sons of Aigyptos are seeking to force the girls into a marriage they oppose—he soon begins to realize that these suppliants are making a request that might be costly to Argos: war with the sons of Aigyptos (342). Also, he is troubled by the question of justice: might not the sons of Aigyptos have authority to wed the daughters of Danaos according to the laws of Egypt (387–91)? The chorus, however, press their claim as suppliants protected by Zeus, god of suppliants (348–53, 381–86), and insist on the justice of their cause (392–96, 402–6).[34] They tighten the screw when they call on Pelasgos to be their "righteous protector" (*eusebês proxenos*) and warn him of the consequences of watching his suppliant being dragged by force from the gods' altar and the gods' images like a horse by the bridle and with a rough hand on her fine garments; he should beware of the requirements of Zeus (418–37).

When Pelasgos shows that he still is troubled by his dilemma, the chorus make what they say is the last of their many appeals for reverence and compassion (*aidoiôn logôn*): they say that if Pelasgos will not pledge to protect them, they will commit suicide by hanging themselves from the statues of the gods (455–67). Pelasgos says that he has heard a word that is "a lash to his heart." He further articulates his dilemma: their suicide would be a "pollution beyond outdoing" (μίασμ' . . . οὐχ ὑπερτοχεύσιμον), but battle with the sons of Aigyptos, alternatively, would involve a cruel expense: men's blood on the ground for women's sake (468–77). And yet he must revere (*aideisthai*) the wrath of Zeus who guards the suppliants.[35] Therefore, he sends Danaos to place suppliant boughs on the other altars of the local gods. It may happen, he says, that some "seeing these and having compassion" (*oiktisas idôn*) will hate the aggression of the male troop and that the people (*demos*) will become more kindly to you; he adds that all people bear "impulses of kindness" (*eunoias*) toward the weaker party (478–89).[36] Here, compassion explicitly comes in: the people will be moved by compassion to aid the helpless girls. Can we deny that Pelasgos himself is moved by such compassion? I think not, although he does not say that he personally experiences such a feeling.[37] Presumably he includes himself in the "every one" (πᾶς τις) of 489. Danaos, moreover, responds: "We think it is worth much to have found and gained a champion so compassionate" (*aidoion*, 490–91). The adjective *aidoios* refers explicitly to Pelasgos's reverence toward the suppliants, but in a broader sense it embraces showing compassion and kindness to those suppliants as well.[38]

We should also note that Danaos's expression of praise and gratitude here functions as a gesture of reciprocity. Pelasgos instructs Danaos on the appeal he is to make before the Argive assembly (516–23). After the Argive people have voted in their favor, the chorus in their song of praise and gratitude pray for recompensing blessing on the Argives as well (625–730). They sing of the Argives who "had compassion for them" (ᾤκτισαν ἡμᾶς), cast a favorable vote for them, and "revere" (αἰδοῦνται) the suppliants of Zeus, "this miserable flock" (ποίμναν τάνδ' ἀμέγαρτον, 639–42). Are we to conclude that the father has been successful in his appeal while the daughters have failed with their threats (as does Naiden 2006: 84–85)? Perhaps so, but the efforts of father and daughters have been directed toward the same end, and, together with Pelasgos's guidance and Danaos's parental control and leadership, they have all succeeded in their supplication and are accordingly grateful.

But in Greek tragedy the course of compassion rarely runs smooth. In this play, the opposition comes, as expected, from the sons of Aigyptos, here represented by their herald. The theme of compassion or, rather, the lack of compassion comes up as the Herald threatens to seize the girls if they don't hasten to the ship (D3).[39] "Dragging [by the hair] (*holkê*)," he says, "shows no respect (*hazetai*) to locks of hair" (884). Then, a moment later, "Tearing [of clothing] (*lakis*) will not pity (*katoiktiei*) the cloth (lit. 'weaving') of your 'tunic' (*chitôn*)." The herald's lack of pity, however, is soon met by the king's resistance. After an exchange in which Pelasgos asserts that he and his people will protect the gods' suppliants, the herald exits to rejoin the sons of Aigyptos. A battle looms in the future, but this play ends short of its performance.[40]

Pelasgos again assures the suppliants that he, along with his people, will serve as their protector (*prostatês*, 963–64). And again the maidens reciprocate in wishing blessings on Pelasgos (966–79); Danaos endorses their prayers as well as libations of thanksgiving to the gods (980–82). To yet another song of praise of Argos (1018–29), the chorus adds a brief prayer to Artemis, that she look upon them and show compassion (*oiktizomena*) and that Aphrodite never be allowed to force them into wedlock against their will (1030–33). This brief prayer to Artemis recapitulates that of 144–53 in the *parodos.*

Two traditional elements evident in the supplications of this play are (1) the invocation by the suppliants of Zeus's special protection of suppliants, with emphasis on his anger and vengeance against those who harm or refuse to protect suppliants, and the king's recognition of this divine protection (211, 385–86, 478–79, 639–42),[41] and (2) the association of heroic behavior with compassion and the protection of suppliants from their persecutors (D1a). Adkins (1960: 157–58) rightly sees the city's obligation to protect suppliants as a continuation of the Homeric *agathos*'s obligation to offer such protection. Adkins interprets this "obligation" as primarily a requirement to exhibit "competitive" *aretê* rather than as a moral obligation: "To fail to protect the suppliant is unworthy of a free unit which must be strong enough to support itself in order to exist." While I agree with Adkins that this differs from what we moderns would consider "moral" action, Adkins here gives too little emphasis to the religious side of the obligation; he gives none at all to compassion. But feelings of compassion, the requirements of Zeus, god of suppliants, and the inducements of martial valor *all* motivate the champion and his city to defend the suppliant.[42] Furthermore, Argos is a sort of democracy, reputed to be favorable toward suppliants (19–29), and in the course of the play the city shows itself compassionate toward the weak (486–89, 639–42). We can assume that the Athenian audience would identify with the citizens of Argos to whom the suppliants were appealing. But although the exhibition of compassion here is viewed positively, as a sign of civic and heroic *aretê* and nobility, there is also an undertone of tension and danger in which such protection necessarily involves a city that opposes the hostile pursuers of suppliants. To be compassionate may involve risk.

Compassion in this play, however, is not truly problematic in that Danaos and his daughters are confident in the justice, if not always of the success, of their cause and the gods' support, and Pelasgos and the citizens of Argos ultimately provide the support and protection they need. The Danaids' claim of kinship to the Argives serves to enhance the arousal of Argive compassion in this play. Also, as we have seen, the Danaids show proper reciprocity in their praise and prayers for blessings on Pelasgos and his city.

As noted in the analysis above, *oiktos* (compassion) and *aidôs* (reverence) are so closely linked in this play as to seem two sides of the same coin. This is especially true of Aischylos's use of the adjective *aidoios*. Pelasgos's compassion in this play is somewhat detached in contrast to what we will find in the compassionate characters of Euripides and Sophokles. Pelasgos tends to justify his actions based on his reverence for Zeus's law and the requirements of *aretê*. Not only does he not express a personal feeling of compassion, but neither he nor the chorus make use of an argument based on the human condition or the fragility of human prosperity, the hallmark of compassion in Sophoklean tragedy, as we shall see. He does, however, comment that all people pity the weaker party. This suggests at least some sense of a universal sympathy for human vulnerability (D2). It will be of interest to see whether compassion is made more personal or more direct in later plays of Aischylos.

Oresteia

Expressions of compassion or appeals for compassion occur several times in the course of the *Oresteia*, but the valuation of compassion per se does not appear to be a major theme in the trilogy, which is primarily concerned with the problems of retaliatory justice and a uniquely Athenian solution to that problem. Still, compassion or its denial occurs at significant moments in this long, complex tragic series. Let's examine the compassion theme in each of the plays in turn.

Agamemnon

The important *parodos* narrates both a response motivated by compassion and an appeal for compassion that is denied. The compassionate response is that of the goddess Artemis in Kalchas's interpretation of the omen of the eagles and hare as reported by the chorus. Kalchas says that Artemis, out of compassion (*oiktos*) became angry at the eagles' feast on the hare and its unborn, that "she hates (*stugei*) the feast of the eagles" (134–38). Her compassion is the strong impulse to protect or defend the innocent sufferer, but in this case it functions in response to a symbolic event (an omen) that has already transpired. Since Artemis is a goddess with great power, her response may have far-reaching consequences, including the sacrifice of Iphigeneia (cf. 146–55, 201).

The appeal for compassion occurs in that act of sacrifice. Aischylos speaks of Iphigeneia striking each of her sacrificers with the "pity-arousing shaft" (βέλει φιλοίκτῳ) of her eyes (240–41). This is an appeal—conveyed by the eyes of the victim to the eyes of the officiants—for a strong inhibiting compassion. It comes after she has already made entreaties (*litai*) to her father that have been rejected and after, at his command, she has been lifted from where she had fallen in supplication about his robes,[43] been put facedown on the altar "like a goat" and had her mouth gagged to prevent curses on the house (228–37). The text says that she tried to speak and adds an ironic reminder of her former happiness as the graceful daughter who had charmed her father and his friends with song at the festive table (242–47).[44] The fall from prosperity to misery is implicit here. Of course, the chorus does not convey whether Iphigeneia's "pity-moving glance" was successful, but the implication is that it was not and that the sacrifice took place, although, again, whether Artemis intervened at the last minute or not is left unclear.

At Agamemnon's entrance with Kassandra, the chorus warn him of words that pretend to express sympathetic joy (*sunchairein*, 793) but conceal true feelings.[45] Such a warning anticipates the deception and death that soon will follow. A sincere expression of human compassion for a fellow human must await Kassandra's exchange with the chorus before the palace. Despite Klytaimestra's impatience with Kassandra's passive resistance in refusing to budge from the chariot, the chorus of Argive elders express their compassion for the girl: "I pity (*epoiktirô*) her, however, and will not be angry."[46] They then advise her to enter the house, as Klytaimestra has requested (1069–71). But as they listen and watch her further, they compare her "possessed by a god and mad" to the nightingale that laments Itys with its "miserable heart" (1140–45).[47] Kassandra herself anticipates the compassion that the chorus will later feel after she meets her fate: "Soon you being present will pity me (*oiktiras*) and say that I was too true a prophetess" (1240–41). Still later, just prior to Kassandra's last words before entering the palace, the chorus say, "Oh miserable one, I pity (*oiktirô*) you for your god-ordained death" (1321). The chorus's compassion for Kassandra is without result, however: since they are powerless, they cannot intervene in her fate.

Kassandra herself brings up a connection between pity and justice. She asks why she "piteous" (*katoiktos*) should lament the fall of Troy, when she can foresee that Troy's captors will themselves come to a bad end, thanks to the gods. Also, based on this, she calmly accepts her own impending death. "I will dare to die," she says. "I greet this door as the gate of Death" (1286–94). Here we find the notion that revenge is a type of compensatory compassion: lamentation can be withheld from the victim (here, Troy and herself, as Klytaimestra's future victim), if that victim is avenged (or will be avenged) by either human or divine agency (cf. intro. p. 19). Troy's captors do come to a bad end, including Agamemnon, and Kassandra can foresee that she herself will be avenged by Orestes' killing of Klytaimestra and Aigisthos. In response, the chorus pronounce her as being a woman both very "pitiable" (*talaina*) and very "wise" (*sophê*, 1295–96). They marvel at her courageous acceptance of her own fated death; they compare her, in fact, to a sacrificial victim that calmly steps forward to the sacrifice (1297–98; cf. their further praise of her courage in 1302).[48]

In her final speech before she enters the palace, Kassandra utters a prayer that she be avenged followed by a reflection on the fragility of human fortune: "Oh, the fortune of mortals! If prosperous (*eutuchounta*), one might compare it to a shadow.[49] If disastrous (*dustuchêi*), the stroke of a wet sponge blots out (*ôlesen*) the picture. And I pity (*oiktirô*) this much more than that" (1327–30).[50] Here, the emphasis is clearly on the fragility of good fortune, the truth of which has been demonstrated by the fate of Kassandra and her family, including Priam and Hekabe (D2). This is an early depiction of humankind's tragic destiny, which the *Oresteia* further highlights with its recurrent them of "wisdom through suffering" (*pathei mathos*).[51]

Libation Bearers

The notion that Agamemnon's murder was "piteous" (*epoiktos phonos*) was introduced by the chorus at *Agamemnon* 1614. This is taken up in *Libation Bearers* at 433 and 511, where, respectively, Elektra and the chorus of slave women complain that Agamemnon's burial or tomb was "unlamented" (i.e., not receiving the appropriate lamentation, ceremony, and care). In contrast, note that Elektra refers to Iphigeneia as having been sacrificed "pitilessly" (*nêleôs*, 242), a characterization that might appear to reflect badly on Agamemnon, who carried out the sacrifice, but Elektra's focus in the context of her speech to Orestes appears to be on the piteousness of Iphigeneia's sacrifice rather than on ascribing responsibility for it.

The children of Agamemnon appeal to Agamemnon's spirit for compassion (help or salvation). Elektra prays to Agamemnon's spirit below: "Show compassion (*epoiktiron*) to both me and beloved Orestes" (130–31). She prays specifically for help in reversing the children's status as slaves and outcasts in the household where her mother has promoted as her mate Aigisthos, her partner in Agamemnon's murder. Elektra also prays for the safe return home of Orestes, who at this point still appears to her to be away, and she furthermore asks Agamemnon to grant that she herself be "more temperate" (*sôphronestera*) than her mother and "more reverent" (*eusebestera*) in her actions (138–41). She adds additional prayers to Agamemnon for an avenger to bring about just retribution for his murder, while for herself and her brother she prays that Agamemnon, along with "the gods, Earth, and victory-bearing Justice," will be a "bringer of blessings" (142–48).

Later, Elektra appeals a second time to her father's spirit to "have compassion" (*oiktire*) on his children—both the female and the male—and to ensure the survival of the line of Pelops (500–503). Her appeal here, however, emphasizes that this will be in Agamemnon's self-interest. She dwells on the archaic notion of the solidarity of the family: that the survival of children accomplishes the survival of their ancestor, even though he is dead. "For even in death you have not yet died" (504). Save us, she says, and you will save yourself.

The chorus express their sympathy for Elektra and Orestes as the children of Agamemnon engage in lamentations around the tomb of Agamemnon and work themselves up to carrying through their retribution on Klytaimestra and Aigisthos. When Orestes at one point utters a plaintive cry of distress and bewilderment, the chorus refer to the "lament" (*oiktos,* 411) that causes their hearts to throb (405–11).[52] They further testify to how their mood is alternately darkened and brightened by words of distress and hope.[53]

Still later, when Orestes is about to kill his mother, Klytaimestra pleads for mercy. She pleads with her son, "Hold back, child, and *aidesai,* my child, this breast" that gave you nourishment as a baby (896–97). Again in Aischylos we have the verb *aideisthai* being used in an appeal, and here again it may combine "have respect for" and "have compassion for," although the appeal here may be as much for "show mercy" as for "have compassion." Klytaimestra's appeal by the mother's breast is, at least on one level, an appeal based on reciprocity. She will soon repeat this type of appeal in 908, saying that she nourished Orestes and wishes to grow old with him. She is clearly asking for kind treatment in return for her kind treatment of him in the past. Furthermore, she is seeking to arouse the inhibiting power of compassion (D1b).[54]

Orestes immediately turns to Pylades and asks, "Should I out of pity/respect refrain (*aidesthô*) from killing my mother?" But Pylades simply insists that Orestes should obey Apollo's oracle and keep his pledge. This persuades Orestes to go through with the killing, which he proceeds to do after a few more verbal exchanges with Klytaimestra. It is retributive justice: no pity for one who showed no pity. But, as scholars have often observed, Orestes' killing of his mother is something he does with reluctance and sorrow; it lacks the joy and the zest of Klytaimestra's killing of Agamemnon.

Eumenides

Pity involves the Furies in the third play. The ghost of Klytaimestra blames the Furies for sleeping and having no compassion (*katoiktizeis*) on her misfortune (*pathos,* 121). What she demands is the punishment of Orestes. Again, we find retribution functioning as compassion: retribution brings relief of suffering. In Klytaimestra's case it is specifically the ghost of the dead person that seeks such compassion. Her statement that she lacks honor among the dead suggests that retribution will restore her honor (95–98). When Apollo comes out of his temple and tells the chorus to leave, he imagines the sort of place that the Furies should inhabit, a place with tortures and mutilations, where men "moan long lamentation" (*oiktismon,* 189), a reference to verbal expression of grief or pain (D3). We can infer here that pity would be lacking in such a place of cruelty. A third reference to compassion or the lack of it occurs when the chorus of Furies envision the lawlessness that will occur if Orestes should be acquitted of his mother's murder. They predict that in such a future, some recently stricken father or mother will "cry out for compassion" or "utter a wail" (οἶκτον οἰκτίσαιτ,' 515)—the context suggests that they will cry out for justice from the Furies, but the Furies whose protection has lapsed will not be able to help. Here there is a linkage between compassion and justice: justice is a form of compassion for those who have been wronged. We should note here that the "justice" sought by Klytaimestra and the Furies and also even that envisioned by Kassandra assume the blind retributory system sponsored by the Furies. The trilogy as a whole challenges the validity of such a system and promotes its reform.

Expressions of compassion or appeals for compassion occur at some critical points in the trilogy, although the expression of compassion is limited to the chorus who pity the victim Kassandra and to the goddess Artemis who pities the victims in the omen. Also, Kassandra herself uttered a summation of the pitiable human condition. The end of the *Eumenides,* however, works out the problems of the cycle of vengeance promoted by the Furies and brings the Furies into a newer, more progressive system of justice under which they will be called the Eumenides and will serve a deterrent function. Compassion is not explicitly mentioned as a component of the new dispensation that Athene proclaims during the play's concluding moments, but we may assume that compassionate treatment of others would have a likely role in such an advanced system. We have seen that it was denied a place in the system of blind retaliatory justice.

Prometheus Bound

We now look at *Prometheus Bound,* a play traditionally attributed to Aischylos but not universally accepted as such. It differs fundamentally from other Greek tragedies in having gods rather than human beings as its primary characters; humans do, however, play a small but significant role.[55] The play is about a conflict between two groups of deities, the Olympians and the Titans. Humans appear in the talk of the divine characters as the beneficiaries of the Titan Prometheus and in the form of a single character on stage, Io. Compassion in *Prometheus Bound,* therefore, is presented in radically different dramatic circumstances than in other Greek tragedies. In fact, to allow compassion to function in the play with regard to divine characters like Prometheus, Aischylos must allow gods to suffer and to experience deprivation, pain, and loss—experiences that we tend to consider more human than divine. Aischylos thus takes on an ambitious task of creating a tragedy among the gods. He can do this in part by introducing two "generations" of gods, the earlier Titans and the later Olympians. Since the Olympians under Zeus are dominant, they are mostly exempt from suffering and loss, whereas the hapless Titans are subject to them. A third race, the humans, is still lower in status and, consequently, most subject to pain and suffering and also to death. In fact, in the trials, sufferings, and small triumphs of humans as presented in this play, we readily recognize our own human condition and can identify completely. Surprisingly, we find expressions of pity in this play in greater abundance than in *Suppliants*.[56] Yet there remains an element of detachment, as we shall see.

The Prologue: Hephaistos's Compassion

Compassion is first enunciated in the opening scene as Hephaistos, Kratos, and Bia engage in the harsh task of shackling with adamantine chains the misbehaving Titan Prometheus upright to a Scythian cliff and then driving an adamantine wedge through his chest. We learn from Kratos that Prometheus is guilty of having stolen fire from the gods to give to humankind. He must therefore pay recompense to the gods, learn to accept the sovereignty of Olympian Zeus, and stop his "human-loving way" (*philanthropos tropos*, 1–11).

One of the three deities, Hephaistos, says that he lacks the heart to bind by force a "kindred" (*suggenê*) god to the wintry chasm, but must muster the courage to do so since it is dangerous to disregard the commands of the father (14–17). He then assures Prometheus that he participates in this harsh task unwillingly (*akôn*); in fact, he juxtaposes his unwillingness to do the task and Prometheus's unwillingness to have it done to him (18–20); he furthermore envisions Prometheus's isolation from mortals, who will be unable to visit Prometheus in this remote and harsh climate, an acknowledgment of Prometheus's association with human beings in the past. Also, Hephaistos predicts the suffering that Prometheus will endure, exposed to the hot sun all day. Time will be eternally exhausting for him.

Hephaistos then rehearses the cause of Prometheus's suffering: his championing of humankind (*philanthropos tropos*, again, 28). He zeroes in on Prometheus's crime: Prometheus, a god, betrayed his fellow gods by bestowing divine honors on humankind "beyond what was due to them" (πέρα δίκης, 30). Because of this, Hephaistos continues, Prometheus must "guard this unpleasant rock, upright, without sleep, and without bending his knee;" he will utter many wailings and helpless laments. Hephaistos then concludes by explaining that the heart (*phrenes*) of Zeus is inexorable (*dusparaitêtoi*) and that whoever newly comes to power is rough (*traxus*). Zeus therefore is depicted as an arrogant tyrant newly come to power, and Prometheus as his subject who must suffer pains much as human subjects sometimes suffer at the hands of their masters.[57]

Kratos asks Hephaistos why he delays and pities (*katoiktizêi*) in vain—since Hephaistos should properly hate a god who gave away to mortals Hephaistos's own privilege (*geras*, 36–38).[58] Hephaistos explains his compassion in terms of his kinship (*to suggenes*) and his companionship (*homilia*) with Prometheus; indeed, he says that these things are "strangely powerful" (*deinon*, 39; cf. intro. pp. 18–19).[59] Kratos acknowledges Hephaistos's reasons but cites as more formidable the prospect of Zeus's punishment if they should refuse to obey his orders. Hephaistos responds that Kratos is always pitiless (*nêlês*) and full of audacity (*thrasos*, 42).[60] Kratos justifies his attitude by asserting that it does no good to lament (*thrêneisthai*) Prometheus and chides Hephaistos to "stop working in vain at a useless effort" (43–44).[61] Hephaistos expresses his loathing of his own handicraft and reluctantly but competently performs the tasks that he has been assigned.

He stops short, however, when Kratos commands him to drive the adamantine wedge through Prometheus's chest: "Ah, Prometheus, how I lament over (*hyper stenô*) your sufferings" (*ponoi*, 66). Kratos is impatient: You're holding back and "lamenting over" the enemies of Zeus? Be warned that someday you don't "pity (*oiktieis*) yourself" (67–68; cf. D6 and see below). Hephaistos: "You see a sight horrible to behold (*dustheaton*) with the eyes" (69). When later Hephaistos charges Kratos for being overly severe, Kratos retorts that Hephaistos should go ahead and "be soft" (*malthakizou*), but not reproach Kratos's stubbornness or his rough anger. Having done his work, Hephaistos exits; soon Kratos and Bia follow, after Kratos utters a final set of insults to Prometheus in his now helpless situation.

This opening scene introduces several important themes relating to compassion that differ from those we have seen in *Suppliants*. Hephaistos's compassion for Prometheus is of the "restraining" or "inhibiting" type, wherein a person charged with a harsh or cruel task experiences a feeling of compassion that inhibits him or her from carrying through that task (D1b). Hephaistos, as we have seen, expresses such inhibiting compassion (14–15, 36, 66). When Kratos chides him for this "useless" compassion, Hephaistos calls Kratos "pitiless" (42, cf. D5) but ultimately realizes that he must perform the tasks. In this case, Zeus's power wins out over the restraining power of compassion to compel Hephaistos's compliance with the orders. This is the more typical situation in tragedy, where duty or authority requiring force or violence effectively trumps the restraint of compassion.

We also have seen how Hephaistos attributes his compassion, in part, to his sense of relatedness to Prometheus (14, 39) as a "kindred" god. As in *Suppliants*, relatedness promotes a sense of similarity or likeness that prompts a compassionate response (cf. D2). Also, the visual horror of Prometheus's suffering prompts Hephaistos's compassion (69, cf. D3).

Finally, there is Kratos's warning that Hephaistos may have to "pity himself" if he does not comply with Zeus's orders (67–68). The verb *oiktizo* here most likely refers to the expression of lamentation rather than what we might call "self-pity," an often long-term self-denigrating attitude associated with low self-esteem. Here, it denotes intense grief for one's own loss or misfortune, typically expressed aloud with moans and laments. Pity or grief for one's own suffering is an emotion to be avoided, if at all possible, primarily because it arises out of dire misfortune. We will see such situations in other tragedies, as we see it here in Prometheus's own suffering.

As a god, of course, Prometheus cannot suffer the ultimate loss and death that a human being can, but Aischylos presents him as capable of suffering tremendous pain.[62] Aischylos gives us a sense of Prometheus's pain in his first speech (88–126). Prometheus seems to feel more sharply the dishonor and shame of his punishment than he does the actual physical pains that presumably beset him: note "disgraceful troubles" (*aikeiaisin*, 93) and "shameful bondage" (*desmon aeikê*, 97). There is no indication in the text that he cried out in agony when the stake was driven through his chest, but he does express woe at his present misery (*pêma*) and that to come (98–99); we therefore can assume that he feels physical pain, as Hephaistos indicated that he would.[63] As a god with prophetic power, moreover, he is in the unique situation of being able to foresee his future sufferings; still, he reasons that he must bear his "doom" as lightly as possible, since the strength of necessity is unconquerable (*adêriton*, 101–4). At the prospect of someone approaching, he characterizes himself as a "manacled (*desmotês*), unfortunate (*duspotmos*) god, the enemy (*echthros*) of Zeus and Zeus's court, because of his too great love (*philotês*) for humankind" (119–22). He also expresses fear at the approach of what turns out to be the chorus of Okeanids (126).

The Parodos: Prometheus and Daughters of Okeanos

The chorus seek to allay Prometheus's fears and explain that they have come out of love (*philia*) and concern for him. When Prometheus asks them to look on his suffering, the chorus express compassion: they say that tears filled their eyes as they beheld Prometheus's body "withering away" on the rocks in adamantine bonds (144–51). Prometheus, again showing sensitivity to shame, expresses a wish to have been buried beneath the earth in Tartaros, so that neither god nor any other could gloat over his agonies. He fears that his exposed, public suffering will allow his enemies to exult over him (152–59).[64] The chorus asks who of the gods is so "hard-hearted" (*tlêsikardios*) as to rejoice at these things or who does not "sympathize indignantly" (*xunaschalâi*) at your troubles, except for Zeus (160–63)?[65]

The encounter with the Okeanids provides an opportunity for Prometheus to unfold for the chorus and for the audience the story of his conflict with Zeus.[66] Prometheus's own compassion comes into play here after the story of the Titanomachy when he comes to the part about human beings. Zeus, now king of the gods, distributed powers and privileges to the various gods, but he took no account of human beings, preferring to destroy them all and create instead a new other race. Prometheus said that only he had the courage to oppose Zeus in this and was successful in saving the human race from oblivion. Because of this, he says, he is tortured by such agonies "painful to suffer and pitiable to see" (πάσχειν μὲν ἀλγειναῖσιν, οἰκτραῖσιν δ' ἰδεῖν, 238). He continues: because he put humans first in his compassion (*oiktos*), he himself "was not judged worthy" (οὐκ ἠξιώθην) of it (i.e., of compassion), but has been "pitilessly" (*nêleôs*) brought into line, a "sight shameful for Zeus" (239–41).[67]

Stanford (1983: 26) sees Prometheus's pity for the human race as an example of *philanthrôpia:* "an emotion . . . akin to pity, but milder, more abstract and more cerebral . . . 'love of humanity.' In contrast with pity, which is chiefly directed toward individuals this emotion, or sentiment, was concerned with humanity in general, but more warmly, it seems, than our 'philanthropy' and almost approaching the Christian concept, 'charity.'" Stanford's interpretation seems fair enough generally: Aischylos, as we have seen, has used "*philanthrôpos tropos*" in lines 11 and 28 to characterize Prometheus's loving care for humankind. But note that Prometheus uses *oiktos* in 239 to describe the compassion he displayed for humankind, but that Zeus did not show to him (cf. 267). Here, Prometheus's pity for humankind does seem to take on a more personal and powerful emotional quality, as though he responded to the powerful emotion of *oiktos* ("compassion") at the sight of human suffering or at the thought of human destruction, and it prompted him to take action so as to spare humanity. This is the sort of heroic, saving compassion that we find in Homer, but of course, here there is a difference in status between Prometheus, a god, and mortals that makes his pity for humankind inherently a transaction between unequal parties rather than one between equals such as we find between humans in Homer and in most Greek tragedies. That the humans here are a group rather than an individual also contributes to the detachment we find in Prometheus's compassion for humanity. Also, as we see below, Prometheus cannot expect reciprocal compassion from humanity, unlike the human hero who benefits his peers. Because of this inherent inequality it is more like Christian charity, which often seems to carry a notion of the superiority of the charitable one (as if god or the special agent of god), in contrast to Greek compassion, which emphasizes the inherent equality in relations between human beings. Prometheus, as a god, is inherently unequal to his human beneficiaries. And this is certainly the way the other gods see it, which results in their use of *philanthrôpos* to describe Prometheus's care for an inferior race of beings.[68]

The chorus repeat their theme that "iron-hearted" (σιδηρόφρων) and "made out of rock" (κἀκ πέτρας εἰργασμένος) would be someone who does not "sympathize indignantly" (*sunaschalâi*, cf. 162) with Prometheus's hardships (242–44). They add that they did not wish to see Prometheus's troubles, but now that they have seen them, they are "pained in their hearts" (ἠλγύνθην κέαρ, 244–45). Prometheus acknowledges their feeling, adding that to his friends (*philoi*) he is pitiable (*eleinos*) to see (246).[69] The "visual" element of compassion here (141, 144–48, 237–46) recapitulates that which we saw earlier (cf. above on 69 and D3).

But when the chorus inquire further and learn of Prometheus's gifts of "blind hope" and fire to mortals and how, because of these gifts, he incurred the punishment from Zeus, the chorus conclude that Prometheus has erred (*hêmartes*, 260) and needs to seek release (*eklusis*) from his ordeal (*athlos*, 262). Prometheus replies that it is easy for someone outside of trouble to give advice to the one in trouble, but then adds that he erred willingly (*hekôn*), repeating the word for emphasis. In helping mortals, he himself "found suffering" (*ponoi*, 267) but adds that he did not envision the suffering he got.[70] He asks them to desist from lamenting his present pains but to witness his fortunes as they unfold. As they do this, he requests that they "sympathize" (*sumponêsate*) with one who now is in distress. He ends with a generalization: "misery (*pêmonê*) wanders broadly and lands on all in turn" (275–76).

We have here a reflection on the universality of suffering reminiscent of that expressed in Akhilleus's story of the two urns of Zeus (*Iliad* 24, cf. D2). Since this principle of universal suffering is typically taken as the essence of the human condition, it is odd to find a deity including gods within its operation. Indeed, in this scene we find that the chorus serves as a sympathetic group who allow Prometheus to explicate his compassion for humankind and how he has suffered as a result of that compassion. But we are seeing here a somewhat anomalous situation: a god who has shown compassion or mercy to the human beings below him receives punishment from a god above him for that compassion. Since the normal expectation is for compassion to be rewarded with compassion, his suffering raises a problem of divine justice.[71]

The chorus raised this problem at 259–62, and it seemed to limit somewhat their continuing expression of compassion. This conforms with the general assumption that compassion requires innocence in the sufferer, but we can note that they do continue to be sympathetic to Prometheus's situation. In fact, in 260–61, they express reluctance to hear more about Prometheus's "error," since it is "not pleasurable" for them and "painful" for him. We can infer here the continuation of their compassion in that it restrains them from continuing a discourse that will be painful for Prometheus (D1b). Their desire is for Prometheus to gain relief from his suffering, as they say at 262. Prometheus's impatience with their advice and his request for them to stop lamenting his suffering suggests that their active expressions of sympathy and concern have reached their useful limit, while his request that they continue to observe suggests that the continuing presence of a sympathetic audience will be comforting to him.

Prometheus and Okeanos

Okeanos is a fellow Titan who has been Prometheus's ally but who now comes as the sympathetic friend determined to fix the problem.[72] When he first enters, he expresses sympathy (*sunalgô,* "I share your pain," 288) for Prometheus's fate, and he adds that kinship (*to suggenes*) and respect for Prometheus force him to this.[73] He furthermore assures Prometheus that he is not a man of empty words, but wants to know how he can help (*sumprassein*) Prometheus; he adds, "for you can never say that you have a friend more loyal than Okeanos" (293–97). Prometheus, however, seems taken aback by Okeanos's arrival: "What? Have you too come to stare at my sufferings?" He goes on to complain about the bad treatment he has received from his ungrateful friend Zeus.

Okeanos is quick to dish out advice: he offers to intercede with Zeus on Prometheus's behalf but warns Prometheus to restrain his speech against Zeus so as not to incur harsher punishment. Instead, Prometheus should defer to Zeus's power and let Okeanos try to help him out. Prometheus is skeptical of Okeanos's ability to persuade Zeus and warns him that he may only get himself into trouble. When Okeanos asserts confidence that Zeus will grant him this favor, Prometheus thanks him for his "eagerness to help" (*prothumia*) but forbids him to expose himself to risk by interceding. Prometheus says that just because he suffers does not mean that he wants misery (*pêmonê*) to be widespread in the world (345–46). He cites as examples of suffering that Zeus has already imposed on the world the misery of his brother Atlas and that of the monster Typhon (cf. the discussion of 275–76, above).[74]

Compassion enters here unexpectedly: Prometheus says that "seeing Typhon he had compassion" (ἰδὼν ᾤκτιρα, 352), because Typhon was defeated by Zeus's violence and now lies "a weak and outstretched bulk" weighed down under Mount Aitna (D3). Typhon, normally the epitome of the terrible monster, is hardly on anyone's list as a poor, pitiful character on the order of Niobe or Hekabe, but for Prometheus he is a fellow sufferer of Zeus's overarching power.[75] Prometheus does not conceal Typhon's terror-inspiring nature here; indeed, that is the height from which Typhon has fallen to his lowly inert status as Zeus's victim. Typhon and Atlas, like Prometheus himself, are exempla of Zeus's power and his willingness to punish those who oppose him.[76] Prometheus does not want Okeanos to subject himself to the risk of such pain. Furthermore, any overtures Okeanos makes to Zeus will redound to Prometheus's disadvantage (386). Disappointed yet relieved, Okeanos departs homeward.

A further point can be made here: Prometheus's unwillingness to subject others to pain—just because he suffers—is a sign of his nobility.[77] Normally, people are happy to have others who share in their misery: "Misery loves company." Prometheus is about the task of relieving suffering in the world, not spreading it.

The choral song that follows is a heartfelt lament for Prometheus's suffering, a lamentation that the chorus say is shared by the world as a whole. They refer specifically to Prometheus's "most lamentable miseries" (*megalostosi pêmasi,* 413–14) and his "pitiable pain" (*algos oiktron,* 435). The lamentations described here have a strongly sympathetic, pain-sharing quality: mortals are said to "share the anguish" (*sugkamnousi,* 414); even the waves of the sea, the depths of Hades, and the streams of rivers utter sympathetic sounds of lamentation.[78]

Prometheus responds with an account of the troubles (*pêmata*) that plagued humankind—their lack of intelligence and reason—and how he, motivated by goodwill (*eunoia*), gave them gifts (442–46). He then details in two recitals his manifold contributions to humanity's cultural development (447–68, 476–506). Prometheus interjects between these accounts an ironic note: although he was able to relieve humankind's suffering by his inventions, he lacks the wit to relieve himself of his present agony (469–71). The chorus echo this irony by envisioning Prometheus as a doctor who cannot heal his own disease. This is sympathetic irony that again points up the injustice of Prometheus's situation as a god who has shown compassion to the human race below him. That race, however, though sympathetic, as the choral song above suggested, is unable to reciprocate in kind so as to relieve Prometheus's suffering.[79] Later the chorus reinforce this point when they say that Prometheus's gifts to humankind have been a "favorless favor" (*charis acharis,* 545), by which they mean that his favors to mortals have not received the expected reciprocity.[80] In ancient Greek society, those who gave gifts expected gifts in return.[81] The problem here is that mortals are not the gods' peers; consequently, the gods cannot expect equivalent returns from their human beneficiaries. Indeed, the text here suggests that Zeus has kept the mortals so feeble that they cannot or dare not attempt to aid Prometheus (547–551). The chorus point up the contrast between Prometheus's current misery and his happier days, when he wed their sister Hesione. As Griffith notes, the chorus's approach here is in the "spirit of *sôphrosunê*," but drawing parallels with Sophokles' Chrysothemis in *Elektra* and Ismene in *Antigone*, he rightly adds that "under a tyranny, such as Zeus's (or Aigisthus's or Creon's), *sôphrosunê* may not appeal to those of free spirit" (1983: *ad* 536–39, also cf. *ad* 526–60). Prometheus may have been imprudent in helping mortals, but he did the right thing as he saw it: the compassionate thing.

Prometheus and Io

The last exhibition of compassion in this play comes during the scene with Io. With Io, the play gains a second sufferer—a human one—to share the stage with Prometheus. Io suffers persecution from Hera (and from Zeus, indirectly) in the form of a gadfly (phantom of the watchman Argos) that stings Io and causes her to wander the earth. Prometheus and the chorus sympathize with this miserable young woman, and she acknowledges Prometheus's benefaction to humankind and his suffering as well (613–14). When she consequently requests that he disclose her future fate, at first Prometheus is reluctant to reveal this, for fear of crushing Io's spirit (628). But she insists on knowing, and he defers to her wish. The chorus, however, request to hear Io's story first. Prometheus allows Io to decide but suggests that the sympathetic tear she will gain from telling her sad story will be worthwhile (637–39)—a reflection on the power of art to arouse sympathy and the comfort of having a sympathetic audience. She, indeed, anticipates Prometheus's pity, when at the end of her tale she pleads with him not to pity (*oiktisas*) her and then flatter her with false words about her future (684–86).[82] When the chorus burst out with extravagant expressions of sympathetic lamentation (687–95), Prometheus alerts them to the fact that that their lamentation is premature in that he will reveal further pains and suffering in Io's future (696–97). He says much the same to Io and the chorus after he relates the first part of Io's wanderings; he characterizes the sufferings he has yet to reveal as "a stormy sea of ruinous misery" (742–46).

When Io expresses the thought that it might be better for her to die rather than to extend her misery, Prometheus reveals that his own suffering is much greater than hers in that his misery lacks the termination of death and will continue until Zeus falls from power. Io attributes her own suffering ultimately to Zeus as well (759). That they both suffer at the hand of Zeus unites Io and Prometheus.[83] Io will ultimately receive rest and compensation from Zeus in Egypt, but there is another important connection that Prometheus reveals: Io's descendant (Herakles) will be the one to release Prometheus from his bondage. At the end of Prometheus's revelation of Io's future, she suffers another attack from the gadfly and exits in distress. In the song that follows, the chorus indirectly express final words of sympathy for Io but in the form of a wish that such a fate of divine love never befall them (887–907). We see here that Prometheus, although a god sympathetic to the suffering human Io, lacks the power to relieve Io's suffering since it is in the hands of Zeus and fate. Prometheus can give her only a "favor" (*kerdos*, 777)—knowledge of that destiny. This is in keeping with the gifts of knowledge he has given other humans as well (cf. 443–44).[84]

Prometheus and Hermes

The play concludes with an encounter between Prometheus and Hermes, who acts as Zeus's agent. Hermes makes threats in an effort to get Prometheus to reveal his secret, but Prometheus remains defiant and confident in the secret that he possesses. At one point he asserts that he will never become "woman-minded" (*thêlunous*, 1003) so as to entreat Zeus to free him from his bonds; "I am far from that," he says (1002–6).[85] In other words, Prometheus refuses to become Zeus's suppliant begging for mercy. Prometheus seems to suggest here that for one god to beg another god for mercy would be shameful. This is especially true since Prometheus and Zeus are enemies. Also, Prometheus can refuse to do so here because he has a weapon that allows him to remain equal to Zeus rather than subservient to him. When Hermes threatens still greater punishment for Prometheus, the chorus advise Prometheus to give up his stubbornness (*authadia*) and listen to reason (1036–39).[86] When Prometheus persists in refusing to yield, Hermes warns those "who suffer with" (*sugkamnousai*) Prometheus to remove themselves lest they be overcome by the thunder that will come (1058–62). But Prometheus's courageous defiance and Hermes' arrogance effect a reversal in the chorus's attitude. The chorus state their unwillingness to betray their friend and insist that they are ready to suffer (*paschein*) any fate with him (μετὰ τοῦδ'). The chorus's sympathy for Prometheus results in their willingness to incur actual pains with him.[87]

Conclusion with Reflections on the Trilogy

Aischylos presents Prometheus and the chorus as characters who are sympathetic, compassionate deities in contrast to the harsh ruler Zeus and his henchman Hermes. Prometheus, above all, is presented as a nobly philanthropic and compassionate character with whom the audience would readily sympathize. But the primary foci of the dramatic action are Prometheus's own suffering at the hand of the overbearing Zeus and responses to that suffering by other characters, including Kratos, Hephaistos, the chorus, Okeanos, Io, and Hermes. Compassion and, conversely, its lack serve to distinguish what this play presents as, respectively, the good and the bad.[88]

I conclude this survey of compassion in *Prometheus Bound* with a brief look at two passages, one from the play and one from an important fragment. Both were brought to my attention by Herington's classic essay, "Aeschylus: The Last Phase."

ΠΡ. οἶδ' ὅτι τραχὺς καὶ παρ' ἑαυτῷ
τὸ δίκαιον ἔχων Ζεύς· ἀλλ' ἔμπας
μαλακογνώμων
ἔσται ποθ,' ὅταν ταύτῃ ῥαισθῇ·
τὴν δ' ἀτέραμνον στορέσας ὀργὴν
εἰς ἀρθμὸν ἐμοὶ καὶ φιλότητα
σπεύδων σπεύδοντί ποθ' ἥξει. (186–92)

PROMETHEUS: I know that Zeus is rough and keeps justice in his own hands; yet someday he will be gentle-minded, when he has been crushed in this way; then having

> soothed his merciless wrath, he someday will come eagerly into friendship and affection with me also eager.

In this passage Prometheus prophesies the reconciliation between Zeus and himself that will come someday. I take this to be programmatic for the trilogy that the audience is watching as well. Note the change of attitude that will come over Zeus: his "merciless wrath" that we have witnessed in this play will be calmed and transformed into eager (*speudôn*) friendship and affection for his fellow deity Prometheus. Also, note that Prometheus will reciprocate that affection perfectly (*speudonti*)—the words denoting eagerness are even juxtaposed in the Greek text. Also, the text suggests that Zeus will become open to compassionate responses in place of his "merciless wrath."

Fragment 199 (Radt) also suggests a similar change in Zeus. In this fragment, most likely from the second play (*Prometheus Unbound*), Prometheus is instructing Herakles on his future travels and alerts him to the trouble he will have confronting the Ligurians, whom he will be unable to defeat. But, Prometheus says, "Zeus, seeing you helpless (*amêchanounta*), will pity (*oiktirei*) you and, holding above you a cloud, will cover the land with a shower of round stones, throwing which you will easily drive back the Ligurian army." Here we have an explicit statement indicating that Zeus will in the future show compassion, in this case toward his own son, who will be the one to kill the eagle and free Prometheus from his bondage.

It therefore seems likely that the *Prometheia* concluded with reconciliation between Prometheus and Zeus; human beings may also have been part of that reconciliation. Herington writes of the possibility of the trilogy ending with a celebratory torchlight procession.[89]

Concluding Reflections on Aischylos and Compassion

Aischylos emphasizes distance and detachment in his portrayal of compassionate behavior. He is capable of capturing the larger tragic view of life, as he does in *Persians* and *Seven Against Thebes,* both of which concern situations of war: both the conclusion of war and when war is impending, respectively. In *Persians,* the Athenian audience sees the war through the portrayal of the enemy Persians in defeat. Compassion is shown by Dareios to his son Xerxes in Atossa's prophetic dream,[90] but overall the play emphasizes the defeat of the Persians and the Athenians as victors. Still, the expectation that the Athenian audience will be able to sympathize with the defeat of their recent enemies is truly remarkable, as is the play's general treatment of those enemies as tragic characters who suffer in world that seems hostile to them. In *Seven Against Thebes,* the conditions of impending war do not allow free expressions of compassion due to the standards of military discipline that apply to states at war. Nevertheless, the play makes the audience aware of the great suffering and lack of compassion inherent in war and of the tragic potential of those who engage in such conflicts.

In presenting compassionate kings, such as Pelasgos in *Suppliants,* Aischylos does not have them openly express personal feelings of pity or compassion even when they act compassionately. This may relate to an assumption on his part that such a king would possess a strong sense of being the representative of his community of citizens, a sense of self that might suppress the expression of personal feelings; Pelasgos does say at one point (see pp. 79–80 above) that people in general tend to pity and show kindness to the weak. In any case, Pelasgos and the citizens of Argos do show compassion in their treatment of their suppliants, the Danaids. Also, the play consistently links compassion with reverence. Aischylos's lesser characters, such as the choruses in *Oresteia,* do express pity more openly and in other ways similar to the choruses of Euripides and Sophokles. In part, this may be attributed to the aristocratic bias of Greek myth, in which the focus of everyone's sympathy is on the kings, masters, and heroes. Even the lowliest slave feels compassion for his master who suffers disaster (see above, pp. 62–63).

In the *Oresteia,* Aischylos's concern is primarily with issues of justice, particularly with deep and violent conflict within a family and with the issues of retributive justice that arise out of such violent conflict. The trilogy concludes, however, with the acquittal of Orestes and with a powerful celebration of social harmony. Compassion per se has virtually no role in the conflict between kin, although compassion presumably is validated in the ideal of social harmony and the resolution of the seemingly endless cycle of "blind" retribution celebrated in the finale of *Eumenides.* Also, compassion is presented in the relation between Kassandra and the chorus of Theban elders and in Kassandra's attitude toward her captors (see above, pp. 84–86), in which she enunciates connections between pity and justice. Also, compassion is linked with innocence early in the trilogy in the examples of both Artemis's omen and Iphigeneia's appeal to her father (D4). *Prometheus Bound* presents something of a special case in that compassion between gods is qualitatively different from that between human beings: divine vulnerability is limited, whereas that of human beings is much less so. Still, *Prometheus Bound* is exceptional among the plays commonly attributed to Aischylos in its open expressions of sympathy and compassion; also, compassion is associated with the good.

Aischylos can consequently be seen as a tragedian who is especially concerned with issues of justice, both human and cosmic. Such a concern with justice accords a somewhat lesser role to compassion as an important element in human interactions, although as we have seen, compassion and justice normally reinforce each other, except in cases where justice may require the denial of mercy to the person seen as a wrongdoer or enemy. Indeed, sometimes Aischylos depicts linkages between compassion and revenge, with revenge being seen as a type of compassion by the person seeking revenge. In any case, based on his extant tragedies, we do not find the open expression of personal compassion by kings or heroes that we saw in Homer and will see in some of Euripides' and Sophokles' heroic types. Also, Aischylos does not emphasize the common human vulnerability so much as the other two tragedians, although he does provide an early reference to it in Kassandra's language (see p. 85); also, he makes at least two allusions to widespread sympathy for suffering (see pp. 82, 93–94). This difference may relate to the earlier era of history in which Aischylos grew up, lived, and wrote and to the personal worldview he acquired during that time. If we had more of his dramas, we might come to a different conclusion, but we necessarily base our analysis on the plays that have survived. He does, however, convey, especially in his later plays, a strong sense of the value of social harmony and a strong sense of the tragedy inherent in human life. He can thus be characterized as a social idealist.

CHAPTER 4

Euripides

Compassion on Trial

We begin with a selection from Aristophanes' *Frogs*, featuring the debate between Aischylos and Euripides:

AESCHYLUS: Your folksy style's for the birds.
For magnificent thoughts and magnificent fancies, we must have magnificent words.
It's appropriate too for the demigods of heroic times to talk bigger
than we. It goes with their representation as grander in costume and figure.
I set them a standard of purity. You've corrupted it.
EURIPIDES: How did I do it?
AESCHYLUS: By showing a royal man in a costume of rags, with his skin showing through it.
You played on emotions.
EURIPIDES: But why should it be so wrong to awaken their pity?
AESCHYLUS: The rich men won't contribute for warships. You can't find one in the city
who's willing to give. He appears in his rags, and howls, and complains that he's broke. (Lattimore 1969: 68)

From his own time to ours, Euripides has been known as the Greek tragedian who most emphasizes the pitiful and the pathetic.[1] This chapter presents him as a playwright who exploits the pathetic and who can present compassion delicately, but who nevertheless presents compassion as often problematical and sometimes subject to question or limitation. This is consistent with our general perception of Euripides as a searcher and inquirer who challenged commonly held beliefs and assumptions. As far as compassion is concerned, this tendency to question and challenge will emerge in our survey as we explore such themes as "Compassion Shown but Problematized," "Compassion Denied or Thwarted," "Compassion Abused," and "Compassion in Defiance of Divine Spite."

Compassion Shown but Problematized

We have seen in our survey of compassion in Aischylos's *Suppliants* that active or saving compassion typically involves risk that the champion must undertake to provide protection or help to his suppliants. Euripides presents us with two suppliant tragedies, *Children of Herakles* and *Suppliants,* in which compassion requires that the champion incur risk, but in which he must also confront other challenges that make the granting of compassionate assistance still more problematic.

Children of Herakles

Compassion becomes an issue in the opening episode of the play. Iolaos and the young sons of Herakles, fleeing the persistent persecution of Eurystheus, have taken refuge as suppliants at the altar of Zeus Agoraios in Marathon, while Alkmene and the daughters of Herakles have sought the protection of Zeus's temple. The chorus of Marathonian elders arrive in response to Iolaos's cry for help when an Argive herald has tried to drag the boys from the altar and has knocked the old man to the ground. The chorus express alarm and sympathy when they see the old man lying there (75–76): "Poor fellow (*ô talas*)! At whose hand do you suffer this miserable (*dustênon*) fall to the ground?" Iolaos asserts that the herald has dishonored the local gods by dragging him from Zeus's altar. Soon the Athenian king Demophon, son of Theseus, enters along with his brother Akamas and immediately inquires about the misfortune (*tuchê*) that has brought the suppliants together (122). The chorus explain that they wept with compassion (*oiktos,* 129) when they witnessed the herald trying to force the children from the altar and throwing the old man down.[2] Demophon immediately responds that the herald's clothing is Greek but that his actions are barbaric (130–31).

The herald explicitly warns Demophon against a display of compassion for the suppliants: "Surely, they don't expect that, being of sound mind, you alone of so much of Greece that they have approached will foolishly show compassion (*katoiktiein*) on their misfortunes (*sumphoras,* 150–52)."[3] He reiterates this when he warns Demophon: "But if you turn soft (*pepanthêis*) beholding their arguments and lamentations (*oiktismata*), then the matter comes to a battle of spears" (158–60). "Turning soft" here obviously refers to being moved by compassion. The root word is used of the ripening of fruit; here, it metaphorically suggests weakness, possibly feminization—qualities that a person like the herald would associate with a compassionate response so alien to his own ways of responding. He ends with the advice that Demophon should not make the mistake—made so often by Athenians—of choosing the weak as friends instead of the strong (176–79). This refers to Athens' reputation and its sense of its own identity as a *polis* that welcomes outsiders and favors the weak over the strong.[4] The Athenian audience would clearly see this "advice" as a challenge to their sense of themselves as noble champions of the weak.

Iolaos then rises to the challenge and argues the case for himself and Herakles' children (181–231). He begins his appeal on the basis of Athens' sense of honor: it will be shameful for Athens to fail to protect its suppliants. In fact, if Athens were to do so, he could no longer regard Athens as free (*eleutherai,* 198). Iolaos adds other traditional appeals, invoking ties of *philia* (Theseus and Herakles were sons of cousins) and reciprocity (Herakles and Iolaos assisted Theseus in fetching Hippolyte's belt; also, Herakles rescued Theseus from Hades).[5] He ends with a vision of the disgrace that

Demophon will incur should he allow the city's suppliants to be dragged off by force, and he reinforces this with a formal supplication to Demophon.

At this point the chorus openly express to Demophon their compassion for Iolaos and the children: "I feel compassion (*oiktirô*) when I hear their misfortunes (*sumphoras*)." They characterize it as a case of nobility (*eugeneia*) defeated by mischance; specifically, the chorus see these children of a noble father as suffering calamity undeservedly (*anaxiôs*, 232–35). As we have seen and will continue to see (D4), undeserved misfortune is the primary condition that stimulates a compassionate response.

In his positive response to Iolaos's appeal, Demophon raises Iolaos to his feet and gives three reasons why the city should protect the suppliants: (1) the religious duty to protect suppliants at the altar; (2) the kinship and the recompense owed to Iolaos and Herakles for their past benefits to Theseus; and (3) the prestige of Athens and the fear of disgrace (236–49). Here again, as in Aischylos's *Suppliants*, the *aretê* of protecting suppliants is emphasized. Although Demophon does not explicitly cite compassion among the reasons why the city should protect the suppliants, it is implicit in his acceptance of their request.[6] Iolaos has asked for rescue from the aggression of the herald, and the chorus has expressed their compassion in response, acknowledging that the children's suffering was undeserved—and thus appropriately pitied. Demophon's assertion of support for them flows directly from this sequence of events (236–49). The protection of suppliants is presented as a form of *aretê*, but compassion entails action; indeed, the action of saving and protecting is the hero's form of compassion (D1a).

But why does the champion not express his personal feeling of compassion? We have observed this phenomenon in Aischylos as well. The answer lies partly in the nature of champions as men of action, not men of words—unlike the chorus, who frequently express their feelings in words but whose potential for action is limited or nonexistent.[7] Yet champions as kings also act for the state as a whole. Therefore, they may have been thought less likely to express their personal feelings as motives than to provide public reasons to justify those actions. Even what might seem like the expression of a personal motive, such as Demophon's second reason cited above (kinship and obligations of reciprocity), is phrased in terms of action rather than personal feelings.[8] Still, these public rationales are compatible with compassion expressed as action.

Demophon sends the herald away with an assurance that he and Athens will defend the suppliants from Argive aggression. Iolaos, addressing the children, praises the Athenians for rescuing him and the children, "even when they could see that we were wandering beggars" (309–19). Iolaos then directs his praise to Demophon for his exhibition of compassion, calling him "noble / well-born" (*eugenês*), "descended from the best" (ἐξ ἐσθλῶν . . . φύς), and one who preserves his father's reputation (*doxa*) by his noble action (320–28). Demophon is being commended for nobility, valor—and his exhibition of compassion in honoring the suppliants' appeals. Iolaos's compliments clearly link nobility and the compassionate protection of suppliants. The chorus responds that Athens always desires to help the weak in accordance with justice (329–30; cf. above on 176–79).[9] Demophon in reciprocal fashion accepts Iolaos's assurance that the children will remember Athenian *charis* (333–34).

This positive outcome is problematized when Demophon discovers that oracles demand the sacrifice to Persephone of a young daughter of a noble father. Demophon, while willing to defend the suppliants to the death, cannot bring himself nor force his citizens to sacrifice one of their own. He nevertheless shows his willingness to help find a solution to this problem that will safeguard the suppliants. That solution comes in the form of the voluntary self-sacrifice by Herakles' daughter called the maiden.[10] Among other reasons she gives for her decision, the maiden specifically mentions reciprocity for Athens' compassion: "What will we say, if this city chooses to run great risks for our sake, but we, who impose labors on others, run away from the prospect of death when we are able to save them" (503–6)? Demophon later assures her that at burial she will be tended by women as she requests, a sign of his care and concern for her; he also praises her courage (567–71).

It is notable that Demophon persists in his determination to find a way to fulfill his pledge of compassionate assistance.[11] That

Demophon's compassion does not continue to be mentioned does not mean that it does not continue to function as part of his motivation until the rescue of the children is accomplished. This is part of the linkage between compassion and action that stems from the heroic tradition of Homer: the suppliant does not appeal merely for the champion's sympathetic sentiment toward him or her, but for the saving action or rescue that heroic compassion entails.[12] Once the appeal for compassion is made and accepted by the champion, any response toward the satisfaction of that appeal can be assumed to involve compassion on the part of the champion, whether or not the champion continues to acknowledge it as a motive. In Demophon's persistent compassion in this play, Euripides provided his Athenian audience with a model worthy of emulation.

There is, however, another expression of compassion in the play, that of Iolaos for the children of Herakles and for Alkmene when the situation seems hopeless in the face of the oracles demanding the sacrifice. Iolaos says that he is willing to die himself but adds: "But I weep for and have compassion for you, children, and for Alkmene, the old mother of your father" (445–46). Here we have a tender expression of compassion for helpless *philoi* who are doomed to die. Note that Iolaos is able to separate his own fate from that of the children and expresses pity for them despite their closeness to him (cf. intro. pp. 18–19).[13] He goes on to compare his own wretchedness to that of Alkmene. In contrast, he speaks of Eurystheus's stupidity (*skaios hanêr,* 458) and hubris; he wishes for a wise enemy, from whom one can rather expect "compassionate regard" (*aidos*) and "justice" (*dikê,* 456–60).[14]

In the end, however, Eurystheus shrewdly manipulates the argument about his own life as he faces Alkmene's determination to execute him despite Athenian objections (cf. 961–80, 1019–20).[15] Eurystheus declines to make an appeal for mercy: "I do not beg you for mercy" (οὐ παραιτοῦμαί σε), although he prophesies a benefit to Athens in return for its merciful behavior toward him (1026–44). We should nevertheless note that his hostility to Herakles' children continues unabated; he surely would have killed the children but for Athenian intervention and the noble self-sacrifice of Herakles' daughter.

Suppliants

The connection between the persistent compassion and the *aretê* of the Athenian protector is continued in Euripides' *Suppliants.* The Argive mothers of the Seven, who died in war against Thebes, have become suppliants to Athens seeking the burial of their sons. As the play opens, Aithra, the mother of the Athenian king Theseus, has come to the temple of Demeter at Eleusis to offer sacrifices; there she sees the chorus of mothers as they surround her holding suppliant branches. Aithra says that she feels constrained by their suppliant branches and that she stays here "out of pity" (*oiktirousa,* 34) for these gray-haired mothers who have lost their sons and "out of reverence" (*sebousa,* 36) for their suppliant wreaths. The chorus of Argive women make a powerful appeal to Aithra for compassionate aid based on both their common old age and on the natural empathy between mothers (42–70; cf. their further lamentation in 71–86 and D2).[16] Vickers (1973) asserts that both here and elsewhere in Euripides tragic characters "unashamedly appeal for sympathy."[17] I agree, although there are a few exceptions, as we shall see.

When Theseus arrives, he sees his mother among the lamenting suppliants. He remarks on their "pitiable tear" (οἰκτρὸν . . . δάκρυ, 96, cf. 49). He asks about the man "weeping pitiably" (στενάζων οἰκτρὸν, 104) at the gates of the temple. This man, the women's spokesman Adrastos, then appeals to Theseus for compassion: "Save these corpses, having compassion (*oiktiras*) on my troubles and on these mothers whose sons have died" (168–69).[18] In the course of his appeal, he asserts that it is wise for the rich man to observe poverty and for those who have good fortune to observe pitiable things (176–79), a reference to human vulnerability as a motive for compassion (D2).[19] He refers to Athens as a "city that knows misery when she sees it" (190), and he calls Theseus, its leader, "noble" (*esthlos,* 191). The chorus add their voice to the appeal—to receive their misfortunes "through compassion" (δι' οἴκτου, 194). But the young Athenian king is at first unwilling to assent because Adrastos was imprudent in pursuing the war contrary to divine warnings (195–249). This denial of compassion is based on the assumption that those who have acted wrongly do not deserve compassion (D4). The chorus, indeed, admit that Adrastos did wrong (*hêmarten*), but then say that Theseus should be understanding (συγγνώμην . . . ἔχειν χρεών, 250–51).

The chorus therefore intensify their appeal for compassion by invoking blood ties (Aithra's father, Pittheus, was a son of Pelops and brother of Thyestes and Atreus of Argos) and Theseus's similarity to their sons who now need burial.[20] These appeals for compassion are made on the basis of the reciprocity of kinship and on the similarity between themselves who have lost their sons and Aithra who has Theseus as a thriving fortunate son (D2, cf. intro. pp. 18–19).

When Theseus sees his mother weeping for the women, he acknowledges that a feeling also has come over him: "Something shot through me as well!" (κἀμὲ γὰρ διῆλθέ τι, 288).[21] It is compassion and grief for the women's suffering that Theseus feels here. The chorus have explicitly appealed for his compassion just before (263–85, esp. 279–81). "Pity!" (οἴκτισαι), they plead, and they utter their "pitiable cry" (οἰκτρὸν ἰήλεμον). Aithra then makes an appeal to her son in which she warns of the gods' vengeance if Theseus should fail to honor the suppliants and calls his attention to the great prestige that Theseus and Athens would gain by upholding the commonly accepted right of burial (297–331). Theseus agrees to become the women's champion, since these arguments justify his compassionate assistance.[22]

Indeed, the fact that he later personally and with great emotion oversees the burial of the dead strongly suggests that compassion continues to function as part of his motivation. The messenger uses the verb *agapaô* ("to show loving care for the dead") to describe Theseus's attitude toward the deceased warriors (764–66).[23] When Adrastos says that the burden of the corpses must have been dreadful and shameful, the messenger counters, "But why should one another's misfortunes be shameful for people?" (767–68).

Later, as Theseus presents the ashes to the mothers and sons of the fallen, he asks them to remember and honor Athens for its good deeds to them. Adrastos assures him that the Argives will remain grateful and seek to return action with action (1165–79). Note the expectation of reciprocal benefit here and Adrastos's easy acceptance of it: it is something expected by both parties and easily dealt with by both (cf. intro. pp. 17–20).[24] The goddess Athene requires that the Argives swear an oath to defend Athens' interests in the future.[25] As we saw in *Children of Heracles*, the valor of the city and the nobility of the leader who protects and honors suppliants are emphasized. Especially in *Suppliants*, however, compassion itself is depicted as a strong personal emotion that motivates the protector. It is also persistent: as in *Children of Heracles*, the fact that pity is not the explicit focus of the argument does not negate its importance as Theseus's ultimate motive.

Compassion Denied

Compassion is not always granted in Greek tragedy. We will look at four plays by Euripides in which appeals for compassion are made or implied but not granted. All these plays happen to involve the Trojan War, although the action of three of them takes place in the aftermath of the war. Of particular interest here will be the arguments used to appeal for compassion and the arguments used to deny those appeals. The character of the hero denying compassion will also receive emphasis. Also, we briefly survey additional examples of pitilessness and extreme denials of compassion in Euripidean tragedy.

Hekabe

Hekabe presents two supplications, both by the play's protagonist.[26] The first is prompted by the decision of the Greek army to sacrifice Polyxena, Hekabe's daughter, to the ghost of Akhilleus. Hekabe learns of this from the chorus of captive Trojan women. In particular, she learns that Agamemnon favored Polyxena in the debate, out of deference to his captive concubine, Kassandra, Polyxena's sister, but that the sons of Theseus and particularly Odysseus had argued that Akhilleus's ghost should be honored to show gratitude to the great hero. The chorus advise Hekabe to appeal to Agamemnon as a suppliant so as to possibly avert the sacrifice of her daughter. Hekabe laments her daughter's impending death, but Polyxena's response is unexpected. She laments for her mother's sorrow and future loneliness, but not for her own death: for Polyxena, death will be better than living as a slave.

When Odysseus arrives to escort Polyxena to her death, Hekabe makes her appeal. She reminds him of the time when he was her suppliant in Troy: at that time she spared him out of pity (239–57). Now she appeals to him to show gratitude (*charis,* 276) as she in turn supplicates him. She then appeals for reverence (*aidesthêti*) and compassion (*oiktire,* 286–87). Hekabe makes full use of the principle of reciprocity in this appeal—emphasizing that her appeal mirrors Odysseus's earlier appeal to her in many ways. As noted above, the appeal to receive compassion in return for compassion granted in the past is one of the strongest available to a suppliant (cf. intro. p. 19).[27] Hekabe also adds an argument based on the fragility of human fortune: that she was once someone important, but now she is not; Odysseus should consequently be cautious in his exercise of power, since he is also subject to the changes of fortune (282–85, cf. D2).

Odysseus employs a legalistic dodge to avoid Hekabe's appeal by asserting that he is obligated only to save Hekabe, not her daughter! He supplements this with the following specious arguments:

1. Our dead friends, who have died nobly, should be honored. Akhilleus was a great warrior and in death deserves great recompense from his friends.
2. In general, it is more important that dead warriors receive honor than living warriors. Odysseus speaks of his own situation: he is happy with little as a living warrior but wants a grand and glorious tomb: "At my death, I want men to gaze at my tomb reverently."
3. You may be suffering pitiable things (*oiktra,* 321), but so do our own mothers and wives back in Greece, many of whom have lost loved ones.[28]
4. We Greeks succeed by treating our friends well. You foreigners are ungrateful.

In this response, Odysseus suggests that the Greeks' primary motive is gratitude to Akhilleus, their great friend. Pleading his obligation of *philia* to his fellow Greek, Odysseus denies Hekabe's appeal for compensatory compassion. Hekabe gives up her suppliant stance and rises to her feet.

She then tells Polyxena to make her own appeal to Odysseus, in case she has greater power of persuasion than her mother. "Throw yourself pitiably (*oiktrôs*) at his knees and persuade him to have compassion (*epoiktirai*) on your fate . . . for he too has children" (339–41). She therefore advises an appeal based on likeness (D2).[29] Polyxena declines to make such an appeal to Odysseus, but her first words to him indicate that he is seeking by his actions to avoid just such an appeal: he hides his right hand under his cloak and turns his face away so that she cannot touch his chin. The right hand and beard were sometimes touched to inaugurate a supplication. "Take courage," she says, "For you have escaped my Zeus of the Suppliants" (342–45). She therefore shows herself to be much braver than this hero who seeks to avoid the ritual contact of supplication.[30] She proceeds to assert that she prefers to die rather than live as a slave. Still, her speech shows that her life illustrates the tragic theme of the fall from high to low: from princess to slave (D3). Her death, however, will spare her the still greater ignominy of a slave's life.[31]

When Talthybios, the Greek herald, comes to fetch Hekabe for Polyxena's burial, he finds her lying in the dust. He responds to this sight with penetrating questions about the instability of human good fortune, which this fallen queen's misery so well illustrates, and reflects on his own advanced age and his own preference for death rather than suffering such a fate (488–98, cf. D3). When Hekabe requests to hear the details of Polyxena's sacrifice, Talthybios replies that telling this will require him to gain a twofold share of tears: he wept with compassion (*oiktos*) as he witnessed the sacrifice, and he will weep with compassion a second time as he relates the story of it (518–20).[32] Also, he notes that Neoptolemos "both willingly and unwillingly with compassion (*oiktos*)" carried out the sacrifice (566–67). Neoptolemos's attitude, as described here, reflects the dilemma of the person with a heinous duty who must carry it out despite the restraining force of his compassion.[33]

Hekabe's speech, which follows, provides further reflections on the fragility of human fortune, of which her own life is a perfect illustration (585–628, D2). In response (629–56), the chorus sing of their own fates as slaves because of the judgment of Paris, but remarkably they are also able to sympathize with the sorrows of Greek (specifically Spartan) wives and mothers who have lost loved ones in the war (D5).[34] Hekabe, at one point in her discussion with her daughter, remarked that Polyxena was pitiable (*oiktra*) but that she herself was miserable (*athlia,* 417). This comparison between the girl's situational circumstance and the mother's internal experience is rich in meaning. It highlights both the daughter's nobility and the mother's complete misfortune (cf. 429).

But poor Hekabe's troubles are not yet over. An old female attendant enters with a covered corpse behind her. Hekabe then learns that the corpse is neither Polyxena, whom she first expects, nor her other daughter Kassandra, but her son, Polydoros. Here the other shoe drops—the other deep concern of her dreams related in the play's beginning. Hekabe soon concludes that Polymestor must have killed him, without showing pity (οὐδ' ᾤκτισας, 720).[35]

When Agamemnon enters from the camp, Hekabe performs her second supplication in the play. She informs Agamemnon that Polymestor had been her and Priam's guest-friend but that now he has murdered her son—hacked him to death—and, furthermore, left his corpse unburied. At first Agamemnon seems quite sympathetic, moved by Hekabe's great losses of her daughter and now her son: "Alas," he says, "what woman was ever so unfortunate?" (785).

Her supplication is for Agamemnon to help her take revenge on Polymestor and thereby enact justice. She asks for respect for her suppliance (αἰδέσθητί με) and for compassion ("pity me," οἴκτιρον ἡμᾶς, 806–7).[36] Here, compassion is the satisfaction of the pressing desire for justice that the severely wronged person feels.[37] Such desire is a powerful, visceral yearning, which can be satisfied only by a sense that justice has been done—that the wrongdoer has been punished as the law or custom requires.[38] She reflects on law (*nomos*) and on the universal requirement that law and justice govern relations in human communities: law is the very foundation of society.[39] "For by law," she says, "we believe in the gods and we live distinguishing right from wrong" (800–801). Her appeal for compassion is for nothing less than the enactment of just revenge: she asks Agamemnon, "like a painter standing apart," to picture her misery and her fall from royalty to miserable slavery and childlessness (807–11, cf. D3).

Kovacs's stage direction is on target here: "Agamemnon turns as if trying to escape from Hecuba's grasp."[40] Hekabe thus encounters a second Greek hero who turns shy at the prospect of a suppliant's ritual contact. But when the Trojan queen sees that her tears fail to move Agamemnon to action, she realizes that she must resort to the art of persuasion (*peitho*) if she is to succeed. She bases her persuasive effort on Agamemnon's love of Kassandra, Polydoros's sister, and on the mutual affection between Agamemnon and Kassandra (cf. intro. pp. 18–19). Or, as Adkins (1966b: 202) phrases it: "Polydorus . . . is Agamemnon's relative by marriage."

Employing a striking image, Hekabe wishes that her body parts (arms, hands, feet, and hair) each possessed a tongue and could supplicate Agamemnon to uphold justice and punish the wicked Polymestor (836–45).[41] Agamemnon's response: he says he is moved by Hekabe's appeal and sees the justice of her cause,[42] but he fears criticism from his Greek allies, who regard Polymestor as a friend and who might criticize Agamemnon for killing Polymestor to please Kassandra.

Hekabe decides that Agamemnon, like all human beings, is a slave (see her comments, 864–67) and decides to undertake revenge on her own. The irony here is that the slave (Hekabe) is free, whereas the master (Agamemnon) is timorous, bound like a slave. She asks him only to restrain the Greeks when she takes her revenge. Agamemnon doubts that she—a mere old woman and slave—can accomplish such a deed, but Hekabe assures him she can, citing the examples of the daughters of Danaos and the women of Lemnos. Agamemnon exits with a platitudinous wish for justice.

There is no need to describe here Hekabe's revenge on Polymestor or the subsequent development of the action up to the end where Polymestor prophesies Hekabe's future fate. I should mention, however, that Agamemnon does ultimately render a judgment in favor of Hekabe against Polymestor and allows the latter's punishment to stand without him receiving recompense or retaliation.[43] Still, we must ask how different the outcome might have been if Agamemnon had undertaken to punish Polymestor either himself or through the agency of his army rather than deferring to Hekabe's acts of vengeance—acts that many critics have seen as bestializing Hekabe and foreshadowing her ultimate transformation into a female dog.[44] This play suggests that when justice and the law are not upheld, people may resort to their lowest, most savage selves.[45]

In addition to developing the theme of compassion and justice to a high level and displaying the shallowness of the Greek leadership in the persons of Odysseus and Agamemnon, this play also provides prime examples of the compassionate motif of the fall from high to low in the fortunes of Polyxena and Hekabe herself. We may, in fact, say that Hekabe provides the archetype of this motif in this play, although we also see her performing a comparable function in our next play, *Trojan Women.*

Trojan Women

This play, produced around 415 BCE, is notable for its simple plot, which moves from misery to still greater misery with no reversals and hardly any relief from that misery.[46] Although Hekabe is the central character here, as in the play that bears her name, the focus of *Trojan Women* is much broader, encompassing the lot of all the women of Troy and, indeed, of Troy itself. There is, however, a prominent subtheme—the guilt and punishment of the Greek conquerors—that both makes us more sympathetic toward the suffering Trojans and gives those same Trojans a bit of recompense for all their hardship in that their conquerors—some of them, at least—will also suffer somewhere down the line. Kassandra makes this explicit, in fact, at 403–5, where she seeks to comfort her mother with the thought that Agamemnon's future destruction, in which she will indirectly have a hand, means that Troy and Kassandra herself will no longer be the objects of pity (*oiktirein*); the defeat of Troy's conqueror in effect removes Troy's defeat. Misery loves company, especially that of one's enemies.

This subtheme, in fact, is the subject of the play's prologue between Poseidon and Athene. The latter, a stalwart divine ally of the Greeks during the war, has now been alienated from them thanks to the misdeed of Aias Oileus. Poseidon is surprised by this change and asks Athene, "Have you now come to have compassion" (νῦν ἐς οἶκτον ἦλθες) for Troy "since it has been burned to ashes?" (59–60).[47] Athene sidesteps this question and moves on to the business of forming an alliance with Poseidon in order to work her vengeance on the Greeks.[48]

Hekabe and the chorus, in their long opening *kommos*, note repeatedly the piteousness of their common situation, wherein none of them knows her future destiny. Hekabe encapsulates her own story in a brief speech (190–96), in which we see how perfectly she typifies the inherently tragic motif of the fall from high to low: she who once was honored as queen of Troy now has become a slave, an old woman who doesn't even know whom she will serve or what her lowly service will be. Later, in making a prayer to the gods (466–510), she is impelled to tell her story in detail. She says that she will begin first with her blessings so that she can "inject greater pity (*oiktos*, 473) into her troubles." Indeed, as Aristotle and many others have observed, the Greeks from Homer to the end of the Classical period saw the transition from earlier good fortune to later bad fortune as most pitiable. The Greeks felt that one suffered more intensely by falling from prosperity to misery than by living one's whole life in a state of misery (D2, D3). It is as if the knowledge of what one has lost gives one's suffering more edge or poignancy. Hekabe's strategy here is a reflection of the tragic poet's own technique and ultimate goal: to tell a story in such a way as to arouse pity and fear in his audience, as Aristotle described it. The story she then tells is a masterful display of compassion-arousing eloquence (474–510). But such eloquence arouses little compassion in those who matter the most in this story: the Greek captors.

Andromache's pathos, as she tells her own story, is just as great as, if not greater than, that of her mother-in-law (643–83).[49] She narrates her happy life as a model Trojan wife with a wonderful husband. But now we see the poignant dilemma that remains for her even after her tragic loss of husband and home: whether to remain faithful to Hektor's memory or accommodate her new master, whoever he may be. Her narrative contains vivid visualization of the tragic future comparable to that expressed by Homer's Andromache in *Iliad* 6 and by Tekmessa in Sophokles' *Aias.* But her pathos so eloquently expressed is not able to prevent the Greeks from dashing her beloved son, Astyanax, to his death from the Trojan wall (D3).

The one Greek who is capable of feeling broadly humane compassion is, as in *Hekabe,* the messenger Talthybios. But here he bears a cruel message: that Astyanax must die. Talthybios is a voice of reason who counsels acceptance of fate so that Astyanax will at least receive an honorable funeral and burial; he says that otherwise the child will be without both burial and lamentation (*oiktos,* 736). Andromache's keening plaint, so movingly rendered by Vanessa Redgrave in Cacoyannis's classic film, is incapable of arousing saving or inhibiting compassion. Talthybios reluctantly escorts the boy off with a parting observation that such heralding is more fitting for someone less inclined to compassion (*anoiktos*) and more inclined to ruthlessness (*anaideia,* 786–89) than he is. That is the extent of Greek compassion in this drama: a subordinate's inclination to compassion that cannot be enacted and must be suppressed. It is the theme of compassion as inhibitor of cruel action (D1b). As we have seen (cf. intro. pp. 15–17), this type of compassion is often overruled—in tragedy as in life—by the authority of those who require the execution of a cruel job or duty.[50]

After the bizarre *agon* between Hekabe and Helen, the lament and burial of Astyanax provides a sense of closure to the almost overwhelming desolation of this drama. In this play compassion goes underground, as it will continue to be in the next two plays we examine, *Orestes* and *Iphigeneia in Aulis.* It will resurface only to be abused in *Medeia* and in one incident in *Orestes,* but it will achieve positive presence and find voice once again in the final Euripidean tragedy we examine: *Herakles.*

Orestes

In his review of my chapter coauthored with Douglas C. Clapp (Johnson/Clapp 2005), David Rosenbloom notes the problematic nature of this play, saying that it "conspicuously elides pity as a value" (2007: 5). Konstan (2000) also has argued that, in contrast to Sophokles' *Philoktetes,* Euripides' *Orestes* does not make use of explicit appeals for pity (*oiktos* or *eleos*).[51] Euripides, that is, does not have Orestes employ the words for Greek pity (*oiktos, eleos,* or their cognates) when he makes an appeal to Menelaos to intercede on behalf of him and his sister with the people of Argos. The larger point that Konstan seeks to support with this contrast is that Greeks did not appeal for pity to their *philoi,* including their kin. But we have seen and will continue to see in Greek tragic drama appeals for pity or compassion by friends and kinsmen to their friends and kinsmen and also expressions of compassion by one friend or kinsman for another (cf. intro. pp. 18–19). In fact, there is even one such explicit appeal for pity of kinsman to kinsman late in *Orestes* that Konstan does not mention (see below on 1337–43). We will look at that example in the next section of this chapter, but here we examine Orestes' appeal to Menelaos to see whether this can be considered an appeal for pity and whether the author's partial avoidance of pity-language in representing it is significant.

In *Orestes,* the protagonist, as a suppliant, makes a strong appeal to his uncle Menelaos to rescue him and his sister from the angry Argives, who seek vengeance for Klytaimestra's murder (380–455).[52] Orestes' first appeal to Menelaos is based on their blood bond and Menelaos's obligation of reciprocity to Agamemnon (448–55). Menelaos had expressed sympathy for his nephew (447; cf. "poor man," *talas,* 387), but Tyndareos, Klytaimestra's father, intervenes and condemns Orestes; Tyndareos furthermore warns Menelaos not to take action on behalf of his young relatives. Although Orestes answers Tyndareos's condemnation with an argument that places primary responsibility for the murder on Apollo, the god who commanded it, Orestes is clearly shaken by his grandfather's threats to argue for condemnation in the assembly.[53] When Tyndareos exits, Orestes renews his appeal to Menelaos. Again, he begins by emphasizing Menelaos's obligation to Agamemnon—the brother who had helped Menelaos retrieve his stolen wife by ten years of fighting at Troy and by the sacrifice of his own daughter, Iphigeneia (640–79). As he nears the end of his appeal, he intensifies it by kneeling in supplication and emphasizing his own misery: he begs and refers to his own misery and "trouble" (*kakon*) and imagines his dead father hearing this and even hovering above, reinforcing his son's pleas (671–79).[54] The chorus of Argive women also add their plea for Menelaos to intervene.[55] Is Orestes' speech not a plea for compassion? Orestes, I would argue, unnerved by Tyndareos's threats, now resorts to a full supplication and appeals for his uncle to pity him and show compassion. It is a plea for compassion in all but word only. After his appeal for aid based purely on reciprocal favor (*charis*) has fallen short, Orestes, still using those claims to buttress his appeal, supplicates his uncle (ἱκνοῦμαι σ,' 670) to show him compassion as a fellow human being in distress. The absence of explicit pity-language seems hardly significant. In fact, might not Euripides have used Orestes' lack of such language to make him seem yet more pitiable?

Menelaos, in his lengthy reply (682–715), begins by expressing his respect for Orestes' claims (*kataidoumai,* 682) and says that he "desires to share in" Orestes' "misfortunes" (ξυμπονῆσαι σοῖς κακοῖσι βούλομαι, 683). And he proceeds to acknowledge the force of his obligation to Orestes: the blood tie that requires him to do all he can to defend his nephew, even at the cost of his own life. But after these initial words of sympathetic support and dedication to his obligations, Menelaos begins to back away from his commitments by pleading weakness and by advocating moderation, diplomacy, and tact. As "reasonable" as such a stance may appear, the sententious, roundabout rhetoric that Euripides has Menelaos employ in defense of this position in contrast to the noble words that began his speech results in a tone that seems false, distant, and insincere: word and deed are not commensurate.[56] Orestes labels Menelaos's hesitancy as betrayal and cowardice (717–24, 736, 745–54; cf. 1056–59), and Menelaos's baseness becomes a foil for Pylades' noble expressions of willingness to suffer for his friend (768–806).[57]

Later, Elektra and Orestes themselves reflect on the pitiableness of their condemnation by the Argives (e.g., 1018–34). Elektra even generalizes: "For all mortals, their dear life is pitiable" (*oiktron*, 1034). But note that Orestes here uses the masculine rejection of "feminine lamentations" (τοὺς γυναικείους γόους, 1022) in favor of heroic endurance in the face of the inevitable self-sacrifice to which they have been condemned (cf. D6). Still, brother and sister find that their mutual love consoles their misery (1041–51).

The explicit appeal for compassion from a family member that I mentioned earlier appears at 1337–43, where Elektra appeals to the returning Hermione: "Pity us" (οἴκτιρον ἡμᾶς, 1341), she says. But note that this appeal is disingenuous in that Elektra is using it to lure Hermione into the trap in which she will become the hostage of Elektra, Orestes, and Pylades. We'll look at this deceptive use of an appeal for compassion a little later (see below, p. 130). I cite it here to show that Euripides has no hesitancy in having a cousin appeal explicitly for compassion from her cousin, even though Orestes had for whatever reason avoided explicitly using *oiktiron* ("pity me") in his appeal to Menelaos earlier.[58] Citing it here also prompts me to make a further point about the failure of that earlier appeal; the play ends with Orestes and company taking desperate action—even kidnapping the innocent Hermione and holding her hostage. One way to interpret this ending would be to conclude that if Menelaos had used his influence to persuade the Argive assembly to show compassion or mercy to his niece and nephew (D1b), his young relatives might not have needed to resort to the desperate measures that they ended up using. Indeed, Apollo, as deus ex machina, resolves the action in a way that rewards Orestes and Elektra and Pylades rather than punishing them; also, he accepts responsibility for the killings of Klytaimestra and Aigisthos and promises to resolve Argive ill will toward Orestes and Elektra. In this case, as in the two cases of Hekabe's appeals to Odysseus and Agamemnon in *Hekabe*, a hero's failure to respond to an appeal for compassion turns out to have devastating or near-devastating consequences.[59]

Iphigeneia in Aulis

In Euripides' *Iphigeneia in Aulis,* compassion functions both as a strong feeling of restraint and as an element of heroic *aretê.* Early in the play Agamemnon has second thoughts about sacrificing his daughter and secretly attempts to warn Klytaimestra not to bring Iphigeneia to Aulis, but the message is intercepted by Menelaos, who confronts Agamemnon with it and accuses him of betraying the Greek mission. As they are arguing, a messenger enters to announce that Klytaimestra and Iphigeneia have already arrived at the army's camp. As the messenger exits, Agamemnon breaks down as he considers the prospect of facing his wife and children with the true reason for their being brought to Aulis. Among the emotions he expresses is a strong feeling of pity for Iphigeneia: "How I pity her!" (ὡς ᾤκτισ'), he says (460–62). Agamemnon's response also has an effect on Menelaos: the sight of Agamemnon's weeping arouses a feeling of sympathy in his brother ("I myself felt compassion," ἐγώ . . . ᾤκτιρα) and causes him to put aside his strife with Agamemnon (477–80). As a further result of his state of empathy (480), Menelaos asks Agamemnon not to go through with the sacrifice of the girl (481–82). He also acknowledges a strong feeling of compassion (*eleos*) for the girl, a feeling that came upon him when he was made to realize the horrible implications of her impending slaughter (489–92). Part of this feeling was due to the kinship between Menelaos and Iphigeneia (492; cf. intro. pp. 18–19).[60] The chorus praise Menelaos for this change (505–6),[61] but in spite of Menelaos's turnabout, Agamemnon comes to the conclusion that there is an unavoidable compulsion to carry out the sacrifice, a compulsion that he imagines the entire army enforcing (511–14). Later, when Agamemnon must face the innocent and unknowing girl, he experiences lamentation/grief (*oiktos,* 653) and can hardly disguise his emotion, which he attempts to ascribe to the feelings of a father about to lose his daughter in marriage (644–53, 681–90, cf. D6).[62] When Klytaimestra and Iphigeneia learn of Iphigeneia's impending sacrifice, they each make speeches before Agamemnon: Iphigeneia's is a supplication in which she earnestly begs her father to show compassion (αἴδεσαί με καὶ κατοίκτιρον βίου, 1246) and spare her life.[63] Such feelings of compassion (*oiktra*, 1255), which Agamemnon acknowledges, cannot, however, overcome Agamemnon's fear of the army's reprisal (1255–75). This is an example of the failure of compassion as restraining force (D1b). It is unusual here in that (1) Agamemnon is a commander with a cruel task rather than a subordinate and (2) the cruel task is the sacrifice of his own daughter. Agamemnon's denial of compassion has the potential of being very tragic, but Euripides' characterization of him makes him a less than fully sympathetic character, and Iphigeneia ends up volunteering to die. But remembering the tradition followed by Aischylos, we assume Agamemnon will pay a price later.

A subtle Euripidean elaboration of compassion as a motive for heroic saving action (D1a) also occurs in *Iphigeneia in Aulis.* When Klytaimestra and Akhilleus learn of the false pretense of marriage and the real purpose for Iphigeneia coming to Aulis, Klytaimestra appeals to Akhilleus to protect Iphigeneia. She assumes the full suppliant position, and she argues that since Iphigeneia is ostensibly Akhilleus's betrothed, her death will reflect badly on his name (900–16). Akhilleus promises his compassion as a protection (*oiktos*, 934),[64] but then he takes up Klytaimestra's suggestion that his own reputation is involved in defending the girl. As his speech proceeds, it becomes obvious that this is a much more important consideration for him than any feelings of compassion that he might have for the girl or her mother; in fact, he explicitly acknowledges as much (959–61). As Akhilleus lowers his voice and begins talking to himself in the next few lines, he suggests that he might have agreed to the deception and entrapment of Iphigeneia, if he had been told *in advance* of the plan to use his name as a lure. But now he has been made a fool of, and his reputation has been damaged. It is the slight to his reputation that he feels here and not so much compassion for Iphigeneia herself. Akhilleus's concern for his reputation and his compassion for Iphigeneia are not necessarily mutually exclusive—indeed, as we have seen, they normally go together in instances of active compassion—but here Euripides points to an imbalance between the weight of the two motives.[65] Nevertheless, Akhilleus does show himself willing to protect Iphigeneia, and this, rather than purity of motive, is what Klytaimestra is looking for.

As she renews her plea for his assistance, Klytaimestra speaks in general terms of the enhancement of reputation that comes to the good man (*chrestos*) who helps the unfortunate (*dustuchountes*, 983–84).[66] "Pity (*oiktire*) us," she says, "for we have suffered pitiable things" (*oiktra*, 985). When she offers to have Iphigeneia herself supplicate him, Akhilleus—ever mindful of appearances—shows his eagerness to avoid any suggestion of immodesty that might inspire gossip among the troops. Akhilleus then backs off a bit and suggests that Klytaimestra should first approach Agamemnon and attempt to use reasonable persuasion (1011–15) and then, as a last resort, she should call on his arms (1016). If he can be left out of the process, he adds, it will spare him the army's reproach (1020). This is somewhat reminiscent of Menelaos in *Orestes*, although Akhilleus does not refuse to take up arms but rather seeks to avoid conflict if possible. Later Akhilleus returns to report that the troops, including even his Myrmidons, insisted on Iphigeneia's sacrifice and even threatened to stone him when he tried to speak in her defense. Iphigeneia, at this point, decides to accept her death by saying she will devote herself to Artemis (cf. D6). Akhilleus leaves, after pledging that he will defend Iphigeneia's life to the very end, should she request it, but, of course, his pledge is never put to the test. The text indicates that Artemis spared the girl at the last moment.[67]

In this play, we find a failure of restraining compassion when Agamemnon cannot withstand the pressures of the army to deny compassion to his daughter Iphigeneia; also, Akhilleus is less than fully heroic in his pledge of heroic compassion to save the young girl from sacrifice. The girl's own courageous acceptance of her need to die permits Akhilleus to avoid confrontation with the army while saving face—his utmost concern.

Summary and Discussion of Other Examples of Compassion Denied or Not Felt

In the four plays we have examined in this section, compassion is denied or appealed for in vain. In some cases, such as *Hekabe* and *Orestes,* the denial of compassion has devastating consequences and reveals the baseness of such characters as Odysseus and Menelaos, respectively. In *Women of Troy,* the lack of compassion is part and parcel of the ruthlessness of war, as indicated by the plethora of laments and the rarity of expressions of compassion. In *Iphigeneia in Aulis,* the failure of compassion reveals the shallow, self-absorbed heroism of Akhilleus. In some cases, those of Talthybios in *Women of Troy,* Akhilleus in *Hekabe,* and Agamemnon in *Iphigeneia in Aulis,* the requirement of harsh duty compels an individual to shunt aside the compassion that restrains him from carrying out a merciless act. We saw this theme in Aischylos's *Prometheus Bound* and will see it again in Sophoklean drama.

Elsewhere in Euripidean tragedy where compassion might be expected, the lack of it may be correspondingly decried. In Euripides' *Ion,* the old man asks Kreousa how she could have exposed her child to die in the cave. When she answers that she did it casting forth "many pitiful words" (οἰκτρὰ πολλὰ . . . ἔπη), the old man accuses her of hard-heartedness (*tolme*), presumably because her compassion did not extend to the *action* of sparing the child (958–60, cf. D6). In *Bacchae,* Pentheus asks his mother to pity him (*oiktire,* 1120), but she, because of her possession by the vengeful god, fails even to recognize her son and exhibits no such emotion. Later, Agaue feels horror, as she comes to realize what she has done. In *Hippolytos,* Theseus explicitly denies that pity (*oiktos,* 1089) has come over him to make him change his mind about banishing his son, although he will later regret the banishment.[68] In these instances, the temporary lack of compassion results eventually in the sorrow of the one who lacked it.

There are also examples of characters who do not seem to feel the restraining power of compassion at all (D1b) but who openly violate the sanctity of suppliants. In Euripides' *Andromache,* Menelaos pries the heroine from her altar of asylum by holding her young son hostage. The chorus of Thessalian women express compassion (*ôiktir'*), explaining that tribulations such as those suffered by Andromache should seem "pitiful" (*oiktra*) to all mortals, even to those who are not kin (421–22). They advise Menelaos to bring about a reconciliation that will spare Andromache misfortune. Menelaos ignores these words of advice, has his men seize

Andromache, and then reveals that he will not necessarily spare her son but will leave the decision up to his daughter, Andromache's bitter rival and the source of her persecution by Menelaos. As a result of this treachery, Andromache scathingly reproaches the Spartans, in general, and Menelaos, in particular, whose heroism in threatening a defenseless woman she ridicules (445–63).[69] Likewise, in Euripides' *Herakles,* Lykos plans to kill Herakles' father, wife, and children, even though they are suppliants at the altar of Zeus. He is condemned by the chorus of elder Thebans as being godless and an alien who has usurped power over the city of Thebes (252–74). Megara characterizes him as brutal and contrasts him with the noble wise men (*sophoi*) who are disposed to show *aidôs* (299–301).[70] Such forthright violators of suppliants are thus painted in villainous guise.[71]

Compassion Abused

We have seen up to now how tragic drama, by the nature of its plots and themes of human frailty and disaster, was disposed toward the arousal of sympathy in its audience and also how—through its presentation of appeals for compassion, by suppliants and others, and the granting of compassionate aid—it tended to commend and depict as noble those who showed compassion to others in need and to decry those who did not. But because the suppliant had such powerful persuasive forces at his or her disposal—religious sanctions as well as claims of reciprocity—and because the exhibition of compassion was reinforced by praise and the attribution of nobility, appeals for compassion also contained the potential for abuse. There was always the risk that a treacherous suppliant would arouse pity to perverse ends. This no doubt caused anxiety and ambivalence on the part of Athenians, since they believed that they were especially subject to being moved by such appeals. What if the person asking for compassion was treacherous or intended harm to those he or she appealed to, or had other devious plans?[72]

Euripides, ever the "realist," explores this possibility at length in *Medeia* and in one incident in *Orestes.* In *Medeia,* we see a treacherous appeal used, not once, but twice. First, after Kreon has announced Medeia's banishment from Corinth, Medeia assumes the suppliant pose and begs Kreon to allow her to stay only one day to make provision for her children before their exile (271–347). Appealing specifically for her children, she pleads, "Pity them!" (οἴκτιρε δ'αὐτοὺς, 344); she strengthens this appeal by noting that Kreon himself has children and by asserting that her concern is for the children's misfortune, not her own (344–347).[73] The king has already expressed twice his fear of Medeia and his need to expel her before she can harm him (282–91, 316–23). When her supplication causes him to relent and to grant the short reprieve (D1b), he again expresses anxiety about his change, remarking how his *aidôs* has harmed him in the past and showing a momentary prescience of the calamity to come (348–51). After Kreon has left the stage, Medeia confirms the deadly duplicity of her suppliant stance (370–75) and sets her plan in motion.[74]

Later in the play, Medeia makes a second supplication: she begs Aigeus to give her asylum in Athens and promises to end his childlessness in recompense (708–18).[75] Aigeus agrees, swears an oath demanded of him by Medeia that he will protect her from her enemies (D1a), and in turn is praised by the chorus as being "noble" (*gennaios,* 762).[76] Aigeus, as king of Athens, no doubt was intended to remind the Athenian audience of Athens' heritage as the sanctuary of suppliants, but any glory that the praise of Aigeus may have reflected on them was likely undercut by their remembrance of the tradition of Medeia in Athens: how she would later plot to murder Theseus.[77] Medeia also sends the children as suppliants bearing gifts to the princess, gifts that will work the latter's gruesome death. Kreon, in his attempt to save his daughter, only ends up sharing her death.[78] All attempts to show compassion in this play sooner or later recoil upon the one who pities.

I do not mean to suggest here, however, that Medeia is totally in the wrong in her use of devious appeals for compassion: as feminist critics have shown, she has considerable justice on her side regarding Jason's insulting mistreatment of her; also, Kreon has ordered her to go into exile. Furthermore, her weakness as a woman who is threatened by the king's far greater power suggests that she must resort to underhanded methods, including the use of poison, to fight back.[79] Above all, I agree with March's sympathetic reading of Medeia's tragic dilemma when faced with killing her children and with March's conclusions about the end of the play, including her statement that Jason becomes in the end a character whom we pity (1990: 38–43; cf. D6).

Orestes (2)

Another example of a treacherous appeal for compassion in Euripides is that by Elektra to Hermione in *Orestes* (1337–43).[80] Here, the young people under duress use deceit to capture an innocent hostage. Ironically, Hermione is the most decent person around; she readily accedes to Elektra's request for compassion. Ultimately, however, she is spared and rewarded at the end of the play with marriage to Orestes, her captor. These examples show that appeals for compassion may be abused by those with hostile ulterior motives and that they are sometimes properly regarded with suspicion.[81]

Human Compassion in Defiance of Divine Spite: *Herakles*

At the end of Euripides' *Herakles,* Theseus comes to the aid of and shows compassion to his friend Herakles. Here, we find an instance of compassion that differs both situationally and qualitatively from the display of compassion in most Greek tragedies. First of all, the recipient of compassion is not a suppliant. Herakles, rather than seeking out Theseus for his assistance, is instead offered that assistance through Theseus's initiative.[82] In fact, Theseus has to impose his assistance on Herakles, in a way: Herakles is resistant to aid and seeks to hide from Theseus at first. Second, the display of compassion, unlike that in most suppliant plays, does not require or anticipate the display of martial *aretê.*[83] When Theseus arrives, there does not seem to be any other immediate human threat to Herakles or to Theseus for assisting him: Herakles himself has decisively defeated Lycos and his friends, and the divine threat seems to have run its course with Herakles' humiliation through the agency of Iris and Lyssa.[84] The threat comes instead from what Herakles has done in his madness, the harm he has done to his loved ones—his wife and children—and, by extension, to himself. Herakles' grief for his loved ones and his guilt and shame concerning his own acts of violence (regardless of Hera's role in causing them) drive him to a suicidal wish.[85]

At the same time, Theseus's exhibition of compassion in this play does maintain some standard features of Greek heroic compassion and *philia,* notably reciprocity. But I shall further argue in part 2 below that this play departs somewhat from the heroic standard of epic and early tragedy by also portraying a more finely nuanced type of friendship between the two characters—one contrasting with the more formal, remote type of *philia* typically enacted in epic and in the tragic drama of Aischylos and early Sophokles and one in keeping with Euripides' acknowledged emphasis on the humanity of his heroes.[86]

1

Let us begin by looking at some of the more standard features of Greek heroic compassion and *philia* that Euripides exploits in the play, especially his use of reciprocity. Theseus's initial motive for assisting Herakles is based on Herakles' previous *euergesia* to him: Herakles' rescue of Theseus from Hades.[87] Theseus's initial mode of action is heroic: he enters, having come on a military exploit to help his friend Herakles defeat Lykos who, he had heard, had usurped the throne of Thebes and was in the process of waging war against Herakles' Theban allies (1163–68). Theseus's motive for bringing such assistance is based on reciprocity, a standard element in Greek *philia* and Greek compassion.[88] Theseus says explicitly that he comes to repay Herakles (τίνων ἀμοιβάς) for saving him from the underworld and that he comes in case Herakles has need of Theseus's personal assistance or that of allies (1169–71).[89] Note that his motive is expressed in explicitly reciprocal terms.[90]

Their friendship, in fact, seems to be founded on Herakles' initial good deed, "of which things Herakles made a beginning" (ὧν ὑπῆρξεν Ἡρακλῆς, 1169).

The reciprocity theme emerges again as Theseus dismisses Herakles' gesture of warning about "pollution" (*musos,* 1219) by asserting that he doesn't care if he shares in Herakles' suffering. He is willing to incur suffering along with his friend—since Herakles had once rescued him from the underworld:

> οὐδὲν μέλει μοι σύν γε σοὶ πράσσειν κακῶς·
> καὶ γάρ ποτ' εὐτύχησ.' ἐκεῖσ' ἀνοιστέον
> ὅτ' ἐξέσωσάς μ' ἐς φάος νεκρῶν πάρα. (1220–22)

> It doesn't bother me to suffer harm, not with you, at any rate. For once I fared well with you: I have to recall that time when you rescued me into the light from the dead.

Note the nature of the reciprocity invoked here: Herakles had saved Theseus's life; consequently, Theseus is willing to risk his life for Herakles, as if the lease on life granted by Herakles has given him a debt that he now gladly will repay.[91]

Theseus then expands upon this ideal of reciprocal *philia* (or *charis*) by describing two types of inadequate or unworthy friendship: he criticizes short-lived *charis,* which soon forgets the benefactions of friends, and he criticizes the fair-weather friendship of one who is eager to share his (or her) friend's prosperity but is unwilling to share his (or her) troubles:

> χάριν δὲ γηράσκουσαν ἐχθαίρω φίλων
> καὶ τῶν καλῶν μὲν ὅστις ἀπολαύειν θέλει,
> συμπλεῖν δὲ τοῖς φίλοισι δυστυχοῦσιν οὔ. (1223–25)

> I hate friends' gratitude that grows old, and anyone who willingly shares in the good things, but won't share the boat of friends who are unlucky.

By contrast, Theseus's friendship shows no such limits. The occasion for this display of *charis* is Herakles' suicidal crisis: Theseus, therefore, is no "fair-weather friend." In fact, as we have seen, he is willing himself to incur suffering, even death, for the sake of his friend (cf. the discussion of 1169–71, above). This willingness to die is in accordance with the willingness of heroes to take risks and even to sacrifice themselves for the sake of others.

In his first address to Herakles at 1214–28, Theseus emphasizes their friendship[92] and also displays his empathy in emphasizing the greatness of Herakles' misery. But he also shows the inadequacy of Herakles' futile attempt at self-concealment: "Your misery is so great and so clearly visible to all that not even the blackest of clouds could cover it," he says, in effect. Theseus is even somewhat impatient with Herakles' refusal to look at him: "Uncover that miserable head of yours (ἄθλιον κάρα) and look at us!" Then a reminder of proper heroic decorum: the truly noble man (ὅστις εὐγενὴς βροτῶν) bears the miseries that the gods send and does not deny them (1227–28).[93] By implication he is accusing Herakles of a kind of cowardice. Herakles' response to Theseus's assertion suggests that he understands and agrees with it and is properly grateful for Theseus's offer of assistance: "Thank you. And I don't regret that I have benefited you [and, therefore, have earned your friendship and your help]" (ἐπῄνεσ'· εὖ δράσας δέ σ' οὐκ ἀναίνομαι, 1235).[94] This statement is a strong emotional expression of gratitude.

Theseus's response keeps their relationship in precisely reciprocal terms and shows that compassion is the appropriate next step: "And I, being treated well by you then, now feel compassion for you" (ἐγὼ δὲ πάσχων εὖ τότ' οἰκτίρω σε νῦν, 1236).[95] Note that compassion here is seen as a benefit or, at least, as an emotion that will motivate beneficial action on the part of the compassionate individual. Theseus explicitly ties the two behaviors together temporally ("then" and "now") and qualitatively (good treatment brings about compassion, i.e., good treatment). This line also makes clear that compassion is an explicit element of Theseus's actions in this scene: it is both part of his motivation to assist Herakles, and it is likely to be an element implicit in his subsequent acts of assistance as well.[96]

Herakles responds to Theseus's expression of compassion by inquiring about the appropriateness of his feeling that emotion for a child-killer: "Am I pitiable, I who have killed my children?" (οἰκτρὸς γάρ εἰμι τἄμ' ἀποκτείνας τέκνα, 1237). With this question Herakles suggests that as the killer of his children, he may deserve, not compassion, but revulsion.[97] But Theseus replies that he weeps for Herakles' sake, "for your worsened circumstances" (ἐφ' ἑτέραισι συμφοραῖς, 1238), a phrase that suggests a concern for the comprehensiveness of Herakles' troubles as well as suggesting the traditional tragic dynamic, the precipitous fall from high to low, which Herakles has just now experienced.[98] Herakles then seeks to gauge his friend's sense of that misfortune when he asks whether Theseus has seen others (ἄλλους) who have had bigger troubles. Theseus's response that Herakles' troubles reach the sky makes it clear that he has not.

Herakles' first long speech of his debate with Theseus shows the depth of Herakles' sorrow and sense of disgrace (1255–1310). Herakles reviews his troubled family background, his birth and Hera's enmity, and his rigorous labors. Herakles regards this, his killing of his children, as his "final labor" (τὸν λοίσθιον . . . πόνον, 1279).[99] He then considers his future prospects: a life to be characterized by exile, shame, and disrepute, a projection that culminates in his imaginative vision of his alienation from even the earth and sea themselves, a truly fundamental alienation from the cosmos: he will have no place to go, no place to hide.

> ἐς τοῦτο δ' ἥξειν συμφορᾶς οἶμαί ποτε·
> φωνὴν γὰρ ἥσει χθὼν ἀπεννέπουσά με
> μὴ θιγγάνειν γῆς καὶ θάλασσα μὴ περᾶν
> πηγαί τε ποταμῶν, καὶ τὸν ἁρματήλατον
> 'Ιξίον' ἐν δεσμοῖσιν ἐκμιμήσομαι. (1294–98)

> I think that someday I will come to this point: the earth will send forth her voice forbidding me to touch the land, and the sea and the river streams [will forbid me] to cross them, and I will imitate Ixion spinning on a wheel in chains.

He is led to conclude that he has no reason to continue living—that suicide is his only option.[100] "Let Hera celebrate in her victory over me—the first man of Greece," he says, but he also asks, "Who can pray to such a goddess?"—a goddess who, out of jealousy for a human rival, has thoroughly ("roots and all") destroyed the innocent benefactor of Greece (τοὺς εὐεργέτας / Ἑλλάδος ἀπώλεσ' οὐδὲν ὄντας αἰτίους, 1309–10).[101]

After beginning with an odd argument about the gods' acceptance of their own fallibility,[102] Theseus then proceeds to offer Herakles refuge in Athens—a place where Herakles will receive purification, hospitality, and even gifts befitting his stature as a great hero and friend of Theseus. Theseus is remarkably generous here, even by heroic standards: he will give Herakles houses and part of his wealth, even the prizes that Theseus received from the Athenians as a reward for his rescue of young Athenians from the Minotaur. Furthermore, Theseus will grant Herakles plots of his own land in the countryside. Finally, Athens will honor Herakles with sacrifices and stone monuments upon his death.[103] He then explains an additional motivation for this beneficence: there will be glory for the city, since benefiting a noble man brings a beautiful crown to a city: καλὸς γὰρ ἀστοῖς στέφανος Ἑλλήνων ὕπο / ἄνδρ' ἐσθλὸν ὠφλοῦντας εὐκλείας τυχεῖν (1334–35). Here, we find the common notion that *euergesia,* seen here as a type of civic *aretê,* brings glory (metaphorically, a beautiful crown, *kalos stephanos*) to the city, just as the *aretê* of the individual hero brings him *timê* and *kleos.*[104] The status of the recipient also has an effect: the greater the nobility of the recipient (here, the noble Herakles), the greater the *eukleia* that comes from benefiting him.[105]

On a more personal level, Theseus characterizes this as a simple reciprocal transaction: by assisting Herakles, he will repay Herakles' good deed of saving his life in the underworld.

> κἀγὼ χάριν σοι τῆς ἐμῆς σωτηρίας
> τήνδ' ἀντιδώσω· νῦν γὰρ εἶ χρεῖος φίλων. (1336–37)

> And I will give this favor to you in return for my salvation;
> for now you have need of friends!

The language he uses emphasizes reciprocity: χάριν is a word that inherently connotes reciprocity, and ἀντιδώσω means literally "I will give in return"; furthermore, the phrase, "this favor/

gift" (χάριν . . . τήνδε), Theseus's gift, neatly encloses the phrase "for my salvation" (τῆς ἐμῆς σωτηρίας), which encapsulates Herakles' benefit to Theseus. Finally, Theseus succinctly summarizes Herakles' need at this point: "For now you have need of friends!" (νῦν γὰρ εἶ χρεῖος φίλων).[106]

Theseus's argument about Herakles' heroic status (and the behavior appropriate to that status) wins the day. Herakles expresses the fear that suicide will give him a reputation of cowardice (1347–48), also that the man who cannot face misfortune (*sumphorai*) cannot face the attack of an enemy (i.e., that misfortune is a less formidable adversary or challenge than an enemy on the battlefield and therefore will bring him disgrace if he fails to meet the challenge it brings). He asserts, therefore, that he will have the courage to face life (ἐγκαρτερήσω βίοτον, 1351).[107] He accepts Theseus's offer of sanctuary in Athens and expresses his gratitude: "I feel immense gratitude for your gifts" (χάριν τε μυρίαν δώρων ἔχω, 1352), in proper reciprocal fashion.

2

A close examination of the play's final episode also reveals an intricate and subtly human interplay of compassion and friendship between the two heroes. As well as being a hero and representative of Athens, Theseus is presented as a compassionate human being, a man of warmth, sincerity, and sensitivity. He is sympathetic to Amphitryon and Herakles. As Amphitryon unfolds to him the horrible truth about what Herakles has done, Theseus shows appropriate shock and sympathetic concern (1179–84). By referring to Amphitryon's pitiable tone of address (οἰκτροῖς . . . προοιμίοις, 1179), Theseus shows his sensitivity to Amphitryon's sorrowful mood. He also displays awareness of the depth of Herakles' misery: "Oh, oh! What man has been so unfortunate?" (φεῦ φεῦ· τίς ἀνδρῶν ὧδε δυσδαίμων ἔφυ, 1195).[108]

Herakles hides his head out of shame before Theseus's friendship and kinship. We can recall Herakles' initial reluctance to be helped by Theseus where he began by calling attention to Theseus's closeness to him as his kin (*suggenês*) and his friend (*philos*, 1154).

Amphitryon here echoes this closeness in referring to their "kin-born friendship" (φιλίαν ὁμόφυλον, 1200).[109] But this very closeness gives rise to two intense fears in Herakles: (1) the fear of being seen in a state of disgrace, a fear that relates to the shame of dishonor, the standard heroic fear,[110] and (2) the religious fear of polluting his closest friend, a traditional guilt-based anxiety.[111] On learning this, Theseus is almost indignant that his sympathy has been undervalued: "But what if I've come to share his pain? Uncover him!" (ἀλλ' εἰ συναλγῶν γ' ἦλθον; ἐκκάλυπτέ νιν, 1202). His immediate call to action displays his decisiveness.[112] Amphitryon refers to Theseus as a "force matching Herakles' tears" that has come "to join Herakles in his struggle" (βάρος ἀντίπαλον δακρύοις συναμιλλᾶται, 1205). He thereby gives a sense of Theseus's power, commitment, and sympathy for Herakles, while also conveying a sense of balance and reciprocity.

Lines 1241–1254 develop Herakles' renewed determination to commit suicide and Theseus's resistance to that intention.[113] When Theseus accuses him of speaking like "an ordinary person," Herakles chides him for giving advice when he feels no pain—the notion that one must share in the suffering to earn the privilege of giving advice.

> Θη. εἴρηκας ἐπιτυχόντος ἀνθρώπου λόγους.
> Ηρ. σὺ δ' ἐκτὸς ὢν γε συμφορᾶς με νουθετεῖς.
> (1248–49)

THESEUS: You have spoken the words of an ordinary person.
HERAKLES: But you, free from misfortune, are giving me advice.

In other words, Herakles says, "Back off, friend."[114] Theseus, however, tries a different tack, an appeal to Herakles' status and reputation as a hero: "Does the Great Herakles, who endured so much, say these things?" (ὁ πολλὰ δὴ τλὰς Ἡρακλῆς λέγει τάδε, 1250), and "Is this the great benefactor and friend of mankind?" (εὐεργέτης βροτοῖσι καὶ μέγας φίλος, 1252). When Herakles claims that he is beyond human rescue since Hera controls his fate (1253), Theseus responds that Hellas will not let Herakles die through an act of stupidity on his part.[115] These are tough words for a tough situation: the impending suicide of a great hero.[116] Theseus's emphasis on Herakles' heroic nature and status provides a handle for pulling the hero out of his self-destructive tailspin.

Theseus's generous offer of sanctuary and honors brings to Herakles a new humility: Herakles admits that, in all his trials and conquests, he has never shed tears as he does now, nor has he had to surrender to fortune as now (τῇ τύχῃ δουλευτέον, 1357).[117] As Herakles addresses his father and gives him final instructions (1358–77), the audience surely must feel great sympathy for the hero. He is very moving as he spells out how he wants his loved ones buried and as he tells his father to live on in Thebes, despite his misery in doing so.[118] The pathos of this speech is then intensified to still another level by Herakles' poignant address to his children and wife, in which he admits his role in their destruction, contrary to what they deserved and to what he wanted for them. This brings him around again to his own grief and sense of separation from them: "How miserably am I unyoked from my children and wife!" (ὡς ἀθλίως πέπραγα κἀποζεύγνυμαι / τέκνων γυναικός τ,' 1375–76).

His mention of the companionship (*koinôniai*) of his weapons is a bittersweet and ironic reminder of his loss of his family's companionship. As Barlow notes, his address to his weapons and personification of them (they even speak!) parallels Philoktetes' address to his bow in Sophokles' *Philoktetes* (1128). His feelings toward his weapons are starkly ambivalent: they are the instruments with which he slaughtered his family, but they are also the instruments of his glorious achievements and his necessary security against future enemies. Consequently, he accepts the necessity of keeping them.

Contrary to what most other scholars say, Herakles' request that Theseus help him convey Kerberos to Argos from Demeter's grove in Hermione (1386–88, cf. 615) does two things: (1) it shows Herakles' willingness to undertake his heroic labor once again, and (2) it provides an opportunity for further solidifying the *philia* between the two heroes by providing them with a joint task.[119] Also, as Chalk (1962) and Bond (1981) note, Herakles does not want to be alone in his grief, possibly due to a lingering fear of suicide. Herakles ends his speech with a final farewell to Thebes and its people, and a final description of his and their shared misery at the hand of Hera.

As Theseus and Herakles depart in the exodos, Theseus bears further witness to the dominating power of fortune: "For fortune brings down even the strong" (καὶ τοὺς σθένοντας γὰρ καθαιροῦσιν τύχαι, 1396). Herakles comes out with a final death wish: I wish I could turn to stone and forget my troubles. Theseus responds with another word of correction and comfort: Stop talking like that! Give your hand to your friend who is here to help. Herakles, still stunned, brings up yet again the possibility of pollution: "But may I not wipe off my blood on your robes!" (ἀλλ' αἷμα μὴ σοῖς ἐξομόρξωμαι πέπλοις, 1399). Theseus, heroically and also somewhat comically, responds to his friend's warning: "Go ahead! Smear me all you like! I don't refuse it" (ἔκμασσε, φείδου μηδέν· οὐκ ἀναίνομαι, 1400). He displays a confident assurance here but also a continuing willingness to accept the costs of friendship (cf. above, n.111).

When Herakles claims Theseus as his surrogate son to compensate for those he lost, Theseus invites Herakles to lean on him, and Herakles does so. Herakles characterizes this "yoking" as something dear to him (ζεῦγός γε φίλιον, 1403), although he also expresses his keen sense of their disproportionate fates. When he then tells his father that Theseus is the sort of man one must have as a friend—in other words, that Theseus exemplifies the ideal of friendship—Amphitryon replies that Athens is blessed (εὔτεκνος) in her sons: ἡ γὰρ τεκοῦσα τόνδε πατρὶς εὔτεκνος (1405).[120] Herakles, still lingering, wavers between moments of deep dejection and grief and moments of tentative but determined persistence; his emotional instability is fully understandable, given what he has been through.

When Theseus yet again calls Herakles back from his dejection by saying that he is acting womanish and risking condemnation, Herakles responds by asking if he has fallen so low and asserts that Theseus did not always think so. When Theseus then says that Herakles is not the illustrious Herakles of former times, Herakles is yet sharp enough to turn the tables on Theseus by reminding him of his own moment of deep despair in the underworld.

> Ηρ. σὺ ποῖος ἦσθα νέρθεν ἐν κακοῖσιν ὤν;
> Θη. ὡς ἐς τὸ λῆμα παντὸς ἦν ἥσσων ἀνήρ.
> Ηρ. πῶς οὖν ἔτ' εἴπης ὅτι συνέσταλμαι κακοῖς.
> (1414–16)

HERAKLES: What sort of man were you when you were in trouble down below?
THESEUS: I was the least of men in spirit!
HERAKLES: How then can you say that I've been lessened by my troubles?

Theseus has to admit that, yes, he acted just as weakly then, when Herakles was the strong rescuer. This exchange restores the emotional equilibrium and equity between the two heroes.[121]

But when Herakles wants to extend this argument further with another question, Theseus cuts him off and says that it is time to go; Herakles accepts his friend's guidance and says farewell to his father. Herakles ends with a striking image and a generalization: he, the utterly destroyed one, will follow Theseus like a small boat being towed by a larger one, an admission of his psychological weakness and dependence, but also an image with a saving irony, as the spectator reflects on the sheer bulk of the hero in Theseus's tow as they begin their exit. The hero also adds that whoever values money or power above friends is foolish, an assertion of the persistent value of *philia*.[122]

In this scene Theseus has played the role of the *aristos philos*. He provides the verbal assurance and comfort that his suffering friend needs;[123] he offers to risk and sacrifice himself to help his friend, if necessary; he provides for his friend's needs by granting him sanctuary and assurance of support; and he also provides the criticism and chastisement that Herakles needs when he becomes overly dejected and self-piteous. His compassion for Herakles is behind all this; it is the compassion and concern of one good friend for another.

This play depicts compassion between heroic *philoi* in a deeply human way: compassion is shown in the course of an interaction between two great heroes who share mutual admiration for each other. This mutual admiration and respect is evident even in the somewhat playful bantering that Theseus uses to persuade Herakles to give up his plan to commit suicide and to accept Theseus's offer of purification and asylum instead. This is not to say that there are not moments of tension and stress in their relationship.[124] The situation in which they find themselves is so critical that there is bound to be stress between any two individuals; we certainly are not surprised to find it in two "prickly-ego" types like Herakles and Theseus. Yes, there are bumps in the road as Theseus maneuvers Herakles from an earnest determination to die to a still somewhat unsteady resolution to live. The seriousness of the crisis, however, is such that the moments of personal give-and-take which we see on stage may be seen as being of minor consequence: what really matters is whether Theseus can get Herakles to survive after the traumatic shock of finding his loved ones murdered by his own hand.[125] This crisis is avoided and Herakles decides to live only because of the intervention prompted by and carried out by Theseus's compassion.

I don't find another close parallel to this play, among extant Greek tragedies at least. *Aias* has been compared by some, but Aias's and Herakles' situations are very different and Aias lacks the heroic compassionate friend who rescues Herakles.[126] A closer parallel is Sophokles' *Philoktetes.* In that play the *philia* between Neoptolemos and Philoktetes has to be developed, largely through the working of Neoptolemos's burgeoning compassion for the older hero.[127] The similarity is that through his compassion, Neoptolemos is instrumental in Philoktetes' salvation from the figurative death represented by his lonely and painful existence on Lemnos.

As many scholars have noted, the end of Euripides' *Heracles* celebrates *philia* as a positive, *redemptive* value in the face of an impersonal and at times hostile universe. That *philia* works largely through the prompting of Theseus's compassion for his desperate friend. Herakles' survival and prospective return to heroism can be viewed, so far as this play's action is concerned, as a final defeat of Hera or, at least, as a thwarting to the greatest extent possible of her will to destroy Herakles.

Concluding Reflections on Euripides and Compassion

In his treatment of the compassion theme, Euripides is remarkable in the variety of ways in which he presents compassion. In the suppliant plays, *Children of Herakles* and *Suppliants,* he shows the risks and problems confronting state leaders to whom the supplication is made. Nevertheless, in both plays the leaders do persist in providing the requested acts of compassion for their suppliants. These plays thereby provide models of heroic compassion for Euripides' Athenian audience.

Several of his other plays (most notably *Hekabe, Trojan Women,* and *Iphigeneia in Aulis*) show instances in which suppliants are denied compassion during the startup or in the aftermath of the Trojan War. Iphigeneia's sacrifice is obviously needed to advance the Greek effort in the war despite her father's understandable reluctance to carry it through. Hekabe's and the other Trojan women's losses of loved ones and subjection to slavery after the war provide a powerful and graphic illustration of the ultimate desolation of war for the losing side. The execution of the innocent young Astyanax is an especially moving example of the cruel denial of compassion by the victors, despite the Greek messenger Talthybios's evidently strong feeling of compassion that he nevertheless must inhibit in carrying through his duty to see to the boy's killing. Euripides' *Hekabe* shows still further personal tragic losses of the defeated queen of Troy in the execution of her daughter Polyxena and in her discovery of her dead son Polydoros, a victim of her supposed friend Polymestor's betrayal. Her supplications to save her daughter from death and to have her son's murderer punished fall on the deaf ears of her captors, Odysseus and Agamemnon, respectively. These three plays show the inherent brutality of war and futility of attempts to seek compassion in the hostile and violent-prone circumstances of war and its aftermath. Euripides' audience must have been sensitive to these issues as they watched these plays during the Peloponnesian War, which Athens itself was undergoing, a war replete with risks and dangers and with acts of cruelty—some of which, such as the massacre of the Melians, were carried out by the Athenians themselves. Spectators seeing these original productions would most likely have been induced to think twice about the activities in which their state was currently embroiled.

Orestes, although it takes place after the Trojan War, is focused primarily on the family situation of the sons of Atreus, more specifically on the issues raised by Aischylos's *Oresteia,* which had been performed in the Theater of Dionysos fifty years earlier. This is an especially subtle play in which an appeal for compassion fails but is eventually met by divine intervention. Also, as we have seen, still other Euripidean tragedies exemplify the tragic potential and horrors of compassion denied or not appropriately felt. Another prominent theme of compassion in Euripides is presented in the play *Medeia,* which shows the potential for abuse that some appeals for compassion may conceal, to the harm of the person who unwittingly shows compassion.

Finally, in *Herakles,* Euripides presents a positive view of compassion between friends, in this case, Herakles and Theseus. Here, Euripides comes close to matching Sophokles' deep explorations of the linkage of compassion with friendship in *Philoktetes* and *Oidipous at Kolonos.*

Can we see a pattern in Euripides' use of the compassion theme? He seems to move from an earlier interest in the traditional suppliant drama to a fascination with the desolation of the war drama in which compassion tends to be overruled by its opposite, cruelty. *Medeia,* an early play, is largely outside this pattern, but it does allow him to explore the human potential for personal cruelty and vindictiveness, including the willingness to abuse compassion as a powerful tool of persuasion. *Orestes* explores the potential of compassion to fail within a family, where it normally should succeed. *Herakles,* probably written after *Medeia* but before *Orestes,* shows Euripides dealing with the related themes of heroic madness and of divine persecution of a great hero. Here, the playwright shows how compassion can come to the rescue of such a hero in a way that restores him to his heroic career and service to humankind.

In sum, we can see that Euripides is keenly sensitive to the pathos of human suffering and also to the cruelties both of fate and of fellow humans that often seem to accompany such suffering. He especially seems conscious of the humiliation and despondency inherent in the fall from high to low (D3). Also, in exploring such suffering and pathos, he is aware of the positive role that compassion can play in such situations. Finally, he is a realist and rationalist who sees compassion's potential for abuse and failure as well as its beneficial potential.

CHAPTER 5

Sophokles

Classic Compassion

In Aristophanes' *Frogs*, Sophokles remains in the wings or, perhaps we should say, in the shadows. He is characterized as deferring to his elder, Aischylos, but at the same time not intending to defer to his junior, Euripides (Lattimore 53, 788–94). Later, when Aischylos, as victor, is about to leave the Underworld to aid Athens, he directs that the Chair of Tragedy be given to Sophokles, the next-best poet, for safekeeping until he himself should return—never to Euripides (Lattimore 90, 1515–23). Nothing is said in the play about Sophokles' use or avoidance of pathos and compassion, but in comic terms, Sophokles comes off as the moderate poet between the two extremes occupied by Aischylos and Euripides. As such, he presents less of a target for a comedian such as Aristophanes and is therefore not accorded the comic treatment that the other two receive. Much like Aristophanes and like many other critics of Greek tragic drama through the centuries, I see Sophokles as exhibiting the golden mean in his treatment of the compassion theme, much as he exhibits it in other aspects of his poetic work. But I'll provide more on this in the discussion below and in the conclusion.

In this chapter, I treat in detail Sophokles' last three extant dramas. I begin, however, with a survey of recurring subsidiary themes of compassion as developed in Sophokles' four earliest extant plays (*Aias, Women of Trachis, Antigone,* and *Oidipous the King*) and as exemplified in fragments attributed to him.[1] Most of these themes will also recur in our study of Sophokles' last three plays with references to the earlier plays.

The last three sections of this chapter, therefore, treat in much greater depth the development of compassion in Sophokles' last three extant tragedies: *Elektra, Philoktetes,* and *Oidipous at Kolonos.*[2] In these plays, as Reinhardt (1979) notes, the focus is primarily on human conflicts and relationships in contrast to Sophokles' earlier tragedies of fate. *Elektra,* I shall argue, develops the compassion theme dramatically and thematically in ways similar to Sophokles' last two extant plays. In *Philoktetes,* Sophokles develops compassion most extensively as a central theme that is integral to the play's dramatic action; in this play, Sophokles "pulls out all the stops" in elaborating the compassion theme in a powerful and moving drama. Since this play's employment of compassion is also highly controversial, it will require especially close examination. In *Oidipous at Kolonos,* which can be seen as a suppliant play, compassion is also integral to the play's action and, furthermore, is employed thematically by the poet to convey to his audience a sense of their civic identity as compassionate Athenians.

Early Sophoklean Plays and Fragments

I have organized this section by subsidiary themes that recur in both these earlier works and in the later Sophoklean plays analyzed below.

S1.1. The motif of the sanctity of suppliants can be observed in Sophokles' *Aias* and *Oidipous the King.* In the former, a sanctity is attributed to the protection afforded by Aias's corpse when Teukros instructs Eurysakes to cling to his father's body as a suppliant (1171–84); also, Eurysakes is to hold locks of his family members' hair, including one of his own locks, as a "treasure of supplication" (*hiktêrios thêsauros,* 1175).[3]

S1.2. In *Oidipous the King,* a group of Theban suppliants come to ask Oidipous's aid. They assume a suppliant posture at the altars before Oidipous's palace, and a priest, as spokesman for the group, makes the appeal. But even before he hears the nature of the request, Oidipous acknowledges his disposition to aid the suppliants and adds that he would be hard-hearted (*dusalgêtos*) not to feel compassion (*katoiktirôn*) at such an appeal (9–13). This scene not only reveals Oidipous's personal feeling of compassion and his pious reverence for suppliants but also adds a religious motivation to his search for the plague's cure. Later, Oidipous again expresses his feeling of compassion for the citizens (ὦ παῖδες οἴκτροι, 58) and describes how his empathy for the suffering people of Thebes has caused him to weep much in his search for a cure.

S2.1. Compassion based on a sense of one's common humanity and on a deep sense of the vulnerability of human fortune is an especially prominent theme in Sophokles (cf. D2). An early "classic" example is Odysseus's feeling of identification with and compassion for the deluded and shamed Aias, even though he is an enemy (*Aias* 121–26; cf. chap. 1, pp. 31–33; cf. intro. pp. 19–20). Stanford calls Odysseus's reflections on the universality of human frailty "the enlightened egoism of classical humanism" (1963: *ad* 124–26). At the end of the play Odysseus again sees in Aias's fate a reflection of his own and therefore requests the hero's burial (1365–67), which he also sees as being in accordance with the gods' laws (1343–44).

S2.2. Likewise, in *Women of Trachis*, Deianeira's joy at the news of Herakles' successful return is tempered by her reflection on the fragility of good fortune: how the fortunate man should fear that he may slip (293–97). The stimulus that gives rise to this reflection on her part is the sight of the captive women who, perhaps once free, will now be slaves in a foreign land. She expresses her strangely powerful feeling of compassion (*oiktos deinos*) for them, emphasizing the extreme change from good fortune to bad that they have experienced (298–302). She then prays to Zeus that such a fate may never befall her children, at least not while she is alive; thus the sight of these women arouses her fear (303–6).[4] Here again we see the connection between fear and compassion that results from a consideration of the unstable lot of human beings (D2). The common Greek tendency to feel compassion for those who have fallen the farthest and are most unaccustomed to suffering is shown by Deianeira's expression of greatest compassion for Iole, who appears to her to be a "person of noble birth" (*gennaia . . . tis*, 307–13); Deianeira suggests that Iole alone of the captured women displays a sensitivity to suffering (*phronein,* 313). Later, Deianeira, although frustrated by her inability to learn the girl's identity, nevertheless says that she wishes to add no further pains to the girl's troubles, which are enough (330–32, cf. D6). Even when she learns that Iole poses a threat to her as a rival for Herakles' affection, she shows no hostility to the girl, but rather seeks a remedy that will allow her to keep Herakles' primary affection for herself. The outcome of Deianeira's "remedy" and indeed the rest of the play's action serve to validate Deianeira's sense of the fallibility of human success—so much so that at the end, Hyllos characterizes the situation as pitiable (*oiktra*) for the human beings concerned, shameful (*aischra*) for the gods (1271–72). Compassion as the appropriate human response to the unpredictability of fate is one of Sophokles' most deeply felt themes.

S2.3. A sense of likeness may be aroused through concern for loved ones or other precious possessions. Compare Priam's appeal to Akhilleus in *Iliad* 24. We will see this motif in Antigone's appeal to the chorus (*Oidipous at Kolonos* 237–53) and in Philoktetes' appeal to Neoptolemos (*Philoktetes* 468–69).

S3. Suppliants who appeal for compassion in Sophoklean drama typically assert claims of reciprocity in support of that appeal (cf. intro. p. 19). Tekmessa, for example, makes such claims in *Aias.* She passionately expresses the claims of *philia* in support of her appeal for compassion (*oiktire,* 510) from the suicidal Aias, and she invokes Zeus of the domestic hearth (*ephestios,* 492). She ends her speech by defining the truly noble man (*eugenês*) in terms of reciprocity: he who remembers and repays kindness (*charis*) that has been done to him (520–24). The chorus of Aias's sailors add their approval of Tekmessa's plea and urge Aias to have pity (*oiktos*) in response (525–26). At this point, Aias is incapable of responding sympathetically: "She will have my approval, if only she follows my commands," he effectively says (527–28). Later, Aias's change of heart in the "deception" speech (646–92) does not, in the end, keep him from committing suicide. It does, however, signal some true feelings of Aias, feelings of compassion and moderation that he can admit only with difficulty and only in rare moments of extreme despair like this, given his tragically dominant, normally uncompromising sense of self.[5] Does Aias's expression of compassion here for Tekmessa and his son serve to answer her earlier request for compassion? Yes, according to Doug Clapp in our joint essay (129); indeed, Aias does answer Tekmessa in an important, emotionally meaningful way. Furthermore, since Aias is determined to die (or he will doubtless be killed by the Greek army, if he doesn't kill himself), he cannot fulfill Tekmessa's basic request that he survive. He has shown, however, how he will attempt to provide for his family's protection: he will entrust his child and presumably his concubine to the care of his brother Teukros, who will see to Eurysakes' return home where the boy will care for Aias's parents in their old age (560–71). He thus meets the basic requirement of compassion toward his *philoi* while still providing for the suicide that his disgrace requires.[6]

S4.1. In Sophokles, sensory perception, particularly the visual, is often employed to intensify the compassion of the spectators and, sometimes, that of other characters in the play (cf. D3). In *Oidipous the King,* the messenger announces a sight (the opening of the doors to reveal the self-blinded Oidipous) that he says "even one who hates" would pity (1295–96). Thomas Gould (1970: 147) notes that the object of the hate is ambiguous: it could be either Oidipous himself or the horrible sight on stage.[7] The former seems to have more merit: that even an enemy would pity the sight of the blinded Oidipous. Earlier in the play, as the chorus of Theban elders survey the desolation resulting from the plague and pray for divine intervention, they witness the children of Thebes lying dead on the ground unpitied (*nêlea genethla*) and not lamented (*anoiktôs,* 180–81); near the altars, they see wives and mothers of the dead lamenting and calling on Apollo, the Healer (182–86).

S4.2. In *Women of Trachis,* the nurse reporting Deianeira's suicide to the chorus remarks that their pity would have been intensified (κάρτ' ἂν ᾤκτισας), if they had seen what Deianeira did (death by the sword) rather than just hearing about it (896–97).[8] The nurse then relates the horrible event in graphic detail, including Hyllos's sorrowful distress. Hyllos by then had come to realize that he had accused his innocent mother wrongly, since Nessos had tricked her unaware into poisoning Herakles.

S4.3. Later in the same play, Herakles lifts the covers so that all, but particularly his son Hyllos, may see (he uses several different verbs of seeing) how pitiable his condition is (ὡς οἰκτρῶς ἔχω, 1076–80).[9] He prays for death, dwelling on the irony that he, the great hero who has conquered all the great monsters of the world, is now in a situation of utter defeat (1081–1111); he ends this speech with a pathetic boast that he will punish Deianeira, in keeping with his fame as the punisher of all evildoers. It is a condition of which he is ashamed, not least, because he is suffering at the hand of a woman, a disgraceful outcome for a male hero, and because he has been reduced to suffering and cries of pain and grief "like a woman."[10]

S4.4. Also, there is the startling, pathetic spectacle of Aias among the slaughtered beasts (*Aias* 346–429). Despite Pickard-Cambridge's (1946) and Stanford's (1963) reservations about the use of the *ekkyklema* (rolling platform) to display Aias sitting among the slaughtered animals, this scene is a perfect occasion for using some such device to present this powerful dramatic image, assuming that he could not be clearly seen by the audience from within the *skênê*.[11] Tekmessa explicitly prepares the audience for a vision of Aias (346–47), and since Aias immediately begins a song in interchange with the chorus and Tekmessa, it would be preferable if he were visible to the audience. In any case, the audience receives a powerful and unforgettable visual image, whether through the eyes or in the imagination (D3).

S4.5. In fragment 659 (Lloyd-Jones 1996), Tyro laments the loss of her hair—the result of mistreatment by her wicked stepmother, I would guess—and compares herself to a foal whose mane has been cut and who sees her image reflected in a river. As the foal laments her loss, "Alas! Even a pitiless person (*anoiktirmôn*) would feel compassion (*oiktireie*) for her." If they saw her, that is. Feeling compassion at seeing the display of intense grief and loss seems to be the point of this image. Tyro, of course, uses the image to elicit compassion for her own pitiable loss of hair (D3).

S5.1. Compassion and heroic action/nobility. Sophoklean heroes to whom appeals for compassion are made typically respond to those appeals with compassionate action (D1a, cf. intro. p. 17). As we have seen already (in S3 above), Aias answers Tekmessa's appeal for protection by summoning Teukros. In the same play, Odysseus acts to bring about the burial of Aias, despite the opposition of the sons of Atreus. In *Oidipous the King,* Oidipous tells his suppliants at the beginning of the play that he has already applied (ἔπραξα) the one remedy he has found: he has sent Kreon to Delphi in order to discover how (whether by deed or word) he might rescue (ἐρυσαίμην) the city (68–72). Later, he takes action by uttering a proclamation designed to lead to the discovery and expulsion of Laios's killer, the source of the plague (216–75). The irony inherent in this speech has been exhaustively analyzed; my point here is that Oidipous is acting to remedy the situation, even though this action and all his further steps to discover the killer's identity (and his own!) will eventually redound tragically on him and on Jocasta as well. Oidipous, therefore, represents a compassionate hero whose actions to aid and protect his city from a terrible plague end up revealing his own role in bringing about that plague; as such, he is an anomaly among compassionate heroes, who more often thrive in return for their compassionate action. In Sophokles' deeply tragic world, some compassionate types, such as Oidipous and Deianeira, suffer in spite of their virtue.[12]

S5.2. Also, Sophokles' characters, especially suppliants, typically ascribe nobility to the protectors or potential protectors of suppliants or to those who otherwise show compassion for them (cf. intro. pp. 17–18). In *Oidipous the King,* the Theban suppliants call Oidipous "most powerful" (40) and "most excellent" of mortals (*aristos,* 46) and even "savior" (*sôtêr,* 48) in their appeal to him for protection. Near the end of the play, after his catastrophe, Oidipous himself calls Kreon "noble" (*gennaios*) in appealing to him to show compassion by bringing Oidipous's daughters to their father and allowing him to touch them (1462–75). He uses *gennaios* of Kreon again when he requests that Kreon see to the girls' welfare (1503–10). Conversely, those heroes or champions who fail to respond with compassionate action would typically be characterized as "shameful" or "ignoble."

S6. Compassion is also occasionally depicted in the earlier plays of Sophokles as a strong emotion that restrains one from doing harm to an innocent person (cf. D1b). The Theban shepherd in *Oidipous the King* explains that a feeling of compassion (*katoiktisas*) motivated him to spare the infant that he was charged with killing and to hand him over instead to the Corinthian shepherd (1177–79). The rescue of another infant exposed to die (Paris himself) may well have been narrated in Sophokles' lost *Alexandros* (see Pearson, *Fragments,* 1: 57–58).

S7.1. As far as compassion or mercy and considerations of justice are concerned, one Sophoklean fragment asserts that no man who unwillingly does wrong is bad (*kakos,* cf. D4).[13] Although compassion is not explicitly mentioned here, it might be assumed that such a person would be considered worthy of mercy. In *Women of Trachis,* Deianeira says she will refrain from harsh words against her new rival because of her sympathy for Iole, whose beauty has ruined her own life: she has unwillingly destroyed and enslaved her homeland (461–67). Also, Deianeira refuses to blame Herakles and expresses understanding for Herakles' desire for Iole by describing it as a sickness that he passively suffers (445–46, 543–44; cf. Lichas's description, 475–77, 488–89). Like a powerful disease, love seems to dominate here, even mastering the great hero, Herakles.[14] The power of Love is the theme of the choral song that follows (497–530); ironically, the love object in that song is Deianeira herself, at a younger age when she was being sought by both Herakles and Acheloos. Later Hyllos seeks to abate Herakles' desire for retribution against Deianeira by asserting that she has erred unwillingly (οὐχ ἑκουσία, 1122–23); Herakles thus at last learns that his true adversary was Nessos, a dead monster from his glorious past. Mercy and understanding for the one who suffers beyond his control or who acts unknowingly is an assumption in these examples, an assumption that we also encounter in Sophokles' tragedies about Philoktetes and Oidipous at Kolonos.[15]

S7.2. With these examples of pathos, we might compare the pathos with which Sophokles portrays the suffering of the innocent Antigone, especially in the *kommos* between Antigone and the chorus (*Antigone* 806–82). Is Antigone innocent? Antigone is guilty of disobeying the king's decree, but innocent and vindicated in upholding the divine laws requiring burial of kin. I accept the interpretation that sees Antigone's actions as more just than not and her punishment by Kreon as more unjust than just. This accords with Teiresias's prophetic interpretation of events, which is clearly authoritative. That being the case, Antigone is in the category of sympathetic characters who arouse the ideal spectator's pity; Haimon and Eurydike are also in that category. Even Kreon, however, elicits some sympathy as the messenger reports him futilely seeking to undo the damage he has done by leaving Polyneikes' corpse "unpitied" (*nêlees*, 1197) and torn by dogs. This is one of Sophokles' darker tragedies, in which the conflict and suffering of the characters is hardly, if at all, relieved by one character's compassion for another. The chorus of Theban elders is hardly sympathetic—at least Antigone does not see them as such (see the *kommos* cited above); Haimon's intense grief for his beloved Antigone would qualify as sympathetic (1224–25), but she is already dead and this is very soon followed by his own suicide.

S8. Pity is connected to the theme of gender in several of Sophokles' plays (cf. D6). As noted above in S4.3, Herakles in *Women of Trachis* is ashamed of his womanly cries of pain. In *Aias* as well, the male hero seems to associate feelings of pity and lamentation with femininity, which he sees as fundamentally alien to his own male nature. "Women are prone to lamentation," he says (580).[16] But later in the so-called deception speech (646–92), he says that he has been softened in his words by the woman (Tekmessa), whereas before he had displayed his more characteristic male hardness; he says that he now feels pity (*oiktirô*) in leaving Tekmessa a widow and his son an orphan at the hand of his enemies. Aias here associates feelings of pity with women and indicates that such feelings are normally alien to his male personality. Indeed, in Greek culture generally, including in Greek tragedy, tears of pity and lamentation are often associated with the laments that women typically displayed at funerals.[17] For male heroes like Herakles and Aias, weeping in lamentation and feeling pity were seen as something appropriate to women and, consequently, not appropriate to males. Note, however, that in these two cases, it is particularly the feeling of self-directed grief and lamentation that they characterize as "feminine" or, alternatively, as the mark of a coward. Earlier, in reporting Aias's uncharacteristic cries of distress upon awakening from madness to see what he had done, Tekmessa recalled that Aias had always said that such cries were characteristic of a cowardly or low-spirited man (*Aias* 318–19). In discussing Sophokles' presentation of these two weeping and moaning heroes, Vickers (1973) offers the following:

> In both cases, Sophocles invokes the Stoic principle in order to draw attention to the fact that two supremely heroic characters have found it to be unworkable. Experience disproves the Stoic *consolatio:* in tragedy, strong men weep. The uninhibited expression of their suffering is natural, right, inevitable.[18]

Herakles in *Women of Trachis* and Aias appear to display "self-pity" in these grim situations (cf. D6). In both instances, the heroes are shown to be very much aware of the images they project—as seen by others. In contrast, as we have seen elsewhere, the actual granting of compassionate assistance by a hero to a suppliant, *also prompted by feelings of compassion,* is typically seen as fully in keeping with the male nature of heroic types.[19]

Elektra

Elektra might seem an odd choice for a drama to illustrate the theme of compassion, but the theme is presented there in a relatively straightforward manner. Also, as we shall see, in *Elektra* Sophokles develops the theme of compassion dramatically in ways that closely anticipate the development of compassion in his last two extant plays, *Philoktetes* and *Oidipous at Kolonos.*[20]

Sophokles' *Elektra* is a play that concludes with two acts of retribution and, as such, has been the source of much debate over the years. The way that compassion connects to the retribution theme relates to what I have said above about the relationships between compassion and justice and also those between compassion and reciprocity. In regard to the former, we have noted that compassion tends to be reserved for the innocent or for those who have erred unwillingly or in ignorance. A corollary of that proposition is that compassion is not granted to those who are guilty or who do wrong knowingly and deliberately. The element of reciprocity comes in here as well: the ancient Greeks assumed that one repays kindness with kindness or compassion with compassion. We are disposed to show compassion to those who have shown compassion to us in the past. But again there is a negative corollary: no compassion for those who have shown no compassion. The Greeks assumed that one repays wrong with wrong, harm with harm, and also a refusal to show compassion with a similar refusal to show compassion.

These negative corollaries tend to be problematical—both for us as moderns and for the ancient Greeks themselves. For us, especially those of us influenced directly or indirectly by Western or non-Western religious teachings that emphasize values such as love, mercy, and forgiveness toward all, the general proposition that one should harm one's enemy or show no compassion or mercy for a wrongdoer is somewhat repugnant to our ethical/religious sensibilities. An exception to this repugnance tends to arise in certain situations, such as war, criminal trials, and situations involving self-defense. In such situations, most of us accept the use of force to deter and sometimes even to punish those whom we regard as an aggressor, a heinous criminal, or, collectively, a nation bent on world domination or genocide. Still, when we are thinking as our "better selves," we are uncomfortable with the old Hebraic adage of "a tooth for a tooth" and with the similar Greek attitude that one naturally should seek to harm one's enemies. Indeed, modern legal codes now tend to allow for exceptions or extenuating circumstances in certain cases. What this means for our appreciation of ancient Greek plays and stories is that we may be uncomfortable with those stories which show retributory justice being enacted and yet do not seem to question the use of retribution and, indeed, may even praise its use. Nevertheless, we can assume that an ancient Greek would not have been as uncomfortable with such stories as we tend to be.[21] Given this cultural difference, we need to be especially cautious when reading an ancient play (or one from a different modern culture) that appears to commend attitudes with which we may be uncomfortable.

I said above that the negative corollaries of these propositions about justice and reciprocity were problematic for the ancient Greeks as well. We have already seen this in plays such as Sophokles' *Aias*, which raises the issue: What do we do when a friend becomes an enemy? Most serious readers of that play, myself included, would agree that Odysseus makes the appropriate responses to that situation: while he no doubt would have defended himself if Aias had assaulted him, he nevertheless pitied Aias when the latter was clearly being destroyed by Athene, and he saw that, once dead, Aias, a great former friend, deserved a decent burial. Sophokles raises a similar issue in *Antigone* regarding the treatment of Polyneikes. Again, most would say that whereas Kreon may have been justified in defending his city against Polyneikes' assault, he nevertheless did serious wrong in denying burial to the dead Polyneikes, his kinsman, and in condemning Antigone to death for her persistence in seeing to her brother's burial. We might also be reminded here of Aischylos's *Oresteia*, which presents the inauguration of deliberative justice at Athens in the mythic form of Orestes' trial. Obviously, the ancient Athenians saw complications and the need for some exceptions in the application of the old standard of justice: help your friends and harm your enemies. Jean-Pierre Vernant has brilliantly theorized a basis for these sorts of problems in his seminal essays about the conflicts inherent between the poetic tradition based in myth and the new social and legal realities of the democratic *polis*.[22] A modern American analogue might be, for example, the western movie. Although many of these films were produced from 1940 to 1970, they typically depict legendary characters and situations representing the century before. Still, Americans, at least, feel that classic films of this genre yet speak to them and raise important issues to which they can relate.

Now, let's examine compassion in *Elektra*. The play presents the reunion of Elektra with her brother Orestes during the execution of the plot developed by Orestes, his friend Pylades, and Orestes' paidagogos to execute Klytaimestra and Aigisthos for their murder of Orestes' and Elektra's father, Agamemnon. In the prologue of the play, we see the arrival of Orestes and friends near the palace of Mykenai. We learn that Orestes has been instructed by Apollo to employ stealth to kill his father's murderers by his just hand (*cheir endikos,* 36–37).[23] Later Orestes adds the assertion that he comes with justice (*dikê*), sped by the gods, to cleanse his ancestral home (69–70). We also note that although Orestes is understood to be the leader of this group and indeed lays out the plans that are to be followed to accomplish their task, the paidagogos plays a pivotal role as senior advisor and prompter of action. At the end of his opening speech the paidagogos asserts that it is time to act, a theme that he will repeat at other points of the drama. In fact, when Orestes hears his lamenting, "unfortunate" (*dystênos*) sister inside the palace, and suggests that they stop to listen to her, it is the paidagogos who insists that no, they should do nothing before accomplishing the will of Apollo.[24]

Throughout the play, Elektra and the chorus of Mykenaian women who are friends of Elektra characterize the killing of Agamemnon as an act without pity. Elektra in her long monody beginning at line 86 laments her father and says that no lamentation (*oiktos*) comes from anyone except from her, even though he died so shamefully (*aikôs*) and so pitiably (*oiktrôs,* 100–102). There is a clear implication here that the pity and lamentation that were appropriate in response to such a cruel death have been denied not only by the murderers but even by others, except for Elektra herself. She brings up the pitiful death again later when she asserts that one who forgets parents who died pitifully (*oiktrôs*) is foolish (*nêpios,* 145–46). She, in contrast, is ever remembering and ever lamenting.[25] She makes these statements in the context of the chorus's concern that Elektra's mourning is immoderate and harmful to her (137–44). As their conversation continues, Elektra reminds them (and the audience) of her own miserable state: that she lives hopeless, weak, childless, without a husband's protection, like a contemptible (*anaxia*) stranger in rags and at empty tables—in her father's house (185–92).[26] The chorus themselves then sing of Agamemnon's cries as having been piteous (*oiktra*) and that it was piteous when the blow of the axe came down on him (193–96).

Elektra says that she persists in lamenting her father because it would be dishonorable not to (236–44);[27] later, she characterizes her lamentation as the mark of a well-bred, noble woman (*eugenês gunê,* 257). Furthermore, she says that her laments serve to remind all that if the murderers fail to pay the penalty, it will result in the loss for all mortals of both compassionate regard among human beings (*aidôs*)[28] and reverence toward the gods (*eusebeia,* 245–50). Her call for retribution on the murderers is a call for justice.[29]

Elektra praises the chorus for showing sympathy and concern for her, calling them *genethla gennaiôn* (children of the noble, 129). She says that they repay her with the kindness (*charis*) of every sort of friendship (*philotês,* 134; i.e., displaying the reciprocity expected in friendship). The chorus themselves later show that they consider their own interest linked to that of Elektra, thereby indicating the mutuality that underlies their concern for her (251–52; cf. intro. pp. 17–19).[30]

Elektra further details the abuses she suffers at the hands of Klytaimestra and Aigisthos in the long speech beginning at 254. In addition to the insults and threats that she receives from her mother, she must withstand the sight of Aigisthos replacing her father in every role, including that of her mother's lover. Also, she notes that every month Klytaimestra commemorates the day that she killed Agamemnon with a festival dedicated to "the gods that saved her" (281). Also, some of Klytaimestra's threats have to do with Orestes: when someone announces that Orestes is about to return, Klytaimestra furiously accuses Elektra of having stolen Orestes from her arms and smuggled him away. Klytaimestra always adds that Elektra will pay a penalty for doing this. A probable implication here is that otherwise, Klytaimestra or Aigisthos would have killed the boy, thereby removing the threat of him as his father's avenger.[31] Elektra concludes that in the midst of such evils, she herself must also resort to evil—an instance of reciprocal justice (307–9).[32]

The first conversation between Elektra and her sister Chrysothemis reveals the differences in personality and position between the sisters. Whereas Elektra, ever faithful to her father and resistant to her mother and Aigisthos, lives a life of hardship, Chrysothemis has decided not to resist those in power with the result that she lives a life of palatial ease and comfort. She wishes her sister would do the same. Chrysothemis realizes, however, that she is being hypocritical: that her sister is in the right and has "justice" (*to dikaion*) on her side; nevertheless, she admits that she is too weak to stand up to the rulers and, furthermore, that it allows her, unlike Elektra, to live "in freedom" (*eleuthera*, 339). Much like the two sisters in Sophokles' *Antigone*, these sisters are at opposite poles. Elektra cannot tolerate compliance and prefers the life of hardship she leads, since it hurts her enemies and gives honor to Agamemnon. She accuses her sister of cowardice and submission to the enemy.[33]

The sisters are at a standoff when Chrysothemis reveals that she possesses new information: that Elektra is about to be sent out of the country to live in a dungeon or tomb. Whether she will be buried alive, like Antigone, or imprisoned is left vague, but in either case it will mean the end of Elektra as a thorn in her mother's side. Elektra is resigned to such a fate, since it will end the limbo of her current life. Burnett (1998: 123) goes further, asserting that Elektra's defiance in the face of this threat "proves that she will not buy her way out of even the greatest physical suffering with even the smallest gesture of complicity with her father's killers."

But Chrysothemis has other news as well: that Klytaimestra, prompted by a bad dream of Agamemnon symbolically being restored to power, has sent Chrysothemis to make a propitiating sacrifice at the grave of Agamemnon. Elektra then convinces her sister to dispose of Klytaimestra's offering and substitute instead an offering of their own together with a prayer that Agamemnon come above to help them and that Orestes return to defeat Agamemnon's enemies. Chrysothemis is impressed by the justness and reasonableness of Elektra's idea and agrees to do it, provided the chorus does not reveal it to Klytaimestra. The chorus, buoyed by Klytaimestra's dream and confident that Orestes will return, sing a song expressing hope that justice will be done (472–501). They end the song with a reflection on the troubles that the house has endured since Pelops's cruel betrayal of Myrtilos.

The entrance of Klytaimestra in the next episode provokes a debate between Klytaimestra and Elektra about the justice of Agamemnon's death. My reading of the debate is that Elektra effectively refutes Klytaimestra's arguments and shows that the murder was more unjust than just.[34] Klytaimestra ends the interchange with an oath by Artemis that Elektra will be punished when Aigisthos returns. She then makes a sacrifice and prayer to Apollo, in which she prays for the well-being of those of her children who have no enmity or bitterness toward her—obviously excluding Elektra from this prayer.[35]

It is at this point that the paidagogos enters and the plot of Orestes and friends is put into motion. Of particular interest to our study here is Klytaimestra's response to the news of Orestes' death, which the paidagogos narrates in vivid detail.[36] At first she shows some disposition not to hate Orestes: "One does not hate one's children, even when they treat you badly" (770–71). But, when pressed by the paidagogos, she adds that Orestes had left her, had reproached her for Agamemnon's murder, and had threatened to do "terrible things" (*deina*). She concludes by claiming that fear of him had made sleep impossible for her. But now, she says that she has been freed from fear—even Elektra's threats will no longer pose a danger. Obviously, she is delighted that her son is dead.

Elektra, seeing that she has no hope with Orestes gone, expresses a wish to die.[37] She and the chorus then sing a *kommos,* lamenting Elektra's misfortune and Orestes' death. In an effort to console Elektra, the chorus bring up the story of Amphiaraos, a seer whose wife also betrayed him. The point of consolation seems to be that since Amphiaraos has relatively good fortune in the underworld, there is hope that Agamemnon does as well. But as the chorus is about to add that Amphiaraos was avenged by his son, Elektra anticipates them but concludes that this is not comforting to her: Amphiaraos had his avenger, but she has lost the one she hoped would avenge her father. They then turn to the death of Orestes, but Elektra notes that he died in a foreign land far from the caring hands and lamentation of his beloved sister.

Chrysothemis, when she enters, however, says that she brings good news: Orestes has returned. Fresh offerings and a cutting of hair at the grave of Agamemnon suggest Orestes and no other. Elektra's response is one of two dramatic displays of compassion in the second half of the play. Elektra blurts out, "Alas! How I have long been pitying you for your ignorance!" (ἐποικτίρω πάλαι, 920). Ignorance makes one vulnerable and prone to error. In this case, Elektra assumes that Chrysothemis is mistaken due to her ignorance of the fact that Orestes is dead. The word *palai* (for a long time) here shows that Elektra's compassion was developing for a period of time before she spoke, presumably referring to the time Chrysothemis took to tell her story.[38] Chrysothemis is also worthy of compassion in that once she learns the bitter truth, her joy will plummet to despair. The audience would likely assume that Elektra's compassion for her sister stems in part from her anticipation of this fall from high to low (D3). Chrysothemis herself confirms this change from ignorant delight to knowing dejection at 934–37.

Yet there is also an element of irony at play here, which we as spectators and readers are aware of, at least in the back of our minds: Chrysothemis in her assumption that Orestes is alive is on firmer ground factually than Elektra who assumes he is dead.[39] Of course, since she is not privy to the plot of Orestes and friends, Elektra has been tricked like Klytaimestra into believing that Orestes is dead. What then are we to make of Elektra's display of compassion for her poor sister's ignorance—ignorance that will soon be confirmed as being knowledge instead? We can still accept Elektra's compassion for her sister as a genuine indication of Elektra's character: she is fully capable of compassion toward her loved ones in circumstances that call for compassion. That Sophokles dwells on Elektra's compassion here as he does suggests that we should take note of it. Furthermore, Elektra's not knowing that Orestes is actually alive should not detract from our estimation of her noble character here. Sophokles implants an irony for the characters and the spectator, but the irony is not a heavy one, since Elektra's care for her sister does not lead to a tragic outcome but rather displays the appropriate care and concern that should exist between the two sisters.[40]

This irony does, however, lend poignancy to the rift that develops between the two sisters as the scene continues. Elektra proposes that they, the two sisters, kill Aigisthos, since they can no longer expect the assistance of Orestes. She assures her sister that they will win praise and a good reputation for themselves; Chrysothemis will have good prospects for a marriage, which Aigisthos would never allow; they will earn gratitude for their piety (*eusebeia*) and assistance from their dead father and brother below;[41] they will save themselves from sorrow; and, finally, they will avoid the shame that is disgraceful for nobles like themselves (947–89).[42] But Chrysothemis, much like Ismene in *Antigone*, sees this as a futile plan against those in power; she pleads with her sister to be sensible. The chorus express their approval of Chrysothemis's advice here (1015–16). The interchange in stichomythia that follows shows that neither will give in to the other. Elektra is determined to undertake the retribution by herself, whereas Chrysothemis is certain that her sister's action will be disastrous and wants to stop her from attempting it. After each persists in claiming the right against the other, Chrysothemis finally exits.

The choral song that follows is broadly about the need for justice. After singing about the mutual care of birds from one generation to the next and vice versa, the chorus decry the lack of such mutual care among humankind, even though Zeus's law of justice requires it. They appeal to a voice that goes below to cry out there a pitiable message (*oiktra / ops*) to the sons of Atreus, announcing joyless disgraces (*oneidê*) to them (1066–69). Some have interpreted these lines as conveying criticism of the dead hero Agamemnon for his delay in using his power to help his children in their struggle against Aigisthos and Klytaimestra.[43] March (2001), however, whose interpretation I favor, sees it as disgrace for the family brought about by Chrysothemis's disloyalty. In any case, the strophe suggests a pitiable situation that requires remedial action lest it become a source of shame for the family.[44] The chorus then mention the discord now prevailing in the house of Atreus between the two sisters. In particular, they lament the betrayal, isolation, and abandonment of Elektra, who is careless regarding death and ready to die, ever lamenting her father's fate; they praise her loyalty to her father as exceptional (1058–81).

In the second strophe the chorus continue to praise Elektra for her choice of a glorious life of lamentation rather than a miserable life without glory; also, they sing that she has won double praise as being both a wise (*sopha*) and noble (*arista*) daughter.[45] They conclude the song with a wish that Elektra come to surpass her enemies in strength and wealth by as much as she now is below them. They assert that her current life is not happy, although she wins accolades by observing the highest laws, by her piety (*eusebeia*) toward Zeus (1082–97).[46]

With Orestes' entrance, we might note that the irony we observed above as lending poignancy to the conflict between Elektra and her sister also has served to undercut somewhat for the spectator the impact of the chorus's urgent expressions of concern and hope about Elektra's future *as a lone actor against Aigisthos's and Klytaimestra's power.* Orestes' and Pylades' entrance reminds us that the plot against Klytaimestra and Aigisthos is already fully in play and apparently on track. Our concern about what Elektra might do next on her own is therefore mitigated by the expectation that any attempt on her part to take action against the killers will be preempted by the actions of Orestes and company. Furthermore, the prospect of her happy reunion with her brother now seems imminent. While the characters we see onstage are being subjected to an emotional roller-coaster ride, we the audience are allowed some relief and indeed some pleasure from the superior knowledge of the circumstances that the poet has allowed us to share.[47]

The recognition and reunion of Elektra and Orestes proceeds forthwith. There is great irony as Orestes recognizes his sister soon after they encounter each other, whereas Elektra's recognition of him is tantalizingly delayed. When she requests to hold the urn said to contain Orestes' ashes, Orestes recognizes that this woman is a friend rather than an enemy (1119–25). She immediately begins, in characteristic form, a lament for her beloved brother (1126–70). In addressing his memory, Elektra asserts that she saved the young Orestes from murder, an explicit confirmation of earlier suggestions of this (1131–35).[48] Elektra laments that she was unable to provide the loving care of his body when he died; instead, he died in a foreign land. She laments that her long care for him has come to nothing: she claims that she acted more as mother and nurse to him than did the women who had those roles. She addresses the ashes: "O pitiable body!" (*O demas oiktron*, 1161). And she concludes her lament with a wish that she herself die and dwell with her beloved brother in the world below.[49]

Elektra's display of lamentation and compassion throws the pretending Orestes off balance.[50] In his astonishment, Orestes comes to the conclusion that this is his sister Elektra before him in rags. Elektra cannot comprehend this stranger's sudden interest in her and concern for her! This richly ironic, tantalizing scene proceeds with Elektra in the dark for another twenty lines before finally Orestes blurts out, "O unfortunate one! Seeing you, how I pity you for a long time now!" (ὦ δύσποτμ,' ὡς ὁρῶν σ' ἐποικτίρω πάλαι, 1199).[51] The phrasing almost precisely matches Elektra's expression of compassion for her sister Chrysothemis in line 920 (see above). In both cases, compassion is a powerful force that over time (*palai*) builds and eventually demands expression. In the earlier instance Elektra's compassion was for her sister's ignorance; here Orestes' compassion for Elektra is in part for her ignorance of who he is. But it is much more than that. When she says, "Then you are the only one who has pitied me," he answers, "I am the only one feeling pain (*algôn*) from your troubles" (*kakois*, 1201).[52] This is the inhibiting power of compassion that does not allow one to harm or continue harming an innocent.[53] Here, Orestes is unable to continue his charade in which not only his enemies but also his dear sister is deceived. Also, in this short time, he has learned much about the sorry plight of Elektra, and for that he feels much sympathetic pain, as he enunciates at 1201. This growing compassion prompts his expression of it at 1199–1201 and then leads him to quickly reveal his identity to Elektra and to confirm it with the signet ring so that her sorrow for his supposed loss can be ended.[54]

The reunion of brother and sister is joyous but must be curtailed at this point since the plot of deception and retribution is already in play. Almost immediately, Orestes must silence his garrulous sister (1236, and again at 1238, 1259, 1288–92, 1322; cf. 1271–72); he shows that he knows her well! There is a light comic tone to these interchanges. Finally, the paidagogos, ever acting as the manager of the plot, must come out of the palace and chide them for their delay and urge them to get on with it (1326–38). Even the paidagogos must be reintroduced to Elektra, and she must exclaim at length on her joy at being reunited with him. He again must cry, "Enough!" and prompt them to save the sharing of memories for later: now is the time to act![55] Klytaimestra is alone and vulnerable. Orestes and Pylades then go in. Before she goes in, Elektra addresses the statue of Apollo with a prayer of supplication to assist in punishing the impious murderers. Apollo, of course, is the divine instigator of the retribution.[56]

After she comes back out, the voice of Klytaimestra is heard from within. At one point, Klytaimestra begs Orestes to pity his mother (*oiktire,* 1411). Elektra makes the requisite judgment: "But neither he nor his father was pitied (οὐκ . . . ᾠκτίρεϑ') by you!" (1411–12). This is reciprocal compassion in the negative mode: no pity for those who show no pity to others.[57] Klytaimestra's execution soon follows. The chorus comment that the curses are functioning and that those long dead drain the blood of the killers; they also express their approval of Klytaimestra's execution (1417–23).[58]

In accordance with typical dramatic efficiency, Aigisthos soon returns, eager to confirm the news of Orestes' death. Elektra sends Orestes and the others inside while she awaits Aigisthos in front of the palace. In fact, at this point she takes control of the situation: "Leave things here to me," she tells Orestes as he is going in. She then proceeds to manipulate Aigisthos. When she tells him that he can see the body itself, he utters an amazing line: "You have given me much joy in your speech—not your usual thing" (1456). Elektra's reply is truly sardonic: "Rejoice, if you really can!" Aigisthos orders the doors opened and utters a gloating warning to any who may have had hopes pinned on Orestes' return; he invites such a person to look on Orestes' corpse and learn to accept Aigisthos's bridle.[59] But his gloating soon turns to horror when he uncovers the corpse to discover—not Orestes, but Klytaimestra. Aigisthos immediately recognizes that he is trapped. Elektra, in her final speech in the play, forbids Aigisthos from making a lengthy speech and demands his immediate death and burial, a series of actions that she says would be her only release (*lutêrion*) from long-suffered woes (*kakôn . . . tôn palai,* 1484–90). I agree with Segal that Elektra's emphasis here is "not upon savoring the vengeance, but finishing it and banishing all sight and memory of it" (1966: 520–21). The notion of release from long woes suggests that the retribution here is seen as a type of compassion: justice as relieving the suffering of the wronged individual.[60] Orestes and Pylades then escort Aigisthos into the house, where his death will soon follow. Elektra exits into the palace, after she hears the chorus's concluding words, which celebrate the end of suffering and beginning of freedom for the seed of Atreus (1508–10).[61]

This play differs remarkably from Aischylos's *Choephoroi:* in that play the children had to work themselves up to the point of being able to carry through with the matricide. Here, the process of retribution is set in motion at the very beginning, and motivation never poses a problem; matricide seems to stir no qualms or misgivings for either Orestes or Elektra.[62] Pylades here does not have to prompt a hesitating Orestes to get on with the matricide; instead, Pylades is completely silent, and the older paidagogos has the task of restraining the young people from celebrating too much at their reunion and urging them to get on with the business at hand. Sophokles does not give us Orestes' reaction to what he has done, unlike Aischylos who makes Orestes' misgivings and sense of sorrow an important part of his "justification" in contrast to Klytaimestra's joy at having killed Agamemnon. In this play, Aigisthos and Klytaimestra clearly deserve to die, and there is no hesitation in giving them what they deserve. Furthermore, the play suggests a divine hand in the outcome.[63] Apollo is cited at the beginning as the divine instigator of the retribution (see my comments above on the prologue); there is Klytaimestra's prophetic dream that prefigures the return of Orestes to power; and at 1264–70, although a line is missing from the text, Orestes asserts and Elektra accepts that a god brought Orestes to Mykenai and prompted his actions there. Several references are made in the play to the spirit of the dead Agamemnon having played a role in motivating the children to avenge him. Kells (1973), for one, seems to accept this as part of Sophokles' vision in the play.[64] Might Sophokles and his audience have accepted this retribution simply as an appropriate, if slow-coming, act of divine justice?[65]

Compassion functions in this play as a strong motivating force between friends, prompting Elektra to end Chrysothemis's "illusion" that Orestes is alive, and prompting Orestes to end Elektra's sorrow and suffering over the apparent loss of her brother. Elektra and Orestes are therefore characterized as being capable of compassion. Aigisthos's and Klytaimestra's contrasting lack of compassion serves to motivate Elektra and Orestes: Agamemnon's death is repeatedly characterized as pitiful, undeserved, and unlamented; this motivates the retribution against his murderers in accordance with the ethic, "no pity for those who show no pity." The play does not problematize that ethic. In fact, Orestes' insistence that Aigisthos die in the same place where he had killed Agamemnon shows that Orestes is adhering to a standard of precise reciprocal justice.[66] Klytaimestra and Aigisthos are depicted as sufficiently evil and Elektra and Orestes and friends as sufficiently good so as to make retribution seem justified.[67] There are no explicit words of alarm or misgiving at the end of the play that would seem to question the justice of what has taken place, although, as I said in introducing the play, in the abstract, we moderns tend to be suspicious of retaliatory violence. It is therefore no surprise that scholars have looked high and low for evidence and implications in the play that would question the justice of what Orestes and Elektra did.[68]

There is certainly the irony in the delay of the recognition and reunion, something that Sophokles makes a distinguishing element of in his dramatic plot. The delay serves to highlight the pathos of Elektra's situation as she suffers for over half the play, unaware of the nearness of her brother and of the liberation that is approaching for her.[69] But in her hardship and suffering and her continuing lamentation for her father and then for the brother that she comes to believe is dead, Elektra grabs our sympathy, and her reunion with her brother, when it comes, is for us a joyful reunion that almost distracts the characters from their mission. Our sense of sympathetic joy, in fact, serves to numb us somewhat to the killings that the paidagogos pushes the children to complete in a timely manner.[70] The play does not end after the death of Aigisthos, but as Aigisthos is being taken into the palace to be executed.[71] Sophokles has constructed the play so that the audience's expectations of the short-term future at the end is focused on the killing of Aigisthos—not the entry of the Furies, as in Aischylos's version of the story. Is this play open-ended, as some have concluded?[72] Perhaps. Challenging? Provocative? Yes. The ending of the play is satisfying, and it conveys a sense of justice having been done, but it is not completely without its unsettling questions and ironies. May we not, in fact, say that a Sophoklean play without irony would be like a spring without rain? But Sophoklean irony does tend to promote sympathy toward those ignorant of the irony rather than disdain or alienation.[73] In this case, we can perhaps rely on Aristotle's theory of the tragic and say that any killing of kin is inherently tragic: you can't kill your mother or your son or your brother, regardless of how rotten they may be, and feel completely good about it forever. This is an issue that we will confront again in our last Sophoklean play, *Oidipous at Kolonos.*

Philoktetes

We may now turn to the role of compassion in Sophokles' *Philoktetes.* Because compassion is so integral to the plot of this drama and so fully integrated with other major themes, such as deception, violence, and persuasion, it will be necessary to employ a close reading of the play in order to analyze fully the development of compassion as a theme and as a motivator of action and to demonstrate its relationship to the play's other major themes. In general, the theme of compassion in this play can be seen as part of the larger issue of man's treatment of his fellow man or fellow human being. At the end, I provide a concluding analysis of the role of compassion in the play along with a discussion of the meaning of that role. Our primary questions here are: How does compassion function in this play, and what is the meaning of that function?

Almost all critics who have written about the play have remarked on the sympathy aroused by Philoktetes' suffering and on the role of pity in motivating Neoptolemos's behavior at various points in the action. In his famous book, *Laocoön,* first published in 1766, Lessing has given perhaps the most influential account of this theme. He emphasizes the theatrical vividness of Philoktetes' cries of pain and external wound and brilliantly defends Philoktetes' intense cries against charges (by Cicero and others) that they are unmanly, violate decorum, or otherwise inhibit the spectator's sympathy by their sheer intensity. He also describes Neoptolemos and the chorus as bystanders whose responses or lack of response to Philoktetes' suffering involve the spectator dramatically and distract him from any embarrassment he himself might feel at witnessing such intense expressions of pain.

A number of critics within the last century have seen pity as part of the play's advancement of a new or unconventional value scheme. Bellinger (1939: 6–8) notes that after having been first schooled by Odysseus and then confronted with Philoktetes, the ambitious young Neoptolemos "is presented with an entirely new set of values in which ambition has no place and justice and mercy bulk inconveniently large." He sees in Neoptolemos's decision to take Philoktetes home at the end a sacrifice of "ambition for principle," which was uncommon in Greek heroes. For Adkins (1960a: 183, 189; 1966: 84–85), *Philoktetes* advances beyond traditional Greek values in having Neoptolemos choose honest behavior (a cooperative value) over the competitive value of success, although Adkins does not mention pity in this regard. Zanker (1992: 25, n.16) sees in the play a tension between the competitive "victory" standard, represented by the character of Odysseus, and what he describes as the "ultimate" standard of generosity, compassion, and fairness, reflected in the character of Neoptolemos. Rose associates the depiction of pity in the play with the influence on Sophokles of contemporary anthropological theories about the development of the "social compact" in early human society. Easterling (1978) argues, most convincingly, that *philia* (friendship), coupled with "right action," is the primary value promoted by the play, that it is "What really matters."

This is not to say, however, that this play's positive depiction of compassion is free from controversy—far from it! Indeed, critics are quite evenly divided on how to interpret the play's ending. This division largely stems from an important passage late in the play when Neoptolemos has returned the bow of Herakles to

Philoktetes and attempts to persuade the older hero to go to Troy. He begins his speech with a pointed criticism of Philoktetes:

> . . . ἀνθρώποισι τὰς μὲν ἐκ θεῶν
> τύχας δοθείσας ἔστ' ἀναγκαῖον φέρειν·
> ὅσοι δ' ἑκουσίοισιν ἔγκεινται βλάβαις,
> ὥσπερ σύ, τούτοις οὔτε συγγνώμην ἔχειν
> δίκαιόν ἐστιν οὔτ' ἐποικτίρειν τινά. (1316–20)

> It is necessary for human beings to put up with misfortunes from the gods; but people like you who are enmeshed in troubles of their own choosing—one ought neither to excuse nor feel pity for such people.

Many scholars have taken a cue from Neoptolemos here and in their reading of the play show that they consider Philoktetes a less than fully sympathetic character.[74] Many have found him to be perversely stubborn and undeserving of pity in his refusal to be persuaded by Neoptolemos to go to Troy. Some have cited his apparent disobedience of the gods' will in so refusing and have criticized his pledge to use the bow of Herakles against his fellow Greeks. Likewise, Philoktetes' and Neoptolemos's decision to go to Greece rather than to Troy has been seen by some as "unheroic" or misguided.[75] Herakles' reversal of this decision is consequently seen as a criticism and welcome correction of it. Other scholars, however, take a more sympathetic view of Philoktetes' refusal to be persuaded by Neoptolemos and view the pair's decision for Greece as carrying a strongly positive meaning, although not necessarily an unqualified good.[76] Most of these agree that the second ending is a desirable turn of events.[77] Careful attention to the play's thematic development of "pity" or "compassion"—the very thing that Neoptolemos seems to deny to Philoktetes in the quotation above—can perhaps help resolve for us these critical differences and answer this important question: Is Philoktetes worthy of compassion?

Through a close analysis of Sophokles' dramatic and thematic employment of compassion in the play, I shall seek to demonstrate that Philoktetes, far from being unworthy of compassion, as Neoptolemos asserts in lines 1316–20, is rather portrayed as the proper and worthy recipient of compassion from Neoptolemos. Furthermore, Neoptolemos's final agreement to escort Philoktetes home (1402–8) is the culmination and demonstration of his development of the compassion that the play characterizes as being appropriate to noble heroic *philoi* (friends) and, moreover, as Neoptolemos's legacy as the son of Akhilleus. In this play, Sophokles depicts compassion (*eleos*) as both a powerful emotion and as a component of the noble *aretê* (excellence) and *philia* (friendship) that are appropriate for heroes. Indeed, the argument of the drama suggests that a lack of such compassion toward one's allies may endanger heroic competitive achievement. Finally, the controversial second ending of the play (with its deus ex machina) reinforces and validates rather than contradicts this concept of heroic compassion and friendship. In other words, the *deus* resolves the apparent conflict between compassion and victory that the play problematizes.

The Exposition of Philoktetes' Need for and Worthiness of Compassion

In *Philoktetes,* Sophokles employs his full theatrical resources in presenting the hero to the audience and to his fellow characters as a noble man in extremely pitiable circumstances. The play presents a masterfully orchestrated development of Philoktetes' need for and worthiness of human sympathy and compassionate aid. The key elements of Philoktetes' situation that are pitiable are the suffering and pain occasioned by his disease, the hardship of his livelihood on the island, and his complete isolation and lack of companionship. His suffering has also been intensified by the cruelty of his abandonment by the Greek leaders and by the sheer length of his ten-year stay on Lemnos.

In the prologue, Odysseus and Neoptolemos have arrived on Lemnos for the purpose of capturing Philoktetes and his bow in order to provide Greek success in the Trojan War. Odysseus then gives a very cursory account of Philoktetes' abandonment on the island: how he himself exposed the son of Poias on the island after his ill-omened cries, caused by his ulcerous foot, interfered with the performance of sacrifices (4–11).[78] A nervous sense of guilt is perhaps meant to be conveyed by Odysseus's insistence that he did this under orders from his superiors (6) and by his apparent eagerness to be done with this distasteful but necessary explanation (11–14).

Odysseus gives a somewhat idyllic cast to the cave for which Neoptolemos is to search: the two entrances make it conveniently warm in winter (by giving a sunny seat on either side) and provide a cooling breeze in summer. Furthermore, there is a nice little spring for drinking water conveniently nearby (16–21). Both Webster (1970) and Jebb (1898) observe that this description of the cave is later contradicted when Philoktetes, who should know better, describes the cave as alternately hot in summer and icy cold in winter (1082); Odysseus, again, appears to be seeking to mitigate the cruelty of abandoning the hero.

Neoptolemos, who does not share Odysseus's motivation for euphemistic description, is more realistic in conveying his impressions of what he sees in the cave: a bunch of leaves trampled down into a primitive bed (33), a rough-hewn drinking vessel of poor craftsmanship, and some kindling (35–36). Odysseus, still intent on putting a sunny face on things, calls these possessions Philoktetes' "treasure" or "store" (*thesaurisma,* 37).[79] Neoptolemos then gets a shock and recoils as he smells and sees some foul rags, full of discharge, that are drying in the sun, presumably, so that they may be used again. Philoktetes' allies, in abandoning him, obviously did not leave him very well provisioned for his long stay. As Kitto (1956: 110) remarks, the pitiable contents of the cave build up "our sense of what Philoktetes has endured and is still to endure." By noting that a man with a diseased foot could not have ventured far away and that he is probably in search of either food or an anesthetic herb (41–44), Odysseus adds yet another pitiable detail to Philoktetes' situation: his very limited mobility.

After this brief delineation of Philoktetes' abandonment and his pitiable circumstances, Sophokles presents an ethical debate between the two men who have come to deal with Philoktetes. This debate results in Neoptolemos's seduction by Odysseus, who by promising him the prospect of glorious victory at Troy, persuades him that they must use deception against Philoktetes rather than persuasion or force, the two methods that the noble son of Akhilleus naturally prefers.[80] In making his argument, Odysseus recognizes that such deception is contrary to Neoptolemos's "nature" (*physis* 79–80) but argues that victory is sweet (81). "At another time (*authis*)," he says, "we will show ourselves to be honest (*dikaioi*); but now (*nun*) give yourself to me in shamelessness for the short space of a day. Then, in the future, be called the most pious (*eusebestatos*) of mortals" (82–85). After further debate, Neoptolemos finally, if reluctantly, accedes to Odysseus's plan to use deception against Philoktetes. By defining the values (victory by any method versus victory by "noble" methods) that are held by Odysseus and Neoptolemos, respectively, the prologue sets the stage for the development of the theme of compassion, which has already appeared implicitly in the two men's contrasting perceptions of Philoktetes' cave.

The chorus of Neoptolemos's sailors enter (the *parodos*), and Neoptolemos invites them to inspect the place where Philoktetes "lies" (i.e., the cave)[81] and tells them to have courage (ϑαρσῶν) as they look, presumably because Philoktetes and the bow are absent (144–46). In the next line, the young hero refers to Philoktetes as a "terrifying traveler" (δεινὸς ὁδίτης), partly because of the terror of his bow, but perhaps also because of the awe that his painful mode of walking must inspire.[82] The chorus's use of the epithet "miserable" (*tlêmôn*) for Philoktetes after they have examined his dwelling suggests that the sight has made an appropriate impression on them (161). Neoptolemos's response to their question concerning Philoktetes' whereabouts has several pathetic touches. Because of his need for food, Philoktetes "plows" (ὀγμεύει) a path nearby; the phrase suggests the track left by the diseased foot being painfully dragged (162–63). Neoptolemos then gives an empathetic description of Philoktetes' mode of livelihood: a painful hunting of beasts and the lack of a "healer" (παιῶνα) for his "ills" (164–68).[83]

The chorus then break into song, expressing at once their feeling of compassion for Philoktetes: "I, for my part, pity him" (οἰκτίρω νιν ἔγωγε, 169–90).[84] Three full lines of their song emphasize his isolation: he has no one to care for him, he has no familiar companion, and he is *always alone* in his misery (170–72). Furthermore, in this state of loneliness and isolation, he is sick with a wild (i.e., savage and uncontrollable) sickness and is at a loss concerning every need that arises (173–75). Philoktetes, therefore, has no "friends" (*philoi*) to sympathize with him and take care of him in his suffering; he has been deprived of all the benefits by which society and friends normally help meet the physical and emotional needs of a person in the desperate straits of sickness.[85] The chorus wonder how he can endure so much misery (175–76) and then conclude the strophe with general complaints about the lot of human beings, specifically those whose fortune in life is not "moderate," "within ordinary limits" (*metrios*, 177–79).

What the chorus mean by *metrios* is shown in the antistrophe, which turns again to the particular case of Philoktetes. "Inferior to perhaps none of the high-born houses this man, deprived of *everything* in life, lies lonely, apart from all companions" (180–83). Philoktetes' life is not *metrios* because he has fallen from the highest, or near highest, social and material status to the lowliest; here is a prime example of the traditional "fall from high to low," which we have seen to be especially pitiable to the Greek way of thinking.[86] Philoktetes' change of circumstance is particularly extreme. Unlike most exiles, he has not merely been exiled from his own society but from all human contact. The chorus emphasize this deprivation: instead of human company, Philoktetes keeps company with assorted beasts; "pitiable (*oiktros*) in his pain and hunger," he suffers "incurable, uncared-for troubles"; also, only "the garbled (*athurostomos*), distant (*têlephanês*) echo responds to his bitter laments" (184–90). Rather than words of sympathy, all he hears is this mocking desolate reminder of his loneliness and pain. And this has been going on for ten years! What this strophe and antistrophe are about is not so much Philoktetes' suffering from the pains of his disease and his difficulties in eking out a primitive livelihood and staving off starvation—devastating as these are—as they are about his lack of and need for human sympathy and compassion. They masterfully portray the nature and intensity of Philoktetes' suffering on Lemnos.

Neoptolemos's cool assertion that Philoktetes suffers by divine design (191–200) is no match for the emotional power of the chorus's song. His characterization of Chryses as "savage," however, suggests that he does not see any justice in Philoktetes' suffering (194). His mention of the fact that Philoktetes suffers "apart from those who care for him" (δίχα κηδεμόνων) is a dissonant reminder of the chorus's preceding song and of Philoktetes' abandonment (195). Neoptolemos's speech serves primarily to signal to the audience that, despite the chorus's outpouring of sympathy, he is still prepared to go through with the deception.

The exposition of Philoktetes' need for and worthiness of compassion is made even more forceful by the hero's first entrance. At one point, the chorus suddenly signal Neoptolemos to keep silent. They hear a sound (presumably a cry) that, they say, is like the familiar companion (*suntrophos*) of a man who is distressed (201–2). *Suntrophos* is an echo of the same word at 171, where the chorus sang that Philoktetes has no familiar human companion; the use of the same word here serves to remind us that Philoktetes' only companion is his own human voice, as the image of the echo (188–90) has already shown. The pitiful vocal sound of complaint of the man who creeps along only with great difficulty "strikes" (βάλλει βάλλει) the chorus even from afar (205–9). The emphasis on the sound of Philoktetes continues in the antistrophe as the chorus hear the man getting closer. Suddenly an imaginative contrast: Philoktetes is *not* playing the panpipes like a typical shepherd returning at the end of the day to the comforts of home and family might do, but rather he is making the cry of a man who is stumbling (again, under necessity, 215–16; cf. 206–7) or who has seen that his harbor is still empty (210–18). The last lines of both the strophe and the antistrophe indicate that Philoktetes is crying aloud, as presumably the actor portraying him would do as he enters.

The representation of Philoktetes on stage must have produced a powerful shock in the audience. As Linforth describes it, Philoktetes enters "a feeble figure of a man, not old, but emaciated and bowed with pain, his hair and beard unkempt, miserably clad, one foot bound in rags" (108–9). Philoktetes' first interchange with the visitors suggests his self-consciousness regarding his savage appearance; he fears that the strangers will abandon him in terror. The imagery in this section suggests the animal-like quality of Philoktetes' existence on Lemnos and implies that he has been reduced from a civilized and human mode of existence to a beast-like level of survival. For the civilized Greeks, who emphasized the gulf between human being and beast, this would represent a most pitiable change of circumstance, as Philoktetes acknowledges. Instead of fearing his "wild" state, he says, the strangers should "feel compassion" for him (οἰκτίσαντες) as a "man" (ἄνδρα) who, "unhappy because of his troubles" (δύστηνον, κακούμενον), is "alone" (μόνον), "deserted" (ἐρῆμον), and "friendless" (κἄφιλον, 226–28).[87] What he desperately wants to hear is a friendly voice. When the strangers hesitate to respond, his insistence that they answer him shows the intensity of his longing for human speech (230–31).

The themes of Philoktetes' isolation and his need for a sympathetic response, introduced so powerfully in the *parodos,* are elaborated in the first long speech of Philoktetes himself (254–316). Philoktetes' pitiable isolation is made to seem even greater to him when he learns that not even a report of his troubles has reached his homeland: he reasons that he must be hateful to the gods. He describes his abandonment: his enemies (Odysseus and the sons of Atreus) cast him out "in an unholy manner" (ἀνοσίως, 257) and shamefully (αἰσχρῶς) threw him out "deserted" (ἐρῆμον, 265, repeated in 269; cf. the discussion of 228, above) and "wasting away" (καταφθίνοντα) from his savage wound. He bitterly imagines that his enemies have conspired to keep their abandonment of him secret and are laughing at him, while his sickness has grown steadily more severe (251–59). The laughter that he attributes to them is because their impiety and shamelessness in abandoning him have gone unpunished. He describes their cruel joy (ἄσμενοι) when he fell asleep on Lemnos and gave them the opportunity to slip off without him (268–72), and how they left him with only a few rags and a little food such as one might give a beggar, presumably, as Jebb and Webster suggest, just enough to avoid the pollution of having starved him themselves (273–75; cf. *Antigone* 775).

He recalls his feelings upon awakening to find that he had been abandoned: his cries of grief at discovering that all his own ships had left and that he had no companion in his sickness except grief itself (276–84).

In the next section of his speech (285–99), Philoktetes describes the hardship of his survival on the island: how he provided himself with the necessities of food, drink, and fire in the winter seasons. The unerring bow of Herakles gave him food, but his diseased foot painfully hampered his mobility in retrieving the game and in searching for firewood. Finally, the provision of fire for his home symbolizes for Philoktetes his success, however primitive and painful, at survival in the hostile, uncivilized environment of Lemnos, even though his wound remains intractable. Philoktetes' own assessment of his suffering on Lemnos recalls and reinforces the empathetic assessment made by the chorus (169–90). This exposition, therefore, together with the *stasimon* (to follow at 676–729) and the portrayal onstage (732–820) of Philoktetes in the throes of his disease at its most virulent, present in graphic detail the nature and intensity of Philoktetes' isolation and suffering on Lemnos.

At line 275 Philoktetes expresses a wish that his enemies suffer the same fate (οἷ'αὐτοῖς τύχοι). During the ten years of his abandonment on Lemnos, he has developed an unwavering enmity toward them, and he wishes them harm at every opportunity. It is critical to note, however, that his wishes for revenge, as here, tend to be expressed in precisely reciprocal, equivalent terms.[88] This expressed enmity is in accordance with the standard notions of Greek reciprocal justice: one wishes harm to one's enemies.[89]

We also learn that Philoktetes had previously requested other visitors to the island to convey him home, but all had refused to do so, had abandoned him, and had left only token gifts of food and clothing. In telling of these incidents, Philoktetes provides a definition of true, meaningful compassion. He uses the word/deed antithesis to distinguish between the minimal compassion of words that previous visitors to the island have shown him and the essential and meaningful compassion of *action,* which consists of conveying him home: λόγοις / ἐλεοῦσι μέν (307–8). Since *eleos* and its cognates most commonly denote compassion expressed by action whereas *oiktos* tends to denote verbal expression of pity, Philoktetes' phrase may be interpreted to mean, "They *do* their compassion *with words*."[90] The linkage of meaningful compassion with action here is significant because action is typical of heroic behavior. Contrast also Odysseus's expressed preference for words (96–99) with Philoktetes' use of the "action" word *drao* below (478).

Positing a basis of shared enmity toward the Greek leaders, Neoptolemos responds to Philoktetes' story with his own deceptive tale (343–90). In contrast to the seemingly shallow pity expressed by Neoptolemos's sailors in 317–18, Philoktetes gives a wholly sincere and sympathetic response to Neoptolemos's tale of his abuse by Odysseus and the sons of Atreus (403–4). Philoktetes' ready sympathy also extends to the news of the death of Akhilleus, Neoptolemos's father, about which he first learns here (331–38). Neoptolemos, in fact, remarks on Philoktetes' expression of sympathy as being exceptional (339–40): "I think that your own sufferings are enough for you, poor man, so that there is no need for you to lament those of your neighbor." It is, of course, natural for a person's own immediate suffering to take precedence over his or her concern for the suffering of others and, thus, for one's own pain to limit one's capacity to empathize with that of someone else. Aristotle remarks that those who are moved by strong emotions (such as great fear) do not feel pity since they are taken up with what is happening to themselves; terror—concerning oneself or close loved ones—tends to drive out compassion for others (*Rhetoric* 1385b, 32–33; 1386a, 17–24). Therefore, the expression of compassion is to be expected only from those who are in a position, however temporary, of strength, soundness, or relative prosperity and free from suffering themselves.[91] For someone who himself is in a state of extreme misfortune to express deep sympathy for others is therefore a sign of that person's outstanding nobility and inner strength (D5). Philoktetes here shows himself to be of such nobility.[92] Neoptolemos's use of the commonplace to dismiss Philoktetes' sympathetic expression (to which Philoktetes graciously defers in 341–42) only serves to call attention to this nobility, which, of course, contributes to Philoktetes' worthiness to receive compassion himself, since his expression of sympathy for Neoptolemos's loved one is a kindness that should be reciprocated. In summary, the play's exposition presents Philoktetes as a worthy hero desperately in need of compassionate assistance, a hero who himself is capable of exhibiting deep compassion and friendship.

Philoktetes' Appeal for Compassion

When Neoptolemos seems to be on the verge of leaving without him, Philoktetes makes his long and important speech of appeal to the son of Akhilleus (468–506). He begins in the traditional way by invoking Neoptolemos's father, mother, and whatever at home may be "dear" to him (468–69)[93] and by claiming that he beseeches Neoptolemos as a suppliant (ἱκέτης ἱκνοῦμαι, 470). His first appeal is that he not be left "alone, deserted" (*monon, erêmon*) on the island in the evil circumstances that Neoptolemos has both heard about and seen. (He thus reminds the audience of the graphic portrayal of his existence developed in the early part of the play.) Philoktetes then mentions the active alternative to being abandoned that he is seeking: to be carried home on Neoptolemos's ship (473–83). He begins by conceding the "great annoyance" (*duschereia . . . pollê*) that will be involved in transporting a man with a disease like his: the stench and piercing cries of pain.

Philoktetes then casts this deed of compassion in terms of noble action: after generalizing that to the "noble" (τοῖσι γενναίοισι) the "shameful, base deed" (τὸ αἰσχρόν) is "hateful," whereas the "useful, noble deed" (τὸ χρηστόν) is "glorious" (εὐκλεές), he asserts that abandoning him will bring "shameful reproach" (ὄνειδος οὐ καλόν) to Neoptolemos, whereas the act of taking him home will bring the "greatest prize of glory" (πλεῖστον εὐκλείας γέρας). Furthermore, he asks Neoptolemos to exhibit the traditional heroic quality of *tolma* (475, 481), which in this case would refer to the endurance required to transport Philoktetes home. We have seen how the protector of suppliants who shows compassion is typically a hero who is praised as noble (*gennaios*).[94] Philoktetes here invests the doer of the compassionate act of taking him home with the same heroic qualities that would traditionally be used to describe the protector of a suppliant against human enemies. The *tolma* required of the protector has shifted from valor against human enemies to endurance of the discomforts incurred by transporting the diseased man. Indeed, Philoktetes emphasizes that the discomforts, although intense, will nevertheless last only the short time of the single day required to get him home (480). But he still sees this service as "noble" and even as a source of "glory" in the sense that it is appropriate to heroes and expected of them, especially in contrast to the alternative of abandoning a fellow hero like Philoktetes as the Greek leaders have done.

Kirkwood (1958: 243, n.23) notes the verbal similarity between these lines and lines 79–85, in which Odysseus sought to persuade Neoptolemos to adopt his tactics (see above). There also Neoptolemos was asked to exhibit *tolma,* but Odysseus meant the daring and insensitivity that Neoptolemos needed to go through with the deception, which was contrary to his heroic *physis.* Like Philoktetes, Odysseus promised Neoptolemos an enhanced reputation: the glory of victory (81) as well as a reputation for being wise and valiant (119), but in return for a *single day's worth* of uncomfortable shamelessness without justice and piety (82–85). Philoktetes, of course, has no knowledge of this counteroffer, but by the way Sophokles phrases Philoktetes' promise of *eukleia* here, the audience can see clearly the contrasting value schemes between which Neoptolemos must choose. Rose (1992: 292–93) sees a "pathetic disparity" between Philoktetes' assumptions in his use of heroic terminology here and the values of the corrupt "real" world presented elsewhere in the play. Blundell (1989: 199–200) similarly asserts that Philoktetes "uses heroic, aristocratic language to urge a course of action that conforms to intrinsic moral standards rather than the approval of the community at large, and to justice rather than heroic accomplishment." I maintain, however, that the horrible effects of Philoktetes' "god-sent" disease are sufficiently dramatized, especially with the staging of the violent attack of the disease yet to come at 730–826, to convince the audience that the ordeal of transporting him is truly requisite of heroic *tolma.* His dreadful cries of pain and the sight and stench of his wound would occasion real fear and discomfort for the sailors on Neoptolemos's ship. Also, the wound's divine origin gives it an unpredictable, awesome quality beyond that of "natural" wounds.[95] Finally, note that the point of contrast here is actually with Odysseus's plan of deception, the heroic quality and appropriateness of which is questioned repeatedly in the play. Odysseus had used the heroic word *tolma* (82) deviously in asking Neoptolemos to "dare" to violate his own noble standards.

Philoktetes continues his appeal with a request that he be stowed in whatever part of the ship will allow him to cause the least discomfort to his shipmates (481–83), again trying desperately to minimize the burden of his transport. He then intensifies his appeal by invoking Zeus Hikesios and by adopting the suppliant posture, in spite of the difficulty in doing so caused by his lameness (484–86). It is likely that Philoktetes here completes the full ritual contact of traditional supplication (there is no converse indication in the text) and that Sophokles means the audience to be impressed by the religious force that this traditional ritual act performed onstage gives to Philoktetes' appeal.[96] Indeed, far from there being any enmity between Philoktetes and Neoptolemos that might obviate the compulsion of the supplication, there is instead an incipient *philia* based firmly on the *philia* between Philoktetes and Neoptolemos's father. This should make the pressure all the stronger.

Then for the second time in the speech, Philoktetes begs not to be abandoned "deserted" (*erêmon*), as he has been, "apart from the paths of men" (486–87), but that Neoptolemos save him, in the way most convenient, by either taking him to Neoptolemos's own home or dropping him off in Euboia, from where he can easily make his way home. By doing so, Neoptolemos will be doing a favor to Philoktetes' father, who, Philoktetes fears, either has died or, because of the indifference of those passing strangers to whom Philoktetes had entrusted messages, has failed to receive any news of his son's whereabouts. The father anxiously waiting for his son's return from war was, of course, a standard image in legends of the Trojan War (cf. Akhilleus and Peleus, Aias and Telemon, Odysseus and Laertes) and a standard source of pathos. After Philoktetes has expressed so much concern for Neoptolemos's father, Akhilleus, he can expect Neoptolemos to have a reciprocal feeling for Poias. Furthermore, the mention of the negligent messengers is yet another reminder of the empty, ineffective compassion to which Philoktetes has become accustomed during the last ten years (cf. 305–13).

Philoktetes then comes to the climax of his appeal, begging Neoptolemos: "Save me, have compassion on me" (σῶσον, ἐλέησον—he emphatically repeats "You (*su*)"; 501), and he adds that Neoptolemos should consider "how frightful all things are and how precarious it is for mortals who at one point fare well but at another suffer the opposite" (502–3). The fickleness of fate is the familiar topos that we have seen so often in Greek literature, especially in appeals for compassion.[97] As is usual in such appeals, Philoktetes focuses on the "pessimistic" dénouement that the prosperous are likely to sink into misfortune rather than that the misfortunate can hope for better circumstances. Philoktetes chooses, of course, the model of transformation appropriate to the situation; he himself is an example of a prosperous man who has fallen into ruin and agony. Neoptolemos, although presently without troubles, should ipso facto identify with Philoktetes by considering that a like fate could happen to him and then show compassion, as he would hope it would be shown to him. Such compassion, in accordance with the traditional Greek concept of heroic compassion, would be shown not merely by words of sympathy but by behavior: the act of taking Philoktetes home. Philoktetes' speech, therefore, is based on extremely strong, traditional appeals, including a complete supplication. His appeals are appropriate to Neoptolemos's heritage and his "supposed" situation; they should move the young man and result in success.

The chorus amplify Philoktetes' appeal by pleading for Neoptolemos to have compassion ("Pity him, lord"; οἴκτιρ,' ἄναξ) and by recommending that he take Philoktetes home (507–18). They speak of his great "labors" (*ponoi*), difficult to bear, and pray that such may not afflict their friends. Neoptolemos then warns the chorus not to overestimate their tolerance now, only to have to go back on their words when continuous contact with the disease proves too much for them to stand (519–21). This warning and the chorus's determined reassurance serve to give Philoktetes the security that, once in motion toward home, he will not be cast out again by these sailors at the first convenient stopping place, as was the case when he was originally abandoned. Neoptolemos then asserts that it would be shameful (*aischra*) for him to be found less ready than his men to labor to meet the need of this *xenos* (524–25), suggesting, as Philoktetes had done (475–79), that shame is involved in failing to help a noble *xenos*.[98] He leads Philoktetes to believe that he has assented to take him home (526), but the ambiguity ("to wherever," ὅποι) of the destination for which Neoptolemos prays to the gods reminds the audience of Neoptolemos's duplicity (528–29).

Philoktetes is understandably ecstatic at hearing these assurances and at once emphasizes his newfound *philia* with these strangers (530–32). Indeed, he is eager to prove his *philia* "in action" (ἔργῳ), thus exhibiting the heroic tendency to display reciprocal behavior rather than express mere words of gratitude. He then invites Neoptolemos to go into his cave to see the harsh circumstances in which he eked out a living and which are evidence of his stouthearted (*eukardios*) nature (533–35). He continues by speculating that no other man could have endured even seeing these things, much less living there, but adds that necessity schooled him so that he could bear such hardship (536–38). By the use of such words as *tlênai* and *eukardios*, Philoktetes gives his struggle for survival on Lemnos a specifically heroic coloration and seeks to display his *aretê* in vanquishing the harsh circumstances of the island. He obviously expects such an exhibition of heroic *aretê* to demonstrate to the son of Akhilleus his worthiness for friendship and compassion.

At this point we can examine the choral *stasimon* (676–729), which is sung after the scene with the false merchant while Philoktetes and Neoptolemos are in the cave making preparations to get on the ship. While they are absent, the chorus sing yet another song about Philoktetes' suffering that begins with a contrast between Ixion and Philoktetes, two sufferers. Ixion is a mythical model of the violent, ungrateful deceiver: after Zeus had done Ixion the favor of purifying him for the cruel murder of Ixion's own father-in-law, Ixion repaid the favor by trying to seduce Hera, the act that Sophokles here uses to identify him (677). The point of the chorus's contrast is that although Ixion's punishment on the wheel was harsh, it was not so harsh as the fate (*moira*) of Philoktetes, a man whose innocence makes his calamity so undeserved (*anaxiôs,* 685), especially in contrast with someone like Ixion. The chorus stress the fact that Philoktetes has harmed no one unjustly, either by force or deceit (as Jebb interprets, 683). Unlike Ixion, who wrongly used both "force" (*bia*) and "deceit" (*dolos*), Philoktetes has always been "fair to the fair" (ἴσος ὢν ἴσοις), that is, scrupulous in his application of positive reciprocity (684).[99] Sophokles makes it emphatically clear in this song that Philoktetes is worthy of compassion by virtue of his innocence and that he should offer no barrier to anyone's sympathy through any wrongdoing on his part.[100]

The chorus next express wonder at Philoktetes' ability to endure the extreme loneliness of the desert island, a loneliness in which he has heard only the sound of the waves on the beach, a life hardly worth living for the sociable Greeks—here, a "life full of tears" (686–90). More specifically, the chorus emphasize that Philoktetes has had no neighbor who (1) might provide a sympathetic audience to his cries of agony[101] and (2) might be an active helper to Philoktetes in alleviating the consequences of his disease (691–700). The wound is described here in graphic terms as "oozing blood," and the foot is said to be "infested" or "having a beast within" (*enthêros*), suggesting that the disease itself is a beast that must be "lulled to sleep" (*kateunaseien*) with drugs, although this will be only a temporary effect, since it will awaken again.[102] The chorus conclude the first antistrophe with another description of Philoktetes' pitiful mode of movement—a painful crawl that is compared to the insecure movements of an infant (701–5). Philoktetes' method of food-gathering and diet are the subject of the next strophe: he kills game with his bow and drinks standing water rather than enjoying crops and wine, the foods of the civilization from which he has been exiled.[103]

The first three stanzas of the *stasimon* thus emphasize Philoktetes' pitiful past sufferings and his endurance in such a way as to arouse the audience's feeling of sympathy to the utmost. As Kitto (1956: 118) observes:

> Sophocles makes his chorus harp on Philoctetes' sufferings because he does not want our minds to be occupied by

> anything else. . . . The point is that these sufferings which fill the minds of the chorus are also filling the mind of Neoptolemus, and must fill our minds too. Sophocles is making us feel the impact and the strain of it. *This* is what Odysseus and the Atreidae have done to a helpless ally.

I interpret the controversial final antistrophe as follows: after having described Philoktetes' *previous* suffering and struggles in the first three stanzas, the chorus continue their song with yet another empathetic lyric, which reflects Philoktetes' *present* psychological state of joyful expectancy. The emphatic νῦν δὲ (718) marks the change of temporal reference. This is how Philoktetes feels and thinks after his encounter with Neoptolemos, although, again, the audience is meant to sense a discrepancy between the chorus's projection of Philoktetes' expectations and the plan of deception that, presumably, is still in effect and on the verge of success.[104] In summary, the entire *stasimon* provides a lyrical recapitulation of Philoktetes' past sufferings and struggles and of his present expectant joy as developed in the first half of the play, while it also sets the tone for the subsequent dramatic action.

Models of Philia *and Compassion*

In the development of their relationship, Philoktetes repeatedly alludes to two models of compassion and *philia:* to Neoptolemos's father, Akhilleus, and to himself, in his own past relationship with Herakles. In the play, Akhilleus is depicted as Philoktetes' noble friend and a hero cut from essentially the same cloth as Philoktetes (242, 336–38, 874–75, 904–5).[105] Philoktetes characterizes him as one who would never have done what Odysseus and the Atreidai have done to Philoktetes, but instead would have opposed their treatment of him. Indeed, the tradition of Akhilleus's independence and opposition to the Greek leadership is exploited effectively here by Sophokles. The playwright also characterizes Akhilleus as a hero noted both for his hatred of duplicity (88–89) and for his compassion for fellow heroes (904–5). Akhilleus's antipathy to duplicity is well known from the *Iliad* (e.g., 9.312–13). Akhilleus as a model of compassionate behavior also stems from the Homeric tradition.

As we have seen, in the *Iliad* he eventually regains his normal compassion for his *philoi* (cf. chap. 1, pp. 40–42). Homer also depicts Akhilleus as a hero who can be moved to compassion in *Iliad* 24, where Akhilleus, despite his deeply felt residual hostility toward Hektor and the Trojans, nevertheless responds compassionately (οἰκτίρων, 516) and humanely to old King Priam's request for Hektor's body (*Iliad* 24.486–551).[106]

Also, Philoktetes himself serves as a model of heroic *philia* and compassion, since as a youth he showed compassion to a suffering *philos,* the great hero Herakles. This association is established in the scene in which Neoptolemos makes a hesitant request to handle the bow (656–70). Philoktetes replies to his request:

> ὅσιά τε φωνεῖς ἔστι τ,' ὦ τέκνον, θέμις,
> ὅς γ' ἡλίου τόδ' εἰσορᾶν ἐμοὶ φάος
> μόνος δέδωκας, ὃς χθόν' Οἰταίαν ἰδεῖν,
> ὃς πατέρα πρέσβυν, ὃς φίλους, ὃς τῶν ἐμῶν
> ἐχθρῶν μ' ἔνερθεν ὄντ' ἀνέστησάς πέρα.
> θάρσει, παρέσται ταῦτά σοι καὶ θιγγάνειν
> καὶ δόντι δοῦναι κἀξεπεύξασθαι βροτῶν
> ἀρετῆς ἕκατι τῶνδ' ἐπιψαῦσαι μόνῳ·
> εὐεργετῶν γὰρ καὐτὸς αὔτ' ἐκτησάμην. (662–70)

> Your words are holy, and it is right for you, my son, who alone have granted me to look upon this light of the sun, to see the land of Oita, to see my aged father and my friends, and have raised me up from beneath my enemies' feet so that I am above them. Take heart, it will be in your power to handle this bow and to give it back to the one who gave it to you, and to boast that you alone of mortals have touched it because of your excellence; for it was in doing an act of kindness that I myself acquired it.

Philoktetes makes it clear that Neoptolemos is entitled to hold the bow, an act that Philoktetes describes as a benefit or kindness to Neoptolemos in recompense for Neoptolemos's compassionate assent to take him home. Philoktetes' language, particularly the use of the verb "give" (δίδωμι) in 668, stresses the notion of reciprocity in granting this request, a notion at the core of popular Greek ethics and of the Greek understanding of the social basis of heroic behavior.[107] Philoktetes' use of the word "excellence" (*aretê*) in 669 to describe Neoptolemos's assent to take him home again suggests that Philoktetes continues to see Neoptolemos's compassionate service as having a noble or heroic quality.[108] Then, when Philoktetes mentions that he himself acquired the bow in recompense by "doing an act of kindness" (εὐεργετῶν, 670), the audience is made to recall Philoktetes' act of compassion for the great Herakles, who had asked Philoktetes to perform the grim task of burning his body when he was in agony. Neoptolemos's compassionate service to Philoktetes would likewise have its grim aspects, as Philoktetes himself has made clear. Rose (1992: 294) rightly remarks that here the bow becomes a symbol of "service to a suffering friend." Indeed, the bow is not only a mythic instrument of superhuman power but also symbolizes noble service between heroes, the mechanism through which the bow, in all its power, is passed from one hero to the next.[109] Sophokles' use of anaphora in Philoktetes' response, signaled by the repetition of ὅς (who) in 663–66, helps convey the warmth of Philoktetes' gratitude.

Neoptolemos responds to Philoktetes in kind by saying that the *philos* who knows how to reciprocate when he has received a kindness is more valuable than any possession (671–73). Webster (1970) sees Neoptolemos's emotion here as genuine: "Neoptolemos feels a natural sympathy for Philoktetes as a like-minded hero." Whether Sophokles intended the audience to think this or not, the son of Akhilleus's heritage and *physis* as depicted in the play so far would suggest to the audience that he *should* be so affected by such behavior and would intensify the suspense as to whether he will actually continue to carry out the deception. Then, when Philoktetes asks Neoptolemos to come into the cave with him as a "helper" (ξυμπαραστάτην, 675) that his sick condition requires, we are reminded of his pitiful lack of such a helper in his long years on the island (170–75, 195), a lack that now seems to be remedied by his new *philos*, Neoptolemos.

Up to this point, we have seen how Philoktetes has modeled for Neoptolemos a type of *philia* that is based on mutual trust, mutual benefit, and compassionate action, a friendship that he characterizes with his highest terms of value, namely those associated with *aretê*. In contrast, Odysseus has offered Neoptolemos a reward of glory to be won by following a plan that entails deceit of Philoktetes. The scene that follows is pivotal in that it shows the development of Neoptolemos's strong, personal feeling of compassion for Philoktetes and also shows his conformity to the model of friendship that Philoktetes has proposed for him.[110]

Neoptolemos's Compassion, Stage 1: Development and Conformity

Sophokles exploits the visual and auditory immediacy of the theater when he presents Philoktetes experiencing one of the periodic attacks that comprise the most intensely painful stage of his disease's cycle. Philoktetes cries out and cannot conceal his intense agony, although at first he tries to do so. The sheer intensity of his pain is shown not only by his agonized cries and his violent writhing, but also by his extreme request that Neoptolemos cut off his foot at once without regard as to whether this would endanger his life (742–50). Philoktetes then suddenly begs Neoptolemos again to pity him (οἴκτιρέ με) and not to abandon him out of fear of the hideous nature of his attack (756–57). Thus far Neoptolemos has heard about Philoktetes' suffering, has seen his pitiable surroundings, and has seen the man himself when the disease was in abeyance. But now, for the first time, Sophokles has Neoptolemos (as well as the audience) witness Philoktetes' suffering at its most intense under the full onslaught of the rabid disease.[111] Neoptolemos is at a loss in the face of what he witnesses and here first gives voice to an unmistakably powerful and unambiguous feeling of sympathy for Philoktetes' sufferings: "Alas, you are miserable, clearly miserable indeed from all your labors!" (ἰὼ δύστηνε σύ, / δύστηνε δῆτα διὰ πόνων πάντων φανείς, 759–60).[112] It is a sympathy in direct proportion to Philoktetes' anguish: the younger hero's use of the word "miserable" (*dystênos*) to describe Philoktetes echoes the latter's use of the same word to describe himself fifteen lines before. He furthermore shows an eagerness to help comfort Philoktetes by offering to hold him (761).

As Philoktetes is being overcome by this attack of his disease, he entrusts the bow of Herakles to Neoptolemos with the request that he keep it and safeguard it from the Greek pursuers whom Philoktetes now expects to arrive after his encounter with the merchant (763–73). He also reminds Neoptolemos of his religious obligation to protect him from his enemies by recalling that he is Neoptolemos's suppliant (*prostropon*, 773). Previously, Philoktetes had supplicated Neoptolemos to endure the unpleasant effects of the disease in the process of conveying him home. Now, as if there were no qualitative difference, he also thrusts Neoptolemos into the customary role of the protector of a suppliant against human enemies. By giving a solemn pledge of his right hand not to abandon Philoktetes (810–13), Neoptolemos further reinforces his role as protector and savior.[113]

After Philoktetes entrusts the bow to Neoptolemos and then experiences a second surge of the disease coming on, he makes a request that Neoptolemos burn his body in the Lemnian volcano nearby—a task that recalls Philoktetes' similar act of service to his mentor, the dying Herakles. After a silence that Philoktetes notices and that betrays Neoptolemos's inner conflict, Neoptolemos openly expresses his deep feeling of compassion for the older hero: he acknowledges that he has been in pain for a long time (ἀλγῶ πάλαι, 806) in his grief for Philoktetes' troubles.[114] The mention of his own pain both stresses the sympathetic quality of Neoptolemos's compassion and also suggests that he feels discomfort in his role as deceiver, a role in which his true feelings and inclinations have had to be suppressed. The word πάλαι reveals that he has had this feeling for a long time and recalls the full range of appeals that Philoktetes has made to the "noble nature" of the son of Akhilleus—pleas that should have been effective, although only now, as he witnesses the full horror of Philoktetes' suffering, does their effect begin to show through unequivocally. While Philoktetes sleeps, Neoptolemos shows his realization that victory at Troy is impossible without Philoktetes himself and that the gods intend for Philoktetes to wear the crown of victory (839–42). Neoptolemos here sees that his own future, specifically any hope of personal achievement at Troy, is linked to that of Philoktetes.

When Philoktetes awakens to find that he has not been abandoned, he continues to characterize Neoptolemos in noble terms:

ὦ φέγγος ὕπνου διάδοχον, τό τ' ἐλπίδων
ἄπιστον οἰκούρημα τῶνδε τῶν ξένων.
οὐ γάρ ποτ,' ὦ παῖ, τοῦτ' ἂν ἐξηύχησ' ἐγώ,
τλῆναί σ' ἐλεινῶς ὧδε τἀμὰ πήματα
μεῖναι παρόντα καὶ ξυνωφελοῦντά μοι.
οὔκουν Ἀτρεῖδαι τοῦτ' ἔτλησαν εὐφόρως
οὕτως ἐνεγκεῖν, ἀγαθοὶ στρατηλάται.
ἀλλ' εὐγενὴς γὰρ ἡ φύσις κἀξ εὐγενῶν,
ὦ τέκνον, ἡ σή, πάντα ταῦτ' ἐν εὐχερεῖ
ἔθου, βοῆς τε καὶ δυσοσμίας γέμων. (867–76)

Light, sleep's successor, and the watch kept by these strangers, a thing beyond my hopes! For never, my son, could I have hoped for this, that you would stay here by me, so compassionately withstanding my miseries and joining in my care. The Atreidai never dared to bear this so patiently—fine commanders that they are! But since your nature is noble and descended from the noble, son, you took these things in stride, even though you were filled full of my screaming and bad stench.

Philoktetes contrasts Neoptolemos' compassionate endurance (τλῆναι . . . ἐλεινῶς) with the Atreidai's inability to bear his suffering "patiently" (εὐφόρως, 872). Indeed, the Greek leaders had used just such an occasion to abandon Philoktetes on Lemnos. In contrast, Neoptolemos's "noble nature, descended from the noble" (εὐγενὴς . . . φύσις κἀξ εὐγενῶν, 874; cf. n.108 above) has enabled him to tolerate easily the horrible effects of Philoktetes' disease. To reinforce this point, Philoktetes sarcastically calls the Atreidai "the fine generals" (ἀγαθοὶ στρατηλάται, 873). That Neoptolemos's behavior is consistent with his father's example is further emphasized by Philoktetes' statement at 904–5: "You neither do nor say anything unlike your father in helping a noble man." Philoktetes' intense gratitude reminds us yet again that he has had no such helper before. The compassion of Neoptolemos for which Philoktetes is so grateful consists of behavior (staying and helping) rather than mere words of sympathy.[115] Also, in being unable to abandon Philoktetes without the bow, we see in Neoptolemos the working of compassion as a restraining force (D1b).

Sophokles here, as elsewhere in the play, relies on a notion of natural—what we might call "genetic"—inheritance (i.e., that Neoptolemos has his most basic nature and character from his father, Akhilleus). Whereas the poet's references to nobility may have suggested connotations of class distinction for members (or some members) of his audience, I believe that the primary meaning of nobility in these lines is to denote and suggest qualities of character rather than class stereotypes. Sophokles' emphasis is not on Neoptolemos's class per se but rather on his character and behavior, that is, whether he acts in a way consistent with his outstanding father's character, behavior, and expressed ideals. The contrast implied by Philoktetes is not with unsavory members of a lower social class but with Odysseus and the sons of Atreus, members of the same heroic, "aristocratic" class as Akhilleus and his son. If anything, Agamemnon outranks them all socially; indeed, the criticism of the Atreidai in 873 is that they are not exhibiting the character which their positions as generals suggests they should. The poet displays an awareness that both natural inheritance and environment/education play a role in the development of character.[116]

Neoptolemos's Compassion, Stage 2: Persistence and Reassertion

Having developed a strong feeling of compassion for Philoktetes and having lived up to Philoktetes' expectation in not abandoning him, Neoptolemos's *philia* with Philoktetes is challenged by his disclosure of the deception and by Odysseus's intervention.

When Philoktetes subsequently shows a noble desire to be as self-sufficient as possible (889–92, 894), Neoptolemos can no longer conceal his inner turmoil and blurts out a cry of indecision (895). Philoktetes notices Neoptolemos's hesitancy, and for the next few lines (896–911) Sophokles develops Philoktetes' anxious misunderstanding of Neoptolemos's language and feelings: whereas

Neoptolemos hesitates to carry out the deception, Philoktetes thinks that he hesitates to take him home. Philoktetes fears that the "offensiveness," "disgust" (*dyschereia*) caused by his disease has suddenly led Neoptolemos to forsake the exceptional compassionate *tolma* that he had just been praising. Neoptolemos speaks of the *dyschereia* that results from forsaking one's *physis* (902–3), by which he means telling lies and deceiving a *philos,* behavior that will make him seem shameful (*aischros,* 906) and base (*kakos,* 908–9; cf. 86–91, 108, 120). Philoktetes, misinterpreting his meaning, asserts that Neoptolemos is not abandoning his *physis* or deviating from the example of his father, Akhilleus, by "helping (ἐπωφελῶν) a noble man" (904–5, cf. 475–79, 670), referring to the traditional expectation of one hero to help another. The empathetic and compassionate nature of Neoptolemos's agony here is shown by his expression of long-term distress (ἀνιῶμαι πάλαι) at the prospect of his deceitful behavior resulting in pain for Philoktetes (912–13, cf. 806).

Neoptolemos can no longer keep the truth of the deception from Philoktetes; his discomfort with lying and his feeling of compassion for Philoktetes force this change. But after he reveals his deception, Neoptolemos nevertheless retains possession of the bow and asserts that Philoktetes must go to Troy, citing his own continuing obedience to his commanders and the imperative for victory as the reasons why he cannot return the bow (915–26). Deception is no longer being used, but so long as Philoktetes is deprived of his bow, there is an element of threat and coercion behind any attempt to persuade him. Philoktetes' response (927–62) to Neoptolemos's disclosure is understandably a mixture of anger, disappointment, and fear. On the one hand, he is angry with Neoptolemos for betraying his trust by using deception. At the same time, he appeals to Neoptolemos to respect his rights as a suppliant: he stresses Neoptolemos's shameful betrayal of his suppliant, whom he now has violated by depriving him of his bow (929–31). Philoktetes also, as one would expect, chides Neoptolemos for acting contrary to his *physis* as the son of Akhilleus, although he sees this as the result of the influence of *kakoi,* who have corrupted Neoptolemos (950, 971–72, cf. 1008–15).

His mention of Herakles in 943 recalls the heroic *philia* that the bow symbolizes, but in violation of which the bow is now being utilized. The speech also conveys Philoktetes' feeling of isolation as well as his desperate need of the bow for survival.

The powerful effect of Philoktetes' speech is revealed by Neoptolemos's response: an "awesome feeling of compassion" (οἶκτος δεινὸς, 965) has befallen him, and not now for the first time, but has done so for a long time.[117] This compassion, at a crucial moment in the play's dramatic action, restrains Neoptolemos from hurting Philoktetes further: he is unable to leave this man defenseless without the bow (D1b). Philoktetes immediately begs Neoptolemos to show compassion (ἐλέησον, 967) and again associates reproach and shame with the use of the unheroic method of deceit (967–68, 971–72, cf. above on 906, 908–9). The compassion that Philoktetes now requests is the act of returning the bow (973).

Neoptolemos experiences a crisis of indecision and seems to be on the verge of handing the bow back to Philoktetes when Odysseus suddenly intervenes to stop him and to take control of the situation. Despite Odysseus's dominance, Neoptolemos's compassion for Philoktetes continues to play a powerful role in the action. To demonstrate Neoptolemos's inappropriateness as Odysseus's assistant, Philoktetes himself points out Neoptolemos's sympathy for him and his pain at performing the actions that Odysseus has compelled him to do (1007–12). Odysseus, when threatening to abandon Philoktetes, acknowledges Neoptolemos's noble tendency to compassion (γενναῖός περ ὤν) by telling him to stop looking at Philoktetes, who is trying to appeal to him (1068–69).[118] Odysseus obviously fears that Neoptolemos's compassion for Philoktetes may result in further obstruction of his own plans. After his long silence during the verbal wrangling of Odysseus and Philoktetes, however, Neoptolemos orders his men to stay with Philoktetes in hopes that he will change his mind while preparations are being made for the voyage to Troy. Neoptolemos does this, although he says he knows that he will be criticized by Odysseus for being "by nature too full of pity" (ὡς ἔφυν οἴκτου πλέως, 1074–75). The reproach that Neoptolemos anticipates from Odysseus for this exhibition of compassion is consistent with the play's characterization of Odysseus as the sort of person who typically sees this emotion as a dangerous threat to competitive success.[119]

Odysseus's behavior during the coercion phase accords with his actions elsewhere in the play and serves to intensify the abuse of Philoktetes. Odysseus's attempt to coerce Philoktetes into coming to Troy includes a threat to force Philoktetes onto the boat (982–83), which Philoktetes rightly regards as equivalent to enslaving him, a free man (995–96). Odysseus shuts off his acrimonious debate with Philoktetes with yet another threat: to abandon Philoktetes on the island without the bow and to use the bow himself to win great glory at Troy. With the loss of his bow and the prospect of abandonment and inevitable death on Lemnos without it, as Beye (1970: 66) notes, Philoktetes has now been denied all value by the Greeks in terms of heroic "reward" (*geras*) and "honor" (*timê*); in Philoktetes' own words, "I am nothing" (οὐδέν εἰμι, 1030).[120] As he contemplates these dire prospects in the play's *kommos,* Philoktetes is at his lowest and most pitiable point. Sophokles thus uses the *kommos* to plumb the depths of his hero's despair and vulnerability. Still, Philoktetes resolutely refuses to surrender to the coercion that is being used against him: he maintains his refusal to go to Troy with the Greeks, despite the chorus's attempts to prevail upon him to bend. In doing so, he maintains his heroic integrity in a way typical of other Sophoklean heroes. After the wrenching despair of Philoktetes' *kommos,* the audience suddenly learns that Neoptolemos has had a change of heart: the compassion that we have seen building in him, rather than being suppressed by Odysseus, has instead driven him into rebellion. Despite the opposition of Odysseus and the Greek army, he will return the bow to Philoktetes, the third major turning point in the play's action (after the attack of the disease and the disclosure of the deception).

Neoptolemos's assertion that he has done wrong by obeying Odysseus and the army (1226) shows that he now agrees with Philoktetes' earlier argument that his *physis* has been corrupted by his superiors (950, 971, 1008–15). At this point, Neoptolemos renounces the loyalty that had earlier allowed Odysseus to control him (93–94, 925–26). His refusal to budge under threat of the army's retaliation and his forthright readiness to do battle with Odysseus, if necessary, show him as exhibiting Akhilleus's independent defiance of the group.[121] Finally, Neoptolemos's actions demonstrate that his compassion consists not only of assistance to Philoktetes but also of the heroic protection of a suppliant against human enemies; also it is action, not just words (D1a). The last we see of Odysseus in the play is when he slinks off the stage in fear that Philoktetes will shoot him with the bow. As Taplin (1971: 36–37) notes, this is a most unheroic exit for a Greek hero and one that signifies the drama's repudiation of him and of the values for which he stands.[122] In summary, Neoptolemos's compassion for Philoktetes, which was challenged by his disclosure of the deception and by Odysseus's intervention, has nevertheless persisted and has reasserted itself to the point that he has returned the bow to Philoktetes despite the opposition of Odysseus.[123]

Failed Persuasion and the Decision for Greece

With Odysseus renounced and the bow returned, Neoptolemos, at last, has established a basis for genuine, uncoerced persuasion. This brings us back to the problem concerning the play's ending with which we began. The debate between Neoptolemos and Philoktetes at this point is a crucial one that involves the issue of compassion in the play both in regard to Philoktetes' worthiness to receive compassion from Neoptolemos and in regard to Neoptolemos's eventual justification in showing compassion to Philoktetes by agreeing to take him home.

Neoptolemos prefaces his argument for going to Troy with the assertion that Philoktetes is being excessively stubborn in refusing to help himself by going to Troy, and that therefore he is not the proper recipient of sympathy (1316–20; see above, pp. 169–70, for the citation of the text). He continues by saying that Philoktetes has become savage and will not take friendly advice, but considers a friend who gives such advice to be an enemy and hates him (1321–23). Only after these assertions, which suggest his impatience and frustration, does Neoptolemos begin his argument proper, which is that Philoktetes should come to Troy willingly, so that he can be healed and so that he and Neoptolemos will gain the glory of victory in the Trojan War. It should be noted that this is the first attempt to persuade Philoktetes to go to Troy, by Neoptolemos or by anyone else, that has not involved deception or the threat of force or other duress, including the threat of abandoning Philoktetes on Lemnos without the bow. Consequently, it is not quite right for Neoptolemos to say that Philoktetes is stubborn and unwilling to listen to friendly advice. As to Philoktetes being savage, I agree with Kitto (1956: 132), who asks, "But who has caused him to become savage?" Indeed, who had isolated him from civilization to begin with, and who has continued to treat him as a beast to be hunted or, at best, an enemy or outcast to be tricked or threatened? Furthermore, Philoktetes' response to Neoptolemos's speech here reveals that he is struggling with a serious dilemma—whether to accept Neoptolemos's advice or not.

> οἴμοι, τί δράσω; πῶς ἀπιστήσω λόγοις
> τοῖς τοῦδ,' ὅς εὔνους ὢν ἐμοὶ παρῄνεσεν (1350–51)

> What will I do? How can I distrust the words of this man,
> who has advised me out of kindness?

This expression of his dilemma shows that Philoktetes accepts his young friend's argument as being in good faith and wants to give in to it. This is not the response of a man who finds hateful those who advise him with goodwill and on a basis of friendship.

Neoptolemos's assertion, in lines 1316–20, seems to be based on a reasonable enough commonplace: that those who are able, but unwilling, to help themselves out of their own difficulties cannot expect to receive sympathy from others. This would seem to be an appropriate criticism for those who—for no good reason—refuse to extricate themselves from their own difficulties. But is this Philoktetes' situation here, and, furthermore, should Neoptolemos's assertion be taken as his (or Sophokles') final assessment of Philoktetes?[124]

The text suggests otherwise. In responding to Neoptolemos's advice, Philoktetes enunciates several reasons that do not allow him to go to Troy. The first reason relates to the shame that stems from the hero's "dishonor" (*atimia*) among the Greeks. Philoktetes has been deprived of all *timê* by the actions of the leaders. In contrast to the somewhat analogous situation of Akhilleus in the *Iliad,* although the dishonor of Philoktetes has been much greater, Odysseus and the Greek leaders in this play have neither apologized to Philoktetes nor made any restitution for the wrongs they have done to him.[125] Philoktetes imagines his own shame, humiliation, and loneliness in the midst of his enemies (1352–57). He even personifies his eyes and asks them how they could endure the sight of such an association, just as he had envisioned the bow's shame at being used by Odysseus (1128–39). If he goes back even now, it will seem as if he is capitulating to their threats out of desperate self-interest, despite their continuing abuse of him. Second, Philoktetes fears still further maltreatment at the hands of the Greek leaders, a fear based on his past and his continuing experience with them. Nothing that Neoptolemos has said and, for that matter, nothing that has happened so far in the play would suggest that this is an unlikely prospect.[126] His third reason concerns the leaders' abuse of Neoptolemos, and although Philoktetes mistakenly asserts that Neoptolemos has been wronged by being deprived of Akhilleus's arms, he still has no reliable assurance that he and Neoptolemos will not continue to suffer abuse at the hands of the Greek leaders. Finally, Philoktetes cannot bring himself to help his enemies. By going to Troy and fighting for the Greek leaders, he would be accomplishing their goals and giving them victory. Although in the ensuing argument (1373–1401) Neoptolemos continues to press Philoktetes to relent for his own benefit and although the elder hero perhaps comes close to giving in to his young friend at 1388, nevertheless Philoktetes maintains his position, which is based on his past experience with the Greek leaders. Kitto effectively argues that the timing of Neoptolemos's revelation of the oracle's promises and his use of arguments directed to Philoktetes' self-interest show that

> what the Atreidae and Odysseus have done to Philoktetes has so bitten into his soul that he will himself willingly endure

his malady to the end rather than rescue his tormentors from the disaster which they so justly merit. (1956: 132)

As much as he would like to give in to his young friend's sincere effort at persuasion, Philoktetes refuses to participate in a society and give assistance to men who violate reciprocity and show no consideration for willing allies, a society that has discarded him as worthless and has abused Neoptolemos's noble inclinations. We want Philoktetes to be healed, but at the same time we understand why Neoptolemos fails to persuade him. Under the circumstances, Philoktetes' refusal is an understandable ethical choice.[127]

Blundell (1989: 215–19) argues that Philoktetes wrongfully chooses "Harm Enemies" over "Help Friends" (and helping himself) in his persistent refusal to be persuaded by Neoptolemos here. She claims that Philoktetes fails "to abide by his own principles of reciprocal friendship and active gratitude" and that he wrongs his friend Neoptolemos by refusing to be persuaded by him. In response, I would argue that Philoktetes' adherence to "Harm Enemies" is restricted here to a refusal to benefit those who themselves have shown no compassion. This is a concept of reciprocity that does not entail active harm to such people but rather a passive refusal to benefit them, a degree of negative reciprocity that was accepted implicitly in Greek popular morality.[128] I would also point out that Philoktetes here is almost persuaded by his newly redeemed young friend, but still not fully so; subsequent events of the play will complete that persuasion. His position, much like that of Akhilleus at the end of the "embassy scene" of *Iliad* 9, while fundamentally unchanged, has nevertheless softened somewhat.

Given what Philoktetes has been subjected to and what he has suffered for the past ten years (and in the first 1300 lines of the play), we should not be indignant or impatient with him for being unwilling to entrust himself to the Greek leadership again or for being unwilling to help those who have so mistreated him. Neoptolemos's characterization of Philoktetes at 1316–23 misses the mark: Philoktetes is not simply a person who stubbornly refuses to help himself and continues in his suffering for no good reason. Indeed, at the conclusion of Philoktetes' speech, Neoptolemos acknowledges that Philoktetes' argument is reasonable (λέγεις μὲν εἰκότ,' 1373), although he still wishes that Philoktetes would change his mind. In sum, the young man's impatient and frustrated assertion of Philoktetes' unworthiness of sympathy at 1316–23 should be understood neither as his own final assessment of Philoktetes nor that which the play's argument supports.[129]

The second problem of the play's ending involves the decision of Philoktetes and Neoptolemos to go home rather than to Troy, a decision that has struck some readers as unwarranted or unheroic. Neoptolemos is at a loss as to what he will do after his words have failed to persuade Philoktetes; he realizes that the only option open is for the argument to cease and for Philoktetes to continue to go without the healing and glory that the oracle had promised (1393–96). The word/deed antithesis employed in these lines signals a transition from the mode of language to the more heroic mode of behavior. Philoktetes asks his friend to allow him to suffer the pain that is his fate, but to relieve that pain as far as he can by performing the essential act of compassion (πρᾶξον, 1399) which Philoktetes has desired all along and that Neoptolemos, in effect, has promised to perform with the pledge of his right hand: transportation from the desert island to the sympathetic community of family and friends (310–11, 468–506, 526, 813, 869–81, 904–5, 941, 1367–71).[130] Neoptolemos's earlier assurance of this act of noble compassion caused Philoktetes to deem him worthy of being entrusted with Herakles' bow, but Neoptolemos's role as deceiver and later his compromised and then sincere efforts to persuade Philoktetes otherwise have kept him from fulfilling Philoktetes' long-standing request. To enforce his request, Philoktetes uses his claim as Neoptolemos's suppliant as well as all the claims of *philia* that he has developed with Neoptolemos throughout the play. Neoptolemos's compassion for Philoktetes (coupled with his own self-interest) had led him to seek to persuade Philoktetes to go to Troy so as to bring about Philoktetes' cure and the benefit of victory for both Philoktetes and himself. But given Philoktetes' unwillingness to go to Troy, conveyance of Philoktetes home is the most compassionate option remaining to Neoptolemos.[131] It does remove

Philoktetes from the isolation of Lemnos to the care of friends and family and the friendlier and more comfortable circumstances of home. Furthermore, it restores Philoktetes' *timê* even as it ensures defeat for the Greek leaders who have denied him *timê.* It does, however, entail both men's loss of greater glory at Troy, the persistence of Philoktetes' painful condition, and Neoptolemos's and his men's discomfort in conveying Philoktetes home. It is, nevertheless, the best that Philoktetes and Neoptolemos can do in their situation. When he says, "Let's go!" (στείχωμεν, 1402), Neoptolemos at last says for real what he had only feigned at 526 and 645. His words and deeds now are finally of a single fabric (D1a). Philoktetes calls his word γενναῖον, the acclamation of nobility with which suppliants traditionally mark their protectors.[132]

After having agreed to take him home, Neoptolemos expresses some fear of incurring the enmity and possibly the military aggression of the Achaians. Philoktetes, however, again showing his commitment to heroic reciprocity, promises him the aid (προσωφέλησιν, cf. 871, 905) and protection of his bow should such an attack occur (1404–7).[133] With this assurance, Neoptolemos, misgivings assuaged, again urges Philoktetes to depart to the ship (1407–8). Here, as when he returned the bow, Neoptolemos shows that he willing to oppose Odysseus and the Greek army, should they threaten him and Philoktetes.

It is important to note that it is Philoktetes who makes the choice not to go to Troy, not Neoptolemos. Neoptolemos fails in his effort to persuade Philoktetes to go to Troy, and he is disappointed, but he fails nobly and in accordance with his statement early in the play that he would rather fail nobly than win ignobly (94–95). After persuasion fails, Neoptolemos's choices are severely limited: (1) he can take Philoktetes home as requested and as he himself has promised; (2) he can abandon Philoktetes on Lemnos again and go to Troy, to almost certain defeat and humiliation, as indicated by the oracle of Helenos and reiterated in his own attempt to persuade Philoktetes; (3) he can even more inhumanely abandon Philoktetes on Lemnos and go home to Greece. Neoptolemos chooses compassion, but he does not choose it over victory as many have asserted, since victory is no longer a possibility unless Philoktetes willingly goes to Troy. In assenting to take Philoktetes home, Neoptolemos completes his development as the heroic peer of Philoktetes and as a son worthy of Akhilleus. Also, he joins with Philoktetes in repudiating the corrupt methods of Odysseus and the Atreidai.[134]

A Great Friend's Act of Grace

One problem with this demonstration of compassion and *philia* by Neoptolemos and Philoktetes is that the pair have shown themselves worthy of the rewards of victory at Troy, rewards that they must now forgo. Also, as Easterling (1978) asserts, Philoktetes has shown himself worthy of being healed of his terrible affliction.[135] It remains for the deus ex machina to provide the most compassionate outcome for Philoktetes and the reward due to Neoptolemos, as well as to resolve the conflict with the accepted mythic tradition of the Greek victory at Troy. Herakles, Philoktetes' great friend and beneficiary of Philoktetes' compassion, now a god, redirects the two heroes toward Troy and validates the heroism of their earlier decision.[136]

Herakles says he comes out of concern for Philoktetes and for his benefit (*charis*, 1413); he does not reprove Philoktetes for refusing to be coerced by Odysseus or persuaded by Neoptolemos.[137] His purpose is to reveal to Philoktetes the "determinations" (*bouleumata*) of Zeus and to delay Philoktetes from his present journey home (1415–16, cf. μήπω γε, 1409). Herakles speaks as if he is showing the deliberations of Zeus to Philoktetes for the first time. Indeed, throughout the play the fulfillment of the oracle has been said to be conditional upon Philoktetes' willingness to go to Troy; now the divine will (that Philoktetes go to Troy) is made unmistakably clear to Philoktetes through the authority of his divine friend.[138]

Herakles begins his revelation of Zeus's determinations with a comparison: he himself, after his great "labors" (*ponoi*), has won "immortal excellence"; likewise, Philoktetes, after (and through) all his "sufferings" (*ponoi*), will make his life glorious (1418–22).[139] Although their rewards will not be precisely equal (the son of Zeus has become divine), the dynamic is the same: like Herakles,

Philoktetes will receive glory after his labors. The word ὀφείλεται (1421), although usually translated "it is your destiny" or "it is ordained," also conveys through its literal meaning a notion that the glory Philoktetes will receive is "owed" or "due" to him.[140]

Herakles reveals that Philoktetes will go to Troy with Neoptolemos, will be healed, will kill Paris with Herakles' bow, and will sack Troy (1423–28). He twice asserts that the army will honor Philoktetes for his *aretê* (1425, 1429), indicating Philoktetes' full reintegration into the military community at Troy. Herakles then assures Philoktetes that he will return home with the spoils of victory to his father, Poias, and the "heights of Oita" (1429–30). Oita, as elsewhere in the play, refers to the homeland for which Philoktetes has longed so intensely and for so long, but its mention also evokes the memory of Philoktetes' association with Herakles. The gratitude and friendly reciprocity that characterize their relationship is shown in Herakles' request that Philoktetes make a memory-offering at his pyre on Oita in recompense for the benefits that Philoktetes will have received from using Herakles' bow, the use of which, as we have seen, was itself a gift given in reciprocity for Philoktetes' compassionate service to Herakles (1428–33).

Herakles then explicitly emphasizes reciprocity when he addresses Neoptolemos with a reminder that victory at Troy depends on the mutual effort and cooperation of him and Philoktetes: neither can win victory alone; they are to guard each other like two lions.[141] This image of friendship validates the reverent treatment of Philoktetes that Philoktetes has sought and that Neoptolemos has developed in the course of the play.[142] These lines in particular emphasize the necessity of such behavior and of such relationships for the success of competitive joint ventures, including war. Herakles' characterization of Philoktetes' and Neoptolemos's interdependence as being essential to the Greek victory thus validates the pair's compassionate and caring treatment of each other as it has developed in the play and in spite of the obstacles put in its path. Furthermore, Herakles' assertions here are in accordance with the drama's theme of heroic compassion.[143]

After Herakles has finished speaking, Philoktetes expresses his affection and respect for Herakles and immediately assents to do what the god says. Philoktetes thus reverses his previous decision. Why does Herakles succeed where Neoptolemos has failed? Herakles, a god, speaks in *mythoi* (1410, 1417, 1447) rather than in *logoi* used by mortals like Neoptolemos (1350).[144] As the son of Zeus, Herakles reveals the divine will unequivocally, and Philoktetes piously does not disobey this clear indication of Zeus's plans.[145] Herakles also, unlike Neoptolemos, can give Philoktetes definite assurance that he will not suffer further at the hands of the Greek leadership or army, but rather will win glory from the army and return home to his father (cf. 1358–61). He promises to send Asklepios himself to heal the hero's wound. Finally, and most important, Herakles is Philoktetes' close and longtime friend.[146] Herakles is a revered hero whom Philoktetes has emulated in the past and someone whose beneficence Philoktetes can trust absolutely.[147] When Philoktetes returns to the Greek army, he will say that Herakles himself has sent him and Neoptolemos. Philoktetes can now assent to the advice of friends like Herakles and Neoptolemos completely (1466–68).[148] Herakles' intervention, as a friend of Philoktetes who has himself participated in and benefited from *philia* of the sort that Philoktetes has advocated, allows Philoktetes to put aside his resistance and to go to Troy with Neoptolemos, in a strongly collaborative mode that reinforces and validates this same type of *philia,* in order to win victory and to receive a divine cure. The deus ex machina, therefore, both reinforces and advances the play's theme of compassion.[149]

Concluding Analysis

In this play, compassion is developed dramatically in at least three ways in the character of Neoptolemos: (1) as a strong feeling of sympathy in response to the noble Philoktetes' suffering; (2) as a powerful force that inhibits him, as a subordinate with a brutal duty, from hurting Philoktetes further (e.g., 912–13) and eventually propels him to return the stolen bow contrary to Odysseus's wishes (D1b); and (3) as the noble protective compassion, traditionally associated with powerful religious and heroic obligations, that impels him to endure the inconvenience of helping a suffering friend and ally and to fulfill Philoktetes' long-standing request to be taken home in spite of the likelihood of the Greek army's retaliation (D1a). Unlike the traditional suppliant drama in which the protector makes a straightforward response to the suppliant's appeal, the fulfillment of Philoktetes' appeal for compassion is made exceptionally suspenseful by Neoptolemos's own wavering between allegiances and his search for "identity" throughout the play. Sophokles thus makes even Neoptolemos's expressions of compassion, which are placed at critical moments in the play's action, highly dramatic.

Compassion is idealized in the play and is depicted in terms of traditional reciprocal service between heroic *philoi.* The particular compassionate service that Philoktetes requests is that Neoptolemos convey him home in spite of the disgust and annoyance occasioned by Philoktetes' disease and its effects and, in the last part of the play, in the face of resistance from the Greek army. Philoktetes makes a distinction between the minimal compassion of word and token behavior and the meaningful compassion involving action, the sort of compassion that is, as we have seen from Homer on, traditionally associated with heroes. Philoktetes enforces his request with traditional methods: a claim of *philia* with Neoptolemos's father, supplication, obligations of pledge and promise, and an appeal for compassion on the basis of likeness and the fear of the instability of fortune. But his strongest appeal is that based on the trust and reciprocity appropriate to noble *philoi.* This ideal is exhibited in the models of Philoktetes' own service to Herakles (670) and Akhilleus's disposition to benefit friends (904–5) as well as by Philoktetes' entrusting the bow of Herakles to Neoptolemos in return for the latter's agreement to take him home and by Philoktetes' later willingness to assist Neoptolemos in warding off an attack by the Greeks. Herakles' final description of the conquest of Troy by the two heroes also reflects this ideal of interdependence. Such reciprocal service is associated throughout the play with nobility and is said to bring *eukleia* (478). It is shown to be alien to such men as Odysseus and the Atreidai, who are depicted as shameless, base, and cowardly in their uncompassionate use of abandonment, deception, and threats of force against an ally. In serving as a model of compassionate reciprocal service, Philoktetes acts as Neoptolemos's instructor in such behavior, teaching him the nature of compassion and what it requires in practical terms. In this way he partly takes up the role and educational function of Neoptolemos's dead father, who also serves as a model of such behavior. Neoptolemos proves himself to be a student worthy of their teaching.

Whereas in most plays compassionate behavior toward suppliants or allies is combined with the exhibition of martial *aretê* by an *agathos,* in *Philoktetes* Sophokles arranges the plot so that these two components of traditional heroism are put into apparent conflict. Odysseus believes and persuades Neoptolemos to believe that the glory of victory at Troy can be won without showing reverence to their ally Philoktetes. Philoktetes, on the other hand, requires that Neoptolemos win *eukleia* by virtue of his compassionate service, which seemingly will result in the sacrifice of both Neoptolemos's and Philoktetes' victory at Troy. The repudiation and near failure of Odysseus and the Atreidai, who are saved only by the gods' will that Philoktetes and Neoptolemos be rewarded with healing and joint victory at Troy, suggest that victory is ultimately dependent on the proper reverence and compassion of allies toward one another.

In *Philoktetes,* therefore, Sophokles was advocating compassion and reverence between allies as an ethical ideal and necessity, in spite of the sacrifice sometimes inherent in true compassion. In doing so, Sophokles was advocating traditional, heroic ethical values, of the sort first found in the Homeric poems, rather than promoting a new or unconventional scheme of values, as some have asserted. Instead, by means of an unconventional plot he brought adherence to traditional, heroic ethical values, such as compassion for *philoi,* into conflict with an unethical pursuit of the traditional goal of heroism, the glory of military victory. Indeed, we have seen that this play contrasts heroism not with the compassion characteristic of Neoptolemos, which is expressed in action, but rather with the words, trickery, and attempts at victory through them characteristic of Odysseus. By doing this, Sophokles portrayed, in a unique manner, the ultimate futility of attempts to achieve heroic success that are devoid of traditional, heroic ethical mores, especially compassionate reverence for and assistance to one's *philoi.*

Philoktetes' powerful advocacy of reverence for humanity and of compassionate mutual service remains of timeless interest. Through the highly dramatic action of the play and especially through his portrayal of Philoktetes and Neoptolemos, Sophokles suggests that without such compassion and mutual service between its citizens, without regard for worth and dignity of the individual, a society becomes corrupt and risks losing the participation of the very people that it most needs to survive and flourish.[150]

Oidipous at Kolonos

The play that perhaps best typifies the ideal of Athenian compassion from an Athenian perspective is Sophokles' *Oidipous at Kolonos.*[151] Oidipous is clearly the protagonist of this play, but an Athenian watching it would be made conscious of his Athenian identity and would see Theseus as representing his culture's ideal, merely by virtue of his being the greatest legendary Athenian hero. In fact, Sophokles does seem to have conceived of Theseus in this play as a man of virtue: there is, for example, Oidipous's praise of Theseus and Athens as displaying piety (*to eusebes*), fairness (*to epieikes*), and honesty (*to mê pseudostomein,* 1124–27). Theseus is, in fact, notable for his display of a number of attributes typical of an ideal hero-king, including wisdom, decisive leadership, and courage.[152] Theseus's compassion, as shown by his treatment of Oidipous and his family, is an integral part of the ideal qualities he displays in *Oidipous at Kolonos.*[153]

The recipient of Theseus's compassion in this play, Oidipous, is somewhat different from other suppliants.[154] This suppliant is Oidipous himself, the archetypal sinner, the man who has committed both patricide and incest with his mother. As a suppliant he presents special problems: Do the expectations of supplication apply to such a suppliant? Can such a suppliant claim divine protection in any sense? These issues are explored in the first 550 lines of the play before Theseus's entrance.

Oidipous's appeal for compassion in this play begins when he and Antigone are in the grove of the Eumenides. In his prayer to the Eumenides (84–110), Oidipous first asks the Eumenides not to be "unsympathetic" (*agnômones*) to Apollo and to him (86). After explaining the prophecy that brought him to Athens and the grove, he calls on the Eumenides and Athens, the "most honored city," to "pity" (*oiktirate*) "this miserable phantom (*eidôlon*) of the man Oidipous" (106–10).[155] The word *eidôlon* that Oidipous uses here to represent himself is the very same word used by Odysseus in *Aias* 126 to characterize the insubstantiality of the human condition.

A typical human response to Oidipous can be seen in the anxious reaction of the chorus, representing the old men of Kolonos, once they know Oidipous's identity. But when the chorus insist that Oidipous leave the country, it is Antigone, a young woman, who makes the supplicatory appeal for compassion to the chorus, asking them to "pity" (*oiktirate*) her as she appeals for her father (237–54).[156] She entreats them as a sighted person who, unlike her blind father, "looks at" their eyes and, "appearing as though one from their own blood," asks them to have compassionate regard for her miserable father.[157] The eyes could eloquently express the suppliant's distress (cf. chap. 3 on Iphigeneia's "pity-moving glance" in Aischylos's *Agamemnon* 240–41); also, the chorus can avoid Oidipous's sight, but not Antigone's. She furthermore appeals as though a child to an elder kinsman (cf. Jebb), thus stressing her similarity to the chorus's young daughters, nieces, and granddaughters—an appeal based on likeness. This type of appeal continues as she then notes her and her father's dependency on them, as on a god, and begs them by whatever they hold dear *from home* (*oikothen:* child, wife, possession, or god) to grant the unexpected favor (*charis*), that is, sanctuary. She concludes by saying that every mortal is subject to the god that drives him, by which she emphasizes Oidipous's human vulnerability—one that he shares with all, including the chorus.[158] The power of Antigone's appeal for compassion allows her to be successful in part: the chorus say that they "pity" (*oiktiromen*) Antigone and Oidipous for their misfortune but that fear of the gods keeps them from granting the request.[159]

Oidipous counters this fearful reaction by insisting on his innocence in the actions he has committed and by disclosing that he, as a suppliant, brings a great benefit to Athens, if it will receive him. In his appeal Oidipous refers to Athens' reputation as a city that reverences the gods and alone saves and protects the hard-pressed stranger (258–62) and argues that this reputation will be harmed if they dishonor a suppliant like Oidipous.[160] The chorus reply that they will defer the decision to the king. After they witness Oidipous's interchange with Ismene, however, the chorus conclude that Oidipous is "deserving of compassion" (*epaxios . . . katoiktisai*) and reciprocate his promise of benefit to Athens with beneficial advice about rituals that Oidipous should perform.[161] After the chorus request and receive yet another version of Oidipous' troubles, Theseus, the king of Athens, enters.

What is most striking about Theseus's entrance is that he immediately expresses his compassion for Oidipous and gives assurance that Oidipous's request will be granted *in advance of* even hearing that request.[162] Theseus's first words in greeting Oidipous merit close attention:

πολλῶν ἀκούων ἔν τε τῷ πάρος χρόνῳ
τὰς αἱματηρὰς ὀμμάτων διαφθορὰς
ἔγνωκά σ,' ὦ παῖ Λαΐου, τανῦν θ' ὁδοῖς
ἐν ταῖσδε λεύσσων μᾶλλον ἐξεπίσταμαι.
σκευή τε γάρ σε καὶ τὸ δύστηνον κάρα
δηλοῦτον ἡμῖν ὄνθ' ὃς εἶ, καί σ' οἰκτίσας
θέλω 'περέσθαι, δύσμορ' Οἰδίπους, τίνα
πόλεως ἐπέστης προστροπὴν ἐμοῦ τ' ἔχων,
αὐτός τε χἠ σὴ δύσμορος παραστάτις.

Hearing from many in the past the story of the bloody destruction (*haimatêras . . . diaphthoras*) of your eyes, I have recognized you, son of Laios, and now seeing you after this journey, I even more thoroughly understand your situation. Your rags and your miserable (*dustênon*) head show clearly who you are, and I pity you (*s'oiktisas*), unfortunate (*dusmoros*) Oidipous, and wish to learn with what request of the city and of me you have appeared—you and your unfortunate helper (*dusmoros parastatis*). (551–59)

Theseus's first words to Oidipous are of a personal nature and show his recognition of Oidipous and his awareness of Oidipous's past sufferings, an awareness that he says he understands even better by seeing Oidipous in his current plight, obviously worn with age and troubles. He first expresses his compassion (*s'oiktisas*) for Oidipous's suffering and then immediately and implicitly acknowledges the status of the strangers as that of suppliants by first asking what their request is. Note also his eagerness to learn what Oidipous needs from him: "I wish to learn," he says. There is no hint on Theseus's part of the hesitancy or wariness that we might expect of someone faced with the demands of such a suppliant.[163]

Theseus then gives Oidipous assurance that he will meet his request.

δίδασκε· δεινὴν γάρ τιν' ἂν πρᾶξιν τύχοις
λέξας ὁποίας ἐξαφισταίμην ἐγώ·
ὃς οἶδά γ' αὐτὸς ὡς ἐπαιδεύθην ξένος,
ὥσπερ σύ, χὠς εἷς πλεῖστ' ἀνὴρ ἐπὶ ξένης
ἤθλησα κινδυνεύματ' ἐν τὠμῷ κάρᾳ,
ὥστε ξένον γ' ἂν οὐδέν' ὄνθ,' ὥσπερ σὺ νῦν,
ὑπεκτραποίμην μὴ οὐ συνεκσῴζειν· ἐπεὶ
ἔξοιδ' ἀνὴρ ὢν χὤτι τῆς εἰς αὔριον
οὐδὲν πλέον μοι σοῦ μέτεστιν ἡμέρας.

Teach me. For you would speak of some terrible labor (*deinên . . . praxin*) for me to stand apart from it—I who know that I myself (*hos oida g'autos*) was reared as a foreigner (*xenos*), just like you (*hôsper su*), and how in a foreign land (*epi xenês*) I, alone of men, struggled with many dangers to my life, so that I could never turn aside from someone who was a foreigner (*xenos*), just like you are now (*hôsper su nûn*), and not save him. Because I know well, human being (*anêr*) that I am, that I have no more a share of tomorrow than you do. (560–68)

Theseus says that Oidipous's labor would have to be dire indeed to cause him to stand apart from it.[164] He strengthens this assurance still further by what he says next: after he reflects on the commonality of his life experiences and those of Oidipous, he asserts that he would *never* turn aside from rescuing *any* exile. His compassionate response to Oidipous's suffering is based on his own experiences as a foreigner and on his deep understanding of the instability of human prosperity.[165] Does Theseus expect a return benefit from Oidipous? If so, he doesn't mention it.[166] Theseus's assurances entail a deeper notion of reciprocity: mutual assistance will make the world a better place. He acts in the implicit hope that if he were in such a circumstance, someone would rescue him.[167] Oidipous praises Theseus's nobility (*to gennaion*, 569), and Theseus then learns of and accepts Oidipous's reciprocal promise of benefit to Athens (cf. intro. pp. 17–20). Tzanetou (2005: 114) notes that Theseus grants Oidipous citizenship.

Furthermore, Theseus not only receives Oidipous and his daughters and provides them sanctuary, but he also acts decisively in his role as heroic protector of the suppliants under his care. When Kreon seeks to coerce Oidipous by kidnapping the daughters, Theseus immediately sends men to block their escape. He then characterizes Kreon's aggression against the daughters of Oidipous as aggression against Athens herself—an insult to it and to its ruler's reputation and honor. Kreon, he says, is treating the city as "manless" and "slave-like" and its king as a "nobody" (911–36). In particular, he chides Kreon for carrying off the gods' suppliants that are under Athens' protection—an unjust act that Theseus says he would never resort to (919–31). As Theseus is leaving to retrieve the daughters after he has assured Oidipous that he will do so, Oidipous praises Theseus for his nobility a second time (1042–43). This episode shows an application of active compassion that protects or helps those who suffer (cf. S5 above and D1a).[168]

But there is yet another supplication in this play: that of Oidipous's son Polyneikes to his father. Theseus, citing religious reasons (specifically, the suppliant's rights), advises that Oidipous give his son an audience (1179–80); Antigone adds her voice of persuasion out of love for the family; Oidipous with great reluctance accedes to this persuasion. Polyneikes makes a supplication with an appeal to Aidôs (Mercy), who sits by the throne of Zeus (1267–68). His appeal is not explicitly for compassion, but for forgiveness of the wrongs he has done to his father. He begins his speech with an admission of his wrongdoing in neglecting and failing to support his miserable old father. When Oidipous does not respond, Polyneikes fears that he will be sent away dishonored without receiving a reply. Antigone intervenes and urges her brother to speak of his need, since words, giving delight or rousing indignation or arousing compassion (*katoiktisanta*) can give voice to the speechless (1280–83); clearly Antigone hopes that her brother's appeal will be able to move her father to feel compassion. Polyneikes then tells the story of his expulsion by his brother, Eteokles, and about how he himself has formed an alliance with Adrastos of Argos to make war against Thebes. Polyneikes then makes his supplication: he entreats his father to renounce his anger and give his support to Polyneikes' side in the conflict. He even buttresses his appeal by saying that he and his father are alike in that both are wandering beggars (*ptôchoi*) and strangers (*xenoi*), that they both are in pitiable circumstances (D2); and he adds that once he conquers Thebes, he will set Oidipous up in a house of his own. Polyneikes, however, reveals that his real motive is to win Oidipous's support, since an oracle has said that the side which Oidipous supports will gain power.

Oidipous returns no pity for one who had shown no pity when it mattered (or, no love for no love): You threw me out when you had power and now make an appeal when you are in the same trouble you put me in (cf. intro. pp. 17–19). He notes that it has been his daughters who have saved him, not his sons, who as men should have done so (cf. D6). He then proceeds to curse both his sons, effecting that they will kill each other, and saying that his curses conquer Polyneikes' supplication, if Justice still sits by the throne of Zeus.

The aftermath for Polyneikes is an example of tragic pathos. He tells his sister that he is unable to stop the war, which is already in motion: to do so would be shameful for him, and his younger brother would laugh. He will not even report the curse to his allies, since the job of the commander is to report only good news. Polyneikes departs hopeless, expecting defeat. As in *Elektra,* we have an example of devastating conflict between family members. Oidipous's curses, though seemingly justified (as the drama proceeds, nothing suggests otherwise), are nevertheless inherently tragic because this kind of conflict means pain for all involved.[169] The play concludes, however, with Oidipous's glorious ascent or descent to the gods, as he leaves his beloved daughters to the care of Theseus, his noble Athenian host and protector. Winnington-Ingram (1980: 274–75) notes the irony of Theseus's assent to the daughters' request to go to Thebes to intervene in their brothers' conflict, an intervention that ultimately will bring about Antigone's death. Yet again, there is no cloudless day in Sophoklean tragedy.

This play depicts Athens as a city of law and justice.[170] In particular, it refers to and dramatically represents Athens as a polis reverent toward the gods and receptive of suppliants such as Oidipous. As Athens' king, Theseus is a mature hero who, unlike Neoptolemos in *Philoktetes,* readily shows the requisite compassionate emotional response to a worthy suppliant's appeal and displays the appropriate heroic behavior that flows from it.[171] Indeed, in Theseus, Sophokles presents the complete Athenian hero, whose response to suffering is emotionally warm and humane as well as being behaviorally effective. Not a cold, dispassionate *pater patriae,* as he has been called; indeed, at points he shows some anger and impatience.[172] Rather, he is a hero who, for Sophokles, represented the best of Athenian qualities and embodied its best hope in the critical final stages of the war with Sparta.[173] Theseus's compassion is at the core of those qualities.

Concluding Reflections on Sophokles and Compassion

Taking a clue from Aristophanes' comic characterization of the three tragedians in *Frogs,* we can see how he and his audience might have seen Sophokles, in a sense, as the golden mean between the extremes represented by Aischylos and Euripides. Certainly, Sophokles is the most traditional of the three in regard to the compassion theme as found in Homer's poetry. He develops this theme most fully in *Philoktetes,* where he shows Neoptolemos's growing compassion for the suffering hero Philoktetes despite the opposition of the powerful Odysseus, who sees Philoktetes and his bow merely as instruments to be captured and used. The mutual heroic compassion exemplified by Neoptolemos and Philoktetes is validated by Herakles' appearance as deus ex machina who rewards the two with assurances that they will be victors in the war and that Philoktetes will at long last be cured of his terrible affliction. They therefore provide a model of heroic cooperative compassion in a way not unlike the ideal of heroic cooperation visualized in Homer's *Iliad* but tragically lost for most of the epic.

Sophokles further presents compassion as a positive ideal in *Oidipous at Kolonos,* in which Theseus gives sanctuary and protection to the blind Oidipous and receives a blessing for Athens in return for his compassion. Here again we see a powerful representation of the common vulnerability of human beings in the face of the vagaries of fate. A similar note is found earlier in Sophokles' *Aias,* where Odysseus is able to have compassion for his fellow Greek warrior Aias in spite of Aias's threat to kill Odysseus and the Atreidai. Odysseus's compassion for his fellow human being allowed him to recognize the god-imposed madness in Aias's threats, the madness that led to his humiliating slaughter of camp animals instead of the Greek leaders he despised. After the suicide, Odysseus's continuing compassion for Aias also allowed him to persuade Agamemnon and Menelaus to grant Aias an honorable burial. Throughout, Odysseus is conscious of the vulnerability of human fortune: in regarding Aias's tragic fate, he says, in effect, "there but for the grace of god, go I." This example of a warrior feeling compassion for his fellow warrior turned hostile recalls somewhat Homer's representation of Akhilleus's compassion for his enemy Priam in book 24 of the *Iliad.* In both cases, the fragility of human fortune is at the core of the compassion felt by one character for another (D2).

In contrast, Sophokles' *Elektra* explores the theme of "no pity for those who show no pity," exemplified by the reciprocal hostility and violence between the older and younger generations of Agamemnon's family, but relieved by the compassion shown, at times ironically, among the younger family members. Sophokles' use of irony in regard to compassion also comes into play in Deianeira's tender feelings for her husband Herakles' captive, Iole, by whom the hero has been smitten secretly with love, and also in Oidipous's compassion for the Thebans suffering under the curse incurred by the murderer of Laius—none other than Oidipous himself. In addition, Sophokles' kings and heroes tend to speak openly of their own personal feelings of compassion, unlike those in Aischylos and some of those in Euripides. All in all, Sophokles emerges as an idealist with powerful humane feelings and a deep understanding of the vulnerable human condition that pervades the life of each of us.

Conclusion

Homer and the Three Tragedians

Homer, especially the Homer of the *Iliad,* sets a high standard for the tragic poets in regard to the thematic importance of compassion and the significance and depth of his portrayal of compassionate action. His characters openly plead for compassion and openly express their feelings of compassion and act on them—either granting or denying the appeal made to them. Furthermore, Homeric compassion is typically grounded in the notion of the vulnerability of human life and the instability of human fortune and happiness. This foundation is evident in such powerful scenes as Andromache's appeal to Hektor in *Iliad* 6 and in Priam's appeal to Akhilleus in *Iliad* 24.

Aischylos, the earliest of the three tragedians, focuses on compassion primarily in the context of the Greek city-state. Pelasgos provides acts of saving compassion based on a strong sense of reverence for his city's suppliants; Prometheus feels compassion for and shows compassion to the suffering human race that he observes from his superior status as a god. Where Aischylos, the Athenian patriot and idealist, most seems to value compassion is in his vision of the ideal state where justice, mercy, and compassion work together to provide social harmony and a just way of living.

Euripides rightly receives the title of the poet who exploits the theme of pathos to the maximum. His portrayal of human suffering and misery in *Trojan Women* is not matched in the extant dramas of the other two great tragedians. Euripides tends to explore extremes of suffering and misfortune and to exploit spectacular effects of pathos, but often those effects are presented in a context of human corruption or heroic failure in ways that call the heroic enterprise and divine justice into serious question. Although Euripides' characters, such as Hekabe, can and, in fact, sometimes do point to their own misfortunes as evidence of the instability of human fortune, nevertheless we often miss in Euripides the deep human sympathy that we found in Homer. Or perhaps we should say that such human sympathy tends to be undercut in Euripides by his use of rhetorical strategies or sophistic arguments typical of the later fifth-century culture in which he produced his dramas. On the other hand, as a "realist," Euripides does expose the treachery and abuse that appeals for compassion may cloak (as in *Medeia,* for example). Also, he is not hesitant to expose the shallowness of an Odysseus or Agamemnon or the vanity of an Akhilleus as they find ways to deny appeals for compassion or, at least, to sidestep them. *Herakles,* however, in my view, reaches a kind of sublimity in its portrayal of the mutual compassion between Herakles and Theseus in the wake of Herakles' tragic downfall at the hands of a spiteful goddess. There is an element of human redemption in that play as perhaps there is in other plays, such as *Hippolytos.* Euripides consequently presents our own time with situations and characterizations that seem to fit modern or postmodern notions of existential doubt or concepts such as "life on the edge."

Sophokles is also capable of deep pathos, as in Herakles' agony at the end of *Women of Trachis* or in Philoktetes' agony as he undergoes an attack of the disease that haunts him on Lemnos. Sophokles is also capable of deep irony and questioning, as at the end of *Women of Trachis* and at the end of *Oidipous the King.* But of the three tragedians, Sophokles is the one who consistently undergirds his tragedies with a deep sense of human vulnerability that makes words and actions deeply ironic but also deeply compassionate. He shares this quality with Homer somewhat more than the other two poets do. Also, his characters, including his heroes and heroines, tend to express their compassion for others openly and often with a sense of their own vulnerability as human beings. Examples include Odysseus in *Aias,* Deianeira, Theseus in *Oidipous at Kolonos,* and

Neoptolemos in *Philoktetes.* Sophokles explores the nobility of these characters' expressions of compassion and their actions that are consistent with that compassion. For these reasons Sophokles is the most "classic" of the three in having a fundamentally compassionate view of life and an ability to convey that view in his tragic dramas. In these respects, he is also the most "Homeric" of the three.

Compassionate Heroes, Gods, and Choruses

Having made these distinctions among the three playwrights, I want to point out some common ground among them. More important than their differences is the fact that all three provide models of compassionate heroes and gods. Aischylos gives us Pelasgos, who provides protection for the Danaids from their Egyptian pursuers. On the divine level, Hephaistos, though subordinate to Zeus, feels compassion for his fellow god, Prometheus. Prometheus, of course, shows compassion to all humans. Aischylos also has the ghost of Dareios pitying his son Xerxes in Queen Atossa's dream.

Euripides provides two Athenian hero/kings, Demophon and Theseus, who, respectively, save the children of Herakles from oppression by Eurystheus and uphold the Argive mothers' rights to have their sons buried. Theseus, also, because of his compassion, saves his heroic friend Herakles from an act of suicide. Also, in response to her request for pity, Aigeus agrees to provide Medeia sanctuary in Athens, although, of course, this will ultimately become a problem for Aigeus.

Sophokles gives us Theseus, king of Athens, who provides sanctuary to the aged Oidipous. Also, he presents on stage the young Neoptolemos, who, through his dramatic development of compassion, befriends and rescues the hero Philoktetes from the island of Lemnos, after which, as the ghost of Herakles promises, Philoktetes will be healed at Troy. Sophokles also presents Odysseus who sees to the burial of the tragic Aias.

Finally, all three poets also provide choruses who typically express compassion for their superiors: notable examples include Aischylos's *Persians, Agamemnon, Libation Bearers, Prometheus Bound;*

Euripides' *Children of Herakles, Hekabe, Trojan Women, Orestes, Iphigeneia in Aulis, Andromache, Medeia, Herakles;* and Sophokles' *Aias, Women of Trachis, Elektra, Oidipous the King, Oidipous at Kolonos,* and *Philoktetes.*

Common Patterns

Regarding compassion generally in the texts I have analyzed, certain common patterns emerge. Within the close family and extended kin, normally appeals for compassion are unnecessary, since both *philia* and *eleos* are readily felt and acted upon for loved ones in need.[1] The exceptions would be when there is alienation between family members, such as between Klytaimestra and Orestes, so that an appeal for *eleos* (compassion/mercy) is necessary; also, if the kinsman is unresponsive, an appeal may be necessary (cf. Orestes and Menelaus in Euripides' *Orestes*). As we move further outside the family, appeals based on reciprocity tend to come into play more often; with nonfamily *philoi* or *xenoi* reminding the champion of past benefits (cf. Euripides' *Herakles*). With complete strangers, more extensive appeals may be needed, with emphasis on likenesses and possible future recompense; likewise with non-Greek strangers that one may encounter, although they prima facie have a still lesser basis for establishing likeness with the person supplicated. Enemies are at the far extreme, since what is owed them is negative reciprocity: an ill return for the ill they have done you, or a cold deafness in response to their cries for compassion. When compassion is shown to an enemy, the result is so extraordinary that it attains a special height or sublimity, to use Longinos's terminology.[2] Examples that we have seen are Akhilleus's compassion for Priam in *Iliad* 24, Kyros's compassion for Kroisos, and Odysseus's compassion for Aias in Sophokles' *Aias.* Almost as extraordinary are those episodes of compassion for strangers, such as Theseus for the elder Oidipous in *Oidipous at Kolonos.* Compassion for *philoi* is made a central issue in Sophokles' *Philoktetes* as well as in Euripides' *Herakles.* More often in tragedy, compassion for enemies is ignored or denied (*Hekabe*) or is made largely futile (Talthybios's in *Trojan Women*); there is also the suffering of females as well as males in war situations (D6). Tragedy reflects the realities of life as we know them: with many a tragic outcome, but with an occasional light of brilliance in the tragic darkness afforded by an unexpected act of compassion.

Compassion and Character

A number of general statements made by characters in tragedy suggest that the tragedians themselves considered a disposition to feel and show compassion to be a requirement of a humane person and the mark of a refined or educated individual. Conversely, a character who is exclusively pitiless or prone to pitilessness is for all three poets a bad character; the inability to feel compassion and the disinclination to show it are signs of barbarity and inhumanity. Some examples: Aischylos's Pelasgos (*Suppliants* 489) acknowledges that all properly feel "kindness" (*eunoia*) toward the weak. In *Prometheus Bound* (242–44), the chorus at one point say that one who "does not sympathize" (οὐ συνασχαλᾷ) with Prometheus's suffering is "iron-minded and made of stone." Such statements are especially common in Euripides, who has the chorus of his *Kyklops* call Polyphemos "Pitiless" (*Nêlês*) for sacrificing the suppliants at his hearth (369–70).[3] In *Iphigeneia among the Taurians,* the Hellenic Iphigeneia is uncomfortable with the pitiless barbarity that is imposed on her because she must sacrifice humans while among the Taurians (225–26) and then with her own incipient savagery after she hears of her brother's death (344–50).[4] In Euripides' *Elektra* (294–95), Orestes remarks that the wise and educated (*sophoi*) tend to feel *oiktos* whereas the ignorant do not. In *Herakles* (299–301), Megara contrasts *sophoi* and nobly reared enemies, who are disposed to show *aidôs* (reverence), with the stupid (*skaios*) enemy, who is not so disposed. A similar idea is expressed in fragment 407 of Euripides (Kannicht 2004): "It is a lack of refinement (*amousia*) not to shed a tear for pitiable things (*oiktra*)."[5] Aristotle (*Rhetoric* 1385b27) later will say that the educated (*hoi pepaideumenoi*) feel pity because they are properly foresighted (*eulogistoi*). These examples from tragedy (and one from Aristotle) show that Athenian tragedians, particularly Euripides, often explicitly associated feelings of compassion with wisdom and civilization in contrast to the barbarity or crudeness of the pitiless.[6] In addition, the feeling that one is exempt from the vagaries of human fortune is seen as a sign of *hybris* (cf. intro. n.38). For some characters this contributes to a tragic downfall (e.g., Xerxes, Aigisthos in *Oresteia* and Sophokles' *Elektra,* Polymestor in *Hekabe,* Lykos in *Herakles,* Kreon in *Antigone*); for others it seems not to matter so much (Medeia, Tyndareos in *Orestes* and Odysseus in *Philoktetes*).

These statements do not necessarily suggest that pity or compassion was seen as an unqualified virtue by the tragedians in the same way one might consider prudence or justice to be virtues. Indeed, Greek compassion was a powerful emotion subject to misapplication, for example, by pitying the wrong person or by pitying someone when another response was more appropriate. In the world of tragedy, even what might have appeared to be a clear case of appropriate compassion sometimes turned out to have disastrous unintended consequences. Also, people could make appeals for compassion when they did not deserve it or when such pity would rebound to the harm of the pitier or his loved ones. We have seen cases of all these misapplications in our study. Also, at several points compassion is linked to revenge in ways that seem problematic to some. We saw, for example, that Sophokles' Philoktetes asserted that vengeance on his enemies would provide compassionate relief to his own suffering.[7] This connection is made through a demanding and painful desire for justice on the part of the wronged person. Justice in the form of punishment of one's wrongdoers brings relief or "satisfaction" to the wronged one. To a sufferer like Philoktetes, that punishment would appear to be a form of compassion, even if it did not cure his disease or otherwise alleviate his suffering. Yet we have noted that Philoktetes' wish for compassionate relief is stated in precisely reciprocal terms—not in hyperbolic measure.[8]

Nevertheless, acts of compassion, properly applied toward the proper recipient in appropriate circumstances, were seen as beneficial by at least the recipient, the pitier, and presumably anyone not hostile to either of them. Tragedy provided examples of this as well. In regard to people's disposition to display compassion, there was a continuum ranging from those people capable of and perhaps prone to be compassionate to, at the other extreme, those who were incapable of feeling or showing compassion or who were actively cruel persons. For the tragedians, compassion's most direct opposite was cruelty. One could, of course, fail to show proper compassion because of a variety of reasons other than sheer meanness; indifference, fear, ignorance, and envy are some of the other possible causes. Still, it seems clear from Greek tragedy and Homer's epics that a good person is capable of feeling compassion and prone to display it when circumstances properly call for it; a bad person, on the contrary, is incapable of feeling compassion and/or refuses to display it when it is properly called for.

Within epic and tragedy, we have seen portrayed acts of compassion, as well as acts of courage and love, along with acts of cruelty, savagery, jealousy, fear, and cowardice. In fact, as expected, portrayals of positive acts of compassion were relatively rare, given the tragic genre's normal mode of emphasizing the errors, violence, and vulnerability inherent in the human condition. We might say the same about an epic poem, such as Homer's *Iliad.* Nevertheless, those few positive acts of compassion that Homer and the tragedians present are worthy of examination, as are those denials or abuses of compassion that Homer and the tragedians also portray. All these portrayals together give us a picture of compassion as an important part of life.

Benefits of Compassionate Behavior

The question of the benefits of compassionate behavior as portrayed in Greek tragedies is largely inconclusive due to the small amount of data that has survived the centuries. Also, in the plays we have it often involves the larger interpretation of the dramas in which compassion appears, so that in some cases, the answers are bound to be inconclusive, unknowable, or subject to disagreement. Still, from what we have seen, we might say that the following characters appear to prosper (or, at least, not to suffer) by virtue of having been compassionate: Odysseus in *Aias,* Talthybios, Theseus in Sophokles and Euripides (*Hippolytos* excepted), Demophon,

Pelasgos,[9] Hephaistos in *Prometheus Bound,* Orestes in Sophokles' *Elektra,* and Neoptolemos in *Philoktetes.* On the other hand, the following suffer or come to bad ends despite their having displayed compassion: Deianeira, Oidipous in *Oidipous the King,* Kreon in *Medeia,* Kassandra in *Oresteia,* Prometheus. In some cases, however, such as those of Deianeira and Kassandra, compassion per se is not depicted as a cause of the downfall. In tragedy, the innocent and the good sometimes suffer.[10]

Still, the reasoning about compassion in the plays sometimes expresses an element of "faith" to the effect that "if I show compassion to X, then perhaps someday in the future when I am in trouble, X or Y will show compassion to me." It almost seems like a kind of insurance: showing compassion now will likely produce future compassionate returns for the compassionate person. This is the basis of my comment in the introduction (p. 20) that compassion is a gift that keeps on giving. Of course, this is likely to work only if compassion is granted to those who are truly deserving and do not have ulterior or hostile motives in requesting it. Also, granting compassion may involve risks for the compassionate party; still, if compassion is given appropriately, the compassionate person will be rewarded with gratitude and an enhanced reputation. The plays illustrate this, as we have seen, but tragedy also shows that fate is often unpredictable.

Compassion and Reciprocity: Concluding Considerations

An issue recently raised is that compassion for another may involve one in acts of violence. At least one scholar links Athens' reputation as a compassionate city with Athens' pursuit of power through war (see Tzanetou 2005). Yes, a champion approached by a suppliant may be asked to act in defense of that suppliant. And that action may take the form of force, even war. This is the case in Sophokles' *Oidipous at Kolonos:* Theseus does retrieve the daughters of Oidipous after the Thebans have captured them. Also, Athens goes to war in defense or support of its suppliants in Euripides' *Children of Herakles* and *Suppliants.* It can be said, however, that in all these cases, the action taken is a defensive response to aggression by others rather than an act of imperialistic aggression.[11] Also, in all these cases, the Athenians consistently apply the minimum amount of force necessary to accomplish their objective and do not press their military advantage further than required by their goal. Furthermore, as we have seen in *Children of Herakles,* the Athenians support reasonable standards of fairness concerning prisoners of war, even though in that play they eventually accede to Alkmene's demand that she be allowed to execute Eurystheus.

But Tzanetou's more important point seems to be that Athens' reputation as a compassionate city-state served as a convenient cover for Athens' domination over its allies. Doubtless, this has been done in real life, even by the Athenians themselves as Tzanetou argues, but it was not done in the stories of Athenian heroes as presented by tragedy. Indeed, why would the tragic poets take such care concerning the justice of Athenian action, if they merely wanted to show that Athens was powerful and that might makes right? American culture in the past produced many pro-American films and books that did not go to that kind of trouble. In those works the opponents (such as the Nazis) were clearly villainous, and the humiliating defeat they suffered was obviously meant to provide the American audience or readers with mostly unthinking pride and self-satisfaction. Such portrayals rarely raised the problems and issues that the Greek tragedies consistently raise.

This is not to deny an Athenian bias in Athenian literature, including Greek tragedy, as scholars such as Froma Zeitlin (1990) have demonstrated. Greek tragedy was obviously written by Athenians for a mostly Athenian audience. As such, it consistently depicts Athenian characters more sympathetically than non-Athenian ones, but this signifies that an Athenian perspective is being communicated, probably without much awareness of it by either the playwrights or citizen spectators. In fact, can we not say that virtually all art and literature to some extent reflects the perspective of the culture in which it was created and first performed or published? Compare Xenophanes' account of how different cultures represent the gods in their own images. Of course, some works of art or literature reveal more cultural bias than others:

propaganda, for example, is at one extreme, whereas works aiming at a more universal perspective, such as classic literature, including most Greek tragedies, are at the other. Even a work critical of an author's own culture's institutions or public figures is nevertheless in part a reflection of the cultural perspective that the author shares with others in his or her society.

What Greek tragedies show is that we can relate to one another based on our common humanity and in spite of differences we may have in regard to politics, religion, national identity, sexual preference, wealth, family, class, professional status, education, taste, language, ethnicity, color, gender, age, attractiveness, personality type, and so forth. If only we lived in a world in which violence and hostile aggression were nonexistent and violence never had to be employed to contain aggression. This is the kind of world we all should be working for. And I believe that compassion and empathy would be integral to such a world. Without compassion, aggression and retaliation run wild and unopposed.[12] Compassion and empathy are needed to remind us of the horrible consequences of human aggression and to motivate saving action, comforting solace, and, when the time comes, dignified treatment of the dead. Fortunately, in most modern "civilized" cultures, society and law have developed to the extent that, in circumstances outside of war, the demand for retribution is channeled through a legal system in which the state enacts justice on behalf of the wronged individual. Yet compassion and a degree of mercy are still beneficial and desirable, even in the rendering of justice. As long as compassion opposes violent aggression and puts a limit on the application of force to stop aggression, it is worth keeping and worth promoting. We can envision and hope for a world without aggression and violence, but it will be a world in which compassion and empathy are prime values. Greek epic and tragedy show us the tragic potentialities of life without compassion, but they also give us glimpses of the positive potentialities of life when compassion is deeply felt and appropriately acted upon.

Notes

INTRODUCTION

1. See, for example, the recent article (and book) by Damasio (2003), a respected researcher and author in the field of neurobiology. He also notes evidence for compassionate responses in lower primates. Modern scientific study, therefore, seems to be confirming—in general, even if not in precise detail—Lucretius's poetic vision (*DRN* 5.1011–27) of early human society as characterized by the development of a sense of justice and compassion for the weak. On the almost universal acceptance of the Golden Rule and compassion as a core value by world religions of the West and East, see Armstrong (2010: 25–64).

2. See Johnson/Clapp 2005. In particular, see p.162, n.89, on the discrepancy between the demands of the real world and the sensitivity to compassion developed by tragedy.

3. This is indicated by discussions of the spectator's pleasure in viewing a tragedy. Also, the concept of *katharsis,* however interpreted, is focused on the spectator's sense of relief, purification, or moral edification. Again, see Johnson/Clapp 2005 for an examination of the educational impact of the compassion theme within Greek tragedy.

4. Of course, to witness suffering in life may also involve a degree of "spectacle," as we shall see, but it more immediately raises the question of how one will respond to that suffering, something the spectator in the theater is never asked to consider.

5. Recent work on pity in Homer, such as Kim 2000, is surveyed in the following chapter. I do, however, make extensive use in this study of Aristotle's writings about pity.

6. For general comparisons, see, for example, Kitto 1961, Knox 1964, C. P. Segal 1966, Lesky 1967, Ferguson 1972, Taplin 1978, Heath 1987, Zimmerman 1991, E. Hall 2010, and Lefkowitz 2012.

7. See, for example, J. H. H. Schmidt 1889, Burkert 1955, Pohlenz 1956, and Chantraine 1974. Burkert's word study has come to be accepted as a standard in the field. Scott (1979: 6–14), Crotty (1994: 44–46), and Kim (2000: chap. 2) also have word studies of pity specifically in reference to Homer. More general studies of the concept of pity in later classical culture include Dover 1974, Stanford 1983, and Konstan 2001. Konstan's introduction (2001: 1–25) focuses on pity as an emotion and the variety of understandings of it afforded by modern theories. Rachel Sternberg's "The Nature of Pity" (in Sternberg 2005) provides a recent overview of the concept, particularly as it applies to oratory and historiography; also cf. Prauscello 2010: 200–203.

8. Burkert (1955: 20) notes a connection between *eleos* and *elegos* (song of lament) in Eur. *IT* 146–47.

9. See Schmidt (1889: 752) and Jebb on Sophocles, *Philoctetes* 307ff.; cf. Burkert 1955: 36, who notes that *oiktos* tends to be a "strong, almost independent emotional state."

10. Examples are given in Liddell and Scott (1996; hereafter LSJ).

11. Compare Burkert (1955: 20, 29, 36); Burkert (69–70) cites four passages from the *Iliad* in which *eleos* for fallen comrades impels a warrior to rush into battle; he interprets the verb *eleein* used in these examples as denoting a "schmerzliches Innewerden der Verbundenheit zum anderen." Compare Scott (1979: 8–14) on the action implicit in *eleos.*

12. She summarizes, "'To pity,' . . . signifies 'to avenge,' 'to save,' 'to heal,' and 'to give burial'; 'to be pitiless,' conversely, is to effect the opposite—to refuse 'to avenge,' 'to save,' 'to heal,' or 'to give burial.'"

13. Of interest is Burkert's observation (1955: 49–51) that tragedy and choral lyric preferred the *oiktos* group, perhaps because of these genres' connection with dirges. The noun and verb forms of *eleos* occur only in Sophokles' *Philoktetes* and the later plays of Euripides.

14. Konstan (2001: 59–60) preferred to use "pity" as the primary equivalent because it implies greater "distance between the pitier and pitied" than does compound words such as "sympathy" and "compassion." As I show below, I agree with him regarding "sympathy" and related words, but not with regard to "compassion," which as indicated above has an element of detachment in its typical modern usage, but more importantly does not convey the tone of contempt that is often communicated by the word "pity." Rather, its modern usage typically implies equality

between the parties involved. That "compassion" is associated by many with Christian charity need not be a problem for its use as a English equivalent of Greek *eleos* in the time of Homer and the Greek tragedians—a time long before the development of Christian thought.

15. Compare Aristotle's statement cited in n.43 below. One normally ignored this equality, of course, in the case of an appeal for compassion by an enemy, where the fact of enmity is dominant and disdain for the enemy is expected—suppliant or not.

16. A good example of this deceptive potential is found in the chorus's use of "sympathetic joy" (*sunchairein,* Aischylos *Agamemnon* 793) discussed by Burkert (1955: 60); cf. below, chapter 3 (on Aischylos), p. 84.

17. See Burkert (1955: 56–66) and Konstan (2001: 58–60) for extended philological treatments of these synonyms.

18. Obviously, by "dramatic" I mean those acted on stage; by "narrative" I mean those "told" either by an epic narrator or within a play by a character, such as a messenger or a chorus.

19. He also includes in this concept of justice the warding off of injury to oneself, which also inhibits the inflicting of harm by another.

20. Kosak (2005: 264), writing on pity in the Hippocratic corpus, cites from Hippocrates' *Epidemics* 1.11 the statement that physicians should practice two things regarding disease: "to be helpful or to do no harm," ὠφελέειν ἢ μὴ βλάπτειν. This corresponds well to Schopenhauer's dichotomy and to the one I am illustrating here in ancient Greek culture. Fundamentally, the physician's job is to treat his or her patients compassionately.

21. Pythagoras (Iamblichus, *De Vita Pythagorae* 33) and Cicero, *De Finibus* 5.23.

22. Burkert (1955: 38) sees an association in Homer between *eleos/oiktos* and *aidôs* (reverence) whereby both function as a "restraint" on a person's "desires and actions." Scott (1979: 8, 10) specifically sees *oiktos* as providing such an inhibition in Homer, but in contrast to the "positive forward drive" of *eleos.*

23. Sternberg and Lateiner also treat this episode in Sternberg 2005.

24. See, in particular, Lateiner 2005; cf. Sternberg 2006 and Konstan 2001.

25. Another well-known example of this is, of course, the compassionate sparing of the infant Oidipous by shepherds in Sophokles' *Oidipous Tyrannos.* The Theban shepherd said that he felt compassion for the infant (*katoiktisas,* 1178), and the Corinthian shepherd spoke of himself as the savior (*sôtêr,* 1030) of the disfigured baby. I should note, however, that in these examples, there are sometimes unintended consequences

in the sparing of an infant: Kypselos, spared by pity, grows up to become a harsh tyrant—ironically confirming the motive of those who sought to kill him as an infant. Oidipous later regrets that he was spared in infancy and thereby fulfilled his father's curse. Ion's sparing becomes temporarily problematic in Euripides' play, but ultimately it is shown to have been a providential benefit to Athens.

26. Compare Kant's "categorical imperative." A term developed by modern philosophers in this regard is "deontological ethics" (*Encyclopaedia Britannica*). See Nussbaum (1986, chapters 1 and 2: esp. 4–6; 12–16; n. 20, n. 21, 424–25; and 25–32) for a persuasive critique of Kantian morality as applied to the decision-making presented in Greek tragic poetry; my assumptions in this work are consistent with Nussbaum's critique of Kant, although my literary approach to ancient texts differs from her philosophical approach.

27. Schopenhauer himself assumes that morality is of this nature. See his comments (1995: 140–43) on the incompatibility of "egoism" and "moral worth." For him, compassion has moral worth because it is done solely "for the sake of another."

28. Compare Gill (1998a: esp. 307–8). Also, see Burkert (1996: chap. 6) on reciprocity as an anthropological phenomenon and as an element in the development and practice of religion; Burkert also discusses the connections between reciprocity, equality, and empathy.

29. For example, see Sahlins (1972: 185–275).

30. Sahlins (1972: 196–204); on compassion, see 213–14; on circles of affiliation regarding compassion in Greek daily life, see Sternberg (2006: 9–10, 176–78).

31. Donlan (1982, see esp. 140, 168–71) deals with economic reciprocities in Homer, but his emphasis on "generosity" seems to accord with what I am describing here; he cites M. D. Sahlins as his source for the concept of "generalized reciprocity." See also Gill (1998a), cited earlier, for a discussion of reciprocity and mutually beneficial behavior.

32. This statement recapitulates my discussion above, pp. 17–18.

33. See John Gould (1973: 85–90) for an analysis of the role of *aidôs* in supplications in Greek tragedy.

34. Compare Burkert (1955: 38), who refers to *aidôs* as being the "higher, more universal, more lasting case" with reference to an "überpersönliche" norm or standard in contrast to the human-to-human motivation behind *oiktos/eleos*.

35. Compare Aristotle, *Rh.* 1385b. Konstan (2001: 49) calls this the "principle of vulnerability." See McCoy 2013 for an extended study of the value of vulnerability in Greek literature and philosophy.

36. Macleod continues, "Schopenhauer was surely right to see this as a truer origin and a sounder basis of morality than Kant's categorical imperative." Compare my use of Schopenhauer's concepts above.

37. Examples include Sophokles *Aias* 121–26; Aischylos *Agamemnon* 1327–30; Euripides *Elektra* 1329–30, *Orestes* 976–81, and *Hekabe* 488–91. Outside of tragedy, similar statements can be found, such as Herodotos 1.86 and 7.46. Demokritos (frag. 107a) says, "It is fitting for human beings not to laugh at the misfortunes of their fellow men, but to lament (*olophuresthai*) them" because of the instability of life. Similarly in Euripides' *Andromache* 421, the chorus says, "Misfortunes, even of a stranger, are pitiful to all mortals" (cf. also Euripides' *Elektra* 290–91). That these sentiments are also found in Greek aristocratic literature, such as Pindar's epinikian odes, suggests their universality in the ancient Greek worldview.

38. Aristotle notes that when a person thinks that he is exempt from suffering misfortune, his attitude is "insolence" (*hubris*) rather than compassion (*Rh.* 1385b).

39. Contrast Konstan (2001: 61–62) on the significance of these examples: "In appealing to Hector's pity, Andromache, Priam and Hecuba reduce him imaginatively to a helpless, spectral bystander of their fates." My emphasis here is on the pity-inducing power that such visualization would normally have on the loved one; in these examples, the appeals fail because of the tragic circumstances involved.

40. Compare Aristotle *Rh.* 1385b, 1386b. This evaluative element is another part of compassion's cognitive side (cf. D2 above) and is central to many, if not all, acts of compassion. Compare Nussbaum (2001: 304–27) on the importance of cognition as a constituent of emotions such as compassion; also cf. Konstan (2001: 5–10) and Johnson/Clapp (2005: 141–54). Contrast Naiden (2006: 88–97) on the use of claims of "fairness" in supplications; he distinguishes these claims from appeals for pity, which he denigrates as being "humiliating and womanish" (98).

41. Note that Aristotle allows such "goodness" to extend to women and slaves (*Poet.* 1454a).

42. This will be especially true if the sufferer and the person to whom he or she appeals have a past relationship. Here, compassion will tend to function reciprocally.

43. Compare Aristotle *Rh.* 1386b. This may tie back into the likeness phenomenon in D2 in that people typically see themselves as virtuous. If the sufferer also shows himself or herself to be virtuous, this will establish a likeness between the two that will promote a compassionate response: "This person is a good person like me and therefore deserves my compassion."

44. The latter qualification also applies to older men, when they are represented in tragic choruses.

45. I will treat Euripides before Sophokles. My focus in Sophokles is on his later plays, which were written after some of the plays of Euripides I treat. Also, since Sophokles presents the consistently deepest and fullest treatment of the compassion theme, it seems appropriate to save him for last.

CHAPTER 1

In the following review of compassion in Greece prior to the fifth century BCE, my debt to other scholars, especially John Gould, A. R. Hands, and Walter Burkert, is considerable and will be noted.

1. Compare Burkert (1955: 71).

2. On the distinction between these two modes, see Gould (1973: 75–78). For a recent broad treatment of ancient supplication as a ritual of submission, see Burkert (1996: 85–90). See also Naiden's (2006) comprehensive survey of ancient supplication, which includes Near Eastern as well as Greek and Roman examples of supplication in its broad overview of the topic; my few points of disagreement with details of Naiden's work will be noted where relevant.

3. As an epithet in Homer, *Hiketesios: Odyssey* 13.213; *Xeinios: Iliad* 13.625; *Odyssey* 14.284, 9.271.

4. *Odyssey* 9.270–71 and 6.207–8 = 14.57–58 (protector of strangers and beggars). Lloyd-Jones (1971: 5, 30) sees Zeus's protection of guests and suppliants as part of his function as guarantor of justice in general. According to this interpretation, Paris and the Trojans (in the *Iliad*) as well as Polyphemos and the suitors (in the *Odyssey*) are eventually brought to justice through Zeus.

5. Whereas Agamemnon dishonored Apollo's priest, note the Achaian army's respect for the priest and his request (1.22–23). I do not share Pedrick's concern that supplications in the epics vary in the completeness with which they are described. Crotty (1994: 21) effectively argues, "Because of the unique and irreplaceable importance to the suppliant of what he or she seeks, and because supplication is a means of persuading another, the ceremony does not consist of a rigid program that must be carried out with minute attention to every detail if the act is to constitute a supplication. Rather, there is a certain repertory of features, not all of which need appear in every supplication."

6. Compare my discussion of the reciprocal nature of compassion in the introduction, pp. 17–20.

7. . . . τοὺς μὴ συ κτεῖνε σιδήρῳ μηδ' ἱκέτας ἀδικεῖν· ἱκέται δ' ἱεροί τε καὶ ἁγνοί (7.25.1). Note that all translations in this work are my own, except where otherwise noted. I have generally used OCT editions of Homer and the tragedians as my standard texts, although at times I have relied on Kovacs's editions of Euripides' plays.

8. προστρόπαιον αἷμα (*Ion* 1260).

9. Compare my brief discussion of compassion and reverence above (intro. p. 20). *Aidôs* is one of the most frequently discussed concepts in Greek literature; see, for example, von Erffa 1937; Cairns 1993; Schadewaldt (1955: 137–38); Pohlenz (1956: 55–56); Gould (1973: 85–90). The last three are specifically concerned with the connection between *aidôs* and compassion or *aidôs* and the suppliant theme; also, cf. Burkert (1955: 38–39, 71–72, 89) and Crotty (1994: passim).

10. *Iliad* 24.503; *Odyssey* 5.447–50, 7.165 = 181, 9.269–71, 14.388–89.

11. *Iliad* 21.74, 22.82, 22.123–24, 24.503; *Odyssey* 14.388–89, 22.312, 22.344. On the distinction between the two, cf. intro. n.34.

12. Compare Burkert (1955: 71).

13. This is not to say that pity is not usually what the suppliant appeals for (Konstan 2001: 79 and n.11). At least in epic and tragedy, pity or, rather, compassion broadly understood or mercy is more often than not what the suppliant seeks.

14. Gould 1973 gives a full description of the supplication ritual itself and also discusses the symbolic role or ritual significance of the body parts (knees, hands, chin) of the supplicated that the suppliant tends to touch (96–97). Crotty (1994: 18–21) offers insightful comments on the meaning of the supplication ritual as asserting a "long tradition of urgent needs"; also, see Burkert (1979: 43–45) for a somewhat different interpretation of the suppliant's gestures and occasional use of twigs and branches (*hiketêria*).

15. The cases of Chryses (*Iliad* 1.8–52) and Odysseus in Polyphemos's cave (*Odyssey* 9.259–71), for example, suggest that "figurative" supplication can be binding. Naiden (2006: 62–64) argues that words may constitute a supplication, especially when the suppliant cannot accomplish physical contact.

16. Also, someone mindful of ritual (unlike the Kyklops) might try to break contact before harming a suppliant, under the assumption that such a break would destroy the suppliant's divine protection.

17. A similar sense of the rightness of recompense can be found in the Roman world of patrons and clients, although certain thinkers, such as the Stoics, developed distaste for such self-interested motivation when involved in the exhibition of compassion. Hands 1968 discusses the concept of reciprocity in Greece and Rome, especially as regards pity and charity, although he gives little attention to the phenomenon in Greek tragedy. See 29–32 and 81–84 for the Stoic reaction and that of others. For more detailed comments on reciprocity in the society of the Homeric poems, see Finley (1965: 62–65 and passim). For comments about the commonality of norms of reciprocity and retaliation in Greek and many other ancient cultures, see Gouldner (1965: 41). Some recent studies on reciprocity in ancient Greek culture generally may be found in Gill et al. (1998b).

18. Examples in which Greek slaves feel compassion for masters who have suffered misfortune or dependents for kings or children for parents are, of course, exceptions. Still, even here, the element of reciprocity is very strong and lessens the sense of detachment that exists when reciprocity and interdependence are not stressed in relationships. Of course, the patron-client dichotomy of the class-conscious Romans shows that a reciprocal relationship can occur between otherwise unrelated persons of unequal class or status.

19. See further in Finley (63, 103–9) and Gould (90–94). Gould (94) notes that *hiketeia* "inverts the procedures of *xenia:* whereas in *xenia* "the 'insider' extends his protection" and the related honor to the stranger (*xenos*), in supplication, "the 'outsider' enforces a claim to the same honour and protection by ritual procedure which enacts the total abdication of any such claim." This observation, of course, concerns the initial contact of the *xenos* and host rather than their later relationship as "guest-friends."

20. He also adds an implied threat (i.e., uses negative reciprocity) in calling the Greeks to respect his patron god, Apollo. Naiden (2006: 56–57) notes that Chryses uses both the bough appropriate to a suppliant and the staff appropriate to an authoritative priest of Apollo.

21. Chryses' old age and his reference to his tears (*dakrua*) in 1.42 suggest that he is to be taken as a pitiable character (cf. Griffin 1980: 107). Chryses' tears would seem to flow specifically from his abuse by Agamemnon, but more generally they also may be taken to reflect his grief for the continuing loss of his daughter. I therefore disagree with Crotty's assertion (1994: 21–22) that Chryses' appeal to Agamemnon is not for compassion; the fact that his appeal is based on reciprocity and involves an exchange does not mean that compassion is not an appropriate response to his supplication. Also, since Thetis's appeal to Zeus is on behalf of

the honor of her son, a mortal prone to suffering and death, I do not accept Crotty's argument (22–23) that her divine status makes her supplication altogether different from that of mortal suppliants. See Slatkin (1991: chap. 1, esp. 38–39) on Thetis's helplessness relative to other gods and goddesses and on the *Iliad*'s use of Thetis's immortality to emphasize the hero Akhilleus's mortal nature and destiny (also, cf. 77).

22. The concept of "shared humanity" also occurs in Sternberg (2006: 177).

23. Οὐ γὰρ οὕτως οἱ πλουτοῦντες ὡς οἱ πένητες τοὺς ἀτυχοῦντας οἰκτίρειν εἰώθασι· δεδιότες γὰρ περὶ αὐτῶν τὰς τῶν ἄλλων συμφορὰς ἐλεοῦσιν (Stobaeus 4.33.21).

24. ἐννώσαντα ὅτι καὶ αὐτὸς ἄνθρωπος ἐὼν ἄλλον ἄνθρωπον, γενόμενον ἑωυτοῦ εὐδαιμονίῃ οὐκ ἐλάσσω, ζῶντα πυρὶ διδοίη, πρός τε τούτοισι δείσαντα τὴν τίσιν καὶ ἐπιλεξάμενον ὡς οὐδὲν εἴη τῶν ἐν ἀνθρώποισι ἀσφαλέως ἔχον, κελεύειν σβεννύναι τὴν ταχίστην τὸ καιόμενον πῦρ. . . . Kyros's action here is an act of compassion, despite Sternberg's use of "empathy" to describe it (2006: 15–16 and n.28); she notes that Xenophon several generations later explicitly wrote "Cyrus pitied Croesus." In Herodotos, however, Kyros's implicit compassion is evident in the act of salvation that he attempts (D1a).

25. οὐδὲν τὸ τούτου μᾶλλον ἢ τοὐμὸν σκοπῶν. / ὁρῶ γὰρ ἡμᾶς οὐδὲν ὄντας ἄλλο πλὴν / εἴδωλ' ὅσοιπερ ζῶμεν ἢ κούφην σκιάν (124–26). See Clapp's extended analysis of the compassion theme in Sophokles' *Aias* (Johnson/Clapp 2005); also, compare Munteanu (2012: 124, 190–92); and see above on generalized reciprocity (pp. 19–20).

26. Such a sense of basic similarity and of common human need very likely motivated people to perform the simple but essential acts of compassion required by the Athenian *arai Bouzygeiai:* providing water for the thirsty, burial for the unburied corpse, fire for anyone who needed it, a crust for a starving man, and so forth (D1a). See Hands (1968: 46–47); Snell (1960: 168); Pearson (1962: 245, n.2).

27. See further in Hands (1968: 78–80). The insistence by some that it is better to be envied than to be pitied suggests that some preferred to take their chances with the gods' (and their fellow man's) *phthonos;* see, for example, Pindar *Pythia* 1.85 and Herodotos 3.52.

28. Compare Konstan (2001: chap. 2) on what he calls the "vulnerability" principle.

29. At least this was so in the *Odyssey.* In contemporary Western societies, at least, it would seem to apply more to the bankrupt than to the beggar. Indeed, later generations did not hold beggars in such esteem

(see Hands 1968: 62–65 and 77–78). On Zeus's protection of beggars, see Adkins (1960b: 24–25).

30. Of course, the fact that Odysseus is not really the beggar and stranger that he pretends to be injects ironies and audience expectations that would not be present if Odysseus's story were true. Still, Eumaios is not made to remark that Odysseus's words are out of the ordinary. For a treatment of this episode that emphasizes the rhetorical elements of supplication, see Gödde (2000: 66–67).

31. The friend-enemy dichotomy is also depicted as working on a human-divine level as well as between humans, as is obvious from Homer's alignment of different gods with different factions of individuals—Athene and Hera with the Greeks, Apollo with the Trojans, Poseidon with the Kyklops, and so forth. These relationships are reciprocal, and the humans both sacrifice to their guardian deities and pray to them when in trouble. Zeus of course, as the leader and mediator of all the gods, is necessarily more neutral in his relation to humans as well, except for his special protection of guests and suppliants. Still, as father of gods and men, Zeus is sometimes criticized for not properly taking care of his own "children" (*Odyssey* 20.201–3).

32. οἱ δ' ἐλεαίροντες δίδοσαν (367). Naiden (2006: 76) asserts that Odysseus does not beg for food as a suppliant here, but his distinction seems forced. It may be that begging for food was seen as trivial compared to what suppliants normally sought; still, both the suppliant and the beggar can arouse compassion in Homer (D1a).

33. This notion becomes a rhetorical commonplace (e.g., Thukydides 3.40.3, Demosthenes 21.100). It will be discussed further in relation to Greek tragic drama.

34. Readers have noted that Odysseus and his men are themselves less than perfect guests of the Kyklops: uninvited, they have ventured into his cave and have partaken of his food. Still, that the Kyklops turns out to be such a savage brute makes their initial incivility seem mild by comparison (cf. Lloyd-Jones 1971: 29–30).

35. The text says that the crowd was gripped by "compassion" (*oiktos,* 2.81) at Telemachos's humiliation (cf. Scott 1979: 7). This is the inhibiting type of compassion: only the suitor Antinoos dared rebuke him with harsh words (D1b).

36. οὐκ ὄπιδα φρονέοντες ἐνὶ φρεσὶν οὐδ' ἐλεητύν (82). The word ἐλεητύς is related to *eleos* and seems to mean "mercy" in the sense of "sparing" or "compunction in using." See *LSJ* and Cunliffe 1963. Here,

the word is used absolutely, but in 18.451–52 it is used in the phrase ἐλεητὺς ἀλλοτρίων χαρίσασθαι (sparing to give at another's expense).

37. The case of Leodes is problematic; see, e.g., Gould (1973: 81); Scott (1979: 11); Pedrick (1982: 134). Homer doesn't give us much help in interpreting it, but his participation with the other suitors, especially in occupying Odysseus's house (ἐν μεγάγροισι, 322), appears to constitute sufficient grounds for revenge.

38. μάλιστα νεμεσσᾶται κακὰ ἔργα (283–84).

39. Compare Scott (1979: 11) on this episode.

40. Even though Lykaon calls for *aidôs* as well as *eleos* (21: 74–75; cf. D1b).

41. Compare Kim's monograph (2000), which specifically analyzes Akhilleus's pity as a theme that gives the *Iliad* unity. Also, compare Macleod (1982: introduction, esp. sections 1 and 2), who provides an insightful and balanced overview of the pity theme in Homer, especially as it relates to the contrast between art and life; indeed, he concludes that pity is "at the heart of Homer's conception of poetry" (14). Finally, Burkert's often-cited dissertation gives a comprehensive philological treatment of episodes involving pity in the *Iliad* and the *Odyssey* (1955: esp. 81–107, 135–48).

42. On these themes, compare the discussions by Pohlenz (1956: 54–55), Lloyd-Jones (1970: 15–23), Thornton 1984, Kim 2000, Goldhill 1991, Hammer 2002, and Most 2003. Most discusses the linkage between pity and anger that is evident in Homer's narration of warriors' responses to fallen comrades and that is central to Akhilleus's particular story. This linkage, however, is not necessarily present in all cases of compassion in Homer, as we have seen.

43. But contrast with Akhilleus's sustained mood of vengeance toward Hektor his graciousness and courtesy—even toward Agamemnon—when he presides over the funeral games in honor of Patroklos (bk. 23).

44. Note that burial is one of those basic requirements of compassion mentioned in n.26 above. In regard to Akhilleus's mutilation of Hektor's corpse, see Segal 1971. Burkert (1955: 101–2) analyzes Apollo's accusation that Akhilleus has "destroyed or lost compassion."

45. Compare Burkert's comprehensive treatment of this scene; also cf. MacLeod 1982; Zanker 1994; King (1987: 37–45); Seaford (1994: 172–76); Crotty (1994: 75–80); Kim (2000: 62–65, 146–51); and Most (2003: 71–73).

46. Crotty convincingly asserts that "in feeling pity for Priam, Achilles attains a kind of insight into the sorrow and anger that have driven

him throughout the *Iliad*"; also, that "the *eleos* that Achilles ultimately feels for Priam is the emotional expression of his insight that Priam's wretched situation is ultimately his as well" (1994: 14). There is, however, no need to import, as Crotty does (15), Aristotle's notion of *katharsis* to account for Akhilleus's response; at least, Akhilleus's response here differs from that of Aristotle's tragic spectator in that Akhilleus is personally involved in Priam's suffering, as is Priam in Akhilleus's. The two do, however, certainly experience a powerful sense of release and relief from this exhibition of compassion, as does the audience member /reader vicariously.

47. Compare Most (2003: 71), who eloquently writes of "a bridge of similarity . . . upon which compassion can travel"; cf. McCoy (2013: 32). Felson (2002: 47) writes, "The yearning to repay ϑρέπτρα to his parent contributes to Akhilleus' sympathy for Priam."

48. See Macleod *ad* 508 on Akhilleus's initial act of pushing Priam away—to give the two of them some space and allow them to weep—before he raises the old man up in compassionate acceptance of his supplication; also, see Lateiner (1995: 36–41) on how nonverbal behavior, especially Priam's self-abasement as a suppliant, functions to make this a particularly powerful scene. Also, Akhilleus's admiration for Priam's bravery and heart in having come alone to his tent (24: 519–21) enhances Akhilleus's compassion for him (cf. Hammer 1002: 223 and my introduction, section D4). All in all, the compassion in this episode ascends to the level of generalized reciprocity (see Gill 1998a: 312–13 and my introduction, pp. 19–20).

49. αὐτὰρ ἐπὴν ἀγάγῃσιν ἔσω κλισίην Ἀχιλῆος,
οὔτ' αὐτὸς κτενέει ἀπό τ' ἄλλους πάντας ἐρύξει·
οὔτε γάρ ἐστ' ἄφρων οὔτ' ἄσκοπος οὔτ' ἀλιτήμων,
ἀλλὰ μάλ' ἐνδυκέως ἱκέτεω πεφιδήσεται ἀνδρός (24.184–87 = 155–58).

50. Crotty 1994, for one, seems to miss this "competitive" aspect of *eleos* in Homer: that it can prompt the saving intervention of one warrior for his fellow warrior or warriors (D1a).

51. Compare Thornton 1984 on the Litai. Her argument is especially applicable to supplications seeking mercy from the person whom one has wronged. This is not the situation in most supplications outside the *Iliad* and does not fit all supplications in the *Iliad;* e.g., it does not apply to Akhilleus's friends' appeal for compassion from him, although it obviously is designed to fit Agamemnon's attempt to compensate and placate Akhilleus's wrath. But see Lateiner (1995: 54) on Agamemnon's "distance"

in the failed appeal to Akhilleus in book 9: "Only an abortive ceremony of restitution of property by proxies occurs. Achilles experiences no complete social and public ritual, no adequate face-to-face personal admission of fault here or even later" (*Il.* 19.51, 76–77). Later Lateiner adds, "Zeus never faults Achilles' behavior in this quarrel with Agamemnon" (55).

52. Compare Burkert (1955: 73–75) on the nonhuman connotations of *nêlees*. McCoy (2013: 25–26) sees Akhilleus's lack of care for his comrades as being due his wound (*pathos*) by Agamemnon, which keeps him absorbed in the past and unable to relate to the present sufferings of his fellow Greeks.

53. Burkert (1955: 94) and Most (2003: 67) observe that this is Akhilleus's first expression of pity for another person in the epic. McCoy (2013: 22) states, "As Achilles slowly acknowledges and accepts his own vulnerability and that of others—particularly in the loss of Patroklos—his capacity to feel pity is actualized."

54. Compare Gill's thesis (1998a: 309–13), cited above, p. 29. Also, compare Hammer (2002: 213–16) and Zanker (1994: 23–25).

55. She requests compassion at 431 (ἐλέαιρε, cf. οὐδ' ἐλεαίρεις, 406). From her perspective, compassion consists of Hektor staying and protecting (D1a). Hektor responds with compassion for his beloved wife (ἐλέησε, 484) but gently explains that he cannot meet her request; cf. Scott (1979: 12); Kim (2000: 175); and Crotty (1994: 47–51). Contrast Konstan's approach to this appeal and expression of compassion between kin (2001: 61–62) and Hammer's similar approach (2002: 214, n.27); see my introduction, pp. 18–19, 22, and n.39. Also, compare Kleopatra's effective use of prospective horror in her appeal to Meleagros (*Il.* 9. 590–96). Note, however, that Kleopatra's appeal, unlike Andromache's, seeks to induce Meleagros to fight.

56. Priam pleads ἐλέησον (59); Hekabe also pleads ἐλέησον (83): both want their son to come inside in order to rescue them and the other Trojans as well as to save himself (22.56–57). Again, contrast Konstan's reading (2001: 61–62) and Hammer's (see previous note).

57. We will see this theme in tragedy as well, especially in Aischylos.

58. For the artist's special ability and tendency to arouse feelings of sympathy in his audience, cf. *Odyssey* 8.521–31, where Odysseus weeps in response to the bard's tale, although here, of course, the tale is about Odysseus himself. See Macleod (1982: 4–5) on the "workings of pity in Odysseus' mind" that Macleod sees reflected in the simile that Homer employs in these lines.

59. Compare the characterization of Patroklos at 18.669–72.

60. A similar view of the *Iliad* and its author's relation to it may be found in Weil's *The Iliad, or the Poem of Force,* as well as in chapter 2 of Segal 1971.

61. For a debate on this matter, see Long (1970: 122) and the reply by Adkins (1971: 1–2).

62. On the worldview of the Archaic age, compare Dodds, chap. 2; Snell, chap. 3; Fränkel, chap. 4; and above, pp. 31–33, 45–46). Also, see Herington (1985: 131–33 and 146–47) for archaic worldviews, particularly those reflecting the interpenetration of the human and the divine, as they may have specifically influenced Aischylos.

63. Aristotle and Homer probably would have agreed that compassion for the undeserving is a "moral flaw"; we know this explicitly from Aristotle, from Homer only because no one does this.

64. Or by Hippokleides or even Solon or some combination of them perhaps; see Herington (1985: 83–87); also Davison 1958.

65. Compare Herington (1985: 96–97).

66. Compare Else (1965: 46–50); Herington (1985: 87–91).

67. On the impact of Homer on tragedy generally, see Herington 1985 (esp. 133–36).

68. Plato *Ion* 535b–e; see Herington for a general treatment of the rhapsode's performance (1985: 10–15).

69. Indeed, as Herington's fine study has shown, tragedy's inheritance from pre-tragic poetry of many kinds were multiple and varied. My focus, admittedly, is intentionally narrow.

70. Herington (1985: 130–33) discusses the great mythic richness—what he calls the "catholicity"—of early tragedy's inheritance from early epic, especially that of Aischylos, in contrast to greater uniformity and lesser exoticism of the later drama of Sophokles and Euripides.

CHAPTER 2

1. The late Douglass Parker brought this passage to my attention.

2. Bolkestein (1939: 112ff.) cites many of these; cf. Dover (1974: 200–201). David Rosenbloom (2012: esp. 275–76) argues that pity (along with the related emotions of fear, anger, and indignation) was fundamental to Athenian democratic political culture both in tragedy and in the courts; also, that pity was viewed positively by citizens of Athens in opposition to *hubris,* which was associated with elite individuals' power and wealth, along with a sense of immunity to fear and suffering that displayed no

pity since it required none. He argues, therefore, that such *hubris* was inherently antidemocratic. I agree.

3. Compare Rosenbloom (2012: 273). More evidence from the fifth century itself will be given in my discussion below. Let me note here that both Diodorus and Plutarch use *philanthropia* (kindness) to characterize the Athenians and, almost, as a general equivalent to compassion (*oiktos*). I discuss this distinction on pp. 93–94 below, in regard to Aischylos's *Prometheus Bound*, but as we see here, *philanthropia* develops later to denote humane kindness and as a rough equivalent to Christian *agape* and courtesy. The Greek epic and tragic authors, however, observed a careful distinction between the personal feeling of *oiktos/eleos* and the more general feeling of *philanthropia.*

4. On the altar, see further in the commentary on Pausanias by Frazer, in Bolkestein (1939: 113), and in Hands (1968: 80), whose note gives still further bibliography. More recently, Loraux (1986: 374, n.308) asserts that the "altar of the twelve gods did not become the altar of Pity until the last quarter of the fifth century" although she notes that Wycherley thought the fourth century more likely. One colorful incident involving the altar at Athens in Roman times is Lucian's report about the philosopher Demonax (second century CE), who, when the Athenians were thinking of holding a gladiatorial show, advised them that they should not do so without first tearing down their Altar of Compassion (Demonax 57).

5. See, for example, Loraux's *The Invention of Athens* (1986) and Tzanetou 2005. Geertz (1973) argues that cultural ideologies stem from systemic strains and are sometimes useful in effecting positive change, especially in the "establishment and defense of patterns of belief and value" (231). If, however, they become too extreme or destructive, competing ideologies, science, and common sense usually defeat and disable them. A recent overview of ideological thinking is Terry Eagleton (1991).

6. See Sternberg (2006) for a comprehensive study of compassion in the daily life of ancient Athens.

7. For a general discussion of the power of *logos* to arouse emotions such as pity, see Solmsen (1975: 47–65).

8. An extreme example of the power of tragedy to affect its audience negatively is the famous response of the audience to Phrynicos's *Sack of Miletos* in 494 BCE. By presenting an impending historical crisis rather than a general mythical story, the playwright here aroused not pity so much as fear, since the audience knew that the Persians wanted them next; see further in Pelling (1997: 18); Loraux (2002: 43–44); Dué (2006: 60); and Lateiner (2005: 75).

9. I have already mentioned some passages of this sort in the previous chapter (see pp. 31–33, 40, 45–46, and n.62). A few of the many others from tragedy are Aischylos, *Agamemnon* 1327–30; Euripides, *Elektra* 1329–30, *Orestes* 976–81, and *Hekabe* 488–91. Outside of tragedy, similar statements can be found. I have already given one example from Herodotos (see above chap. 1, pp. 31–32); cf. also Herodotos 7.46. Demokritos (B 107a, Diels-Kranz 2: 164) says that "it is fitting for human beings not to laugh at the misfortunes of their fellow men, but to lament (ὀλοφύρεσθαι) them" because of the instability of life. Similarly in Euripides' *Andromache* (421), the chorus says that "misfortunes, even of a stranger, are pitiful to all mortals"; cf. also Euripides' *Elektra* 290–91.

10. For a fuller treatment of compassion in this play, see the chapter on Euripides below.

11. As we shall see in chapter 5, Sophokles also did not flinch from the use of such obvious means of arousing sympathy in his audience. I might mention here, for example, the use of wedding imagery in the young Antigone's "funeral-song" (806–82), the use of the burial motif in *Aias,* and the messenger's speech in *Eurypylos* (see Lloyd Jones, *Fragments*). It seems to me that generally Sophokles showed somewhat more restraint and subtlety than Euripides in exploiting such powerful pathos-arousing motifs.

12. Dover (1974: 201) cites Aristophanes' frequent ridicule of "skin- or eye-diseases" as partial evidence for his contention that the Athenians were lacking in compassion "in certain important respects." Another way of looking at this, however, as suggested to me by David Armstrong, would be that they reserved their compassion for truly catastrophic circumstances.

13. Perhaps here begins the distrust of emotions such as compassion that becomes part of the philosophers' promotion of reason in Sokrates, Plato, and the Stoics. See an argument against Plato's general distrust of compassion in Johnson/Clapp (2005: 141–54).

14. For Gorgias and Thrasymachos, see further in Schadewaldt (1955: 139), Pohlenz (1956: 58), and, especially, Solmsen (1975: 47–48). For rhetorical commonplaces about pity, see E. B. Stevens (1944: 1–25). For a survey of pity and law in the ancient world, see Konstan (2001: 27–48).

15. Compare Rosenbloom (2012: 282–87). In the fourth century, Lykourgos suggested an antidote to the defendants who bring wife and children into court: in cases of treason let the jurors also bring their wives and children into court so that they may better imagine the threat which the traitor posed and thus be more severe in their judgment (1.141; cf. Lysias 28.14).

16. In his renunciation of such techniques, Sokrates also implies that the jurors expected them (Plato, *Apology* 34–35). The sheer repetition of the use of such techniques suggests that they must have sometimes, at least, been effective in gaining acquittals. On *Wasps*, compare Rosenbloom (2012: 283–84, 287–92).

17. Compare Dover (1974: 195–96), who cites Lysias 18.1 and 19.53.

18. Compare the varied accounts of this debate by Solmsen (1975: 62–64), Macleod 1977, and Lateiner (2005: 84–87); also, Naiden (2006: 87 and n.350). Here the Plataians are defendants before the Spartan judges; the Thebans, now allied with the Spartans, are prosecuting the Plataians, their old Boeotian enemies. I have put this debate in the category of assembly debates, although properly it is judicial rather than deliberative in nature; also, although the Athenians are not directly involved in the debate as parties, they have long been allies of the Plataians. It is interesting, nevertheless, that the arguments using compassion here are similar to those we see used in Athenian institutions.

19. The Thebans seek to refute the Plataians' claims to receive compassion by claiming that the Plataians' old alliance with the Spartans is now obsolete and by arguing that the Plataians have forfeited their right to the status of suppliants by their own slaughter of Theban suppliants whom they had promised to spare (3.61–67, esp. 66–67). On the notion of no pity for those who show no pity, see intro. pp. 17–19.

20. Compare Macleod (1983c: 52–67, esp. p.58).

21. Stevens (1944: 1–3) uses this speech as the starting point for his discussion of rhetorical commonplaces of pity. The second section of his article (15–19) concerns the rhetorical topic of the leniency of the Athenian character mentioned here by Kleon.

22. Compare Rosenbloom (2012: 280–81). Note that a close reading of Thukydides' text reveals that Diodotos cautioned them not to be swayed too much (*pleon*) by the emotions of *oiktos* and *epieikeia* (fairness) rather than that they should not feel these emotions at all (Kleon's preference).

23. See contrasting views on this debate in Pearson (1962: 24–26), Macleod (1977: 118–22, 1978: 64–78); Lateiner (2005: 81–84), and Konstan (2001: 80–82). The reasoning of realpolitik typically seems to focus on immediate or short-term interest rather than on long-term considerations of past and future.

24. See, for example, Ferguson (1972: 335–39). Of course, the *Persians* by Aischylos and the *Sack of Miletos* by Phrynichos had clear connections to the Persian War, as we will see in chapter 3. Enterprising scholars have developed a few other salient connections between plays and contemporary

events, particularly in regard to the tragic developments of the Peloponnesian War that Thukydides described. We will note these as we discuss the relevant plays.

25. Here, I mean to contrast Vietnam and World War II to more recent wars such as Iraq, since the former wars involved major mobilizations of American troops through the draft.

26. This phenomenon has been well documented in the work of Jonathan Shay. A dramatic reading of *Theater of War,* a script based on Sophokles' *Aias* and *Philoktetes,* was performed for American combat veterans at a recent combat stress-control conference hosted by the Marine Corps in San Diego, California (*Dallas Morning News,* Aug. 15, 2008). Since 2008, this project has grown so that there are now (as of June 2015) numerous scheduled live performances (see the website for details: www.outsidethewirellc.com/projects/theater-ofwar/overview).

27. See further in (Bolkestein 1939: 112–13), Ehrenberg (1974: 243–45), Hands (1968: 62ff.), and Dover (1974: 197).

28. Cited by Dover (1974: 197), who also gives other examples of the fall from good fortune arousing pity (D2).

29. Compare Hall (2010: 116–17) on how the "civic male consciousness at the heart of the theatrical experience" made every citizen see himself "in some sense as a monarch."

30. See further on reciprocity in liturgies in Ober (1989: 226–30).

31. Lysias's speech defending the cripple's pension (24) indicates that disabled Athenians unable to work did receive a small pension from the state (D4). In the course of the speech, the speaker explicitly associates *hybris* with the wealthy, strong, and young (15 ff.); cf. Rosenbloom's comments cited in n.2 above.

32. See further on this and related fragments of Demokritos in E. A. Havelock's classic work, *The Liberal Temper of Greek Politics* (1957: 142–47).

33. Compare Hands (1968: 80) and Sternberg (2006: 139–40).

34. It is interesting to note here the "emotional" side of the Sophists' speculations about society and the social contract. As we shall see, Euripides frequently participated in the "sophistic" speculations of his time concerning compassion by his treatment of the theme on the tragic stage. In his later plays, Aischylos also emphasized social harmony.

35. Indeed, revenge seemed so justifiable that "wronged" Greeks would call for the gods' pity and vengeance in a single breath (Aischylos *Eumenides* 121; Euripides *Elektra* 671–75). Vengeance is sometimes described as a relief of grief and lamentation (e.g., Euripides *Trojan Women* 403–5), and it is perhaps because people felt a need for such vengeance so sharply

and painfully that they saw the vengeance performed by divine or human avengers as a type of compassion. This theme will be highlighted in our study of Euripides' *Hekabe* and Sophokles' *Philoktetes.*

36. Whether Kleon applies this principle appropriately in the case of Mytilene is certainly questionable; Thukydides does not seem to think he does.

CHAPTER 3

1. This text is from Richmond Lattimore's translation of *The Frogs,* pp.64–68 (excerpted), based on Aristophanes' Greek original, lines 1012–62.

2. Lattimore exercises some liberty with the text in this last line: Aischylos says that Euripides dressed his royals in rags "so that they would appear piteous (*eleinoi*) to people" (1064). Euripides then asks: "What's the harm in this?"

3. I shall treat *Seven Against Thebes* first, even though *Persians* (472 BCE) predates it by five years.

4. I make the following assumptions about dates: the *Suppliants* (ca. 463), *Oresteia* (458), and *Prometheus Bound* (post 458, cf. Herington 1972). I also subscribe to Herington's view of the three trilogies to which these plays belong as marking a change in Aischylos's career as a writer of tragic drama.

5. Rosenmeyer (1982: 170–71), speaking of compassion in Aischylos, remarks: "Compassion for the sufferings of one's fellow men is not expressed by the principals; it is reserved for the chorus. . . . And it should not come as a surprise that the shedding of tears, also, is in Aischylos a strictly choral business. . . . But no character refers to himself in the process of weeping." Also, he notes that even in response to the extended messenger's speeches in *Persians,* "Pity and fear are maintained at their proper level of moderation and do not degenerate into an excess of empathy, which Aeschylean tragedy shuns" (200).

6. Vickers (1973: 467–69) emphasizes the ill omen of the chorus's prayers. On the pity and gender issues raised here, cf. introduction, section D6.

7. οἰκτρὸν γὰρ πόλιν ὧδ' ὠγυγίαν / Ἀΐδαι προϊάψαι, δορὸς ἄγραν / δουλίαν, ψαφαρᾷ σποδῷ / ὑπ' ἀνδρὸς Ἀχαιοῦ θεόθεν / περθομέναν ἀτίμως

8. LSJ recommends this way of writing this cry of distress.

9. τὰς δὲ κεχειρωμένας ἄγεσθαι, / ἐέ, νέας τε καὶ παλαιὰς / ἱππηδὸν πλόκαμων, περιρ- / ρηγνυμὲνων φαρέων·

10. Reading στυγεράν rather than στυγερῶν (335).

11. Compare Rosenmeyer (1982: 187). Also, see Gaca (2014: 305–10) on the mistreatment of women and girls in war.

12. As Thalman (1978: 58) observes, "The chorus's ὀξύγοοι λιταί [prayers with shrill wailing] to the gods (line 320) are replaced by the γόοι [wailings] of grief at the end (lines 854–56, 917–18, 964, 967)."

13. Rachel Sternberg's recent survey of examples of pity in history and oratory (Sternberg 2005: 20) suggests that people captured or defeated in war provided the largest single category of cases seen as pitiable.

14. According to Stanford (1983: 24). Contrary to the view that Greek "pity" did not extend to kin, this is a Persian pitying his son, but if Aischylos intends his audience to sense a discrepancy between Greek and Persian ways here, he does not call attention to it. Also, Dareios is presented in the play generally as a respected elder Persian king; cf., e.g., Pelling (1997: 14–16), Leahy (1969: 173).

15. Hall (1996: *ad* 199), tracing the motif of Xerxes' torn robe throughout the play, interprets it as a component of the play's feminization of the Persians.

16. Here the appeal is to a former king's ghost, as though to a god.

17. This is the view of Hall (1989: 83–84), who sees the Persian lamentation as excessive and barbaric. Compare Loraux (1986: 50): "The only laments that might be mentioned in an [Athenian] *epitaphios* were those of an enemy bemoaning its ill fate." Indeed, she adds that in *Persians,* "Aischylos had made a tragedy out of those Persian tears that were the finest praise of Athens." In her later work (2002), however, Loraux's view of this play changes. See notes 19 and 21 below.

18. For an interpretation that emphasizes the identification of the Athenian audience with the suffering of the Persians in Aischylos's play, see Dué (2006, chap. 2). She associates the chorus's lamentations in the play with the tradition of women's lamentations in epic and song.

19. Compare Loraux (2002: 44–49); also, Pucci, introduction to Loraux (2002: xi). Also, see Hall (1996: esp. 11–13).

20. Gagarin (1976) prefers to see Persia's downfall more as the results of the gods' effects on the nation as a whole. Probably our agreement is greater than our disagreement.

21. Again, compare Loraux (2002: 48), who revisiting her earlier "political" reading of the play, now asserts, "In other words, they [the audience of Athenian citizens] were able to resist the immediate pleasure of being the cause of the suffering represented on the stage, because, in the cries of the defeated enemy, tragedy taught them to recognize something that

touched them above and beyond their identity as Athenians." Also, cf. Pelling (1997: 16) and Gagarin (1976: 52–56).

22. Compare Pelling (1997: 13–19), who refers to the "intrinsic paradox" in presenting "a play with nothing but Persian characters" (13). Gagarin (1976: 54) refers to the "simultaneous presentation of opposed perspectives." Munteanu (2012: 151–63) also develops this ambiguity in her detailed analysis of the play's historical context, with particular emphasis on the role of fear in the play.

23. For detailed treatments of supplication emphasizing the ritual in tragedy, see John Gould (1973: 85–90), Vickers (1973: 438–94); Kopperschmidt 1971 emphasizes the structural elements in suppliant plays; Gödde 2000 stresses the interaction of ritual and rhetoric; Bernek 2004 focuses on political elements. Both *aidôs* (reverence) and *oiktos* (compassion) were typically sought by suppliants in Greek tragedy, although we will see in Aischylos that *aidoios* and its cognates sometimes carry a meaning of "having compassion for the suppliant's misfortune" as well as "having reverence" or "respect" for the suppliant's person.

24. It is, of course, with the latter that Plato was so concerned in the *Republic;* see Johnson/Clapp (2005: 141–54) for our attempt to defend tragedy against Plato's critique.

25. Compare Konstan's recent treatment of pity in this play (2005a: 60–62).

26. They say that the marriage is "unholy" (*asebê*); also, they claim that it is contrary to "right" (*themis,* 37) and "righteousness" (*to dikaion,* 78). At other times, the chorus emphasize that this marriage is contrary to their will: see, for example, the song of 776–824, where they express their dread of being forced into a "heart-rending marriage" (δαικτὼρ καρδίας γάμος, 798–99). These reservations, based in large part on the "aggressive nature" (*hybris,* 81) of their cousins, seem sufficient to justify their refusal to marry and to motivate their father's support of that refusal. Contrast Turner, who argues that the Danaids opposed marriage generally versus marriage with the sons of Aigyptos and therefore appealed to Pelasgos for a "dubious cause" (2001: 33).

27. In Greek, the child's name is Epaphos; *epaphê* is the word for the "caress" or "touch" by which Zeus embraced Io. The chorus also mention the *epipnoiê* ("breathing on" or "inspiration," if you will) of the divine lover. The story of Io and Epaphos and the Danaids' connection to this hereditary line is later elaborated in lines 40–48 and 291–324. Gödde (2000: 187–97) argues that Io's story is also paradigmatic for the story of the Danaids in the drama.

28. This meaning of *kêdemôn* does not exclude the meaning favored by Lembke (1975: 82) of one who sees to the care and proper burial of the dead, but the Danaids' need here is primarily for someone who will protect them from their aggressive suitors.

29. They strengthen their claim on the gods' protection by asserting that even those fleeing from war have an altar of asylum that provides them with divine protection (83–85); cf. Rosenbloom (2012: 276–77); also, see Gödde (2000: 147–76) for an extended analysis of "images of flight" in the play, which she sees as Aischylos's way of characterizing the Danaids' extreme situation and as providing a powerful emotional foundation of the Danaids' supplication.

30. Contrast the herald's disdain of the Greek gods (922–23, 927).

31. Danaos's caution to the young women to be restrained and submissive suggests that they may not be naturally so disposed. Indeed, the *parodos* has already given the audience a sense that these girls are capable of hostility as well as plaintive distress. For an interpretation of Danaos as exemplifying "Egyptian cunning," see Hall (1989: 123).

32. LSJ assumes that *aidoios* embraces "compassion" as well as "reverence"; cf. n.23 above and on lines 28–29, where the chorus sing of the "compassionate/reverent spirit" of the land of Argos. Both meanings seem to be implied in Aischylos's use of *aidoios* in this play. In fact, this linkage suggests a fusion of the two emotions as motives for the human characters; cf. above, introduction, p. 20; also, cf. Burkert (1955: 38).

33. Some take it as the more ritualistic "raise from sanctuary" (e.g., Smyth 1973 *ad loc.*), but the former meaning fits this context better. Page 1972 prints an alternative reading: *antêsas,* meaning "having encountered," but that verb commonly takes a genitive or dative object rather than an accusative as here; also, the meaning seems weaker than Smyth's text printed above.

34. As Gödde (2000: 180) notes, they avoid the question of justice raised by Pelasgos and rephrase the issue as one of the "brutal violence of men over women."

35. Compare Bednarowski, who notes that Pelasgos "does not accuse [the Danaids] of wrongdoing" in their threat of suicide (2010: 202); indeed, Bednarowski gives a balanced view of their suicide threats both here and elsewhere in the play and demonstrates the ambiguity and openness of Aischylos's portrayal of these suppliants.

36. Compare D3 on the connection between sight and compassion. Also cf. Gödde (2000: 178, n.478) on Aischylos's use of the motif of compassion-arousing sight in the play. The assertion that all have an inclination

of kindness toward the weaker appears to be a generalization about human nature that Aischylos's democratic audience, at least, would likely accept regarding themselves.

37. Rosenmeyer (1982: 171) denies compassion as a motive of Pelasgos: "Aeschylean principals who might be expected to voice a similar compassion [to that of the chorus], like Pelasgus pondering the application of the fugitives, do not. Pelasgus's thinking is guided only by his interest in his community. He is not a free agent." Cf. Sandridge (2008: 439), who sees "reverence" rather than "pity" as Pelasgos's motive.

38. LSJ gives the word such a broader range; cf. above n.23.

39. See Gödde (2000: 148–49, n.406) on Aischylos's use of imagery to portray the hybris of the sons of Aigyptos and its relation to the flight imagery used of the Danaids.

40. Winnington-Ingram (1961) argues that whereas the Danaids are able to appeal to Zeus *Hikesios* in *Suppliants,* later in the trilogy they offend Zeus *Xenios* in the killing of their new husbands and, in their polluted state, are again in danger of exile and perhaps become suppliants a second time. Winnington-Ingram speculates plausibly that the situation was resolved by a purification ordained by Zeus and by Aphrodite's reconciliation of the women to marriage with Argives. Of course, one of the daughters, Hypermestra, was unable to bring herself to murder her Egyptian husband. See further on these and other issues in Garvie 1969; also see Gantz (1993: 203–7) for another plausible reconstruction of the trilogy; for a contrary reading that makes Pelasgos the victim, the Danaids the aggressors, and Danaos a tyrant, see Turner 2001.

41. Compare introduction, p. 20 on appeals for *aidôs* and divine protection.

42. A new element here, as Adkins suggests (cf. Gould 1973: 89–90), is the transfer of the supplication from a "domestic" to a "public" situation. Pelasgos tells the suppliants that they are not suppliants at his own hearth ("domestic" supplication) but at a public altar and must therefore appeal to the city for protection (365–69).

43. I follow Lloyd-Jones 1952 in my interpretation of "falling about robes" (πέπλοισι περιπετῆ, 233); cf. Denniston/Page.

44. Fraenkel (1950: *ad* 245 ff.) sees the girl's participation at her father's libation among the men as "hardly conceivable within the limits of Athenian custom" and assumes that Aischylos has "Homerized" here. Denniston/Page (1957), however, don't find any Homeric parallels. But would Aischylos have disturbed his audience's concentration at this critical point by introducing an absurdity? More likely, social practices and gender

restrictions were not as consistent as they may appear to have been. See Loraux (1987: esp. 43, n.42) for further comments on this virgin sacrifice. In this trilogy, the suffering of women is a primary theme (D6).

45. Compare Burkert (1955: 60).

46. Compare Rosenmeyer (1982: 170–71).

47. A variant reading at 1143 for ταλαίναις (miserable) is φιλοίκτοις (piteous).

48. Leahy 1969 argues that Aischylos depicts Kassandra as personally guilty in *Agamemnon* by virtue of her refusal of Apollo's love, but he still judges her as deserving of pity (176).

49. A more common manuscript reading, with *skia* (shadow) in the nominative case and the verb *trepô* (turn) instead of *prepô* (resemble), yields the meaning, "A mere shadow could overturn it."

50. The meaning of her last sentence has troubled critics: to what do "this" and "that" refer? Denniston/Page offer the two most likely interpretations: (1) "this" refers to the second of the general alternatives she mentions, the extreme tenuousness of misfortune, which can easily change to total annihilation, whereas "that" refers to the second alternative, the precariousness of prosperity, which can easily change to misfortune; (2) "this" refers to the "universal misery of man" as presented in Kassandra's reflection on human fortune, whereas "that" refers to Kassandra's and Agamemnon's particular cases. The latter interpretation seems more difficult to grasp and might suggest that Kassandra sees herself as exempt from the tragic human dynamic, whereas the play shows her fate to be a prime illustration of it. The change from misfortune to annihilation is, in fact, the change that she herself is about to undergo.

51. Kassandra earlier made one more "pathetic" or perhaps "macabre" reference in calling Thyestes' children's internal organs and entrails a "pitiable load" (*epoiktiston gemos*, 1221), which she envisions the children holding before themselves and which Thyestes will "taste"; see Denniston/Page for more details. The use of *epoiktistos* here conforms to Aristotle's prescription that we pity the misfortune of others, whereas we grieve or lament our own. The "pitiable" image here is of Thyestes' children—not of Kassandra or the chorus.

52. *Oiktos* is used here to denote verbal lamentation (cf. D6). Smyth translates it here as "piteous plaint."

53. Burkert (1955: 60) notes that Elektra uses the compound *sumpenthein* ("suffer with," *Cho.* 199) only in the context of an external ritual.

54. Contrast Segal (1986: 351–53), who argues that Aischylos's choice of *aidos* over *eleos* here significantly makes Klytaimestra's breast and milk "symbols of a suprapersonal female principle in conflict with the male."

55. Gods, of course, do appear in other tragedies by all three playwrights, but not as principal characters whose conflicts with one another are dramatized directly onstage rather than though human intermediaries (Euripides' *Hippolytos* and *Bacchai* are exceptions in limited ways). This play takes its audience back to the epic world of Hesiod's *Theogony* rather than to the more normally paradigmatic human-centered world of Homer's epics (cf. Griffith 1983: 6 and n.17).

56. Compare Vickers's treatment of sympathy in the play (1973: 70–76).

57. On Zeus's negative portrayal as young tyrant in this play, see Griffith (1983: 7–8).

58. Aischylos here uses Kratos to point out the irony that Prometheus's theft of fire most directly infringed upon Hephaistos's prerogative as the blacksmith god, the god of fire. Hephaistos consequently should be the god most incensed by Prometheus's theft, but instead turns out to be the Olympian most intensely sympathetic to the Titan. Of course, compounding the irony is the fact that Hephaistos is the god with the technology to bind Prometheus to the rock; Kratos and Bia are only "toughs" who escort Prometheus to the place where Hephaistos must exercise his craft. Indeed, technology is an area in which Hephaistos and Prometheus share an expertise.

59. Perhaps Hephaistos recalls here Prometheus's alliance with the Olympians in the war against the Titans. Also, as mentioned in the previous note, they share knowledge of technology. Both exemplify the trickster as well. Griffith (1983: 2–3) notes that Prometheus like Hephaistos and Athene had special honors in Athens; in particular, both Prometheus and Hephaistos were honored by potters (*OCD*).

60. Vickers (1973: 71) notes the polarity presented by the pitiless Might and the sympathetic Hephaestus.

61. Compare Loraux (2002: 57), also Munteanu (2012: 173–75).

62. Can we compare his pain qua pain to that of Herakles in *Women of Trachis* or to that of Philoktetes in Sophokles' play, or is it superhuman even beyond that of Greek heroes? I take this to be a theological question beyond the scope of this study.

63. Also, compare 112–13, 237–38, and 435; see Griffith (1983: 19) on words of pain and suffering in the play.

64. Compare the sensitivity to shame exhibited by Homer's heroes.

65. Burkert (1955: 59–60) discusses how in this play Aischylos first employs the new compound expressions such as *sunaschalan* to express the chorus's long-lasting bond with Prometheus based on pure feeling in

contrast to the poet's use of *oiktirein* to denote an impulse that is realized in action. As Vickers (1973: 72) notes, Aristotle's suggestion that "pity for the oppressed can produce indignation" is relevant here.

66. In this scene, we learn among other things that Prometheus has a resource in his struggle with Zeus: secret knowledge desperately needed by Zeus as to how and by whom Zeus will be stripped of his power as king of the gods. Prometheus therefore expresses confidence that Zeus will neither persuade him nor force him to reveal his secret until Zeus releases him from his bonds and willingly offers him restitution for this mistreatment (168–85).

67. Compare D4 on compassion and worthiness and D3 on the connection between sight and compassion.

68. Compare Stanford (1983: 27).

69. Swanson (1994–95: 224) observes: "Pity . . . seems to be the defining statement of both justice and friendship, according to Prometheus." Contrast Konstan (2001: 60–61), who sees Prometheus as responding "indignantly" to the Okeanids' pity at 246. But any indignation that he expresses here is directed against Zeus and company rather than against the sympathetic daughters of Okeanos; cf. Munteanu (169–70).

70. Swanson (1994–95: 225) notes that Prometheus "indicates his belief that malice, not justice, motivates Zeus" and compares 97 and 525. Indeed, the stake driven through one's chest is consistent with such a belief!

71. Compare Swanson (1994–95: 221).

72. Presumably Okeanos came over to the Olympian side with Prometheus in the war with the Titans since he continues his function in the world above rather than being consigned with the other Titans to Tartaros. Line 331 also suggests that Okeanos may also have supported Prometheus's rebellion against Zeus, but probably only as a sympathetic friend rather than an active participant. Okeanos's proposal here that he himself intercede with Zeus suggests that he has still been able to maintain cordial relations with the chief god.

73. Note the linkage here between sympathy and kinship: kinship prompts sympathy. Both are Titans. Also, Okeanos is Prometheus's father-in-law; cf. Griffith (1983: *ad* 284–396), *contra* Swanson (1994–95: 226) who identifies Okeanos as Prometheus's grandfather; also Hephaistos as a Titan (221). Munteanu (2012: 168 and n.18) mistakenly attributes 288 to the Okeanids instead of the actual speaker, Okeanos.

74. According to Hesiod's *Theogony* 507–25, Atlas, Menoitios, Prometheus, and Epimetheus were sons of the Titan Iapetos. That text describes how Menoitios and Prometheus came to bad ends because of their

opposition to Zeus, but says only that wise Zeus assigned Atlas the task of holding up the sky. The implication seems to be that by doing so Zeus not only provided stability to the orderly division of sky and earth but also neutralized Atlas as a potential troublemaker: because he is ever occupied with his task, Atlas never joins the Titans in opposition to the Olympians. Aischylos's Prometheus emphasizes the suffering that Atlas must endure.

75. Rosenmeyer (1982: 106) finds in Prometheus's speech here "a splendor and a sweep" expressive of his "anger and sympathy with one who had fought Zeus and failed."

76. Compare Griffith (1983: *ad* 347–72).

77. Compare Vickers (1973: 73–74). Also, cf. D5 (pitier's situation).

78. Compare Munteanu (2012: 169).

79. Compare Griffith (1983: *ad* 446).

80. Compare Griffith (1983: *ad* 545–46); also, Stanford (1983: 102–3) on oxymora in Greek tragedy.

81. Compare chapter 1 above, and introduction, pp. 17–18.

82. Swanson (1994–95: 232): "She wants the honest truth." Swanson rightly sees Io as a "relentless seeker of information" who seeks to "take responsibility for herself."

83. Compare Griffith 1983, introduction to Third Episode (561–886).

84. Contrast Swanson (1994–95) for a somewhat different reading of Prometheus's interaction with Io. I am more comfortable with Griffith's assessment of Io's character (12). Also, compare Munteanu's analysis of this episode (2012: 170–72).

85. In Greek culture, lamentation and expressions of weakness are associated with the female gender. For a male to act in a way normally associated with females was considered shameful. Here, Prometheus sees that his own supplication with upturned hands would be an admission of weakness and therefore inherently feminine; cf. Naiden (2006: 51); also, cf. introduction, D6.

86. Vickers (1973: 74–75) attributes the chorus's weakness here and at points earlier in the play (526–60, 887–905) to fear. Griffith (1983: 9 passim) emphasizes Prometheus's "self-willed stubbornness" (*authadia*), but primarily his opponent Hermes charges him with this "flaw"; of course, the masters to whom he refuses to yield see him as stubborn; he himself denies that this motivates him at 436. Yes, he refuses to yield to Zeus's threats, but the care he has shown for humanity, including Io, shows that he is not completely self-absorbed (cf. above on 345–46; also cf. 542–43). Should we not see persistent opposition to oppression and cruel power

as virtuous integrity rather than a vice? Also, see Munteanu (2012: 179–80) on the political implications of pity and fear in the play.

87. Compare Munteanu (2012: 168–69).

88. Swanson (1994–95) takes a mostly negative view of Prometheus's inclination to pity, including his *philanthrôpia* for humankind. But would it have been better for Prometheus to have allowed Zeus to annihilate the human race (cf. above, pp. 92–94) or to have withheld from them (from us) the gifts of reason and civilization? I acknowledge Swanson's view that Prometheus is not perfect and that his advocacy of pity needs eventually to be reconciled with Zeus's view of justice based on "desert," and my reading of the trilogy anticipates such a reconciliation.

89. See Herington, Winnington-Ingram, Rosenmeyer, Griffith, and others on the trilogy as a whole.

90. Compare Elektra's appeal for compassion to the spirit of her father, Agamemnon (see pp. 85–86).

CHAPTER 4

1. Thus de Romilly (1985: 78–80); see further in de Romilly 1961. On Euripides as excelling in presenting the pathetic, also see Quintilian 10.1.68.

2. The chorus's compassionate response toward the old man Iolaus is no doubt due in part to his being an old man like themselves (D2).

3. Burnett (1998: 147) notes that Argos threatens the divine institution of supplication itself in seeking to deny these suppliants a place of sanctuary anywhere.

4. Compare Herodotos 9.27, a still earlier reference to this story as well as to that of Euripides' *Suppliants,* another example of this Athenian tradition, which also is central to the story of Athens' reception of Oidipous; see the section on Sophokles' *Oidipous at Kolonos* in chapter 5. See Tzanetou 2005 and 2012 for an interpretation of Athenian suppliant plays that emphasizes the ideological uses (political and civic) of Athenian pity and generosity.

5. See introduction, pp. 17–19 on the use of past benefits and *philia* to support appeals for compassion.

6. Conacher 1967 interprets the play in terms of *charis* (reciprocal favor) rather than pity or compassion. There is some necessary overlap here, in that appealing to a *philos* for compassion also entails an appeal based on *charis;* the two motives reinforce each other, but the urgency of the suppliants' situation indicates that compassion is the primary thing being sought.

7. This, however, did not keep the Homeric heroes from expressing their pity for others. The answer may partly lie in Athenian notions of masculinity: women, not men, were seen as being prone to emotions such as pity and grief (cf. Konstan 2001: 20).

8. It is impossible to know, since Sophokles' kings, such as Oidipous in *Oidipous the King* and Theseus in *Oidipous at Kolonos*, readily acknowledge their deep feelings of compassion.

9. On the expressions of gratitude here, cf. pp. 17–18. Further choral songs in praise of Athens' protection of suppliants and defiance of Argos occur at 353–80, 748–83, and 892–927. The messenger describes Athenian participation in the battle at 824–66.

10. She is named Makaria by later tradition. See Loraux (1987: chap. 2) for an analysis of this and other virgin sacrifices in tragedy (cf. D6); also, cf. Gödde (2000: 131–42) on the interrelation of supplication and sacrifice in the play.

11. Note Demophon's eagerness to find a solution as he and Iolaos consult about the problem (471–72). Konstan 2005a, in contrast, denies pity a role in Demophon's motivation here; Tzanetou 2005 emphasizes somewhat more than I do the limitation of Athenian pity in the play.

12. Pity, in other words, entails behavioral assistance or compensatory action (i.e., *aretê*). Adkins (1960: 157) cites lines 285–87 of this play, Demophon's last words to the herald, as illustrating the continuation of the *aretê* of the Homeric warrior in the fifth-century king who protects suppliants. Cf. above introduction, pp. 11–12 and chapter 1.

13. Iolaos is Herakles' nephew and the children's cousin.

14. Demophon had earlier described the herald as "a fool" (*skaios*) who thinks he is "stronger than god" (258), that is, who dares to try to carry off Zeus's suppliants (cf. Burnett 1998: 147).

15. See Burnett (1998: 145–57) for a full treatment of the revenge theme in this play. The chorus's subsequent acquiescence to Alkmene's vengeance (1021, 1053–55) after having objected to it earlier is troubling, as scholars such as Vickers (1973: 479–80) and Allan (2001: *ad loc.*) have noted, but not so much as to undercut Athens' positive presentation in this play. Rather, as Burnett argues, Athens persists in being prudent and just; also, see my concluding sentence below. Tzanetou (2005: 116–17) notes that Eurystheus's prophecy envisions the contemporary situation in Athens, namely, that, ironically, the future descendants of the rescued children will become the Spartan enemy of the Peloponnesian War.

16. They refer to their "pitiable tears" (οἰκτρὰ . . . δάκρυ(α), 49) and their pitiable suffering (οἰκτρὰ . . . πάσχουσ(α), 68). The temple of

Demeter is a particularly fitting site for an appeal by mourning mothers on behalf of their children since Demeter is the archetypal mother who grieves and cares for her child, Persephone; cf. Ferguson (1972: 309) who notes that Demeter was "the type of *mater dolorosa*" from whom the suppliant women could expect sympathy.

17. Vickers (1973: 87–88). He also compares appeals by Iphigeneia to Agamemnon (*Iphigeneia in Aulis* 1278, although he mistakenly cites *Iphigeneia among the Taurians*) and Helen's "song of deep wretchedness" (*Helen* 164–78).

18. He expresses his shame at having to adopt the humiliating posture of the suppliant, he who formerly was prosperous (164–66). Cf. introduction, p. 12 on the suppliant's tendency to experience shame.

19. The middle two lines here (177–78)—which prompt the poor to observe the rich to acquire a desire for money—seem out of place and have been deleted by modern editors.

20. I prefer giving lines 263–85 to the chorus. Kovacs gives 263–70 to Adrastos, which I find acceptable provided the chorus receive 271–85.

21. Compare Vickers (1973: 90–91, 459).

22. Compare Zuntz (1955: esp. 7–10), who also sees "compassion" (*oiktos*) and "reason" (*logos*) working in harmony to motivate Theseus here. Burian (1985: 133–35), to the contrary, argues that Aithra's argument is not "a plea for pity at all," but since her arguments promote the same end as the mothers' pleas and reinforce those pleas, both are directed toward Theseus's performance of an act of compassion: the burial of the mothers' sons. As Zuntz (16–17) concludes, Athens is seen in this play as "prompted by compassion to succor the injured. . . . Their pity was active help." Heath (1987: 14–15) also sees compassion as motivating Theseus here; cf. Rosenbloom (2012: 276–77). Again, contrast Konstan (2005a), who overlooks the appeal based on kinship and Theseus's likely identification with the mothers' sons.

23. See Scully's introduction (11–12) to the new Oxford translation for further discussion of these lines. Mendelsohn (2002: 185–87) notes that Theseus appropriates a typical feminine role in tending to the Argive dead, but he sees Theseus as having achieved "enlightenment" in doing so based on "an ability to 'feel' others' suffering."

24. Compare Mills (1997: 167), who discusses Athens' idealization as a city that "will always take risks, and be rewarded for doing so." For a positive reading that nevertheless uncovers the ironies and subtle undercutting of the Athenian democratic ideal, particularly in the context of contemporary Athens as portrayed by Thukydides, see Macleod (1983b: 147–51).

25. Vellacott (1975: 30–32, 157–59) rightly accords Theseus high praise for his restraint in not pressing the Athenian victory over Thebes and sacking the city, but he is troubled that Theseus does not rebuke the sons of the fallen Argives when they pledge to someday avenge their fathers. But when Athene then predicts that the young boys will take vengeance (1213–16) and encourages them to do so, Theseus must accept this as the standard Greek ethic of "harm your enemy" and as the working of fate. Shaw (1982: 10) also notes Theseus's admirable restraint in not sacking Thebes, and argues (16–18) that Theseus's and Athene's views at the end of the play are compatible.

26. Vickers (1973: 81–83) also gives a sensitive reading of suffering and sympathy in this play.

27. Gregory (1999: *ad* 287) correctly notes that Hekabe's plea for pity here is a plea for action, not just sympathy; also, cf. Gödde (2000: 86–87).

28. Gregory (1999: *ad* 321–26) observes, "Even as Odysseus acknowledges the representative aspect of Hecuba's suffering, he perversely makes it a reason *not* to pity her" (also, cf. Love 2012: 84).

29. Compare above; also compare Priam's appeal to Akhilleus based on his likeness to Akhilleus's father.

30. On Polyxena's nobility, compare Nussbaum (1986: 405–6). Reckford shares my view of Odysseus in this play: "Odysseus, deaf to Hecuba's pleas, blind to her as a real person, illustrates how old-fashioned values like decency, honor, and gratitude may be laughed at and may disappear altogether" (1990: 38).

31. See Reckford (1990: 31–33); also, again see Loraux 1987 on this and other virgin sacrifices (cf. D6).

32. Compare Vickers (1973: 82); also, Gödde (2000: 91–94).

33. Compare, for example, Hephaistos in *Prometheus Bound* (chap. 3 above). Also, on Talthybios's and Neoptolemos's responses, compare Hogan (1972: 252); also, see Love (2012: 79–80), especially on the idealization of Polyxena in this scene.

34. Compare Reckford (1990: 41–42) and Love (2012: 80–81). Ferguson (1972: 301) notes that this reflection on Spartan suffering takes place "before an audience that has been at war with Sparta for almost a decade." Compare the chorus's earlier reflections on the unpredictability of their own future lives (444–83), which they expect to be "pitiable" (*oiktros,* 457); also, their later, highly personal remembrance of the final night of Troy (905–51)—a city that has suffered the "most pitiable (*oiktrotatos,* 912) stain" of destruction. This play, like Euripides' *Trojan Women,* provides an eloquent discourse on the cruelty and misery of war.

35. Nussbaum (1986: 408), along with others (see her n.35), traces Hekabe's "moral change" from this moment rather than from Agamemnon's later denial of her supplication. As the rest of my argument will show, I agree. Also, see Love (2012: 82–83) on this scene, which he characterizes as the "First Shock" of the play.

36. The language of her appeal for compassion here mirrors precisely that of her appeal to Odysseus on behalf of Polyxena in 286–87. The parallelism provides a sense of unity to the two supplications and to the play as a whole. Hogan (1972), making a comparison with Thukydides' report of the Plataian debate with the Thebans, argues that appeals for pity in *Hekabe* carry some weight, countering Adkins's tendency (in 1966b) to diminish the significance of such values.

37. The general theme of compassion and justice is applicable here (cf. intro. p. 19). We will see this linkage of compassion with revenge again in Sophokles' *Philoktetes.*

38. Hekabe's desire for justice is especially intense because a betrayal of *xenia* is involved; also the viciousness of her son's murder, the heartless exposure of his corpse, and her discovery of it in the immediate aftermath of Polyxena's sacrifice make it all the more unbearable.

39. Compare Ferguson (1972: 302).

40. Kovacs (1995: 473), post line 811. See Mercier (1993) for an extended treatment of Hekabe's supplication of Agamemnon; also, Love (2012: 83–87).

41. This is followed immediately by the chorus's reflection on the mutability of friends and enemies. On Euripides' use of images of the body in this play, cf. Gödde (2000: 87–89).

42. "I hold you and your son and your fates and your suppliant hand in pity (δι' οἴκτου)," he says (850–51).

43. Compare Nussbaum (1986: 418–19) and see Love (2012: 87–91) on the scene, which he characterizes as the play's "Second Shock."

44. See further in Vickers (1973: 83), Reckford (1990: 33–37), and Nussbaum (1986: chap. 13, esp. 409–18) on Hekabe's revenge and consequent dehumanization.

45. Ferguson: "Only Polyxena rises above the violence." Also, cf. Reckford 1990 and Love (2012: 92–93). Macleod (1983b: 154–57), comparing the Plataian and Melian debates in Thukydides, emphasizes the tragic futility of appeals made by the weaker to the stronger.

46. Vickers's analysis of sympathy and suffering in this play (1973: 91–96) by and large accords with mine.

47. On the pitiableness of Troy, cf., for example, 585–86 and 602.

48. Compare Konstan (2001: 108–9).

49. Also, the *pathê* of Kassandra (306–461) and Polyxena (620–43, as narrated by Andromache) are hardly less moving.

50. Talthybios also takes part in the burial of Astyanax—further evidence of his basic kindness and compassion; compare Theseus's role in the burial in *Suppliants;* also, cf. Suter (2003: 12).

51. Konstan 2000; reprised in Konstan (2001: 51–58).

52. Menelaos's interview with Orestes also indicates that friends of Aigisthos as well as enemies from the Greek army at Troy have played a role in motivating Argos to condemn Agamemnon's children (427–46).

53. In their debate, Tyndareos asks Orestes why he did not show pity /mercy to his mother when she bared her breast in her appeal (526–29); Orestes responds that for him to have done so would have given license to wives to kill their husbands and seek "pity" (*eleos*) from their children (566–71). Orestes' response to Klytaimestra was an instance of "no pity for those who have shown no pity" (cf. above, p. 87, on Aischylos's *Libation Bearers*). Also, note that this example likewise works against Konstan's thesis about kin not seeking pity from kin: Klytaimestra in her desperate situation appealed for pity/mercy from her son. Also, Tyndareos says that he himself cries tears—presumably tears of compassionate grief—for his daughter's misfortunes (528–29). Compare Munteanu (2012: 220–21) on how this scene may have affected the audience.

54. According to the *Scholia in Euripidem* (*Or.* 671), "Orestes speaks gently about himself, pitying (οἰκτείρων) himself (ἑαυτόν) that misfortune advanced upon him to this degree." If we keep line 677, with its mention of tears and laments and misfortunes, the pitiableness of Orestes' plea is emphasized even more.

55. They explicitly pity Orestes' and Elektra's misfortune throughout the play (e.g., 333, 832) and that of the house of Atreus (815).

56. Menelaus describes how a demos—here meaning the Argive assembly, but also applicable to the Athenian assembly members watching the play—will eventually change from a mood of anger to one of pity, if only one is patient and waits for the right mood (696–703). But his suggestion that the people "have compassion in them" (ἔνεστι δ' οἶκτος), followed by his hesitancy to seek to persuade the Argive assembly himself, alerts Orestes and us to Menelaos's own lack of that noble emotion. I agree with Kovacs that lines 704–5 are better deleted (see Kovacs 2003: *ad* 696–716). Orestes later does decide to put his case before the people and to appeal to their compassion: "Someone might have compassion (ἄν οἰκτίσειε) on me," he says (784). Rosenbloom (2007) observes that Orestes

"refuses to depict his condition as pitiable before the Argive Assembly." Actually, the messenger quotes some of Orestes' speech, but Orestes also seems to have persuaded the crowd not to stone him and his sister directly by promising that they would kill themselves. He might have resorted to an explicit appeal for pity in doing so, but the messenger does not say so. Alternatively, Rosenbloom's suggestion that Orestes "is loath to seek pity from the 'mob'" is possible as well. Obviously, as shown by 784, his intention had been to persuade the assembly to pity him and his sister, but he failed to do so, apart from the crowd's small concession not to stone the siblings.

57. I am not surprised that Orestes does not have to resort to a supplicatory plea for compassion to enlist Pylades' assistance. Pylades, unlike Menelaos, readily and gladly accepts the obligations of *philia* (cf. Konstan 2000: 52). Based on the messenger's later report, Menelaus did not appear before the assembly to make an appeal for compassion on behalf of Orestes and Elektra. On Menelaos's "baseness" (*pôneria*), compare Aristotle (*Poetics* 1454a28–29, 1461b21, cited in Rosenbloom 2007); also compare Munteanu's somewhat similar treatment of this episode (2012: 221).

58. Possible reasons for Orestes' avoidance include reluctance to state the obvious, although an element of guilt may also have been assumed as a possible motive, since Orestes did express a sense of guilt for the matricide (284–93, 646–47; cf. Konstan 2000: 55; 2001: 57); compare Herakles' doubts about his worthiness of pity by Theseus (see below, pp. 133–35). Sandridge (2008, n.14) suggests that Orestes' avoidance may have been that other grounds of *philia* were "more rhetorically compelling."

59. This is not to say that Orestes and friends are blameless in their aggressive actions late in the play; my focus here, however, is on Menelaos's failure to respond with compassionate action and the consequences of that failure. In contrast, Munteanu (2012: 223–25) interprets the ending of the play as downplaying the tragic element and as introducing features more appropriate to comedy than to tragedy.

60. Compare Vickers (1973: 80) on this scene.

61. They also had expressed compassion for Agamemnon's family (469–70).

62. Diggle has marked the latter set of lines as "perhaps not Euripidean." They fit my argument well enough, but are not essential to it.

63. She even brings her little brother Orestes into her appeal. See Gödde (2000: 84–86) on Euripides' use of imagery in portraying Iphigeneia's appeal to her father.

64. His pledge is grandiose: "I enclose you with my compassion and weep for you," although he qualifies it: "as much as a young man is able to do so" (933).

65. Compare Norwood (1960: 288), Ferguson (1973: 458–59), Vellacott (1972: 92–94).

66. Klytaimestra's assertion (981–82) that her troubles have nothing to do with Akhilleus is odd, since his interest in Klytaimestra's calamity has just been emphasized. Is there possibly a textual problem here? Vellacott (1972: 93) offers a reasonable explanation: "Clytemnestra feels her way, plays to his vanity."

67. Of course, there are serious textual difficulties regarding the ending of this play, but Euripides is generally assumed to have followed the mythic tradition as I have indicated.

68. Compare Johnson/Clapp 2005 for Clapp's extended treatment of the compassion theme in *Hippolytos.*

69. She also warns him that he may suffer misfortune someday just as she has.

70. See below for an extended treatment of compassion in *Herakles.*

71. Compare Vickers (1973: 84–85), who notes that "oppressors need a hard heart."

72. Another source of anxiety would be a suppliant who was polluted or who otherwise might bring harm to the *polis,* even unknowingly. We will see in the next chapter that this is the problem that the chorus in *Oidipous at Kolonos* initially has with the suppliant Oidipous.

73. The appeal is based on likeness (D2). March (1990: 36) notes that Medeia exploits Kreon's "weak spot, his love for his children."

74. Gould (1973: 85–86) discusses Medeia's supplication of Kreon in terms of the religious significance of the ritual act: Medeia's taking of Kreon's hand, along with the lowering of her demands, forces Kreon to consent.

75. "Pity, pity me," she says (οἴκτιρον, οἴκτιρόν με, 711). March (1990: 37) shows how Medeia again exploits the "child-motif" in appealing to Aigeus and also how Aigeus's childlessness gives Medeia the idea of how to hurt Jason the worst.

76. Just before Aigeus's entrance, the chorus had sung of life in exile as the "most pitiable of distresses" (οἰκτρότατον ἀχέων, 649) and had openly expressed their sympathy for Medeia's lack of a city and friends to pity (*oiktirein*) her "in these most terrible of distresses" (656–58).

77. Compare Vickers (1973: 476–77) on Medeia's supplication of Aigeus.

78. Rachel Sternberg alerted me to this irony; cf. March (1990: 37) and Munteanu (2012: 226–27).

79. Of course, the end of the play reveals that she has special divine support.

80. Compare Munteanu (2012: 223–24) on this scene. See above on the compassion theme in *Orestes* generally.

81. Also, we might compare the charge against Alkibiades in Andokides 4.39, that he is ruthless in bringing about the death and exile of others but ready to use supplications and appeals for pity on his own account. The speaker here actually claims that Alkibiades is inconsistent or hypocritical in being ruthless toward others while pleading for others to show compassion for him, but would we not expect that his pleas for compassion might at times be treacherous as well as hypocritical? In any case, he is presented as someone who does not deserve the pity for which he pleads, as one who should incur a response of no pity for one who does not show pity (cf. D4).

82. Compare Mills (1997: 145–46).

83. For example, Aischylos, *Suppliants;* Euripides, *Suppliants* and *Children of Herakles;* Sophokles, *Oidipous at Kolonos.*

84. At 1382–84, Herakles does mention the prospect of dying at the hands of his enemies should he abandon his weapons, but these enemies at this point in the play seem remote. There is no suggestion of a threat of immediate reprisal from Lykos's friends.

85. Compare D6. Adkins (1966b: 214) emphasizes Herakles' desire to administer justice on himself (1150).

86. See, for example, Gould (1990: 181–83); Michelini (1987, esp. 61–65); also cf. the contrast between Sophokles and Euripides in Aristotle's *Poetics* 1460b33–34.

87. *Herakles* 619–21, 1169. Herakles is referred to as "benefactor" (*euergetes*) by the chorus (877), by Theseus (1252), and by himself (1309).

88. On reciprocity in relation to compassion (in both appeals and grants), see introduction, pp. 17–20.

89. Herakles himself made an earlier reference to his rescue of Theseus at 619–21.

90. Contrast Mills (1997: 147–48), who emphasizes that Theseus repays Herakles by an even greater service in order to appeal to the Athenians' uneasiness about Theseus's need to be rescued from Hades.

91. Heroic reciprocity in this play operates through a series of mutual benefits, but the hero's motivation to return the benefit seems to be driven by feelings of friendship and compassion (if the friend is suffering or in danger) more than by what we moderns might consider a "moral sense of obligation." Heroes seem to *want* to return favors by doing heroic deeds

rather than seeing them as acts that they reluctantly are obliged to perform. Note Theseus's willingness here and his confidence in himself as a hero. Indeed, the mutual benefits of *philia* and compassion could be said to bring about a willing disposition to help one another. See, for example, Dover (1974: 277), who refers to the Athenian ideal of generosity in Thukydides 2.40.4–9; cf. Blundell (1989: 35–36).

92. "I call on you to show your face to your friends" (1214–15).

93. Gregory (1991: 142–43) asserts that Theseus here is redefining nobility (*eugeneia*) in terms of patience and endurance as opposed to "pride" and *aretê.* I doubt that the Greek audience would have perceived a difference: heroism requires endurance of suffering as well as active *aretê.*

94. Compare Halleran's translation; alternatively, Bond 1981 interprets: "I do not refuse (your help) because I benefited you."

95. Compare Pucci (1980: 176–77); also, Mills (1997: 143): "This is the pity which is a part of Athenian ἐπιείκεια, the opposite of inflexibility and hubris, and which derives from intelligent awareness of one's own vulnerability."

96. We might expect *eleos* rather than *oiktos* in reference to acts of compassion, but by the late fifth century a hard and fast distinction between the two words no longer was rigidly observed. See introduction, pp. 10–12.

97. This concern is consistent with the general assumption by Greeks that compassion should be reserved for undeserved suffering, not for wrongdoers (cf. D4 and, e.g., Aristotle *Poetics* 1453a3–5, *Rhetoric* 1385b13–14). That is why Theseus's expression of compassion prompts this question. Herakles himself will deal with the issue of his innocence at 1255–1310, esp. 1309–10. See n.101 below.

98. Herakles' fall is not exactly the stock tragic *peripeteia* of status (e.g., from king to beggar), but psychologically and socially it would be analogous (cf. D3). Aristotle (*Poetics* 1452b28–53a39, cf. *Rhetoric* 1385b13–16, 1386a5–16) makes the fall from prosperity to misery the change of fortune that arouses compassion. By emphasizing Herakles' misfortune, Theseus diverts, or at least seeks to divert, Herakles' attention from his role in the killings. Some take the phrase ἑτέραισι συμφοραῖς to mean "external to you," so as to suggest that Herakles' misfortunes are alien to his nature (i.e., foreign to the person for whose sake Theseus feels compassion). Such a reading is also consistent with and provides even more support for the way I interpret the line above. See Bond 1981 for further discussion of this phrase.

99. He employs the architectural metaphor of the capstone or finishing touch to emphasize the importance and finality of this most horrific "labor," (lit., coping-stone: θριγκῶσαι, 1280). Note that πόνον ("labor," 1279) is a conjecture accepted by Diggle. See Gibert 1995 for insightful reflections on Herakles' last labor.

100. Compare Philoktetes' despair in the *kommos* of Sophokles' *Philoktetes* 1081–94, 1101–15, 1123–62.

101. Note Herakles' emphasis on his own unique achievements and status as a hero; cf. 1252 and earlier references (348–425, 673–700, 877) to Herakles as a great champion and benefactor to humanity. By his question, Herakles calls attention to the fundamental injustice of his ruin at the hands of Hera, a question that, of itself, would seem to open the possibility of redemption by suggesting his worthiness of such.

102. Theseus asserts that mortals should do the same (i.e., bear their own fates, τὰς τύχας, 1321). The assumption here seems to be that if gods in their greater power and knowledge make mistakes and put up with them, then we humans should not hold ourselves to such an unreasonable standard of perfection (which even the gods can't uphold) but should forgive ourselves our failings. Theseus perhaps is calling Herakles to be intellectually aware of his innocence and to forgive himself of an action for which he was not ultimately responsible (cf. de Romilly 1980: 4–5). Theseus realizes that Herakles' greatest need is for self-forgiveness. Other views: Gregory (1991: 144–45) argues that Theseus's main point here is Herakles' need to accept his destiny as a mortal, an attitude that is "the mark of the *eugenês*." Pucci (1980: 232, n.6) sees these lines as having a sophistic ring and compares them to Euripides' *Hippolytos* 456ff.; Walker (1995: 130) sees Theseus's argument as "aristocratic."

103. These would include possibly a tomb, but presumably also sculptural representations, such as those on the Hephaisteion. The sacrifices and monuments appear to signify a hero cult of Herakles rather than the cult of a god (Bond 1981: *ad* 1331–33). The text (1331) explicitly says that Herakles will go to Hades. Woodford 1971 argues that worship of Herakles was both older and more widespread in Attica than that of Theseus. Verbanck-Piérard (1992: 63–64) interprets Theseus's "false" generosity as an attempt to appropriate Herakles' already established claim to divinity and as part of a broader Athenian effort: "l'héracléisation" of Theseus.

104. Compare introduction, p. 17 and D1a. Another scholar has pointed out to me the very similar language and thought at the end of Euripides' *Iphigeneia in Aulis:* "Iphigeneia will be Ἑλλάδος εὐεργέτις (1446), acquire

glory (1376, 1383–84) and reputation (1398), a memorial (1398, 1444), and a crown (1479–80, 1512), which will enable Agamemnon to wear the crown of victory (1529)."

105. Compare Sophokles' *Philoktetes* 475–79. On generosity as a competitive means of acquiring prestige and power, cf. Seaford (1998: 5); for reservations about the Athenian acceptance of Theseus's debt to Herakles, see Mills (1997: 135–36), although Mills (1997: 139) also adds: "By rescuing the great civilizer from suicide, Theseus will be upholding Athens' reputation as the civilizing city." This was obviously something meant to appeal to Euripides' democratic audience (ἀστοῖς, 1334); also note that the praise will come from the Greeks as a whole (Ἑλλήνων ὕπο). See Barlow (1996: *ad* 1334) for further parallels; cf. Tarkow (1977: 31–33), although I find no evidence that we are to take Theseus's offer to Herakles as an example of "hasty compassion" (i.e., as suggesting some future risk for Athens).

106. Lines 1338–39 seem extraneous at this point and, if spoken in performance, would end the speech weakly, but see Michelini (1987: 259, n.123); Gregory (1991: 142, n.43); and Walker (1995: 131, n.56) for arguments to the contrary.

107. Compare Chalk (1962: 13) on the renewal of Herakles' *aretê;* also, Michelini (1987: 259) on how Theseus's human *timai* will replace those taken from Herakles by the gods; such replacement, she notes, is "the office of a friend." See Yoshitake (1994: 143–45) on Herakles' motives here: the hero will still have to deal with the suffering of grief and self-reproach, the avoidance of which would be disgraceful. See Gibert 1997 for an argument to retain the manuscript reading θάνατον (death) at 1351. For a critical view of Herakles' choice of survival over suicide, see Garrison 1995; contra, see Arrowsmith (1956: 55–58), Furley (1986: 108–12), and Mills (1997: 153) for arguments in support of Herakles' choice.

108. Amphitryon, in response, shows his concord by employing two outsized polysyllables to characterize his son: οὐκ . . . ἕτερον / πολυμοχθότερον πολυπλαγκτότερόν τε θνατῶν ("no other / of mortals having more troubles or more wanderings," 1196–97); cf. above on 1237–40. The polysyllables obviously evoke the *Odyssey.*

109. The two heroes are related both through their mortal mothers (both granddaughters of Pelops) and their divine fathers (the brothers Zeus and Poseidon).

110. He uses the word ὀφθησόμεσθα ("we will be seen," 1155); cf. αἰσχύνομαι ("I am ashamed," 1160). Cf. Parker (1983: 316) that Herakles' "dominating emotion is one of shame, shame above all that his

'child-killing pollution' should be seen by Theseus, his dearest friend." See further on *aidôs* in the play in D. Cairns (1993: 293–95).

111. Specifically, he fears polluting his closest friend (φιλτάτῳ ξένων ἐμῶν) with the possibility of uncleanness or defilement, i.e. miasma (τεκνοκτόνον μύσος, 1155), a religion-based fear: "And I do not want to injure the innocent by casting my blood guiltiness on this one" (καὶ τῶιδε προστρόπαιον αἷμα προσβαλὼν / οὐδὲν κακῶσαι τοὺς ἀναιτίους θέλω, 1161–62). Theseus takes up the issue of pollution from blood-guilt when he denies that Herakles, a mortal, can pollute the divine (τὰ τῶν θεῶν, e.g., the gods or the sun) by showing his face (1232; cf. Sophokles' *Oidipous Tyrannos* 1410–15, where Oidipous's fears, similar to those of Herakles here, are dramatized, and *Oidipous at Kolonos*, where others' fear of Oidipous's pollution will eventually be allayed, somewhat as Theseus allays Herakles' here; see further in Parker 1983: 316–21, 109–11). This issue is resolved in the succeeding lines of this stichomythic interchange: Theseus meets Herakles' fear of his own "unholy pollution" (ἀνόσιον μίασμα, 1233) by asserting that the "avenging spirit" (*alastor*) cannot pass from friends to friends (1234), that is, that the pollution of blood-guilt cannot infect one's friends. Barlow (1996: *ad* 1234) remarks: "In this one sentence Theseus rejects the old superstitions and asserts the most important positive element in human life—that of friendship." Theseus projects here an enlightened notion of divinity as (1) invulnerable to harm from humans (in the form of pollution) and (2) as either unconcerned with the interchange between friends (i.e., indifferent) or as supportive of such interchange (i.e., possessing a degree of mercy or indulgence). Compare Bond (1981: *ad* 1232–34), Michelini (1987: 258–59), and Parker (1983: 310–11), the last of whom notes that the need for purification is still felt here by Theseus, who makes provision for it in 1324.

112. Compare Bond (1981: *ad* 1163), who refers to Theseus here in terms of "fifth-century Athenian 'dynamism,' a.k.a. *polupragmosune* to its opponents. Theseus' use of *sunalgein* here emphasizes the closeness of their *philia*."

113. Compare 1146–52, where Herakles first raised the prospect of suicide, but note that 1247 is the first indication to Theseus that Herakles is planning this. Herakles' sense of the enormity of his suffering leads him to express defiance toward the gods, against which Theseus prudently, if perhaps somewhat piously, cautions him for fear that Herakles may incur further divine wrath.

114. Compare Michelini (1987: 261), who asserts that Theseus shows here "only a superficial understanding of the tragic situation." We should recall, however, Theseus's expressed intention of sharing Herakles' pain

(συναλγῶν) at 1202 and his explicit assertion that he has compassion for Herakles in 1236.

115. The Greek word is *amathia,* 1254. See Mills (1997: 131–32) on this word and its cognates in the play; also, Yunis (1988: 144, n.10).

116. Theseus's words also express the value that Herakles represents as a hero to the Hellenic people and to the world—giving some notion of the loss that Herakles' death will represent as well as reminding Herakles of his courage in confronting the great monsters and enemies of his famous labors. See Conacher (1967: 86–88) on how the memory of the labors contributes to Herakles' survival; also, cf. above, n.101 and n.107.

117. Compare de Romilly (1980: 4–5). See Yunis (1988: 155–69) on how Herakles' rejection of the divinity (i.e., the moral authority) of Hera (and Zeus) in 1340–46 allows him to see his act of madness as a misfortune rather than as a divinely imposed stigma.

118. I agree with Barlow (1996 *ad loc.*) that 1366 is better kept, contra Nauck's deletion.

119. Are we to assume that Herakles' heroic career is ending (as does Wilamowitz 1895: 2.109)? Galinsky 1972 sees Herakles as having achieved a new heroism requiring spiritual endurance in place of the external achievements of his heroic past; cf. Yoshitake (1994: 145). Walker (1995: 132–34) sees Herakles' future in Athens as being restricted to that city's hoplite-style warfare, in which he will function as the protector of ephebes; cf. Tarkow (1977: 31) and Foley (1985, esp. 193–94). Chalk (1962: 13–14), contra, argues that Herakles needs Theseus's companionship in his grief, not his help in handling Kerberos; also, that he will continue to need to use violence (*bia*), although he will do so with a new understanding of its tragic implications; cf. Barlow (1996: 13–14 and *ad* 1340–85); also, Adkins (1966b: 218). Lee (1980: 42–43) also argues that Herakles does not in the end renounce his old heroism for a newer, inactive type. I agree with Chalk and Lee here.

120. This provides a note of explicit Athenian ideology, as Mills 1997 and others have interpreted it.

121. Mills (1997: 158), contra, emphasizes the "gulf in heroism" between the two heroes. Cf. Chalk (1962: 13) and Michelini (1997: 261–62), who seem to agree with my point here.

122. See Konstan (1998: 288, n.16) for parallels.

123. Silk (1985: 16) gives an especially vivid account of Herakles' humanization in this final scene. Walker (1995: 129) argues that Herakles "is reduced from a superman to mere humanity, but that change is presented

as a great improvement on the old Heracles, just as the human friendship offered by Athens (1404–5) is preferable to any relationship with the unreliable gods." Lee (1980: 42), on the contrary, sees Herakles' fate at the end of the play as tragic, "very far from a victory" (i.e., as making the best of a very bad situation).

124. For example, in lines 1410–17, also cf. 1226–28, 1248–54.

125. Contrast Padilla 1994, who reads the stresses in Herakles' and Theseus's relationship as reflections of the larger, much more serious conflict that he finds in the parent-child relationships in the play.

126. Compare de Romilly (1980: 2): for Aias, it is a matter of dishonor; for Herakles, a matter of suffering.

127. See the next chapter for a detailed analysis of the compassion theme in *Philoktetes.*

CHAPTER 5

1. For a fuller treatment of the compassion theme in Sophokles' *Aias,* see section 1 by Clapp in Johnson/Clapp 2005; also, cf. Sandridge (2008: 440–41).

2. Reinhardt's argument that *Elektra* belongs with the later rather than with the earlier plays of Sophokles is convincing to me (1979: chap. 5); also, cf. Kells (1973: 1–2 and n.2): a date of around 413, suggested by Dale, seems probable; so also March (2001: 20–22).

3. I interpret the phrase *hiktêrios thêsauros* as an oxymoron: the locks are paltry in and of themselves, but carry power as an element of the ritual. See further in Stanford (1963: *ad loc.*) on the religious significance of the ritual that Teukros sets in motion. *Aidôs* is obviously of concern; cf. introduction, p. 20.

4. Compare Vickers's analysis of suffering and sympathy in this play (1973: 76–78).

5. Compare Clapp's analysis in Johnson/Clapp (2005: 129 and n.28). Also, compare Winnington-Ingram (1980: 30–32 and 47–49) on Aias's psychological conflict as presented in his response to Tekmessa and in the deception speech; and see Munteanu (2012: 192–98) on the theme of "mourning a former self" that she discusses in reference to these scenes.

6. Winnington-Ingram (1980: 31) asserts that Aias's confidence in Teukros is "unrealistic," as the outcome of the play suggests. Indeed, it is Odysseus who saves Teukros and Aias's loved ones in the end. Aias's enlistment of Teukros as a replacement for himself is the best that Aias can do in his desperate situation.

7. Critical opinion is divided: Jebb prefers "while loathing the sight—not hating," whereas Dawe assumes that this line is parallel to *Aias* 924, where Tekmessa asserts that Aias is worthy of lamentation, even among his enemies.

8. See Loraux (1987: chap. 1) on the significance of the manner (by the sword) and place (the bedroom) of Deianeira's death. Compare Vickers (1973: 78) on the "see my suffering" trope and Falkner (2005: 181–82) on the element of spectacle here.

9. Again, cf. Vickers (1973: 78). The severity of Herakles' sickness, including the variations of the intensity of the pain that Herakles experiences from his diseased condition anticipate quite closely the similar intensity and variations of suffering that Philoktetes will experience in the play that bears his name; see below. Also, his suffering in this play recalls (or perhaps anticipates, depending on which play was produced first) the suffering of the great Herakles—for quite different reasons—in Euripides' *Herakles.* See chapter 4 for my analysis of compassion and friendship in that play.

10. See further on the gender issue in S8 below, and cf. D6 on "self-pity." See Faulkner 2005 for an extended treatment of gender in this play.

11. Pickard-Cambridge (1946: 109–10); Stanford (1963: *ad* 348ff.). I am assuming here that, if used, the *ekkyklema* would have been understood by the audience as a conventional device used to reveal interior spaces. For scholars agreeing with my view here, see Taplin (1978: 11–12, 108); Heath (1987: 178 and n.23); and Wiles (1997: 162–64).

12. This is not to say that Oidipous is a paragon of virtue in every respect, but only that he is a character who shows compassion to his people. Compare Winnington-Ingram (1980: 327), who notes that in Sophokles a disposition to compassion, even when based on a sense of the human condition, does not necessarily save a character such as Deianeira or, in *Oidipous in Kolonos,* Antigone.

13. Fragment 665 in Pearson, who cites parallels; cf. Adkins (1960a: 114, n. 28.

14. On love as disease being a characteristic Greek idea with parallels elsewhere, see Easterling (1982: *ad* 445–47). On love as a force from the outside, see Davies (1991: *ad* 476–77).

15. We might also be reminded here of Aristotle's later assertion that *eleos* (pity) is felt for those who suffer undeservedly (*anaxiôs, Poetics* 1453a, *Rhetoric* 1385b, cf. below on *Philoktetes* 685).

16. Also, the chorus imagine the intense grief and lamentation that Aias's mother will display when she learns of her son's mental distress

(621–34); in contrast to her outward expression of grief, they imagine Aias's father merely suffering when he hears the news of his son's ruin. The chorus also hear Tekmessa's cries of alarm and see her as "deeply involved in her lament" (οἴκτῳ τῷδε συγκεκραμένην) when she first discovers Aias's body (891–95). Cf. above in S4.1, where the chorus report the wives and mothers—all women—lamenting at the Theban altars.

17. See further in Loraux 2002, Dué 2006, and Munteanu (2012: 197).

18. Vickers (1973: 68–69). I also quote this comment in my argument referenced in the following note.

19. This is a set of issues that Plato will take up later in his critique of poetry in the *Republic.* See my argument against Plato's view in Johnson /Clapp (2005: 141–54).

20. See Reinhardt (1979: chap. 5) for a penetrating analysis of the stylistic qualities that he uses to align *Elektra* with Sophokles' last two extant plays rather than with the earlier ones. On the question of the play's date, see note 2 above.

21. Compare Burnett (1998: xvi–xvii).

22. See chapters 1–3 of J. P. Vernant and P. Vidal-Naquet 1988.

23. Despite Kells's (1973: *ad loc.*) suggestion that the attribution of justice here might have been Orestes' own characterization of the revenge rather than the oracle's, I take it as the latter and assume Sophokles' audience would have as well. Blundell (1989: 172–73) mistakenly criticizes Orestes for his use of deception and compares him to Odysseus in *Philoktetes,* but, as we see below, Odysseus's deception is wrongly employed against an ally, whereas Orestes' use here is against an enemy and at the direction of Apollo himself; cf. Burnett (1998: 120, n.2).

24. Kaibel (66–67) says that Orestes' characterization of his sister here as *dystênos* will "remain alive in Orestes and influence his mood" (cited by Segal 1966: 515).

25. On Elektra's unceasing devotion to lamentation, see Seaford 1985.

26. Compare 119–20, where she expresses her inability to keep bearing the burden of grief alone and her consequent deep need for her brother's return. Ironically, Orestes had just missed this expression of need for him by his sister. Her sense of isolation—always something pitiable for the Greeks (cf. D3)—is further conveyed in 226–28, where she laments her lack of a comforting word from others.

27. I take "not honoring" (ἐκτίμους, 242) as proleptic, meaning "if I restrain the sharp wings of lamentation *so that they do not honor* my father."

28. In Loraux (2002: 22), *aidôs* here is translated as "pity"; cf. Stanford (1983: 36).

29. Compare March (2001: *ad* 245–50).

30. Compare Kells (1973: *ad loc.*), who also notices that the chorus's concern is not conceived as "altruistic," as we moderns might conceive it; also compare Kells on the reciprocity inherent in their concern at 134. On the chorus's sympathy for and solidarity with Elektra in this play, compare Gardiner 1987 and Foley (2001: 157).

31. Compare Kells (1973: *ad* 296ff.).

32. Contrary to moderation (*sôphronein*) and reverence (*eusebein*)—here filial piety, according to March—which suggests that such justice is a harsh necessity in which normal virtues must be abandoned. March: "She deplores her conduct, but cannot avoid it."

33. See further in Whitman (1951: 165–66).

34. Kells (1973: *ad* 626ff.) concurs: "Electra has won the *agon*"; cf. Reinhardt (1979: 149); Whitman (1951: 157–58). Kitto (1961: 137) argues that, in contrast to Aischylos, Sophokles makes Agamemnon much more "to be pitied than to be blamed" for the sacrifice of Iphigeneia.

35. Also Orestes, according to Kitto (1961: 133). Segal (1966: 478) notes the irony of Klytaimestra praying to the god who has sanctioned the plot that soon will be her undoing.

36. There is an instance of misfortune and compassion in the paidagogos's narration: Orestes' horrible accident (743–63). Although it is a fictional account, it contains a number of the elements of Greek compassion we have observed elsewhere: pathetic details of the accident, the crowd's compassionate cry (ἀνωτότυξε, 750) at the sight of Orestes' misfortune, and reflections both on Orestes' tragic fall from high to low (the victor laid low by fate) and on the intensity of pathos occasioned by seeing rather than hearing about misfortune (761–63).

37. See Reinhardt (1979: 150–52) on Sophokles' use of the paidagogos's narrative to prolong Elektra's torment. Kitzinger (1991) sees Orestes' use of *dolos* as detracting from Elektra's positive use of language and, in effect, as demeaning her role in the rest of the play. I understand and appreciate this perspective, but the play continues to present her sympathetically in her ignorance and then in her participation in Orestes' plan once she realizes that he is still alive.

38. We shall see a similar expression of compassion, but for different reasons, in the following episode.

39. Compare Whitman (1951: 158); Webster (1969: 118); Budelmann (2000: 80–87). Note that since Chrysothemis does not appear again after the reunion of Orestes and Elektra, this earlier "mistake" on Elektra's part is never acknowledged.

40. Contrast Wright (2005: 180–81), who emphasizes the sisters' "emotional incompatibility. . . . There is no rapport, no tenderness between them, but only impatience and abuse. Electra makes no attempt to comfort or empathize with her sister in their loss of Orestes."

41. Kells (1973: *ad* 986ff.) notes that Elektra also conceives of the spirits of Agamemnon and Orestes as continuing to work for vengeance against Aigisthos; compare the prayer Elektra had sent Chrysothemis to offer at the grave earlier.

42. Burnett (1998: 125–26) is careful to note that Elektra's attempt will be directed against Aigisthos alone.

43. Kells, for instance, argues along these lines (1973: *ad* 1066). Winnington-Ingram (1980: 244) suggests that Orestes, assumed by the chorus to be in the underworld as well, might be understood as a son of Atreus referred to here. Such an understanding would allow Orestes' entrance soon after to be seen as an answer to the chorus' prayer.

44. Compare in S5.2 above.

45. Following March (2001: *ad* 1087–88), I interpret τὸ μὴ καλὸν καθοπλίσασα as "having armed herself against dishonor." See Burnett (1998: 122) for a somewhat different reading. Contra Kells, I see no serious inconsistency in the chorus at one point approving Chrysothemis's argument for caution, but later, after her exit, choosing to sympathize with and admire Elektra's resolute devotion to her father's cause; cf. Winnington-Ingram (1980: 241).

46. Dare we compare Antigone's resolute devotion to the laws of Zeus demanding burial of kin? I think so. We may be helped in doing so by recalling that in Homer, proper compassion for dead *philoi* entailed avenging their deaths; cf. introduction above, p. 12; also Kim (2000: 67). Burnett (1998: 123–25) notes Elektra's display of "manly courage" (*andreia*) here.

47. Whitman takes a somewhat different tack here, although his interpretation and mine are ultimately compatible. He sees Elektra's decision to undertake the vengeance on her own as the ultimate development of Elektra's heroic endurance. For him, Orestes will serve primarily a symbolic role as the instrument of Elektra's ultimate triumph and salvation, a kind of deus ex machina (1951: 166–71). Woodard 1966 also sees Elektra as the dominant, triumphant character of the play; he focuses on the dialectic of "word" (*logos*) and "deed" (*ergon*) and on gender differences in the play. Burnett (1998: 123–28) argues that Elektra here develops a heroism that is "pure potentiality . . . empty of content" but that this content will be supplied by Orestes' arrival; their very different types of

heroism will then work together to bring about the retribution. In short, Elektra is heroic in this play.

48. Compare above, pp. 158, 160 (Klytaimestra's hostility toward Orestes); also, compare 964–66 on Elektra's assumption that Aigisthos will not tolerate Chrysothemis having children.

49. Burnett (1998: 129) rightly observes: "This is not the harsh, almost theoretical grief that caused Electra's lamentations for her father. This is the living anguish that bespeaks a tender and cherishing love."

50. Compare Reinhardt (1979: 155–61) for a detailed analysis of the pathos in this recognition scene; also, compare March 2001.

51. Segal (1966: 516) notes that Elektra's speech of lamentation gave Orestes a sense of his own suffering: "I was not then aware of any of my own ills" (1185).

52. Konstan (2001: 142, n.9) is probably correct in saying that Elektra infers a kinship connection in 1202 because Orestes has said that he shares her feelings: "Common feeling suggests the bond of friendship." Still, compassion is expressed between *philoi* both here and in 920–37 (between the sisters; see above); cf. pp. 18–19.

53. Compare S6 above and D1b.

54. Segal (1966: 513) observes, "Orestes' cool practicality becomes touched by a true and deep compassion for Electra," but he adds that their reunion occurs "under the shadow of the deed they must perform"; thus, life must, as elsewhere in the play, "be submerged in death." Likewise, Blundell (1989: 174) mentions the pity in the play but downplays it: "The most striking aspect of this pity is that it is so short-lived." I prefer Burnett's assessment (1998: 129): "The Orestes who watches [Elektra's] bereaved tenderness is no longer a vengeful automaton bereft of emotion. He feels pity and finds a new dimension of himself as he groans over someone else's sufferings as if they were his own." Again, contrast Wright (2005: 186–89), who sees Orestes as a "cold and unsympathetic character" and finds "no affinity whatsoever" between brother and sister.

55. This is an explicit prediction within the text of a positive future after the play's action concludes: Elektra, Orestes' tutor, Orestes, and Pylades will have time to share memories of their past in loving fellowship; also see Orestes' view (1299–1301); cf. March *ad* 1364–66.

56. I cannot agree with Foley (2001: 167–71) that Elektra's role is subordinated to Orestes' in the play's ending, even though he is the one who performs the killings. They work as equals and collaborators; their roles are fused into a concerted effort that leads to achievement (cf. March 2001: *ad* 1319–21). I also do not agree that Elektra deteriorates at the end, nor,

as De Wet (1977: 31–36) argues, that "the main responsibility for the matricide is that of Elektra" (35). I do, however, see the matricide as somewhat problematic, despite being fundamentally just; see n.68 and pp. 167–68.

57. Noted here also by Blundell (1989: 150); cf. Segal (1986: 353–54). Also see Vickers (1973: 83) on the justification of pitilessness here and the difficulty that we moderns have in accepting it. For other parallels in Sophokles, see S7.3 above.

58. Compare Burton (1980: 218–24) and Gardiner (1987: 157–60) on the chorus's approval of the vengeance here, at both 1437–41 and at 1508–10.

59. Compare Blundell (1989: 154–55).

60. Segal is correct in saying that there is no reason to assume, as some have interpreted the lines, that Elektra is asking that Aigisthos's body be thrown to the birds and dogs.

61. I follow Calder (1963) here in having Elektra exit last; cf. March (2001: 13) and Foley (2001: 157). The phrase "seed of Atreus" (σπέρμ' Ἀτρέως) may refer primarily to Elektra, but it includes Orestes as well.

62. This difference is the key to the interpretation of Winnington-Ingram (1980: ch.10), who interprets the play specifically in light of the Aischylean model. For him the Erinyes and the operation of the *lex talionis* are central to the play's action and to the characterization of Orestes and Elektra as well as Klytaimestra and Aigisthos. In fact, he sees Orestes more as a chthonic avenger (235–38) than as the deus ex machina suggested by Whitman (cf. above, n.47). I accept Orestes as being sent by the gods below: Elektra prays for such in 110–20, but the play does not depict those gods as more negative than those above; in fact, Elektra prays for help from both Apollo, an Olympian, and from Hermes, Agamemnon, and other deities of the underworld (so also Burnett 1998: 132 and 137, n.60). Both gods above and those below can support the working of justice. In this play, they seem to function in harmony rather than conflicting as they did in *Eumenides*.

63. Compare March (2001: 16–17).

64. Compare above, n.41 and n.43.

65. Kitto (1961), not so simply perhaps, sees in this play the operation of a principle of universal law (*dikê*). De Wet (1977: 23–31) argues persuasively for the justice of Aigisthos's execution, although he sees the execution of Klytaimestra as much more problematic (cf. above, n.56).

66. Compare S7.3 above.

67. Compare March (2001: 12). See Burnett (1998: 132–36) for a detailed account of Klytaimestra's and Aigisthos' viciousness; see Reinhardt (1979:

138–39) for an appreciation of Elektra's character. Still, I agree with Kitto's assertion that the revenge at the end "is a grim and a bloody business, and Sophocles does not try to pretend that it is anything else"; even Burnett (1998: 138–41) must conclude: "For all its recovery of order . . . the *Electra* leaves its audience with the simple conviction that no human achievement will ever be perfectly clean."

68. Compare Whitman (1951: 159); also Burnett (1998: xv–xvi). For negative and ironic readings of the play, see Kells (1973: 1–2) and Winnington-Ingram (1980: chap. 10); also, Segal (1966 and 1981) takes mostly this view.

69. Reinhardt compares the exposition of Elektra's long and intense suffering in this play to that of Philoktetes' suffering in the play that bears his name (see further in my section on *Philoktetes* below). Stanford (1983: 26) notes the scholiasts' implication that Elektra is the most pitiable of Sophokles' characters (cf. D3). Yet despite her suffering, Elektra, a female character (D6), both shows compassion for both her sister and brother and denies it to her mother and Aigisthos, in keeping with the principle of reciprocity.

70. Compare Burnett (1998: 140), who notes that the retribution on Klytaimestra "seems to follow as much from grief and love as it does from anger and vindictiveness."

71. Compare March (2001: 13, 18).

72. According to Zimmermann (1991: 81); cf. Buxton (1984: 29).

73. Compare Winnington-Ingram (1980: 327–29) on this larger topic.

74. For example, Bowra, Reinhardt, Harsh, Alt, Knox, Avery, Vidal-Naquet, Nussbaum 1976–77, Blundell, Hawkins, Lefèvre, and Sandridge. Poe describes Philoktetes as being too passive to be considered a hero of "high tragedy." Segal (1977: 137; 1981: 315, 360) emphasizes what he sees as Philoktetes' impiety and savagery so that for him the hero undergoes "a bitter eclipse of God and a long immersion in the subhuman life of the beastlike, ensavaged self."

75. For example, Vidal-Naquet and others perhaps influenced by him see the decision of Philoktetes and Neoptolemos for Greece as unpatriotic or contrary to civic virtue; cf., more recently, Lefèvre 2001.

76. For example, Whitman, Kitto, Linforth, Robinson, Taplin, Garvie, Gellie, Kott, Poe, Rose, Easterling, Gill, Kirkwood 1994, and Carlevale. Winnington-Ingram (1980: 296–97), while fundamentally sympathetic to the character, characterizes him as irrationally driven and tragically controlled by his heroic enmity.

77. Some, however, see the reversal as an unsatisfactory but necessary addendum (Robinson and Kott) or even as a hollow, pessimistic conclusion (Poe and Gellie).

78. The verb used here is commonly used for exposing unwanted babies (cf. Webster 1970: *ad loc.*).

79. Jebb calls this description "ironical."

80. Garvie (1972) provides an analysis of the themes of deceit, violence, and persuasion as developed in the play, including their use as structural elements of the plot.

81. Jebb notes that κεῖται (145), while basically neutral, is also suggestive of Philoktetes' limited mobility.

82. A sense of "clever" or "skillful" for *deinos* would, of course, be ironic. The use of "halls" (μελάθρων, 147) and "courts" (αὐλάς, 152) by Neoptolemos and the chorus, respectively, to refer to Philoktetes' dwelling ironically suggests the palace that the typical hero inhabits.

83. Thus Webster's (1970) interpretation of παιῶνα, that is, whether it refers to a drug or a person. In either case it means that Philoktetes has no cure, but if we take it as a personal "healer" (the word's literal meaning), it also emphasizes his isolation.

84. Reinhardt (1979: 182) deals with the apparent discrepancy between the chorus's willing assistance in Neoptolemos's deception of Philoktetes and its expressions of compassion throughout the play by positing a double function for the chorus: it both gives "resonance" to the intrigue by assisting Neoptolemos and creates "dissonance" by its expressions of sympathy for Philoktetes.

85. Aristotle, in *Rhetoric* 1385, mentions the extreme pitifulness of being deprived of friends.

86. See S2 above; introduction, D2 (Likeness) and D3 (Intensity of Suffering); chap, 1, pp. 31–33; also, cf. Jebb.

87. Compare 1018, where Philoktetes describes himself as having been an *aphilos, erêmos, apolis* corpse when the Greeks abandoned him. In describing himself as "wild" (ἀπηγριωμένον, 226), he is describing his uncouth, shaggy appearance, not his inner nature. What "savagery" he displays is the result of what the Greeks have done to him; they, in fact, continue to regard him as a beast to be hunted; see Rose (1992: 308–9) on Odysseus as "hunter of human beings." For an opposing view that posits Philoktetes' inherently savage nature, see Segal 1981, esp. 314–18.

88. Compare 795, "for the same length of time" (τὸν ἴσον χρόνον), and 1114–15: may Odysseus "chance upon my agonies for the same length of time" (τὸν ἴσον χρόνον ἐμὰς λαχόντ' ἀνίας). Also recall the chorus's assessment of Philoktetes as a "man fair among the fair" (ἴσος ἐν ἴσοις ἀνήρ, 684). Later, in his confrontation with Odysseus, he will show the intensity of his feelings by linking retribution with divine compassion

(1040–44): he prays for the gods to punish his enemies, "if you pity me at all" (εἴ τι κἄμ' οἰκτίρετε); such "compassionate" revenge would make him seem to have escaped his disease. In other words, the sweetness of retribution and the proof of divine justice shown by it would adequately recompense his great suffering.

89. See Blundell 1989, also Schein (2005: 41–42), who characterizes Philoktetes' conception of justice as "a moral absolute guaranteed by the gods" and based on the validity of social standards, including those of friendship and reciprocity. Contrast Winnington-Ingram's view of Philoktetes' enmity as tragic (1980, esp. 290–97).

90. Compare Jebb *ad loc.;* Burkert (1955: 42 and 51, n.6); and also Prauscello (2010: 206), who adds, "The disappointment and mismatch in terms of expectations between *eleos* and *oiktos* could not be pointed out more ironically." See the introduction on the general distinction between *eleos* and *oiktos.*

91. Compare, for example, Thukydides' statement (2.51.6) that those who showed the most compassion for the suffering of others in the plague were those who had themselves recovered from the plague and so knew what it was like, but who were now immune from it.

92. Compare, for example, the defeated king Psammenitos (Herodotos 3.14, cf. Aristotle *Rhetoric* 1386a20), who, in spite of the humiliation of his daughter and the impending death threatening his son, nevertheless felt and exhibited compassion at the sight of an aged friend who had been reduced to beggary; he thereby amazed Kroisos and Kambyses. Even more remarkable is Kroisos's compassion (*katoiktirei*) for the very man, Adrestos, who had killed Kroisos's beloved son Atys. Herodotos remarks that Kroisos pitied Adrestos in spite of his own great personal trouble (1.45). Also, see Lessing (29) on Philoktetes' nobility here.

93. Compare Antigone's use of this type of appeal in *Oidipous at Kolonos* 237–54; cf. D2.

94. Compare pp. 17–18; for examples from earlier plays of Sophokles, see S5 above and cf. D1a. Also, as we see in *Oidipous at Kolonos,* Theseus will provide a model of such protective compassion.

95. Compare Knox (1964: 130–31) on the "intolerable" nature of Philoktetes' pain as presented on stage; also Worman (2000 passim) for a different perspective. Stephens (1995: esp. 158–59) focuses on the graphic horror of Philoktetes' wound but argues that Odysseus had valid reasons for abandoning Philoktetes on Lemnos. The intolerable nature of Philoktetes' wound requires a heroic response, which Neoptolemos ultimately will provide, but which Odysseus and the Atreidai failed to perform.

96. Belfiore (1994: 120) interprets this supplication in a similar way. Her further suggestion that Neoptolemos takes Philoktetes by the hand and raises him up from his kneeling position to complete the supplication ritual is an attractive one; cf. Heath (1999: 149). Kosak (1999: 115–17) argues that Philoktetes does not complete full ritual contact here, but her interpretation requires that we read 485–86 in a way other than the most obvious, which is, "I supplicate you (either 'by your knees' or 'on my knees'), even though I am powerless and lame (i.e., it is hard for me to do so)." In any case, when Philoktetes later claims to be Neoptolemos's suppliant (773, 929–30), the latter does not deny it. On the sanctity of suppliants, compare above, chapter 1, pp. 25–28; in earlier plays by Sophokles, see S1.1 above.

97. On compassion and the human condition in other plays of Sophokles, see S2.1–2.2 above and cf. D2. Lloyd-Jones and Wilson, following Reeve, bracket 504–6, but these lines expand this important Sophoklean theme and are appropriate to the situation; also cf. Sandridge (2008: 443). Prauscello (2010: 204–5) uses this passage to illustrate her argument that whereas Philoktetes tends to use *eleos*-related words in his appeals to be rescued from Lemnos, the chorus and Neoptolemus tend to use *oiktos*-related words in their responses, which indicate their sympathy for him but not necessarily their commitment to the action he requests.

98. Compare 265, where the Atreidai and Odysseus are said by Philoktetes to have "shamefully" (*aischrôs*) abandoned him. On *xenia* and compassion, see pp. 17–18.

99. Kosak (1999: 120) notes that ἴσος ἐν ἴσοις also suggested to Sophokles' contemporary audience that Philoktetes was a good citizen, since *isotês* ("equality") was an Athenian democratic value.

100. On compassion and the issues of worthiness and justice, compare D4; also, regarding earlier plays of Sophokles, see S7 above. Lefèvre, on the other hand, sees Philoktetes as one who suffers on Lemnos in recompense for his arrogance toward the goddess Chryses. The text does not say so. Furthermore, if the playwright wished us to think of Philoktetes as such a "sinner," he would hardly have the chorus depict him as the archetypal innocent sufferer presented in the *parodos* and this *stasimon.* Likewise, Sandridge (2008: 444) does not recognize Philoktetes' "merit" as a basis for Neoptolemos's feeling of compassion toward him.

101. Jebb interprets ἀντίτυπον, the epithet of στόνον (lament), to mean "awakening response" (i.e., in the longed-for listener). Another option is to interpret it as "echoing" (as does LSJ), a more obvious meaning for the word that would more clearly emphasize the reality (that Philoktetes'

lament actually arouses no sympathetic response, but only an echo) and would recall the echo-image of the chorus's earlier song (188–90).

102. See further on the beast-image in Fuqua (1964: 149) and Segal (1981: 303).

103. Compare Webster 1970 and Rose (1992: 295).

104. Schein (2005: 34) notes that references to the apotheosis of Herakles in the last stanza recall the *philia* of Herakles and Philoktetes, as well as looking "forward to Heracles' reappearance at the end of the play, at Zeus's prompting and on the basis of this old friendship" (1413, 1445–47, 1467). Also, see further in Linforth (1956: 120–23); Burton 1980; Gardiner 1987; and Tarrant 1986 on the *stasimon.*

105. In lamenting Aias, Patroklos, and Antilochos as good comrades and warriors who, along with Akhilleus, have died at Troy (410–52), Philoktetes associates them with the type of warrior that he himself is, but through their association with Akhilleus, they also represent the paternal heritage of Neoptolemos. In *Odyssey* 11.465–70, the ghosts of Akhilleus, Patroklos, Antilochos, and Aias appear together in the underworld. See further in Schmidt (1973: 94–95) on these warriors and Nestor as representing heroic and ethical standards to which Neoptolemos should aspire.

106. He also accedes to Priam's sanctity as a suppliant and to the will of Zeus as conveyed to him by Thetis. See chapter 1, pp. 39–40. Contrast Blundell (1988: 143–44), who emphasizes Akhilleus's lack of compassion in contrast to Neoptolemos's self-sacrifice in this play. Early in the play, however, Odysseus does exploit the competitive-warrior, glory-seeking side of Akhilleus's model and his son's *physis* to lure the young man into using deception against Philoktetes (50–53, 112–20).

107. See S3 above; cf. introduction, pp. 17–20; chapter 1, pp. 28–31. On the use of δίδωμι in 668, cf. Belfiore (1994: 122).

108. The chorus reinforces this characterization by referring to Neoptolemos as the "son of good men" (ἀνδρῶν ἀγαθῶν παιδὸς, 719) in his anticipated rescue of Philoktetes (cf. p. 17). Adkins (1960: 174) cites the use of *agathoi* in this line as according with the traditional expectation of the *agathos* to protect suppliants. Blundell (1989: 192, n.36) sees Sophokles' use of *aretê* in 669 as an "exception" to its normally heroic, military meaning in Sophokles. The important thing here is the word's heroic connotation and its connection to Neoptolemos's compassion.

109. Compare Taplin (1978: 90); Segal (1981: 318–22); and J. A. Johnson (1988) on the symbolism of the bow. Compare Avery (1965: 294–96) on the Herakles-Philoktetes-Neoptolemos connection.

110. Compassion comes into play in a relationship of *philia* when one *philos* is in desperate straits (cf. intro. pp. 18–19). Such a critical situation

applied when Herakles needed help from Philoktetes to end his misery, and, as we have seen, it is an integral part of what Philoktetes now requests from his new *philos,* Neoptolemos. Indeed, compassion and *philia* will continue to be linked in the rest of this play.

111. On Sophokles' use of sensory perception to intensify compassion in other plays, see S4 above; cf. D3. Easterling's account of the emotional response that an audience would experience includes the following: "It is overwhelmingly a reaction of pity: for his brute physical suffering, lavishly described and enacted on stage, and for his mental anguish in his isolation" (1978: 36).

112. Compare Adams (1957: 148–49) and Erbse (1966: 192).

113. Kamerbeek (*ad* 813) compares *Trachiniai* 1181, *Oidipous at Kolonos* 1632, and Aristophanes' *Clouds* 81, where Dover 1970 notes that the clasping of the right hand signifies a pledge of good faith. The three occurrences in Sophokles all suggest that such a pledge is what heroes use, rather than an oath; cf. *Oidipous at Kolonos* 650–51 on the implication of distrust inherent in oaths.

114. Compare Nussbaum (1992: 268) on Neoptolemos's use of the language of physical pain to describe his response to Philoktetes' suffering; also, Worman (2000) on the use of *alg*-cognates in the play (28) and on Neoptolemos's growing identification with Philoktetes (23–24). See McCoy for an argument that Sophokles presents "Philoktetes' weakness as contributing to the growth of Neoptolemus' virtue and to the growth of the political community" (2013: 64).

115. Compare Prauscello (2010: 205–6); also, compare the connection between compassion and action expressed in 307–8 and discussed above.

116. Compare Carlevale (2000: 46–47). Contrast Rose's view (see esp. 1992: 320–22) of the nature/paternity theme as primarily an "aristocratic slant" and a "Pindaric overlay"; he sees Sophokles using this to subvert the egalitarian thrust of the sophistic anthropology that Rose sees as the basis of the type of cooperative relationship that Philoktetes and Neoptolemos develop in the play. Griffith (1995: esp. 62–75, 107–24) provides a balanced view of how social issues and perspectives relate to tragedy as a "democratic" genre. Easterling (1997: 24) offers the view that "heroes could serve as paradigms for anyone to identify with." On the use of *eugenês* and *gennaios* as general terms of commendation that do not necessarily refer to social class, see Dover (1974: 93–95).

117. Rose (1992: 298–99) notes the contrast between Neoptolemos's psychic wound and the physical distress that Philoktetes both suffers and stimulates in others with his wound. Rose capably argues against

those who see Philoktetes' wound as a symbol of a psychic incapacity on his part. Hawkins (1999: 353) sees compassion as exerting "moral authority" here; this is in keeping with her interpretation of the play as an "ethical tragedy," which she seeks to fit into a "moral" framework based on Aristotelian concepts. In contrast, my interpretation seeks to define the play's values in terms of fifth-century and earlier concepts.

118. Compare Sophokles' use of *gennaios* at 475 and my discussion above.

119. Blundell (1987: 307–29) concludes that Odysseus is best described as an amoral opportunist comparable to the Athenian politicians of the late fifth century, such as the Athenian spokesmen at Melos and those who debated the fate of Mytilene; cf. Gardiner (1987: 48).

120. Especially galling to Philoktetes is the prospect of the use of the bow—the symbol of heroic *philia*—by Odysseus, the abuser of heroic *philoi* (1123–39). Philoktetes, in fact, proceeds to address the bow itself as if it were a *philos* who pities the noble friend from whom it has been taken and must now be handled by an ignoble enemy and witness his tricks; cf. Prauscello (2010: 205). The mention of Herakles at 1131–32 recalls the bow's association with compassionate service between *philoi* and points up the special inappropriateness of its being in the employ of a man who abuses friends.

121. See Heath (1999: 152–53 and n.28) on the voluntary nature of Neoptolemos's commitment to the Greek army's cause at Troy.

122. Compare Kreon's exit in *Oidipous at Kolonos* 1036–41. For Lefèvre (2001: 207–12), Odysseus is the hero of this play and Philoktetes and Neoptolemus are its wayward sinners. In applying his standard of *sophrosyne,* Lefèvre concludes that Odysseus is the only major character in the play who "knows himself." But the person who possesses a true knowledge of himself or herself and his or her situation as a human being should also possess a deep understanding of the fragility of life and good fortune for fellow human beings and for himself as well. Such a person is capable of compassion for the misfortunes of others and expresses such compassion in word and deed. In Sophoklean tragedy, Odysseus of *Aias* and Theseus of *Oidipous at Kolonos* stand out as characters who possess deep self-knowledge along with an understanding of life's fragility and a capability of feeling and exhibiting compassion for unmerited suffering and misfortune. The Odysseus of this play is far other than such a character. Indeed, Neoptolemos and Philoktetes himself come much closer to such an ideal than does the Odysseus presented here.

123. Compare McCoy (2013: 75): "Neoptolemus' experience of pity significantly informs his exercise of reason, for the experience of witnessing

the suffering man leads to his reasoned judgement that the proper moral response is to abide by his promise and to return the bow to Philoctetes. He manages to integrate his reasoned judgement about the best course of action with his affective response to the man."

124. Lefèvre interprets it thus (2001: 198).

125. Compare Beye (1970: 65), who remarks that whereas Akhilleus retires from the group, Philoktetes has been "forcibly expelled."

126. Later Neoptolemos tries to assert that the leaders "will save" Philoktetes (1391), but this comes too little and too late.

127. As Easterling (1978: 36) describes it: "We badly want him to be cured and to be rescued from isolation. At the same time we understand his hostility toward the Greeks, and we do not want him to sacrifice his self-respect at the price of being healed." Contrast Winnington-Ingram (1980: 297), who writes of the negative aspect of the heroic code dominating Philoktetes' reaction here "so that he is bound to reject the plea of Neoptolemus' friendship—and even the prospect of heroic glory."

128. Dover (1974: 192) writes simply: "Returning positive good for ill, an important stage beyond mere refraining from requiting ill, does not seem to be exemplified in the available literature"; cf. Heath 1999: 157, n.37.

129. A friend has suggested to me that Neoptolemos's calling Philoktetes savage and undeserving of pity at 1316–23 could plausibly be seen as a tactic used to aid his persuasion of Philoktetes rather than as a serious effort to characterize Philoktetes objectively. Compare Patroklos's accusation of Akhilleus at *Iliad* 16.33–35.

130. Actually, as scholars have noted, Neoptolemos has not actually promised this, although he has implied as much by his pledge not to abandon Philoktetes (810–13) and by his other actions, such as telling Philoktetes to get on the boat; cf. Taplin (1987: 71–72).

131. Gill (1980: 142) notes that Neoptolemos is asked "to respond to . . . the claim that he respect his friend's wishes rather than act for what seems to him his friend's good"; cf. Robinson (1969: 51); Nussbaum (1976–77: 47); Sandridge (2008: 444).

132. Compare pp. 17–18 and S5.2 above.

133. Note that the bow will be used only defensively. Rose (1992: 304) observes the bow's continuation as a symbol of "mutual aid" and characterizes it as "the final basis of their compact"; cf. Newman, who sees Philoktetes' offer to use the bow in Neoptolemos' defense as a significant step on his part in establishing *philia* with Neoptolemos. Note that Sophokles is careful here not to depict Philoktetes and Neoptolemos as "deserters" of their country or army (contra Bowra and Vidal-Naquet, also Goldhill

1990: 120–23, who seeks to analyze Neoptolemos's dilemma from the perspective of the fifth-century Athenian collective ethos, but see n.134 below). The play poses no suggestion that Neoptolemos, much less Philoktetes, is being "unpatriotic" or even disloyal to the army. The basis of Philoktetes' action is that the army has rejected him, a loyal soldier. And Odysseus's threats are not that he will bring Neoptolemos to justice for wrongdoing or desertion, but that he will resort to bodily force and military aggression to get the bow and the man to Troy (1241–59, 1293–98).

134. Compare Schmidt (1973: 246). I should also note that my interpretation of Neoptolemos's development is not inconsistent with the general argument of Vidal-Naquet, who sees Akhilleus's son as developing from ephebe into a mature warrior worthy of victory at Troy. He does not, however, mention the role of compassion in this development, and we differ on the "first ending" of the play. Likewise, my argument is not incompatible with Goldhill's reconstruction of military ceremony at the City Festival of Dionysos. The play, as I read it, supports civic and military cohesion in a way consistent with Athenian democratic values.

135. Easterling (1978: 37). She and Clare Campbell, whom she cites, also see that Philoktetes is in need of a psychological or spiritual cure as well as a physical one after ten long years of hardship and isolation.

136. Compare Gill (1980: 142–43).

137. Compare Rose (1992: 324), who also notes the designation of Herakles' purpose in coming by the word *charis,* which, he says, typically conveys "the reciprocity of concern characteristic of heroic friends" as well as divine grace reserved for heroes.

138. Compare Jebb on 1336ff.: "The son of Zeus comes from heaven to declare, with his own lips, that Zeus ordains the return of Philoktetes to Troy. Thus a wholly new motive is brought to bear on Philoktetes, who hitherto merely knew (at second hand) what Helenos had prophesied."

139. Webster (1970) remarks that the analogy here is helped by the ambiguity of *ponos,* which can refer to Philoktetes' suffering (and labors) on Lemnos as well as to the labors of Herakles (cf. the references to Philoktetes' *ponoi* at 195, 508, 760). Indeed, this befits the genre of Attic tragedy with its emphasis on the heroes' sufferings rather than their triumphs; cf. Else's classic study, chap. 3.

140. Compare Blundell (1989: 222) and Kamerbeek *ad loc.* McCoy makes an interesting comment: "Herakles shows Philoctetes that his life's meaning is connected to the Greek story of victory against Troy that is to be told; a narrow concept of justice as revenge will not fulfil that larger, divinely sanctioned narrative" (2013: 85).

141. Winnington-Ingram (1980: 303) emphasizes the ferocity of the lions implicit in this image, in which he finds a typically Sophoklean use of irony. Along similar lines, Schein (2005: 38–39) sees in the simile an ominous allusion to *Iliad* 10.297, where Odysseus and Diomedes are compared to "two lions" going on their mission against Dolon and Rhesus; I doubt that very many of Sophokles' audience would have picked up on this "allusion" or that they would have interpreted it this way. I see Sophokles' simile rather as recalling the Homeric sense of compassion as mutual protection between *philoi* (cf. above, introduction, pp. 18–19, and chapter 1, pp. 40–42).

142. Compare Schmidt (1973: 247); Easterling (1978: 37–39); Hawkins (1999: 356); Kosak (1999: 133).

143. Herakles' admonition concerning the need to observe *eusebeia* (1440–44) is, presumably, in recognition of the mythic tradition of Neoptolemos's and the other Greeks' impiety in the course and aftermath of the final battle at Troy. Is this meant to discredit or cast an ominous shadow over Neoptolemos's or Philoktetes' actions in the play up to this point? I think not, contra Bowra (1944: 304) and Segal 1977, although it does ironically open what has been called a "window upon a tragic future" (Winnington-Ingram 1980: 302–3, cf. Easterling 1978: 39). Roberts (1988: 192) insightfully argues that such allusions to the future at the end of Sophokles' plays suggest that "the forces that set tragedies in motion continue unabated, and stories, though they may be serious and complete, are always part of larger stories." In this feature of his drama, Sophokles reflects the nature of his mythic material as a complex, inter-referential, never-ending patchwork of narratives.

144. Compare Winnington-Ingram (1980: 299).

145. Compare Akhilleus's deference to divine will in *Iliad* 1 (to Hera and Athene) and *Iliad* 24 (to Zeus). McCoy (2013: 85) asserts that Herakles' presence "assures Philoctetes that the gods are just and capable of friendship" with him.

146. Compare Winnington-Ingram (1956: 634); Blundell (1989: 222).

147. In contrast, Winnington-Ingram (1980: 301) and Rabel (1997: 301–3) emphasize the role of Herakles' paradigmatic heroism in Philoktetes' persuasion here. I would add that Herakles' use of his own paradigmatic career here is analogous to Philoktetes' use of his past and that of Akhilleus as models for Neoptolemos.

148. Kirkwood (1994: 434–36), in discussing the theme of persuasion in the play and the phrase "counsel of friends" (γνώμη φίλων, 1467) uttered by Philoktetes in his final speech, interprets Neoptolemos's agreement

to convey Philoktetes home as a necessary step in the overall process of Philoktetes' persuasion, a process that culminates in Herakles' persuasive words and Philoktetes' willing assent. This interpretation makes sense in my view.

149. Lefèvre 2001 and Prauscello (2010: 207–9) see Herakles' redirection of Philoktetes and Neoptolemos and the end of the play as a victory for Odysseus and the Atreidai. But we must ask why Odysseus is never mentioned in Herakles' speech and why he is not brought back onstage for the celebration at the end. Instead, the poet frames the victory and celebration at the end strictly in terms of Philoktetes' and Neoptolemos's heroism and mutual concern, including Philoktetes' future cure and reintegration into the Greek army. Odysseus and the sons of Atreus are notably absent.

150. Because compassion in this play is linked so integrally with solidarity and mutual benefit between allies, it attains the level of generalized reciprocity (see intro. pp. 19–20).

151. For interpretations exploring issues of ideology related to the representation of Athens in this play, see Zeitlin 1990; Tzanetou 2005 and 2012; and Bernek 2004.

152. Compare, for example, recent book-length studies on Theseus by Walker 1995 and Mills, both of whom present insightful treatments of his mythic career.

153. See Irwin (1977: passim, esp. 54–56, 86–90, 134–36, and 206–8) on Plato's concepts of the inseparability and unity of virtues See J. F. Johnson /Clapp 2005 for how Theseus's compassion in this play forms part of Sophokles' education of his fellow Athenians; cf. Sandridge (2008: 436–40) for a somewhat similar analysis.

154. Compare Burian 1974 on Sophocles' adaptation of the conventions of the suppliant drama in this play.

155. Later, when Ismene reports to Oidipous the conflict enveloping his two sons, she concludes that she is unable to discover how the gods will pity (*katoiktiousin*) Oidipous's troubles (*ponoi*, 361–84); cf. Konstan (2001: 109).

156. Her mention of Oidipous's deeds as being "unwilling" (*akonta*) provides an assurance of Oidipous's innocence that should allow the chorus's compassion to flow. Cf. S7 on this theme in earlier Sophoklean plays; also, D4 (Worthiness).

157. The word *aidôs* in 247 means "regard for the helpless, compassion," according to LSJ; cf. Stanford (1983: 36).

158. Compare in S2.3 above; also, D2 (Likeness and Vulnerability).

159. Compare D4 on anxiety regarding unworthy or treacherous suppliants. The chorus express fear of some burden, possibly pollution, that Oidipous may impose on the city; cf. Jebb *ad* 235ff.; Blundell (1990: 30, n.31).

160. Jebb and others, including the *Scholia Oidipous at Kolonos* 260, note the transition from Antigone's emotional pleas for compassion to Oidipous's more rational appeal based on justice. Note that they each fit the expected gender roles in this distinction, but also that Antigone both here and in Sophokles' *Antigone* shows the love for kin as well as the compassion that was commonly associated with women (cf. D6).

161. Few scholars seem to have noted this change in the chorus's receptivity to Oidipous; Tzanetou 2005 is one of those few.

162. Compare Mills (1997: 171).

163. Also, note the interconnection, mostly personal, that Theseus lays out in the last two lines: between "the city and me" and "you and your daughter." Burian (1974: 414) notes the contrast between Theseus's ready acceptance of Oidipous and the chorus's earlier resistance and hesitation toward him.

164. The word *praxis* (560) is ambiguous: it could refer either to Oidipous's past activity, which Theseus might shrink from supporting (Jebb), or to the hardship or danger Theseus and Athens might incur in meeting Oidipous's request (Kamerbeek 1984). I prefer the ambiguous "labor" to "fortune" as a translation.

165. In regard to the former, note the emphasis Theseus places on his own life experiences (*hos oida g'autos,* 562), the parallelism he perceives between his upbringing in a foreign land and that experienced by Oidipous (*hôsper su,* 563), and his emphasis on Oidipous's present participation in the class of "strangers" (*xenon . . . hôsper su nûn,* 565), a class that Theseus says he would never refrain from rescuing. Compare Burian (1974: 415), who writes of "Theseus' spontaneous assertion of a common human bond between himself and his suppliant." Burian notes that, unlike the chorus, who are horrified by Oidipous's past, Theseus sees Oidipous as merely "ill-fated" (557). Also, cf. Reinhardt (1979: 207–8); Mills (1997: 172–73); Munteanu (2012: 203–6); McCoy (2013: 54–55).

166. Oidipous has told the chorus that he bears a benefit for Athens, but Theseus does not yet know it. Compare lines 288–90 and Jebb's note on 309. In lines 307–8, in reference to the benefit he is bringing, Oidipous comments on the noble's tendency to benefit himself by helping others. We might, indeed, note the common expectation of the noble man's behavior: that it will be appropriate and beneficial both to others and to himself (and his own). Jebb comments: "Does not experience teach us

that the benefactor of others is often his own. . . . The generous man, though he acts from no calculation of self-interest, actually serves himself by making zealous friends."

167. In Monroe's *The Heart of Altruism* (1996), a study of rescuers of Jews from Nazi persecution in World War II and other life-risking rescuers, her modern "heroes" deny that any sense of self-interest motivated their actions, and Monroe carefully concludes that their behaviors should be called "altruistic." What they seem to share with Theseus here, however, is a deep sense of common humanity. Monroe (206) writes, "Altruists have a particular perspective in which all mankind is connected through a common humanity, in which each individual is linked to all others and to a world in which all living beings are entitled to a certain humane treatment merely by virtue of being alive. It is not any mystical blending of the self with another; rather, it is a very simple but deeply felt recognition that we all share certain characteristics and are entitled to certain rights merely by virtue of our common humanity. It constitutes a powerful statement about what it means to be a human being." The Greeks did not explicitly express such a value of universal human dignity, although something close to it seems implicit in the phenomenon of supplication and in the Greek understanding of the fragility of life shared by all human beings (cf. pp. 19–20 and D2).

168. Compare his later reference to his goal of seeking distinction through his actions rather than by words (1143–44). But also note that both here at 1040 and later at 1210, when he assures Oidipous that he will be protected against Polyneikes, Theseus adds a qualification—"if I don't die first" or "provided the gods keep me safe"—that suggests his continuing sense of his own basic human vulnerability (D2).

169. Oidipous's own long-term suffering from his hate for his sons is shown in 1360–64. In 1189–94, Antigone argued that Oidipous should give Polyneikes a hearing, saying that it would be wrong for him to return evil for evil to a son. But her argument was aimed at getting Oidipous to listen to the plea of his son, a suppliant. Once he has heard Polyneikes' plea, however, his judgment becomes free. When he has uttered his curses, Antigone and Polyneikes can only deal with them as best they can.

170. On the Athenian-Theban contrast in this play, see Zeitlin 1990; Loraux (2002: 44). Scholars have noted that Sophokles has Theseus carefully distinguish Kreon's bad behavior from that of the good Thebans back home (919–23).

171. See the previous section on Neoptolemos's compassion in *Philoktetes.* Compare McCoy's observation that Theseus's compassionate acceptance of Oidipous shows that his rationality includes an "affective element" (2013:

58); McCoy also argues that Theseus's openness in accepting this outsider reflects Athens' democratic inclusion of "'all' in its community" (60).

172. He, for example, chides Oidipous at 592–94 and at 1208–9, although in both instances he quickly moderates his response.

173. Compare Blundell (1993: 299–300, 305–6). Although ancient testimony indicates that the poet did not live to see the play produced and, furthermore, that its first production occurred after Athens had lost the war with Sparta, still the play depicts an Athens undaunted and full of hope for the future.

CONCLUSION

1. Compare pp. 18–19.

2. Compare pp. 19–20. In Homer's *Iliad,* compassion was sometimes possible on the battlefield, but only if the victor was so inclined and if ransom was offered.

3. Compare the *Iliad* 9.629–32, where Aias calls Akhilleus "cruel," one who has made his heart "savage" (*agrion*), for his refusal to show compassion to his *philoi* in need, a characterization that is suggested by others as well (cf. above, pp. 40–42 and n.52); in *Odyssey* 9.475–79, 23.312–13, Odysseus and his men repay the barbarous Kyklops for eating his guests rather than pitying them. Also, in Aischylos's *Suppliants,* the sons of Aigyptos are depicted as pitiless in their behavior (cf. above, pp. 80–81 and n.39).

4. Vickers (1973: 84) interprets the latter passage as one of two cases in tragedy "where the death of pity is presented sympathetically," the other being Sophokles' *Elektra* (see chapter 5 above).

5. The quotation continues with the philanthropic sentiment that "it is evil, when there is abundant wealth, to benefit no mortal out of base stinginess."

6. Compare Vickers (1973: chap. 2), who interprets pity in tragedy as generally a virtue, pitilessness generally a vice. He writes, "Pity—or 'sympathy,' or 'compassion'—is a quality fundamental to humanity; . . . pity is in no way a weakening, condescending, or 'unmanly' reaction to suffering in life or art, . . . it is, rather, the only proper humane response. Not to feel pity when confronted with the sufferings of a Hecuba or Heracles—*that* is unmanly, unnatural: indifference to suffering 'is the one true, terrible and lasting form of cruelty'" (69–70). His last clause quotes Proust.

7. See chap. 5, p. 177 and n.88. Also, see chap. 2, n.35; furthermore, compare Hekabe's supplication to Agamemnon for revenge on Polymestor

(chap. 4, pp. 116–17) and Elektra's sense of relief in gaining retribution on Aigisthos (chap. 5, pp. 165–66).

8. Burkert (1996: 133–34) remarks on the element of measure as the "epitome of rationality" in ancient applications of the *lex talionis.*

9. Pelasgos's ultimate fate is unclear at the end of *Suppliants,* the first play of a trilogy; cf. above, chapter 3, n.40.

10. Compare Winnington-Ingram (1980: chap. 13, esp. pp.327–29). With regard to Oidipous in *Oidipous the King* we might note that Sophokles' later play (*Oidipous at Kolonos*) provides redemption for Oidipous and seems to have been used by the playwright to correct some people's negative impressions of Oidipous based on the earlier play.

11. Compare Griffin (1998: 51 and n.46). Tzanetou herself grants as much in regard to the representation of Athenians in tragedy (2005: n.28). Euripides' *Suppliants* is exceptional in this group of plays in that there the Athenians act in support of the Argive women's request that their kinsmen receive burial rather than because the suppliants are under aggressive threat themselves. Still, the ancient Athenians saw the denial of burial as justifying active intervention.

12. Compare the cycle of pitiless retribution that Aischylos portrays in *Oresteia.*

Bibliography

Adams, S. M. 1957. *Sophocles the Playwright.* Toronto: Toronto University Press.

Adkins, A. W. H. 1960a. *Merit and Responsibility.* Oxford: Oxford University Press.

———. 1960b. "'Honour' and 'Punishment' in the Homeric Poems." *British Institute of Classical Studies* 7: 23–32.

———. 1963. "'Friendship' and 'Self-Sufficiency' in Homer and Aristotle." *Classical Quarterly* n.s. 12: 30–45.

———. 1966a. "Aristotle and the Best Kind of Tragedy." *Classical Quarterly* n.s. 16: 78–102.

———. 1966b. "Basic Greek Values in Euripides' *Hecuba* and *Hercules Furens.*" *Classical Quarterly* n.s. 16: 193–219.

———. 1971. "Homeric Values and Homeric Society." *Journal of Hellenic Studies* 91: 1–14.

Allen, William. 2001. *Euripides. The Children of Heracles.* Warminster, Eng.: Aris & Phillips.

Alt, Karin. 1961. "Schicksal und φύσις im Philoktet des Sophokles." *Hermes* 89: 141–74.

Armstrong, Karen. 2010. *Twelve Steps to a Compassionate Life.* New York: Anchor Books.

Arrowsmith, W. 1956. "Introduction to *Heracles,*" in *Euripides,* vol. 2 of *The Complete Greek Tragedies,* ed. D. Grene and R. Lattimore. Chicago: University of Chicago Press.

Avery, H. C. 1965. "Heracles, Philoctetes, Neoptolemus." *Hermes* 93: 279–97.

Barlow, S. A. 1996. *Euripides. Heracles.* Warminster, Eng.: Aris & Phillips.

Bednarowski, K. Paul. 2010. "The Danaids' Threat: Obscurity, Suspense and the Shedding of Tradition in Aeschylus' *Suppliants*." *Classical Journal* 105: 193–212.

Belfiore, Elizabeth. 1994. "*Xenia* in Sophocles' *Philoctetes*." *Classical Journal* 89: 113–29.

Bellinger, A. R. 1939. "Achilles' Son and Achilles." *Yale Classical Studies* 6: 3–13.

Bernek, Rüdiger. 2004. *Dramaturgie und Ideologie: Der politische Mythos in den Hikesiedramen des Aischylos, Sophokles und Euripides*. München: K. G. Saur.

Beye, C. R. 1970. "Sophocles' *Philoctetes* and the Homeric Embassy." *Transactions of the American Philological Association* 101: 63–75.

Biggs, Penelope. 1966. "The Disease Theme in Sophocles' *Ajax, Philoctetes,* and *Trachiniae*." *Classical Philology* 61: 223–35.

Blundell, M. W. (a.k.a. Ruby Blondell). 1987. "The Moral Character of Odysseus in Sophocles' *Philoctetes*." *GRBS* 28: 307–29.

———. 1988. "The *phusis* of Neoptolemus in Sophocles' *Philoctetes*." *Greece & Rome* n.s. 35: 137–48.

———. 1989. *Helping Friends and Harming Enemies: A Study in Sophocles and Greek Ethics*. Cambridge: Cambridge University Press.

———, tr. 1990. *Sophocles' Oedipus at Colonus*. Newburyport, MA: Focus Classical Library.

———. 1993. "The Ideal of Athens in *Oedipus at Colonus*." In *Tragedy, Comedy, and the Polis*, ed. A. H. Sommerstein et al., 287–306. Bari: Levante Editori.

Bolkestein, Henrik. 1939. *Wohltätigkeit und Armenpflege im vorchristlichen Altertum*. Utrecht: A. Oosthoek.

Bond, G. W. 1981. *Euripides, Heracles*. Oxford: Clarendon Press.

Bowra, M. 1944. *Sophoclean Tragedy*. Oxford: Clarendon Press.

Budelmann, Felix. 2000. *The Language of Sophocles: Communality, Communication and Involvement*. Cambridge: Cambridge University Press.

Burian, Peter. 1974. "Suppliant and Saviour: Oedipus at Colonus." *Phoenix* 28: 408–29.

Burkert, Walter. 1955. *Zum altergriechischen Mitleidsbegriff*. PhD diss., Universität Erlangen.

———. 1979. *Structure and History in Greek Mythology and Ritual*. Berkeley: University of California Press.

———. 1996. *Creation of the Sacred: Tracks of Biology in Early Religions*. Cambridge, MA: Harvard University Press.

Burnett, Anne P. 1998. *Revenge in Attic and Later Tragedy*. Berkeley: University of California Press.

Burton, R. W. B. 1980. *The Chorus in Sophocles' Tragedies.* Oxford: Clarendon Press.

Buxton, R. G. A. 1984. *Sophocles.* Greece and Rome: New Surveys in the Classics. No. 16. Oxford: Clarendon Press.

Cairns, D. L. 1993. *Aidôs: The Psychology and Ethics of Honour and Shame in Ancient Greek Literature.* Oxford: Clarendon Press.

Calder, W. M. 1963. "The End of Sophocles' *Electra.*" *Greek, Roman, and Byzantine Studies* 4: 213–16.

Campbell, Clare. 1972. "A Theophany." *Theoria to Theory* 6: 81–85.

Campbell, Lewis, ed. 1879, 1881. *Sophocles: The Plays and the Fragments.* Oxford: Clarendon Press.

Carlevale, John. 2000. "Education, *Phusis* and Freedom in Sophocles' *Philoctetes.*" *Arion* (3s) 8.1: 26–60.

Chalk, H. H. O. 1962. "*Aretê* and *Bia* in Euripides' *Herakles.*" *Journal of Hellenic Studies* 82: 7–18.

Chantraine, Pierre. 1974. *Dictionnaire Etymologique de la Langue Grecque.* Paris: Editions Klincksieck.

Conacher, D. J. 1967. *Euripidean Drama: Myth, Theme and Structure.* Toronto: Toronto University Press.

Cook, Albert. 1971. *Enactment: Greek Tragedy.* Chicago: Swallow Press.

Crotty, Kevin. 1994. *The Poetics of Supplication: Homer's Iliad and Odyssey.* Ithaca, NY: Cornell University Press.

Cunliffe, Richard J. 1963. *A Lexicon of the Homeric Dialect.* Norman: University of Oklahoma Press.

Damasio, Antonio. 2003. "The Very First Foundation of Virtue: Neurobiology and Ethical Behaviors." *Cerebrum: The Dana Forum on Brain Science* 5.1: 91–106. An excerpt from Damasio, *Looking for Spinoza: Joy, Sorrow, and the Feeling Brain* (Harcourt).

Davies, Malcolm, ed. 1991. *Sophocles / Trachiniae.* Oxford: Clarendon Press.

Dawe, R. D., ed. 1982. *Sophocles / Oedipus Rex.* Cambridge: Cambridge University Press.

Denniston, J. D., and D. Page, eds. 1957. *Aeschylus: Agamemnon.* Oxford: Clarendon Press.

De Wet, B. X. 1977. "The *Electra* of Sophocles—A Study in Social Values." *Acta Classica* 20: 23–36.

Diels, Hermann, and Kranz, Walter. 1966. *Die Fragmente der Vorsokratiker.* 11th ed. 3 vols. Berlin: Weidmannsche Verlagsbuchhandlung.

Diggle, J. 1981–94. *Euripidis Fabulae, Tomi I–III.* Oxford: Clarendon Press.

Donlan, Walter. 1982. "Reciprocities in Homer." *The Classical World* 75: 137–75.

Dover, K. J., ed. 1970. *Aristophanes, Clouds.* Abridged ed. Oxford: Clarendon Press.

———. 1974. *Greek Popular Morality in the Time of Plato and Aristotle.* Oxford: Basil Blackwell.

Dué, Casey. 2006. *The Captive Woman's Lament in Greek Tragedy.* Austin: University of Texas Press.

Eagleton, Terry. 1991. *Ideology: An Introduction.* London: Verso.

Easterling, Patricia E. 1967. "Oedipus and Polynices." *PCPS* 13: 1–13.

———. 1978. "*Philoctetes* and Modern Criticism." *Illinois Classical Studies* 3: 27–39.

———, ed. 1982. *Sophocles / Trachiniae.* Cambridge: Cambridge University Press.

———. 1997. "Constructing the Heroic." In *Greek Tragedy and the Historian,* ed. C. Pelling, 21–37. Oxford: Clarendon Press.

Elftmann, G. B. 1973. *Nobility of Birth in Sophoclean Drama.* PhD diss., University of Pennsylvania.

Else, G. F. 1967. *The Origin and Early Form of Greek Tragedy.* New York: Norton.

Encyclopaedia Britannica. 2005. "Deontological Ethics." Encyclopaedia Britannica Online. 11 May 2005. <http://search.eb.com/eb/article?tocld=9029972>

Erbse, H. 1966. "Neoptolemus und Philoktet bei Sophokles." *Hermes* 94: 177–201.

Erffa, C. E. von. 1937. *Aidos und verwandte Begriffe in ihrer Entwicklung von Homer bis Demokrit. Philologus,* Suppl. 30, 2. PhD diss., Universität Leipzig.

Falkner, Thomas. 2005. "Engendering the Tragic *Theatês:* Pity, Power, and Spectacle in Sophocles' *Trachiniae.*" In *Pity and Power in Ancient Athens,* ed. R. Sternberg, 165–92. Cambridge: Cambridge University Press.

Fedder, Lilian. 1963. "The Symbol of the Desert Island in Sophocles' *Philoctetes.*" *Drama Survey* 3: 33–41.

Felson, Nancy. 2002. "*Threptra* and Invincible Hands: The Father-Son Relationship in *Iliad* 24." *Arethusa* 35: 35–50.

Ferguson, John. 1972. *A Companion to Greek Tragedy.* Austin: University of Texas Press.

Finley, M. I. 1965. *The World of Odysseus.* Rev. ed. New York: Viking.

Foley, Helene P. 1985. *Ritual Irony.* Ithaca, NY: Cornell University Press.

———. 2001. *Female Acts in Greek Tragedy.* Princeton: Princeton University Press.

Fränkel, H. 1975. *Early Greek Poetry and Philosophy,* tr. M. Hadas and J. Willis. Oxford: Basil Blackwell.

Fraenkel, E. 1950. *Aeschylus: Agamemnon.* 3 vols.. Oxford: Clarendon Press.

Fuqua, C. J. 1964. *The Thematic Structure of Sophocles' Philoctetes.* PhD diss., Cornell University.

Furley, D. 1986. "Euripides on the Sanity of Heracles," in *Studies in Honour of T. B. L. Webster,* ed. J. H. Betts, J. T. Hooker, and J. R. Green, 1: 102–13. Bristol: Bristol Classical Press.

Gaca, Kathy L. 2014. "Martial Rape, Pulsating Fear, and the Sexual Maltreatment of Girls (παῖδες), Virgins (παρθένοι), and Women (γυναῖκες) in Antiquity." *American Journal of Philology* 135.3: 303–57.

Gagarin, Michael. 1976. *Aeschylean Drama.* Berkeley: University of California Press.

Galinsky, G. Karl. 1972. *The Herakles Theme.* Oxford: Basil Blackwell.

Gantz, Timothy. 1993. *Early Greek Myth.* Baltimore: Johns Hopkins University Press.

Gardiner, Cynthia P. 1987. *The Sophoclean Chorus. A Study of Character and Function.* Iowa City: University of Iowa Press.

Garrison, E. P. 1995. *Groaning Tears: Ethical and Dramatic Aspects of Suicide in Greek Tragedy.* Leiden: Brill.

Garvie, A. F. 1969. *Aeschylus' Supplices: Play and Trilogy.* Cambridge: Cambridge University Press.

———. 1972. "Deceit, Violence, and Persuasion in the *Philoctetes,*" in *Studi classici in onore di Quintino Catudella I,* 213–26. Catania.

Geertz, Clifford. 1973. "Ideology as a Cultural System," in *The Interpretation of Cultures,* 193–233. New York: Basic.

Gellie, G. H. 1972. *Sophocles: A Reading.* Melbourne: Melbourne University Press.

Gibert, John. 1995. *Change of Mind in Greek Tragedy.* Göttingen: Vandenhoeck & Ruprecht.

———. 1997. "Euripides' *Heracles* 1351 and the Hero's Encounter with Death." *Classical Philology* 92: 247–58.

Gill, Christopher. 1980. "Bow, Oracle and Epiphany." *Greece & Rome* n.s. 27: 137–46.

———. 1998a. "Altruism or Reciprocity in Greek Ethical Philosophy?" in Gill et al. 1998b: 303–28.

Gill, Christopher, Norman Postlethwaite, and Richard Seaford, eds. 1998b. *Reciprocity in Ancient Greece.* Oxford: Clarendon Press.

Gödde, Susanne. 2000. *Das Drama der Hikesie: Ritual und Rhetorik in Aischylos' Hiketiden.* Münster: Aschendorff.

Goldhill, Simon. 1990. "The Great Dionysia and Civic Ideology." In *Nothing to Do with Dionysos?*, ed. J. J. Winkler and F. Zeitlin, 97–129. Princeton: Princeton University Press.

———. 1991. *The Poet's Voice: Essays on Poetics and Greek Literature.* Cambridge: Cambridge University Press.

Gould, John. 1973. "Hiketeia." *Journal of Hellenic Studies* 93: 74–103.

Gould, Thomas, ed. and tr. 1970. *Oedipus the King by Sophocles.* Englewood Cliffs: Prentice Hall.

Gouldner, A. W. 1965. *The Hellenic World: A Sociological Analysis.* New York: Harper Torchbooks.

Gove, P. B., et al., eds. 1973. *Webster's New Dictionary of Synonyms.* Springfield, MA: G. and C. Merriam.

Gregory, Justina. 1991. *Euripides and the Instruction of the Athenians.* Ann Arbor: University of Michigan Press.

———. 1999. *Euripides, Hecuba: Introduction, Text and Commentary.* Atlanta: Scholars Press.

Griffin, J. 1980. *Homer on Life and Death.* Oxford: Clarendon Press.

———. 1998. "The Social Function of Attic Tragedy." *Classical Quarterly* 48: 39–61.

Griffith, Mark, ed. 1983. *Aeschylus / Prometheus Bound.* Cambridge: Cambridge University Press.

———. 1995. "Brilliant Dynasts: Power and Politics in the *Oresteia.*" *Classical Antiquity* 14: 62–129.

———. 2005. "The Subject of Desire in Sophocles' *Antigone.*" In *The Soul of Tragedy: Essays on Athenian Drama,* ed. V. Pedrick and S. M. Oberhelman, 91–136. Chicago: University of Chicago Press.

Grube, G. M. 1961 [orig. 1941]. *The Drama of Euripides.* London: Methuen.

Hall, Edith. 1989. *Inventing the Barbarian.* Oxford: Oxford University Press.

———, ed. 1996. *Aeschylus. Persians.* Warminster, Eng.: Aris & Phillips.

———. 2010. *Greek Tragedy.* Oxford: Oxford University Press.

Halleran, M. R., tr. 1988. *The Heracles of Euripides.* Newburyport, MA: Focus.

Hammer, Dean. 2002. "The *Iliad* as Ethical Thinking: Politics, Pity, and the Operation of Esteem." *Arethusa* 35: 203–35.

Hands, A. R. 1968. *Charities and Social Aid in Greece and Rome.* Ithaca, NY: Cornell University Press.

Harsh, P. W. 1960. "The Role of the Bow in the *Philoctetes* of Sophocles." *American Journal of Philology* 81: 408–14.

Hawkins, Anne H. 1999. "Ethical Tragedy and Sophocles' *Philoctetes.*" *Classical World* 92: 337–57.

Heath, Malcolm. 1987. *The Poetics of Greek Tragedy.* Stanford: Stanford University Press.

———. 1999. "Sophocles' *Philoctetes:* A Problem Play?" In *Sophocles Revisited: Essays Presented to Sir Hugh Lloyd-Jones,* ed. J. Griffin, 137–60. Oxford: Oxford University Press.

Herington, C. J. 1971 [1965]. "Aeschylus: The Last Phase." In *Aeschylus: A Collection of Critical Essays,* ed. Marsh McCall, 148–63. Englewood Cliffs, NJ: Prentice Hall.

———. 1985. *Poetry into Drama: Early Tragedy and the Greek Poetic Tradition.* Berkeley: University of California Press.

Hinds, A. E. 1967. "The Prophecy of Helenus in Sophocles' *Philoctetes.*" *Classical Quarterly* 17: 168–80.

Hogan, James C. 1972. "Thucydides 3.52–68 and Euripides' *Hecuba.*" *Phoenix* 26: 241–57.

Hornblower, S., and A. Spawforth, eds. 1996. *The Oxford Classical Dictionary.* 3rd ed. Oxford: Oxford University Press.

Irwin, Terence. 1977. *Plato's Moral Theory: The Early and Middle Dialogues.* Oxford: Oxford University Press.

Jameson, M. H. 1956. "Politics and the *Philoctetes.*" *Classical Philology* 51: 217–27.

Jebb, R. C., ed. 1885–1902. *Sophocles: The Plays and Fragments.* Cambridge: Cambridge University Press.

Johnson, J. A. 1988. "Sophocles' *Philoctetes:* Deictic Language and the Claims of Odysseus." *Eranos* 86: 117–21.

Johnson, James F. 1980. "Compassion in Sophocles' *Philoctetes:* A Comparative Study." PhD diss., University of Texas at Austin.

———. 2002. "Compassion and Friendship in Euripides' *Herakles.*" *Classical Bulletin* 78.2: 115–29.

Johnson, James F., and Douglas C. Clapp. 2005. "Athenian Tragedy: An Education in Pity." In *Pity and Power in Ancient Athens,* ed. R. Sternberg, 123–64. Cambridge: Cambridge University Press.

Kamerbeek, J. C. 1980. *The Plays of Sophocles: Part VI, The Philoctetes.* Leiden: Brill.

———. 1984. *The Plays of Sophocles: Part VII, The Oedipus Coloneus.* Leiden: Brill.

Kannicht, Richard. 2004. *Euripides.* Vol. 5 of *Tragicorum Graecorum Fragmenta.* Göttingen: Vandenhoeck & Ruprecht.

Kells, J. H., ed. 1973. *Sophocles: Electra.* Cambridge: Cambridge University Press.

Kim, Jinyo. 2000. *The Pity of Achilles: Oral Style and the Unity of the Iliad.* Lanham, MD: Rowman & Littlefield.

King, Katherine C. 1987. *Achilles: Paradigms of the War Hero from Homer to the Middle Ages.* Berkeley: University of California Press.

Kirkwood, G. M. 1958. *A Study of Sophoclean Drama.* Ithaca, NY: Cornell University Press.

———. 1994. "Persuasion and Allusion in Sophokles' 'Philoctetes.'" *Hermes* 122: 425–36.

Kitto, H. D. F. 1956. *Form and Meaning in Drama.* London: Methuen.

———. 1957. *The Greeks.* Baltimore: Penguin.

———. 1961. *Greek Tragedy.* 3rd ed. London: Methuen.

Kitzinger, Rachel. 1991. "Why Mourning Becomes Elektra." *Classical Antiquity* 10.2: 298–327.

Knox, Bernard M. W. 1964. *The Heroic Temper.* Berkeley: University of California Press.

Konstan, David. 1998a. "Reciprocity and Friendship." In *Reciprocity in Ancient Greece,* ed. C. Gill, N. Postlethwaite, and R. Seaford, 279–301. Oxford: Clarendon Press.

———. 1998b. "Philoctetes' Pity: Commentary on Moravcsik." *Proceedings of the Boston Area Colloquium on Ancient Philosophy* 13: 276–82.

———. 2000. "Pity and Two Tragedies." In *Dramatische Wäldchen: Festschrift für Eckard Lefèvre zum 65. Geburtstag,* ed. E. Stärk and G. Vogt-Spira, 47–57. Hildesheim: Georg Olms.

———. 2001. *Pity Transformed.* London: Duckworth.

———. 2005a. "Pity and Politics." In *Pity and Power in Ancient Athens,* ed. R. Sternberg, 48–66. Cambridge: Cambridge University Press.

———. 2005b. "Aristotle on the Tragic Emotions." In *The Soul of Tragedy: Essays on Athenian Drama,* ed. V. Pedrick and S. M. Oberhelman, 13–25. Chicago: University of Chicago Press.

Kopperschmidt, Josef. 1971. "Hikesie als Dramatische Form." In *Die Bauformen der Griechischen Tragödie,* ed. Walter Jens, 321–46. Munich: Wilhelm Fink.

Körte, Alfred. 1957. *Menandri quae supersunt.* 3rd ed. Leipzig: B. G. Teubner.

Kosak, Jennifer C. 1999. "Therapeutic Touch and Sophokles' *Philoktetes.*" *Harvard Studies in Classical Philology* 90: 93–134.

———. 2005. "A Crying Shame: Pitying the Sick in the Hippocratic Corpus and Greek Tragedy." In *Pity and Power in Ancient Athens,* ed. R. Sternberg, 253–76. Cambridge: Cambridge University Press.

Kovacs, David. 1995. *Euripides II.* Cambridge, MA: Harvard University Press.

———. 1998. *Euripides III.* Cambridge, MA: Harvard University Press.

———. 2003. *Euripidea Tertia.* Leiden: Brill.

Kranz, Walter. 1933. *Stasimon, Untersuchungen zu Form und Gehalt der griechischen Tragödie.* Berlin: Weidmann.

Lateiner, Donald. 1995. *Sardonic Smile: Nonverbal Behavior in Homeric Epic.* Ann Arbor: University of Michigan Press.

———. 2005. "The Pitiers and the Pitied in Herodotus and Thucydides." In *Pity and Power in Ancient Athens,* ed. R. Sternberg, 67–97. Cambridge: Cambridge University Press.

Lattimore, Richmond, tr. 1969. *The Frogs.* In *Aristophanes: Four Comedies,* ed. W. Arrowsmith. Ann Arbor: University of Michigan Press.

Leahy, D. M. 1969. "The Rôle of Cassandra in the *Oresteia* of Aeschylus." *Bulletin of the John Rylands Library* 52: 144–77.

Lee, K. 1980. "Human and Divine in Euripides' *Heracles,*" in *Vindex Humanitatis: Essays in Honor of John Huntly Bishop,* ed. Bruce Marshall, 34–45. Armidale, N.S.W.: University of New England.

Lefèvre, Eckard. 2001. *Die Unfähigkeit, sich zu erkennen: Sophokles' Tragödien.* Leiden: Brill.

Lefkowitz, Mary R. 2012. *The Lives of the Greek Poets.* 2nd ed. Baltimore: Johns Hopkins University Press.

Lembke, Janet, ed. and tr. 1975. *Aeschylus: Suppliants.* New York: Oxford University Press.

Lesky, Albin. 1967. *Greek Tragedy,* tr. H. A. Frankfort. 2nd ed. London: Ernest Benn.

Lessing, G. E. 1962. *Laocoön,* tr. E. A. McCormick. Indianapolis: Bobbs-Merrill.

Liddell, H. G., and R. Scott. 1996. *A Greek-English Lexicon,* rev. H. S. Jones, 9th ed. Oxford: Clarendon Press.

Linforth, I. M. 1956. "Philoctetes, the Play and the Man." *University of California Publications in Classical Philology* 15.3: 95–156.

Lloyd-Jones, Hugh. 1952. "The Robes of Iphigeneia." *Classical Review* n.s. 2: 132–35.

———. 1971. *The Justice of Zeus.* Berkeley: University of California Press.

———, ed. 1996. *Sophocles: Fragments.* Cambridge, MA: Harvard University Press.

Lloyd-Jones, Hugh, and N. G. Wilson, eds. 1990a. *Sophoclis Fabulae.* Oxford: Clarendon Press.

———. 1990b. *Sophoclea: Studies in the Text of Sophocles.* Oxford: Clarendon Press.

Long, A. A. 1970. "Morals and Values in Homer." *Journal of Hellenic Studies* 90: 121–39.

Loraux, Nicole. 1986. *The Invention of Athens,* tr. Alan Sheridan. Cambridge, MA: Harvard University Press.

———. 1987. *Tragic Ways of Killing a Woman,* tr. A. Forster. Cambridge, MA: Harvard University Press.

———. 2002. *The Mourning Voice: An Essay on Greek Tragedy,* tr. E. T. Rawlings. Ithaca, NY: Cornell University Press.

Love, Harry. 2012. "Polyshocks: The Dramatic and Rhetorical Functions of Polyxena, Polydorus, and Polymestor in Euripides' *Hecuba*." In *Greek Drama IV: Texts, Contexts, Performance*, ed. D. Rosenbloom and J. Davidson, 72–94. Oxford: Oxford University Press.

Lynn-George, M. 1996. "Structures of Care in the *Iliad*." *Classical Quarterly* n.s. 46.1: 1–26.

MacDowell, Douglas M., ed. 1971. *Wasps*, by Aristophanes. Oxford: Clarendon Press.

Macleod, C. W., ed. 1982. *Homer, Iliad, Book XXIV.* Cambridge: Cambridge University Press.

———. 1983a. "Homer on Poetry and the Poetry of Homer." In Macleod 1983c: 1–15.

———. 1983b. "Thucydides and Tragedy." In Macleod 1983c: 140–58.

———. 1983c. *Collected Essays*. Oxford: Oxford University Press.

March, Jennifer. 1990. "Euripides, the Misogynist?" In *Euripides, Women, and Sexuality*, ed. A. Powell, 32–75. London: Routledge.

———, ed. 2001. *Sophocles. Electra.* Warminster, Eng.: Aris & Phillips.

McCoy, Marina B. 2013. *Wounded Heroes: Vulnerability as a Virtue in Ancient Greek Literature and Philosophy*. Oxford: Oxford University Press.

Méautis, Georges. 1957. *Sophocle: Essai sur le Héros Tragique.* Paris: Albin Michel.

Mendelsohn, Daniel. 2002. *Gender and the City in Euripides' Political Plays.* Oxford: Oxford University Press.

Mercier, Charles E. 1993. "Hekabe's Extended Supplication (*Hec.* 752–888)." *TAPA* 123: 149–60.

Michelini, A. N. 1987. *Euripides and the Tragic Tradition*. Madison: University of Wisconsin Press.

Mills, Sophie. 1997. *Theseus, Tragedy and the Athenian Empire*. Oxford: Oxford University Press.

Monroe, Kristen. 1996. *The Heart of Altruism*. Princeton: Princeton University Press.

Most, Glenn W. 2003. "Anger and Pity in Homer's *Iliad*." In *Ancient Anger: Perspectives from Homer to Galen*, ed. S. Braund and G. W. Most, 50–75. Yale Classical Studies 32. New York: Cambridge University Press.

Munteanu, Dana LaCourse. 2012. *Tragic Pathos: Pity and Fear in Greek Philosophy and Tragedy*. Cambridge: Cambridge University Press.

Naiden, F. S. 2006. *Ancient Supplication*. Oxford: Oxford University Press.

Newman, R. J. 1991. "Heroic Resolution: A Note on Sophocles, *Philoctetes* 1405–1406." *Classical Journal* 86: 305–10.

Norwood, Gilbert. 1960 [orig. 1920]. *Greek Tragedy*. New York: Hill & Wang.

Nussbaum, Martha. 1976–77. "Consequences and Character in Sophocles' *Philoctetes.*" *Philosophy and Literature* 1: 25–53.

———. 1986. *The Fragility of Goodness.* Cambridge: Cambridge University Press.

———. 1992. "Tragedy and Self-sufficiency: Plato and Aristotle on Fear and Pity." In *Essays on Aristotle's Poetics,* ed. A. O. Rorty, 261–90. Princeton: Princeton University Press.

———. 2001. *Upheavals of Thought: The Intelligence of Emotions.* Cambridge: Cambridge University Press.

Padilla, M. W. 1994. "Heroic Paternity in Euripides' *Heracles.*" *Arethusa* 27: 279–302.

Page, Denys, ed. 1972. *Aeschyli Septem Quae Supersunt Tragoedias.* Oxford: Clarendon Press.

Parker, Douglass, tr. 1962. *The Wasps,* by Aristophanes. Ann Arbor: University of Michigan Press.

Parker, Robert. 1983. *Miasma.* Oxford: Clarendon Press.

Pearson, A. C. ed. 1917. *The Fragments of Sophocles.* Cambridge: Cambridge University Press.

Pearson, Lionel. 1962. *Popular Ethics in Ancient Greece.* Stanford: Stanford University Press.

Pedrick, V. 1982. "Supplication in the *Iliad* and the *Odyssey.*" *TAPA* 112: 125–40.

Pelling, Christopher. 1997. "Aeschylus' *Persae* and History." In *Greek Tragedy and the Historian,* ed. C. Pelling, 1–19. Oxford: Clarendon Press.

Pickard-Cambridge, A. W. 1946. *The Theatre of Dionysus at Athens.* Oxford: Clarendon Press.

Podlecki, A. J. 1966. "The Power of the Word in Sophocles' *Philoctetes.*" *Greek, Roman and Byzantine Studies* 7: 233–50.

Poe, J. P. 1974. *Heroism and Divine Justice in Sophocles' Philoctetes. Mnemosyne* suppl. 34. Leiden: Brill.

Pohlenz, Max. 1956. "Furcht und Mitleid?" *Hermes* 84: 49–74.

Pratt, N. T. 1949. "Sophoclean 'Orthodoxy' in the *Philoctetes.*" *American Journal of Philology* 70: 273–89.

Prauscello, Lucia. 2010. "The Language of Pity: *Eleos* and *Oiktos* in Sophocles' *Philoctetes.*" *Cambridge Classical Journal* 56: 199–212.

Pucci, P. 1980. *The Violence of Pity in Euripides' Medea.* Ithaca, NY: Cornell University Press.

Rabel, Robert J. 1997. "Sophocles' *Philoctetes* and the Interpretation of *Iliad* 9." *Arethusa* 30: 297–308.

Radt, Stefan. 1985. *Aeschylus.* Vol. 3 of *Tragicorum Graecorum Fragmenta.* Göttingen: Vandenhoeck & Ruprecht.

Reckford, Kenneth. 1990. "Pity and Terror in Euripides' *Hecuba*." *Arion* (3s) 1: 24–43.

Reinhardt, Karl. 1979 [orig. 1947]. *Sophocles*, tr. Hazel and David Harvey. Oxford: Basil Blackwell.

Roberts, Deborah H. 1988. "Sophoclean Endings: Another Story." *Arethusa* 21: 177–96.

Roberts, W. Rhys, tr. 1941. "Aristotle, Rhetorica." In *The Basic Works of Aristotle*, ed. Richard McKeon, 1317–1451. New York: Random House.

Robinson, D. B. 1969. "Topics in Sophocles' *Philoctetes*." *Classical Quarterly* 19: 34–56.

Roisman, Joseph. 1988. "On Phrynichos' *Sack of Miletos* and *Phoinissai*." *Eranos* 86: 15–23.

Romilly, Jacqueline de. 1961. *L'Evolution du pathétique d'Eschyle à Euripide.* Paris: Presses Universitaires de France.

———. 1980. "Le Refus du Suicide dans l'Héraclès d'Euripide." *Archaiognosia* 1: 1–10.

———. 1985. *A Short History of Greek Literature*, tr. Lillian Doherty. Chicago: University of Chicago Press.

Rose, Peter W. 1992. "Sophokles' *Philoktetes* and the Teachings of the Sophists: A Counteroffensive." In *Sons of the Gods, Children of Earth*, 266–330. Ithaca, NY: Cornell University Press.

Rosenbloom, David. 2007. Review of *Pity and Power in Ancient Athens*, ed. Sternberg. *Bryn Mawr Classical Review*, July 21.

———. 2012. "Athenian Drama and Democratic Political Structure." In *Greek Drama IV: Texts, Contexts, Performance*, ed. D. Rosenbloom and J. Davidson, 270–99. Oxford: Oxford University Press.

Rosenmeyer, Thomas G. 1982. *The Art of Aeschylus.* Berkeley: University of California Press.

Sahlins, Marshall. 1972. *Stone Age Economics.* New York: Aldine de Gruyter.

Sandridge, N. B. 2008. "Feeling Vulnerable, but Not Too Vulnerable: Pity in Sophocles' *Oedipus Coloneus, Ajax, and Philoctetes*." *Classical Journal* 103.4: 433–48.

Schadewaldt, W. 1955. "Furcht und Mitleid?" *Hermes* 83: 129–71.

Schein, Seth L. 2005. "Divine and Human in Sophocles' *Philoctetes*." In *The Soul of Tragedy*, ed. V. Pedrick and S. M. Oberhelman, 27–47. Chicago: University of Chicago Press.

Schmidt, J. H. H. 1889. *Handbuch der Lateinischen und Griechischen Synonymik.* Leipzig: Teubner.

Schmidt, J.-U. 1973. *Sophokles Philoktet, eine Strukturanalyse.* Heidelberg: C. Winter.

Schopenhauer, Arthur. 1995 [orig. 1860]. *On the Basis of Morality*, tr. E. F. J. Payne. Indianapolis: Hackett.

Scott, Mary. 1979. "Pity and Pathos in Homer." *Acta Classica* 22: 1–14.

Scully, Stephen. 1995. Introduction to *Euripides. Suppliant Women*, tr. Rosanna Warren and Stephen Scully, 3–19. Oxford: Oxford University Press.

Seaford, R. 1985. "The Destruction of Limits in Sophocles' *Electra*." *Classical Quarterly* 35: 315–23.

———. 1994. *Reciprocity and Ritual*. Oxford: Oxford University Press.

———. 1998. Introduction to *Reciprocity in Ancient Greece*, ed. C. Gill, N. Postlethwaite, and R. Seaford, 1–11. Oxford: Oxford University Press.

Seale, David. 1972. "The Element of Surprise in Sophocles' *Philoctetes*." *British Institute of Classical Studies* 19: 94–102.

Segal, Charles P. 1966. "The *Electra* of Sophocles." *TAPA* 97: 473–545.

———. 1971. *The Theme of the Mutilation of the Corpse in the Iliad*. Leiden: Brill.

———. 1977. "Philoctetes and the Imperishable Piety." *Hermes* 105: 133–58.

———. 1981. *Tragedy and Civilization: An Interpretation of Sophocles*. Cambridge, MA: Harvard University Press.

———. 1986. *Interpreting Greek Tragedy: Myth, Poetry, Text*. Ithaca, NY: Cornell University Press.

Seyffert, H. 1959. Review of *Zum altergriechischen Mitleidsbegriff*, by W. Burkert. *Gnomon* 31: 389–93.

Shucard, S. C. 1973. "Some Developments in Sophocles' Late Plays of Intrigue." *Classical Journal* 69: 133–38.

Silk, M. S. 1985. "Heracles and Greek Tragedy," *Greece & Rome* 32: 1–22.

Slatkin, Laura M. 1991. *The Power of Thetis: Allusion and Interpretation in the Iliad*. Berkeley: University of California Press.

Smyth, H. W., tr. 1973. *Aeschylus I* (Loeb). Cambridge, MA: Harvard University Press.

———, tr. 1957. *Aeschylus II* (Loeb). Appendix by H. Lloyd-Jones. Cambridge, MA: Harvard University Press.

Snell, Bruno. 1960 [orig. 1953]. *The Discovery of the Mind*, tr. T. G. Rosenmeyer. New York: Harper Torchbooks.

Snell, Bruno. 1971. *Tragicorum Graecorum Fragmenta*. Göttingen: Vandenhoeck & Ruprecht.

Spira, Andreas. 1960. *Untersuchungen zum Deus ex machina bei Sophokles und Euripides*. Kallmunz: Michael Lassleben.

Stanford, W. B., ed. 1963. *Sophocles, Ajax*. London: MacMillan.

———, ed. 1965. *The Odyssey of Homer*. London: MacMillan.

———. 1983. *Greek Tragedy and the Emotions: An Introductory Study*. London: Routledge & Kegan Paul.

Stephens, J. C. 1995. "The Wound of Philoctetes." *Mnemosyne* 48: 153–68.

Sternberg, Rachel, ed. 2005. *Pity and Power in Ancient Athens.* Cambridge: Cambridge University Press.

———. 2006. *Tragedy Offstage: Suffering and Sympathy in Ancient Athens.* Austin: University of Texas Press.

Stevens, E. B. 1944. "Some Attic Commonplaces of Pity." *American Journal of Philology* 65: 1–25.

Suter, Ann. 2003. "Lament in Euripides' *Trojan Women.*" *Mnemosyne* 56.1: 1–28.

Swanson, Judith A. 1994–95. "The Political Philosophy of Aeschylus's *Prometheus Bound:* Justice as Seen by Prometheus, Zeus, and Io." *Interpretation* 22.2: 215–45.

Taplin, Oliver. 1971. "Significant Actions in Sophocles' *Philoctetes.*" *Greek, Roman and Byzantine Studies* 12: 25–44.

———. 1978. *Greek Tragedy in Action.* Berkeley: University of California Press.

———. 1987. "The Mapping of Sophocles' *Philoctetes.*" *British Institute of Classical Studies* 34: 69–77.

Tarkow, T. A. 1977. "The Glorification of Athens in Euripides' *Heracles.*" *Helios* 5.1: 27–35.

Tarrant, R. J. 1986. "Sophocles, *Philoctetes* 676–729: Directions and Indirections." In *Greek Tragedy and Its Legacy,* ed. M. J. Cropp, E. Fantham, and S. E. Scully, 121–34. Calgary: University of Calgary Press.

Thalman, William G. 1978. *Dramatic Art in Aeschylus' Seven Against Thebes.* New Haven: Yale University Press.

Thornton, Agathe. 1984. *Homer's Iliad: Its Composition and the Motif of Supplication.* Göttingen: Vandenhoeck & Ruprecht.

Torrance, R. M. 1965. "Sophocles: Some Bearings." *Harvard Studies in Classical Philology* 69: 269–327.

Turner, Chad. 2001. "Perverted Supplication and Other Inversions in Aeschylus' *Danaid Trilogy.*" *Classical Journal* 97.1: 27–50.

Tzanetou, Angeliki. 2005. "A Generous City: Pity in Athenian Oratory and Tragedy." In *Pity and Power in Ancient Athens,* ed. R. Sternberg, 98–122. Cambridge: Cambridge University Press.

———. 2012. *City of Suppliants: Tragedy and the Athenian Empire.* Austin: University of Texas Press.

Vellacott, P., tr. and ed. 1972. *Euripides / Orestes and Other Plays.* New York: Penguin.

Verbanck-Piérard, A. 1992. "Héraclès héros ou dieu?" In *Héraclès: d'une rive à l'autre de la Méditerrané,* ed. C. Bonnet and C. Jourdain-Annequin, 51–65. Brussels and Rome: Institut historique belge de Rome.

Vernant, J.-P., and P. Vidal Naquet. 1988 [orig. 1972]. *Myth and Tragedy in Ancient Greece,* ed. J. P. Vernant and P. Vidal-Naquet, tr. J. Lloyd. New York: Zone.

Vickers, Brian. 1973. *Towards Greek Tragedy.* London: Longman.

Vidal-Naquet, Pierre. 1988 [orig. 1972]. "Sophocles' *Philoctetes* and the Ephebeia." In *Myth and Tragedy in Ancient Greece,* ed. J. P. Vernant and P. Vidal-Naquet, tr. Janet Lloyd, 161–79. New York: Zone.

Waldock, A. J. A. 1951. *Sophocles the Dramatist.* Cambridge: Cambridge University Press.

Walker, Henry J. 1995. *Theseus and Athens.* Oxford: Oxford University Press.

Webster, T. B. L. 1969. *An Introduction to Sophocles.* London: Methuen.

———, ed. 1970. *Sophocles, Philoctetes.* Cambridge: Cambridge University Press.

Weil, Simone. 1945. *The Iliad, or the Poem of Force,* tr. M. McCarthy. New York: Politics.

Weinstock, H. 1931. *Sophokles.* 3rd ed. Leipzig and Berlin: Teubner.

West, M. L., ed. 1972. *Iambi et Elegi Graeci.* 2 vols. Oxford: Clarendon Press.

Whitman, C. H. 1951. *Sophocles: A Study in Heroic Humanism.* Cambridge, MA: Harvard University Press.

Wilamowitz-Moellendorf, U. von. 1895. *Euripides. Herakles.* Berlin: Weidmann.

Wiles, David. 1997. *Tragedy in Athens.* Cambridge: Cambridge University Press.

Wilson, Edmund. 1959. "Philoctetes: The Wound and the Bow." In *The Wound and the Bow,* 272–95. New York: Oxford University Press.

Winnington-Ingram, R. P. 1956. Review of "Philoctetes: The Play and the Man," by I. M. Linforth. *Gnomon* 28: 632–34.

———. 1961. "The Danaid Trilogy of Aeschylus." *Journal of Hellenic Studies* 81: 141–52.

———. 1969. "Tragica: *Philoctetes* 839–42." *British Institute of Classical Studies* 16: 48–50.

———. 1980. *Sophocles: An Interpretation.* Cambridge: Cambridge University Press.

Woodard, Thomas. 1966. "The *Electra* of Sophocles." In *Sophocles: A Collection of Critical Essays,* ed. T. Woodard, 124–45. Englewood Cliffs, NJ: Prentice Hall.

Woodford, Susan. 1971. "Cults of Heracles in Athens." In *Studies Presented to George M. A. Hanfmann,* ed. D. G. Mitten, J. G. Pedley, and J. A. Scott, 211–25. Cambridge, MA: Fogg Art Museum.

Worman, Nancy. 2000. "Infection in the Sentence: The Discourse of Disease in Sophocles' *Philoctetes.*" *Arethusa* 33: 1–36.

Wright, Matthew. 2005. "The Joy of Sophocles' *Electra.*" *Greece & Rome* 52.2: 172–94.

Yoshitake, S. 1994. "Disgrace, Grief, and Other Ills: Herakles' Rejection of Suicide." *Journal of Hellenic Studies* 114: 135–53.

Yunis, H. 1988. *A New Creed: Fundamental Religious Beliefs in the Athenian Polis and Euripidean Drama*. Hypomnemata 91. Göttingen: Vandenhoeck & Ruprecht.

Zanker, Graham. 1992. "Sophocles' *Ajax* and the Heroic Values of the *Iliad.*" *Classical Quarterly* n.s. 42: 20–25.

———. 1994. *The Heart of Achilles.* Ann Arbor: University of Michigan Press.

Zeitlin, Froma I. 1990. "Thebes: Theater of Self and Society in Athenian Drama." In *Nothing to Do with Dionysos?,* ed. J. J. Winkler and F. I. Zeitlin, 130–67. Princeton: Princeton University Press.

Zimmermann, Bernhard. 1991 [orig. 1986]. *Greek Tragedy: An Introduction,* tr. T. Marier. Baltimore: Johns Hopkins University Press.

Index

For Greek words that appear as various parts of speech derived from the same root (e.g., a noun and a verb), the index typically refers to only the most basic form.